Participating in Developme

Developme
The polici
have frequ
Developme
approaches
aims to n
increasingl
and accept

It is self
will benefi
therefore p
This volur
address. Fi
should def
definition
interdiscip
developme
while not

The ne
in the ch
contexts a
this debat
collection. Its authors both define and validate the role of the anthropologist in
development as well as that of development in anthropology.

Paul Sillitoe is Professor of Anthropology at the University of Durham.
Alan Bicker is a research fellow at the University of Kent. **Johan Pottier** is
Professor of African Anthropology at the School of Oriental and Asian
Studies, University of London.

ASA Monographs (vol. no. 39)

Participating in Development

Approaches to indigenous knowledge

Edited by Paul Sillitoe, Alan Bicker and Johan Pottier

London and New York

First published 2002
by Routledge
11 New Fetter Lane, London EC4P 4EE

Simultaneously published in the USA and Canada
by Routledge
29 West 35th Street, New York, NY 10001

Routledge is an imprint of the Taylor & Francis Group

Typeset in Bembo by Taylor and Francis Books Ltd
Printed and bound in Great Britain by St Edmundsbury Press,
Bury St Edmunds, Suffolk

British Library Cataloguing in Publication Data
A catalogue record for this book is available from the British Library

Library of Congress Cataloging in Publication Data
Participating in development : approaches to indigenous
knowledge / edited by Paul Sillitoe, Alan Bicker, and Johan Pottier.
p. cm.
Includes bibliographical references and index.
1. Ethnoscience–Developing countries. 2. Technical
assistance–Anthropological aspects. 3. Community development.
4. Applied anthropology. I. Sillitoe, Paul. II. Bicker, Alan. III. Pottier,
Johan.
GN476 .P37 2002
307.1'4–dc21
2002021956

ISBN 0–415–25868–5 (hbk)
ISBN 0–415–25869–3 (pbk)

We dedicate this book to the memories of
Darrell Posey and Michael Warren,
vigorous advocates of indigenous knowledge and rights.

1-20

Contents

Illustrations

Figures

Tables

Contributors

Alan Bicker, Anthropology Department, University of Kent, Eliot College, Canterbury, CT2 7NS

John R. Campbell, Anthropology Department, School of Oriental & African Studies, Thornhaugh Street, Russell Square, London, WC1H 0XG

John Clammer, Department of Comparative Culture, Sophia University, 4 Yonban-cho, Chiyoda-ku, Tokyo, Japan 102–0081

David A. Cleveland, Anthropology Department/Environmental Studies Program, University of California – Santa Barbara, Santa Barbara, California, USA

Peter Croal, Environment Assessment and Compliance Division, Scientific, Technical and Advisory Services Directorate, Canadian International Development Agency Policy Branch, 12th Floor 200 Promenade du Portage, Hull, Quebec, Canada

Wes Darou, Environment Assessment and Compliance Division, Scientific, Technical and Advisory Services Directorate, Canadian International Development Agency Policy Branch, 12th Floor 200 Promenade du Portage, Hull, Quebec, Canada

Roy Ellen, Anthropology Department, University of Kent, Eliot College, Canterbury, CT2 7NS

Aneesa Kassam, Anthropology Department, University of Durham, 43 Old Elvet, Durham DH1 3HN

Elizabeth Akinyi Onjoro, Community Mental Health Department/ Center for HIV Education and Research, University of South Florida, 13301 Bruce B. Downs Boulevard, MHC – 1431, Tampa, Florida 33612, USA

The late Darrell Posey, Oxford Centre for the Environment, Ethics and Society, Mansfield College, Oxford University, Oxford, OX1 3TF

Johan Pottier, Anthropology Department, School of Oriental & African Studies, Thornhaugh Street, Russell Square, London, WC1H 0XG

Trevor Purcell, Anthropology Department/African Studies Program, University of South Florida, 4202 E Fowler Avenue, SOC 107, Tampa, Florida 33620, USA

Michael Schönhuth, Ethnologie Department, Universität Trier, D-54 286 Trier, Germany

Paul Sillitoe, Anthropology Department, University of Durham, 43 Old Elvet, Durham DH1 3HN

Daniela Soleri, Anthropology Department/Environmental Studies Program, University of California – Santa Barbara, Santa Barbara, California, USA

Acknowledgements

The organization of a large event such as the Association of Social Anthropologists' conference in 2000 at London University, and the subsequent collection of papers into a volume like this one, depends on the support and assistance of several people. We wish to thank in particular Jackie Sillitoe for her support and help throughout; Jennifer Law and her band of postgraduate volunteers for efficient conference administration; and Matt McLennan for dedicated assistance with copy editing and close attention to detail.

Chapter I

Participant observation to participatory development

Making anthropology work

Paul Sillitoe

There is a revolution occurring in the pursuit of ethnography (Sillitoe 1998). Few anthropologists are involved! It has to do with the shift in emphasis that is occurring in the development world from a 'top-down' intervention to a 'grassroots' participatory perspective. Development agencies have been casting around for several years with mounting evidence of resources wasted in ill-conceived, frequently centrally imposed schemes that have not only failed to improve matters in less developed countries but which have also on occasion made them worse, arrogantly sending in the eggheads to sort out local problems (Hobart 1993). The time has come for anthropology to consolidate its place in development practice, not merely as frustrated post-project critic but as implementing partner. There are growing demands for its skills and insights to further understanding of agricultural, health, community and other issues, and so contribute, as this volume argues, to positive change in the long term, promoting culturally appropriate and environmentally sustainable interventions acceptable to 'beneficiaries'. The conference from which this work derives – the millennial Association of Social Anthropologists of the United Kingdom and Commonwealth Conference (at London's School of Oriental and African Studies, April 2000) – aimed to further the involvement of anthropologists in this challenging work.

Anthropology needs to turn from overinterest in postmodern mindgames to engaging more with development's dilemmas, as Darrell Posey (chapter 2) argues passionately, or face further probable diminution in the current political and economic climate, (with its accountancy demands) as some of the proliferating commentaries on the discipline's future suggest. Its identity is at stake. The topic of identity features prominently in contemporary anthropological discourse, aptly perhaps given its focus on subjectivity (although it exposes the discipline devastatingly to postmodern critiques by appearing ethnocentrically again, in the name of theory, to impose its concerns on those it studies). But there is more at stake here than disciplinary self-interest. Many of those communities anthropologists study are explicitly the target group of development agencies, the 'poorest of the poor' as they say, and, where the discipline can, it should surely do something to assist them. Until recently we could argue that the issue of development (whatever that is conceived to be – a question about which several contributors to this volume puzzle – though people around the world seem to desire it in some form or another) shuts us out with its concern for top-down transfer of technology, without the need to hear much from its assumed 'beneficiaries'. But this no longer pertains. We are obliged to take up the challenge, with all of its difficult ethical dilemmas, as Posey (chapter 2) goes on eloquently to advocate. The discipline has yet fully to acknowledge and act on these opportunities. It needs to build on its maligned applied tradition, according some priority and giving disciplinary creditability to this work (Gardner and Lewis 1996; Grillo and Stirrat 1997). It will doubtless be difficult, as Michael Schönhuth (chapter 7) points out. There is a need for mutual professional support, guidelines for practice, contributions to new and appropriate methodologies, institutional capacity building and assistance networks, and so on. Anthropology should bid to become the intellectual home of participatory development (Farrington and Martin 1988; Bass *et al.* 1995), affording it disciplinary pedigree and coherence. It is time that we put anthropology to work.

The focus of the revolution that directly concerns anthropology is the appearance, within the broad context of participatory development, of a new field of specialism called, among other things, 'indigenous or local knowledge'. This is in the process of establishing itself within development practice, where it has recently become popular to point out that indigenous peoples have their own effective 'science' and resource use practices, and that to help them it is necessary to understand something about their knowledge and management systems (Kloppenburg 1991; DeWalt 1994). It also relates to identity issues (Sillitoe 2000), featuring here in peoples' fights against cultural imperialism, as they take the opportunity to assert a place for their knowledge. The philosophy underlying local knowledge research is unexceptionable (Warren *et al.* 1995). The proposition that an understanding and appreciation of local ideas and practices should inform development work is self-evident to any anthropologist. This growing acknowledgement that effective development assistance benefits from some understanding of indigenous knowledge and practices is gratifying for anthropology, as it has argued along these lines for decades. It puts anthropology on the development team.

Anthropology needs to give attention, or else others will cuckoo it. There is evidence that many are ready to do so; agricultural economists and human geographers, even foresters and plant pathologists are taking over our disciplinary role, as some of this volume's contributors show. This is unfortunate for anthropology and development, the discipline having wide experience of the issues. There is a danger that others might unwittingly sell it short, using its intellectual capital in attempts to further their work, as evidenced in practices such as rapid rural appraisal (RRA) and participatory rural appraisal (PRA). The problems encountered in trying to understand something about others' sociocultural traditions are not to be glossed over in glib methodologies. Anthropologists have been wrestling with them since their discipline emerged, and should be there to ensure that recent enthusiasm results in successful incorporation into development practice; misrepresenting the difficulties will not further this in the long run but will lead to disillusionment on the part of other development professionals. It demands engagement with the paradox of interdisciplinary research, which on the one hand comes naturally to anthropology while on the other threatens further to compromise the discipline's currently insecure identity.

Anthropology's opportunity: changes in development perspectives

The emergence of development's interest in indigenous knowledge and practice has depended crucially on a recent sea-change in the paradigms that structure development (Preston 1996; Potter *et al.* 1999). The dominant ones until a decade or so ago were modernization, the classic transfer-of-technology paradigm associated with the political right, and dependency, the Marxist informed paradigm associated with the political left. They are both blind to local knowledge issues.

- The *modernization* approach – not only dismisses local knowledge but also views it as part of the problem, being non-scientific, traditional and risk-adverse, even irrational and primitive.
- The *dependency* approach – portrays poor farmers as helpless victims; local knowledge is again sidelined, this time as the view of the powerless.

The new bottom-up oriented development paradigms, which have recently emerged to challenge these top-down perspectives, are the market-liberal and neo-populist. Both give more credence to local perspectives but otherwise mirror the same political divide, the former associated with the political right, and the latter associated with the political left.

- The *market-liberal* approach – although this gives more attention to local knowledge, it is largely as market information relating to available technical options, how it will influence choice and the appropriateness of the various options to farmers' environments and households.
- The *neo-populist* approach – the participatory focus gives potential prominence to local knowledge, which is taken seriously and granted a role in problem identification, research and so on.

The correspondence between these paradigmatic shifts and the end of the so-called Cold War is improbably coincidental, overseas aid no longer being imposed so blatantly to advance hegemonies in different parts of the world with the collapse of one of the superpowers, allowing for the potentially more politically volatile voice of the poorest to be heard.

These different paradigms are not mutually exclusive (Simon 1999). They are often mixed up in policy and programmes, as illustrated in several of this book's contributions. Sometimes those who subscribe to one view of the development process borrow ideas from others, sometimes intentionally making an alliance, other times unintentionally with confused or fortuitously beneficial results. Regarding the more recent market-technical and populist-empowerment approaches that allow for a grassroots perspective and advocate indigenous knowledge research, both technological and sociopolitical issues feature to an extent, inextricably entwined. It is a matter of emphasis. And participation, facilitated by outsiders, does not necessarily accommodate cultural diversity but may rather encourage people to enter the contemporary capitalist world, here sharing modernization's assumptions, albeit shifting responsibility locally for decisions and, ultimately, project failure. The eclectic mixing of assumptions is laudable, as it strives to reach a consensus between different views, symbolized initially by the right and left political poles. There is perhaps nothing new here represented by, on the one hand, the association of technological advances and improvements with natural scientists and central governments, and, on the other, the association of empowerment of the poor and disadvantaged with social scientists and non-governmental orga-nizations. And while there is nothing new in applauding attempts to encourage a rapprochement between these two positions, promoting creative tension and understanding of the issues raised by each, this in no way dimin-ishes the perennial difficulties and frustrations of such work, which at root come down to differences in values and priorities, as the contributions of Clammer (chapter 3), Kassam (chapter 4) and Croal and Darou (chapter 5) show.

A new third way for the twenty-first century

The implication from an anthropological perspective of these shifts in devel-opment practice is a demand for a third way forward to structure cross-cultural enquiries. Up until now two perspectives have dominated the discipline (Boon 1982). The first, which can be traced back to the discipline's nineteenth-century ancestors, is the *generalist approach* which uses evidence from a range of cultures to search for cross-cultural comparisons applicable to all humankind, in a search for 'laws' or universal postulates about humanity grounded in our own social philosophy and assumptions and elaborated into sociological theories. The second, instituted in the early twentieth century, is the *relativist approach*, the in-depth ethnographic study of small communities as unique cultural formations, by fieldworking anthropologists striving again to use their discipline's largely sociological theories and assumptions to account for and make sense of what they think they see, hear, experience and so on.

The new third way taking off for the twenty-first century is an *action approach*, as opposed to a purely academic one. It is pioneering ways to facilitate others' expression of their understanding of the rapidly changing world, while informing them about our thoughts (e.g. the scientific understanding that underpins the technology that drives development and its implications from our experience). It struggles to allow for these others' culturally conditioned knowledge and expectations; that is, not forcing our view or understanding down their throats but trying to advance mutual comprehension and allowing them to speak effectively for themselves. We have to evolve new collaborative research arrangements. The oft-cited process of globalization is forcing this third approach on anthropology as it becomes increasingly untenable to pretend to know or represent others' interests. We can detect three interrelated contemporary intellectual trends that intimate the discipline's move down this new third way.

First, there is the burgeoning *intellectual property rights* debate, where the issues are equally ethical and intellectual, as Darrell Posey (chapter 2) makes clear, using the metaphor of *terra nullis* to critique anthropology's engagement with development. It has arisen, on the one hand, from a realization that local people may know of natural resources that have commercial potential (Chadwick and Marsh 1994), fuelling fears that their knowledge may be unfairly expropriated for commercial gain, even patented by foreign companies after industrial intervention (e.g. genetic manipulation), without due acknowledgement and a fair share of the profit going to the original owners (Brush and Stabinsky 1996). On the other hand, it relates to the growing desire of people to control their own cultural property and destiny in the modern world, which relates closely to concerns of protecting cultural identity, and extends from demands for the repatriation of artefacts from museums to demands for a voice in various bodies that make decisions affecting their regions and lives, including development agencies. Aneesa Kassam (chapter 4) illustrates this point of view, as the Oromo of Ethiopia seek to define their view of development. There are increasing calls for a strengthening of rights generally, including human rights, intellectual and cultural property rights (Gupta 1991; Brown 1994), but these are proving not only difficult to police effectively but also to define. There are issues about inherent versus contingent rights and conflation of rights with practice, for example in conservation (Cleveland and Murray 1997). The idea that knowledge can be owned is in itself a cultural construct, as are the contrasting notions of private ownership and communal property, such that it may not even occur to people that they may receive monetary or other benefits from it. These controversial issues are currently under heated debate internationally, nationally and regionally by governments and non-governmental organizations, including indigenous peoples' organizations (Posey and Dutfield 1996; Gustafsson 1996; Posey

2000). The implications are large for anthropology, which has disseminated information widely according to open Western scholarly tradition, without explaining to local communities its possible use by others, nor how this might affect local rights to either control or benefit from it.

Second, the *participation movement* in development is forcing a change of direction, to the role of cultural facilitator and knowledge broker. Participatory approaches have emerged as an attempt to bring development practice nearer to the people it is intended to assist, arising from growing dissatisfaction with expert-led top-down approaches (Farrington and Martin 1988; Bass *et al.* 1995). They are flexible and fast-evolving suites of methods, the most widely cited being Participatory Rural Appraisal, 'a family of approaches and methods to enable rural people to share, enhance, and analyse their knowledge of life and conditions, to plan and to act' (Chambers 1995: 4). Advocates of participatory development recommend more time spent in the field, not hurried and intrusive questionnaire-driven survey visits. They aim to involve a range of people from any community, seeking to include those who may be marginalized such as the very poor and women. The intention is to empower all (Wright and Nelson 1995), which predictably has profound implications, as Trevor Purcell and Elizabeth Onjoro (chapter 8) make clear in their methodological discussion. Participation is methodologically eclectic, mixing semi-structured interviews with observation, particularly favouring techniques that draw in local people with innovative games, diagramming, mapping exercises, focus-group discussions and so on (Pretty *et al.* 1995). The outsider team, preferably comprising a range of disciplinary backgrounds to promote different perspectives on problems, seeks to catalyse and facilitate reflective action, and serve as a conduit to report the findings to policy makers, planners and politicians. The further it can withdraw and hand over to the community the better, allowing people to follow their own lines of enquiry. The extent to which participation occurs varies from 'window dressing', outsider-directed and manipulated interaction, to the promotion of 'self-mobilization', genuine insider collaboration and collegiate interaction (Bass *et al.* 1995; Martin and Sherington 1996). The team constantly reviews findings, focusing on issues as they emerge, working to synthesize findings and discuss conclusions, not away somewhere in an inaccessible institution, but in the village with local people.

Third, there is the undermining of the discipline that has occurred with *postmodernism*, which argues that anthropology as currently practised is not possible anyway (Gellner 1992). An Englishman self-evidently cannot know New Guinea culture like a New Guinean. The anthropologists' claim to understanding is founded on the flawed Enlightenment assumption that they can explain human actions and beliefs by detached analysis and objective reason. They are mistaken in this – the 'essentializing' categories they use misrepresent others. As John Clammer (chapter 3) argues, the Cartesian paradigm prioritizes cognitive understanding above other important dimensions of perception such as the emotive, affective and corporeal. Anthropological analysis oppresses and dominates, is part of an imperialist and self-seeking agenda, as Posey (chapter 2) argues vehemently. Instead of striving to use comparative methods to formulate and validate theoretical generalizations about the human condition through research into other sociocultural heritages, we should aim to give space to a multiplicity of narratives, allow for 'heteroglossia' and 'plural authorship' (Rabinow 1986: 286). We should realize that the anthropological voice is only one of countless independent perspectives no more authoritative than any other, and merits no privileged space (Geertz 1984; Clifford and Marcus 1986); as several contributors argue – for example, Schönhuth (chapter 7), and Purcell and Onjoro (chapter 8) – in their attempts to devise approaches giving an equal say to all. We have no grounds for preferring any attribute above another in discussing something. The relativism may be extreme. Any issue may in principle have countless attributes. It is the way an observer sees and codes them, which is both a culturally informed and idiosyncratic subjective act, that constitutes reality (Shweder 1984). There is support nonetheless for the idea that a universal external 'reality' exists at some level independently of human minds, although never understood in exactly the same way by any two minds. Cleveland and Soleri (chapter 10) try to connect postmodernist relativism with scientific positivism through a straightforward model of plant–environment relationships, comparing indigenous and scientific knowledge without privileging either one. There is a transcendental aspect to postmodern deconstruction that is reminiscent of Eastern philosophy in trying to pass beyond scientific rationality to some higher plane of consciousness inaccessible 'to ordinary people who are locked in the chains of their own culture-bound perceptions' (Lindholm 1997: 750). I attempt to explore this analogy further (chapter 6) in modelling relations between various knowledge traditions, the indigenous and the scientific. There are strong parallels between postmodernism and participatory approaches to development in the struggle to nullify the expert's assertion of power, reject any judgement by others or imposition of domination – a liberal egalitarianism seeking space for the expression of all equally valid agendas.

The challenge of indigenous knowledge

The challenge to anthropology is exciting. At the meeting that resulted in this volume it was suggested that anthropology should explore some of the following new opportunities and their methodological implications. They touch upon many contemporary issues, as the following chapters make clear.

* The status of ethnography in respect of intellectual property rights – who has the right to know what and control the flow of knowledge (chapters 2, 8)?

- The crisis of representation in anthropology – who can write with authority about whose problems in an increasingly globalized world (chapters 3, 4, 5)?
- The meaning of indigenous knowledge – is it legitimate to identify such knowledge and use such a term (chapters 6, 8, 10)?
- The demand for action research to facilitate participation – to what extent is it appropriate for foreign researchers to involve themselves in empowerment debates and politics elsewhere (chapters 3, 7, 8)?
- Conflicts with academic demands – are these working against involvement in development and action research (chapters 2, 6, 7)?
- The demand for interdisciplinary research – how might we more effectively facilitate it and what are the implications for anthropology (chapters 6, 9, 10)?
- Conflicts with the demands of development – how can we accommodate to these (e.g. the short-term demands of development agencies) without courting unacceptable misunderstanding (chapters 8, 9)?
- The promotion of meaningful participation – how can we ensure the knowledge and aspirations of all stakeholders have equal opportunity to inform development (chapters 4, 7, 8, 10)?

This collection of essays seeks to explore some of the conceptual issues that face indigenous knowledge within a range of ethnographic and development contexts. It identifies two major issues that anthropology needs to address regarding indigenous knowledge research. One concerns the definition of this rapidly expanding field: what is indigenous knowledge – indeed what is development – and what are the implications, notably political, of any definition? The other is the need to evolve appropriate methodologies to meet the challenge: how to pursue cross-culturally informed interdisciplinary research in development contexts and what are the possibilities and pitfalls? These two questions broadly structure the contributions to this volume.

What is indigenous knowledge?

When is knowledge indigenous? It is by no means clear, particularly at this time, with the search for whatever it is growing rapidly in development circles (Antweiler 1998; Purcell 1998; Semali and Kincheloe 1999). This is shown by the range of alternative terms used for indigenous knowledge by different writers vying for prominence and claiming to be more representative as they argue over the content of, and approaches to, this field. They include local knowledge, rural people's knowledge, insider knowledge, indigenous technical knowledge, traditional environmental knowledge, peoples' science and folk knowledge. It is difficult to draw lines between these; even the words indigenous and local are fraught with obscurity. But they all share a certain common semantic load and address the same broad issues. Some writers contrast this knowledge with scientific knowledge, even implying that it applies only to non-Western knowledge, prompting others to query the status of 'non-scientific' Western beliefs and the implications of contemporary accelerating globalizing trends. These differences take us into difficult eggshell terrain with a contentious political edge which has connotations of superiority and inferiority. The absence of any consensus over terms intimates the flux that characterizes this fast-moving and exciting field in development practice.

We need a working definition (Ellen and Harris 2000: 2–6). Indigenous knowledge in development contexts may relate to any knowledge held more or less collectively by a population, informing understanding of the world. It may pertain to any domain, particularly natural resource management in development currently. It is community based, embedded in and conditioned by local tradition. It is culturally informed understanding inculcated into individuals from birth onwards, structuring how they interface with their environments. It is also informed continually by outside intelligence. Its distribution is fragmentary. Although more widely shared locally on the whole than specialized scientific knowledge, no one person, authority or social group knows it all. There may be a certain asymmetry here, some clustering of certain knowledge within populations (e.g. by gender, age etc., or according to specialist status, perhaps reflecting political or ritual power). It exists nowhere as a totality, there is no grand repository, and hence no coherent overall theoretical model, although it may achieve some coherence in cosmologies, rituals and symbolic discourse (which are notoriously difficult to access convincingly). It is equally skill as conscious knowledge, as John Clammer (chapter 3) points out, transmitted orally and through experience, and repetitive practice characterizes its learning between generations. It is the heritage of practical everyday life, with its functional demands, and is fluid and constantly changing, being dynamic and subject to ongoing local, regional and global negotiation between people and their environments.

According to this definition, indigenous knowledge equates with much anthropological research. While defined in dictionaries as 'the study of humankind', the discipline has largely concerned itself with the documentation and understanding of sociocultural traditions worldwide, which encompasses local knowledge by default. In this case, what is the difference between them? It would appear to be one of focus. Research in anthropology is more of an academic pursuit, its objective being to further understanding of the human condition, ultimately to elucidate how our sociocultural and biological heritage contribute to our uniqueness among animals. Research in local knowledge, on the other hand, relates to development issues and problems. Its objective is to introduce a locally informed perspective into development, to challenge the assumption that development is something outsiders have a right to impose, and to promote an appreciation of indigenous power structures and know-how. In some regards it is, many would argue – such as the contributors to this volume – the long overdue introduction of a more overt anthropological perspective and awareness into development, bringing anthropology to bear on its urgent problems. It is an opportunity to take anthropology in exciting new directions, although some may see it as a threat to its intellectual integrity, as Michael Schönhuth (chapter 7) argues in the context of German academia.

The current debate over whether it is justifiable to talk of indigenous knowledge illustrates the need for an anthropological contribution, for it questions the discipline's existence. Some writers argue that to conflate others' knowledge traditions into an indigenous category and contrast it with Western scientific knowledge is insupportable because it overlooks differences within and similarities between various local and scientific perspectives (Agrawal 1995; Parkes 2000). It is criticized on four grounds. First, these different knowledge systems may be similar in essentials and content. Second, there are certain parallels in the methods they use to investigate reality. Third, science is no less culturally located than other knowledge traditions. And fourth, and perhaps most disturbing, it privileges the scientific perspective to distinguish it from others' knowledge traditions.

Should we abandon our attempt to discuss indigenous knowledge in development, which necessarily involves some distinction between it and scientific knowledge, in the face of these criticisms, given the differences within, and similarities between, these knowledge traditions? I think not. This dichotomy overlooks anthropological knowledge, which sits uneasily between the scientific and indigenous perspectives. It is a strange hybrid curate's egg form of understanding, involving both others and our occidental selves, as the reflexive debate of the past decade has affirmed. Its existence challenges any attempt to dispose of our notions of the scientific and indigenous, or the global and local. First, most anthropologists would agree that there are substantial similarities and overlaps in the substantive contents of various knowledge systems; if this was not so, it is difficult to conceive how we could communicate with one another. Second, it is undeniably questionable to attempt to distinguish scientific from any other knowledge on formal grounds, that it is more objective for example, or exclusively tests ideas using experimentation while others do not; local farmers are among some of the world's most avid experimenters. The contribution of David Cleveland and Daniela Soleri (chapter 10) illustrates this, and the previous point, in a comparison of Mexican maize farmers' practices with those of scientific plant breeders. Third, scientific knowledge is indisputably anchored culturally in Western society, where it largely originated, although with the contemporary communications revolution and associated cultural globalization processes, hybridization is occurring and blurring distinctions between it and other knowledge on sociocultural grounds. The contribution of John Clammer (chapter 3) illustrates this in the context of a discussion of Japanese attitudes to science in development. And fourth, any privileging that occurs in distinguishing between different knowledge traditions, whether different folk ones or indigenous and scientific, is not necessarily inevitable; it is indeed dubious to privilege scientific discourse as its costs become increasingly evident, both environmental, with pollution, non-sustainability, etc., and social, with redundancy, alienation, etc. My contribution (chapter 6) illustrates this by proposing a model of relations between different knowledge traditions that subverts any hierarchical arrangement, putting all on a par in a complex multidimensional network.

It is undeniable that scientific knowledge has underpinned great technological change, allowing human beings to interfere with, and extend considerable control over nature, and that it is the dissemination of this technology for the betterment of humankind that underpins the notion of development. It is the wish of the majority of the populations of lesser developed countries to share in this technological advance, not just to increase their standard of living, but sometimes to stave off starvation, sickness and death, particularly given the relentless expansion of some populations. We find people demanding development, if we put them first and listen to them, as contemporary participatory approaches advocate. It is not helpful in striving to meet this demand to argue in effect that we should not distinguish between different cultural traditions, of which knowledge systems are a part. Well-intentioned arguments to the contrary, seeking to redress the power imbalance between scientific and other perspectives, may open themselves up to charges of ethnocentrism, for implying that the 'they' of contemporary cultural discourse are the same as 'us'. We are not all the same, although the current trend towards a global culture and history is eroding the distinctions between different culturally specific knowledge systems.

In allowing local populations to inform the development process with their own knowledge and aspirations, we open up the prospect ultimately of a redefinition of the meaning of development itself and its aims. This is where the indigenous knowledge in development agenda inexorably leads, although until now we have avoided speaking of it, anxious at the reaction of international funding agencies. It represents the reduction of foreign hegemony, the promotion of what some call endogenous development (Haverkort and Hiemstra 1999). Development agencies are likely to see it as subversive because it will diminish their control. When we interpret indigenous knowledge in this wide sense, we have local stakeholders contributing equally to the determination of development objectives alongside foreigners mindful of their funding agencies' policy initiatives, reducing the control of the latter, whether or not disguised by participation rhetoric. Several of the contributions to this volume intimate what the contours of such development might look like. In their chapter, Peter Croal and Wes Darou (chapter 5) sketch some of the thoughts of the First Nations of Canada about development and the values that inform their engagement with it, notably a profound respect for the Earth and sustainability. The piece by Clammer (chapter 3) makes some similar points but from a Japanese perspective informed by Buddhist aesthetics and emotions. In her paper, Kassam (chapter 4) outlines a view of development in which people are struggling against a situation of 'internal colonialism' in order to bring about an order of development based on their own indigenous democratic principles.

The definition of indigenous knowledge, and hence development, is no straightforward endeavour in the rapidly changing contemporary world with its forces of globalization (Antweiler 1998; Semali and Kincheloe 1999). Currently, in different regions of the globe we find people with unique cultural traditions and histories, which continue to condition in significant regards their views of the environment, life and so on. The Canadian Indians illustrate this well, as Croal and Darou (chapter 5) show, continuing to hold onto their sacred view of nature in the face of generations of materialistic European dominance. Their views give precedence to different issues and priorities, reflect different experiences and interests, and will be codified in different idioms and styles, which we come to understand to varying extents. While not replicating one another, individuals share a sufficient but indeterminate amount in common to comprise a distinct cultural order with common historical tradition, values, idioms, etc. They are informed by different cultural repertoires that have evolved over generations, albeit not in isolation, being influenced by others, having some points of similarity and overlap, yet maintaining a distinctiveness, with the contrast between different traditions correlating closely, until recently, with geographical distance. So long as different cultures have differingly formulated and expressed understandings of the world, the tussle for prominence – of which the indigenous versus scientific knowledge debate is an aspect – looks set to be on-going with continuing battles over the 'big' intractable issues such as ideology, values and belief, defining who we think we are, why we are here, the proper way to live, and so on.

It follows that the high-tech 'we' and indigenous 'them' dichotomy is inescapable in some measure and to argue in effect that we should not distinguish between different intellectual traditions is unrealistic, however laudable the grounds to overcome intellectual imperialism. The distinction between indigenous and scientific, local and global knowledge is defensible, differences within, and similarities between knowledge traditions notwithstanding. What is made of the differences apparent between scientific-technical and indigenous knowledge depends on one's view of development. The transfer of technology, 'normal science' and 'normal professionalism' approaches all emphasize difference; whereas the 'farmer first', 'action research', and 'new professionalism' approaches all downplay difference, encouraging an open, intercultural approach (Chambers 1993). The stark discrimination between the scientific and indigenous that characterizes current development literature is inadequate, if not misleading, as to the relationship between the two, as I contend in detail later (chapter 6), even where it is used to argue for a reversal of the relationship in favour of participation and local knowledge. All knowledge potentially passes into the local pool and blends with what is known to inform today's understanding and practice. Rural peoples' understanding of natural resource management issues is a blend of knowledge from various sources, which it is difficult to disentangle. The understanding that farmers of Oaxaca have of genetic processes, as recounted by Cleveland and Soleri (chapter 10), may sometimes be informed by interaction with plant breeders, formal education and so on. It is syncretic knowledge, in constant process of change, being continually influenced by outside ideas.

Advocates of local knowledge in development argue that we should aim to play off the different perspectives, the strengths and weaknesses, advantages and disadvantages of different knowledge traditions to improve our overall understanding of issues and problems by generating synergy between them. Indigenous knowledge research attempts to facilitate some communication from local people to policy makers and all those stakeholders in between, as both I (chapter 6) and Schönhuth (chapter 7) argue. But conflict is inherent in the process too because we are not just talking about furthering understanding, of advancing more rounded views, but of employing the knowledge to effect some action, and sometimes the values that underpin them are not readily reconcilable. Heads become 'as full of quarrels as an egg is full' (*Romeo and Juliet*, III.i.23). The aim, we argue, should be equitable negotiation, a central tenet of local knowledge in participatory development. The negotiations become far more complex but the development initiatives are more likely to be appropriate for more people, and hence more sustainable. The methodological implications are large.

Some methodological challenges

When we have decided what indigenous knowledge is, we have to face the question of how best to undertake research into it. We need to devise a methodology that mediates effectively between the contradictions that characterize the promotion of development research from an indigenous knowledge perspective, epitomized in the contrast between local indigenous knowledge and global scientific understanding (Grenier 1998). The one is more narrowly culturally contextualized, whereas the other is cosmopolitan and has universal theoretical aspirations. The methods of the former are more inductive with a 'relative' model of the world underlying the knowledge tradition, which to outsiders involved in development is largely unknown (even unknowable according to postmodern thinkers), whereas the methods of the latter are more deductive, with a 'general' model of the world and established methods for investigating it. Consequently, we cannot assume that the one will be congruent with the other; rather, we have to seek the contrasts and parallels. We have to reconcile indigenous knowledge – wide holistic knowledge and systemic understanding of 'every person' – with scientific knowledge – the narrow and in-depth understanding of highly trained specialists – and in so doing promote cross-culturally informed research. It puts anthropology on the spot.

Like any opportunity, putting anthropology to work presents us with some challenges. Indeed the advent of indigenous knowledge research portends a discipline-shaking shift in method. We need urgently to explore some of the methodological issues that flow from an engagement with it, as Schönhuth (chapter 7) argues in referring to inconsistencies between participatory and academic anthropological research. This research has grown rapidly since its take-off in the early 1980s, when some provocative works appeared, with a proliferation of conferences, symposia, edited volumes and technical reports, and the founding of international networks and newsletters. A great deal of this work has been associated with the Intermediate Technology Movement and bears the mark of its solid concern for addressing practical issues in appropriate contexts, technically, culturally and environmentally (Warren et al. 1995). It is difficult as a consequence to define the intellectual stance of local knowledge studies, which are currently very heterogeneous in their approaches, reflecting a healthy interest in any academic paradigm if relevant to enquiries and pertinent to developmental problems in any region, although the majority have affinity to descriptive ethnographic accounts. The result is that local knowledge research currently lacks conceptual or methodological coherence (Simpson 1997); indeed it is caught in a battle of perspectives (Long and Long 1992), as practitioners tussle in arguments characterized as right versus left, natural versus social science, hard versus soft systems and so on. This book seeks to advance needed theoretical and methodological debate, to address ontological and epistemological issues, and to put this vital research on firmer intellectual foundations to rebuff critics and justify its place in development practice.

The challenges that currently face local knowledge centre on its effective incorporation into the development process, which implies the formulation of appropriate methodologies (Sillitoe et al. 2000). While it is increasingly acknowledged as sound sense in development contexts that where we think we can offer technical assistance to others based on science they are more likely to respond to it positively if presented sympathetically, with regard for their knowledge and understanding, this position has still to be comprehensively validated to gain wide acceptance. This is no straightforward endeavour involving the import of tried and tested approaches from anthropology, such as participant observation, sample surveys, case histories, etc. It involves the formulation of research strategies that meet the demands of development – to be cost effective, to be time effective, to generate appropriate insights, to be readily intelligible to non-experts, etc. – while not compromising anthropological expectations, so downplaying the difficulties attending the excogitation of others' knowledge as to render the work effectively valueless.

The issues are considerable and are addressed in the coming chapters. They include the following:

- The need to develop a coherent local knowledge intellectual framework to interface effectively with Western science. The promotion of facilitatory anthropological research methods to foster meaningful interdisciplinary dialogue between natural resources scientists and local people to establish what research may have to offer (chapters 6, 7, 9, 10).
- The advancement of a methodology that recognizes that local knowledge is neither static nor uniform, but subject to continual negotiation between stakeholders; part of the on-going globalization process. This involves the constant revision of knowledge and understanding, with people interpreting and modifying for themselves any information that reaches them in the light of their sociocultural tradition and experience (chapters 8, 10).
- The development of methods that facilitate adoption of interventions by promoting partnership and an awareness of local perspectives. Negotiations will be difficult, not only because of cross-cultural communication and understanding difficulties, but also because it will inevitably have a political aspect to it (chapters 2, 8, 9).
- The implications of variations in knowledge within local communities demand assessment and the advancement of appropriate methodologies to gauge them. Local knowledge is not locally homogeneous. Differences exist along gender, age, class, occupational and other lines, and between individuals of similar social status; and the interpretation that people put on shared knowledge may differ, depending on how it affects their interests (chapters 3, 4, 5).
- The variations in knowledge within local communities will oblige us to address the issue of whose knowledge we are going to privilege, or whether we can represent everyone's knowledge, and if so, what would be the intellectual status of such all-encompassing – standard normative anthropological – knowledge (chapters 4, 5, 6)?
- The local knowledge initiative, engaging with peoples' lives in ways not heretofore entertained by anthropology, will need to address some contentious ethical issues, for in contributing to development which aims to assist certain people over others it is inevitably interfering in their lives. Indigenous knowledge research is not socially neutral (chapters 2, 3, 7).
- The time-scale involved in ethnographic research will present problems in development contexts with their short-term orientation and politically driven considerations demanding immediate returns. It will require some methodological compromises, and the effect of these on ethnographic data (reliability, etc.) will need to be assessed (chapters 9, 10).
- The difficulties encountered in formulating generalizations applicable on a large scale also present a considerable barrier to local knowledge research in development, and there is a need to evolve methods and formulate

principles that will allow some reliable anthropological input beyond the local and into wider policy debates (chapters 8, 10).

An issue revisited several times during the ASA 2000 conference was the promotion of interdisciplinary research in intercultural contexts. Its further-ance captures the contradictions that anthropology has to resolve in contributing to the formulation of methods that will advance indigenous knowledge research in development, for it pertains directly to anthropology's changing identity (Figure 1.1). Development agencies are increasingly promoting interdisciplinary approaches to problems in their programmes. In its review of natural resources research, for example, the Department for International Development's Renewable Natural Resources Research Strategy (Research Task Group 1994) prescribes a 'livelihood systems perspec-tive' throughout its research programmes to further a comprehensive understanding of natural resources management and reduce the likelihood of development initiatives inappropriate to poor beneficiaries (Wilson 2001). It makes interdisciplinary research mandatory.

Figure 1.1   Disciplinary tribalism or interdisciplinary collaboration?

Note: Reproduced from *Times Higher Education Supplement*, by kind permission of Andrew Birch

There is nothing new in demands for interdisciplinary research (Chubin *et al.* 1986; Klein 1990); these have occurred repeatedly for many years (e.g. Gluckman 1964), even recurring periodically as an intellectual fashion (Storrer 1972). The history of anthropology shows its cyclical nature, the discipline coming into being in the UK partly through the work of a multi-disciplinary team of scientists (zoologist, psychiatrist, linguist, etc.) following the 1898 Cambridge Expedition to the Torres Straits (Sillitoe 1977; Herle and Rouse 1998) and the emergence of development's indigenous knowledge demands signalling a revival of interest. It is thought that the promotion of interdisciplinary research will help solve some pressing issues, such as the promotion of sustainable resources use (Lockeretz 1991; Anders and Mueller 1995), it being argued that problems surrounding their management can only be properly addressed in this way (Janssen and Goldsworthy 1996: 259). The way people relate to and manage their natural environments to derive liveli-hoods requires integrated study. This routinely involves several disciplines in both the natural sciences (agronomy, soil science, forestry, fisheries science, animal production, etc.) and the social sciences (agricultural economics, anthropology, small business management, geography, development studies, rural sociology, etc.), often organized in farming systems research teams.

The call for interdisciplinarity has become a mantra. The assumption is not only that it is good but also that we can do it, whereas my experience of attempting to work in interdisciplinary contexts is that the contradictions thrown up can stymie the research effort (Rhoades *et al.* 1986; Crow *et al.* 1992). The methodological problems of working in teams are large and not to be underestimated, as John Campbell (chapter 9) shows in his study of range-land management in Botswana, where team dysfunction undermined effective integration. The indigenous knowledge debate is a new, unexplored context in which to reflect on the well-rehearsed problems of interdisciplinarity. While the issues have been extensively explored in other contexts (Faber and Scheper 1997), they have yet to be investigated from the viewpoint of this newly emerging field. We should promote it as the driver for meeting the demands of interdisciplinary research, investigating feasibility, limits and contradictions from this perspective. On first appearances it lends itself partic-ularly to interdisciplinary endeavours, being by definition interdisciplinary. Local people do not think in terms of soil, crops, fish and forests, but exploit and manage their natural environment as whole systems. They hold their knowledge holistically, are interdisciplinary practitioners (Sillitoe 1998; Ellen and Harris 2000), as reflected in their understanding of health and sickness, among other fields. Furthermore, the embracing of the anthropological tradi-tion implies a systems or holistic approach. We are well placed to further interdisciplinarity with our all-encompassing view of culture.

The call for interdisciplinary research in development highlights some of the methodological challenges and rethinking facing anthropology. One of the ironies of anthropology is that it is an interdisciplinary endeavour without

teams, for various methodological and historical reasons. The lone anthropologist, acting like the structuralists' *bricoleur* 'jack-of-all-trades', has striven for a
holistic view. The discipline can no longer afford to work only in this way
without appearing unacceptably amateurish to specialists in the fields on
which it inevitably encroaches. It has not only to come to terms with research
teams, but also to facilitating these, given its suitability to take on the role of
generalist coordinator through indigenous knowledge research. To mention
some issues briefly, and there are many, as the contributions to this volume
show. There is the problem of disruption to a small community if a team of
outsiders descends on it. The 'fly on the wall' anthropological method is in
danger of being compromised (although the anthropologist may stay longer in
the field than others, various team members are likely to visit regularly).
Anthropologists, traditionally having worked alone, are notoriously bad team
members, with their possessive attitudes to their often painfully won knowledge about 'their people' and disdain for others' inability to understand the
different cultural contexts in which they have immersed themselves. The
contribution of Cleveland and Soleri (chapter 10) illustrates the frustrations
and potential benefits of mixing in anthropological understanding with
botanical theory to promote collaboration between Mexican farmers and
plant breeders. The discipline has also evolved a daunting jargon armoury to
fend off outsiders from its impenetrable debates. The demands of interdisciplinarity require the reverse.

Back to the future

A perennial problem with interdisciplinary research is juggling the contradictory demands of depth and breadth (Petrie 1976). We need to evolve a
research methodology that contextualizes narrow scientific enquiries within a
broad perspective. It was George Monbiot who compared scientists with
autistic savants, brilliant in narrow areas but not necessarily wise regarding the
world. Interdisciplinary indigenous knowledge research seeks to incorporate
wisdom (Haverkort and Hiemstra 1999). What is the nature of the trade-off
between disciplinary depth and insight to achieve interdisciplinary breadth
and context? The anthropological experience of relating small-scale studies to
large-scale issues, evident in the earlier relativist and generalist distinction,
should prove useful. The discipline, with interdisciplinary instincts and doubts
about superficiality, seeks universals in particulars in its quest to uncover
human significances in relative differences. The spectre of superficiality haunts
broadly constituted interdisciplinary work, making those who engage in it feel
vulnerable. Anthropology today illustrates the danger of lack of intellectual
identity or clear purpose. We see this as the discipline's core subject matter –
namely small-scale, largely independent societies – finally disappears at the
start of the twenty-first century under the relentless pressure of colonization
and subsequent globalization, and it is left searching for an identity.

We have a fourth reason to heed the twenty-first century's beckoning third anthropological way. Traditionally holistic and interdisciplinary by default – for no other discipline claimed such societies for study, so anthropology encompassed all aspects of them – the subject is left looking as if it tries to study everything, down to the trivial. The discipline is analogous to a broken fried egg, its yolk running indistinguishably into the albumen of surrounding disciplinary eggs. It is becoming increasingly difficult to see what characterizes anthropology as it merges with the many other cognate disciplines with which it overlaps (nearly all the social sciences and emerging cultural studies – sociology, geography, archaeology, politics, development studies, to name a few). Is it wise today to appear to study everything? The burgeoning literature on the future of the discipline reflects these worries. Geertz, for example, was among the first to talk of 'blurred genres' from his thoughts on the future of the discipline's identity, perceiving not only of disciplinary boundaries breaking down and becoming increasingly permeable, but also that, 'Something is happening to the way we think about how we think' (1980: 166). But there always has been flux in the disciplining of knowledge (Gluckman 1964). The traditional departmental ordering of academies masks the turmoil and confusion, and does not do justice to the profusion and variety that characterizes scholarly enquiry, where nothing is known for certain and beyond question. But the impediments to interdisciplinarity are deeply rooted in our intellectual culture, where disciplinary boundaries seem as rigid as ever for many currently in academia (Becher 1989). This is certainly the experience of many contributors to this volume, such as Campbell (chapter 9) and Cleveland and Soleri (chapter 10). What holds disciplines together and hinders more egg-breaking interdisciplinary research? It is to this question, among others, that any methodological advances will need to address themselves, using indigenous knowledge led team research as a lever to manoeuvre other disciplines together.

Interdisciplinary research with a local knowledge perspective involves the reconciliation of tensions evident between the natural and social sciences, assuming that outsiders have something to contribute to the development process elsewhere, and that indigenous knowledge needs to be conveyed to technocrats and policy makers such that they can appreciate its relevance. This is the way to dismantle the divide between indigenous and scientific know-ledge: not to contend that it is bogus to distinguish between them. It is widely agreed in development circles that it is necessary to know local people; the problem is how to achieve this and contribute meaningfully to development. There is considerable scope, and increasing demand, for the refining and reforming of anthropological methods to meet development requirements – methods which recent postmodern debates have strangely ignored when their criticisms of what the discipline has achieved relate in no small measure to fieldwork practice. The element of scientific collaboration in local knowledge research may strike some anthropologists as contentious, inviting unnecessary distortion. Any interpretation of another culture is unavoidably distorting, an inevitable limitation of our research methods, as current deconstructive critiques affirm, and this development-oriented indigenous knowledge work is no different from any other ethnographic enquiry in this respect. It differs in its struggle to accommodate hard technological science and soft social science perspectives in understanding and interpreting other cultures and their environments, which has the virtue of not pretending to aspire to some insider's interpretation. It admits that anthropology has to work more with other disciplines, to draw on its interdisciplinary instincts, not in isolation as previously, but together with others, with the noble aim of affording a voice to the previously marginalized and postcolonialized, notably helping the very poor. It is in this spirit that we have contributed to this book.

Bibliography

Agrawal, A. 1995. Dismantling the divide between indigenous and scientific knowledge. *Development and Change* 26: 413–439.

Anders, M. M. and R. A. Mueller. 1995. Managing communication and research task perceptions in interdisciplinary crops research. *Quarterly Journal of International Agriculture* 34: 53–69.

Antweiler, C. 1998. Local knowledge and local knowing: An anthropological analysis of contested 'cultural products' in the context of development. *Anthropos* 93: 469–494.

Bass, S., B. Dalal-Clayton and J. Pretty. 1995. *Participation in Strategies for Sustainable Development*. London: International Institute for Environment and Development, Environmental Planning Issues no. 7.

Becher, A. 1989. *Academic Tribes and Territories*. Oxford: Oxford University Press.

Boon, J. A. 1982. *Other Tribes, Other Scribes: Symbolic Anthropology in Comparative Study of Cultures, Histories, Religions, and Texts*. Cambridge: Cambridge University Press.

Brown, K. 1994. Approaches to valuing plant medicines: The economics of culture or the culture of economics? *Biodiversity and Conservation* 3: 734–750.

Brush, S. and D. Stabinsky. 1996. *Valuing Local Knowledge: Indigenous People and Intellectual Property Rights*. Washington DC: Island Press.

Chadwick, D. J. and J. Marsh (eds). 1994. *Ethnobotany and the Search for New Drugs*. CIBA Foundation Symposium no. 185. Chichester: John Wiley and Sons.

Chambers, R. 1993. *Challenging the Professions: Frontiers for Rural Development*. London: Intermediate Technology Publications.

——. 1995. *Participatory Rural Appraisal. Recent Developments in Rural Appraisal: From Rapid to Relaxed and Participatory*. Ottawa: Notes for an Aga Khan Foundation Workshop.

Chubin, D. E., A. L. Porter and F. A. Rossinin. 1986. *Interdisciplinary Analysis and Research: Theory and Practice of Problem Focused Research and Development*. Lomond: Mt Airy.

Cleveland, D. A. and S. C. Murray. 1997. The world's crop genetic resources and the rights of indigenous farmers. *Current Anthropology* 38: 477–515.

Clifford, J. and G. Marcus (eds). 1986. *Writing culture: The Poetics and Politics of Ethnography*. Berkeley: University of California Press.

Crow, G. M., L. Levine and N. Nager. 1992. Are three heads better than one? Reflections on doing collaborative interdisciplinary research. *American Education Research Journal* 29(4): 737–753.

DeWalt, B. 1994. Using indigenous knowledge to improve agriculture and natural resource management. *Human Organization* 53(2): 123–131.

Ellen, R. and H. Harris. 2000. Introduction. In R. Ellen, P. Parkes and A. Bicker (eds) *Indigenous Environmental Knowledge and its Transformations* (pp. 1–33). Amsterdam: Harwood Academic.

Faber, J. and W. J. Scheper. 1997. Interdisciplinary social science: A methodological analysis. *Quality & Quantity* 31: 37–56.

Farrington, J. and A. Martin. 1988. *Farmer Participation in Agricultural Research: A Review of Concepts and Practices*. ODA Agricultural Administration Unit Occasional Paper no. 9. London: Overseas Development Institute.

Gardner, K. and D. Lewis. 1996. *Anthropology, Development and the Post-Modern Challenge*. London: Pluto Press.

Geertz, C. 1980. Blurred genres: Refiguration of social thought. *American Scholar* 49: 165–179.

———. 1984. Anti anti-relativism. *American Anthropologist* 86: 263–278.

Gellner, E. 1992. *Postmodernism, Reason and Religion*. London: Routledge.

Gluckman, M. (ed.). 1964. *Closed Systems, Open Minds: The Limits of Naivety in Social Anthropology*. Edinburgh: Oliver and Boyd.

Grenier, L. 1998. *Working with Indigenous Knowledge. A Guide for Researchers*. Ottawa: IDRC.

Grillo, R. D. and R. L. Stirrat (eds). 1997. *Discourses of Development: Anthropological Perspectives*. Oxford: Berg.

Gupta, A. 1991. Peasant knowledge: Who has rights to use it? In B. Haverkort, J. van der Kamp and A. Waters-Bayer (eds) *Joining Farmers' Experiments: Experiences in Participatory Technology Development* (pp. 17–20). London: Intermediate Technology Publications.

Gustafsson, R. 1996. *The Way We Work with Indigenous Peoples*. Geneva: ILO Publications.

Haverkort B. and W. Hiemstra (eds). 1999. *Food for Thought: Ancient Visions and New Experiments of Rural People*. London: Zed Books.

Herle, A. and S. Rouse (eds). 1998. *Cambridge and the Torres Straits: Centenary Essays on the 1898 Anthropological Expedition*. Cambridge: Cambridge University Press.

Hobart, M. (ed.). 1993. *An Anthropological Critique of Development: The Growth of Ignorance*. London: Routledge.

Janssen, W. and P. Goldsworthy. 1996. Multidisciplinary research for natural resource management: Conceptual and practical implications. *Agricultural Systems* 51: 259–279.

Klein, J. T. 1990. *Interdisciplinarity: History, Theory and Practice*. Detroit: Wayne State University Press.

Kloppenburg, J. 1991. Social theory and the de/construction of agricultural science: Local knowledge for an alternative agriculture. *Rural Sociology* 56(4): 519–548.

Lindholm, C. 1997. Logical and moral dilemmas of postmodernism. *Journal of the Royal Anthropological Institute* 3: 747–760.

Lockeretz, W. 1991. Multidisciplinary research and sustainable agriculture. *Biological Agriculture & Horticulture* 8: 101–122.

Long, N. and A. Long (eds). 1992. *Battlefields of Knowledge: The Interlocking of Theory and Practice in Social Research and Development.* London: Routledge.

Martin, A. and J. Sherington. 1996. *Participatory Research Methods: Implementation, Effectiveness and Institutional Linkages.* Paper presented at ODA Natural Resources Systems Programme Socio-economic Methodologies Workshop.

Parkes, P. 2000. Enclaved knowledge: Indigent and indignant representations of environmental management and development among the Kalasha of Pakistan. In R. Ellen, P. Parkes and A. Bicker (eds) *Indigenous Environmental Knowledge and its Transformations* (pp. 253–291). Amsterdam: Harwood Academic.

Petrie, H. G. 1976. Do you see what I see? The epistemology of interdisciplinary inquiry. *Journal of Aesthetic Education* 10: 29–43.

Posey, D. A. 2000. Ethnobiology and ethnoecology in the context of national laws and international agreements affecting indigenous and local knowledge, traditional resources and intellectual property rights. In R. Ellen, P. Parkes and A. Bicker (eds) *Indigenous Environmental Knowledge and its Transformations* (pp. 35–54). Amsterdam: Harwood Academic.

Posey, D. and G. Dutfield. 1996. *Beyond Intellectual Property: Toward Traditional Resource Rights for Indigenous Peoples and Local Communities.* Ottawa: IDRC Books.

Potter, R. B., T. Binns, J. A. Elliott and D. Smith. 1999. Part 1. Theories of development. *Geographies of Development.* Harlow: Longman.

Preston, P. W. 1996. *Development Theory: An Introduction.* Oxford: Blackwell.

Pretty, J., I. Gujit, M. Thompson and I. Scoones. 1995. *Participatory Learning and Action: A Trainer's Guide.* London: International Institute for Environment and Development.

Purcell, T. W. 1998. Indigenous knowledge and applied anthropology: Questions of definition and direction. *Human Organization* 57(3): 258–272.

Rabinow, P. 1986. Representations are social facts: Modernity and postmodernity in anthropology. In J. Clifford and G. Marcus (eds) *Writing Culture: The Poetics and Politics of Ethnography.* Berkeley: University of California Press.

Research Task Group, 1994. *Renewable Natural Resources Research Strategy 1995–2005.* Report of the Natural Resources Research Department, Overseas Development Administration (now Department for International Development), London.

Rhoades, R. E., D. E. Horton and R. H. Booth. 1986. Anthropologist, biological scientist and economist: The three musketeers or three stooges of farming systems research? In J. R. Jones and B. J. Wallace (eds) *Social Sciences and Farming Systems Research: Methodological Perspectives on Agricultural Development* (pp. 21–40). Boulder: Westview Press.

Semali, L. M. and J. L. Kincheloe. 1999. Introduction: What is indigenous knowledge and why should we study it? In L. M. Semali and J. L. Kincheloe (eds) *What is Indigenous Knowledge: Voices from the Academy* (pp. 3–57). New York: Falmer Press.

Shweder, R. 1984. Anthropology's romantic rebellion against the Enlightenment, or there's more to thinking than reason and evidence. In R. Shweder and R. Levine (eds) *Culture Theory: Essays of Mind, Self and Emotion.* Cambridge: Cambridge University Press.

Sillitoe, P. 1977. To Mabuiag, Mer and Murray: The Torres Straits Expedition 1899. *Cambridge Anthropology* 3 (2): 1–21.

——. 1998. The development of indigenous knowledge: A new applied anthropology. *Current Anthropology* 39(2): 223–252.

——. 2000. Introduction: The state of indigenous knowledge in Bangladesh. In P. Sillitoe (ed.) *Indigenous Knowledge Development in Bangladesh: Present and Future* (pp. 3–20). London: Intermediate Technology Publications and Dhaka: University Press.

Sillitoe, P., P. D. Dixon and J. J. F. Barr. 2000. *Indigenous Knowledge Methodology*. Discussion paper for the Natural Resources Systems Programme, Department for International Development.

Simon, D. 1999. Development revisited: Thinking about, practising and teaching development after the Cold War. In D. Simon and A. Närman (eds) *Development as Theory and Practice* (pp. 17–54). Harlow: Longman.

Simpson, B. M. 1997. Towards a conceptual framework for understanding the structure and internal dynamics of local knowledge systems. Paper presented at *Creativity and Innovation at the Grassroots* Conference, Ahmedabad, January.

Storrer, N. W. 1972. Relations among scientific disciplines. In S. Z. Nagi and R. G. Corwin (eds) *The Social Contexts of Research* (pp. 229–268). London: Wiley-Interscience.

Warren, D. M., L. J. Slikkerveer and D. Brokensha (eds). 1995. *The Cultural Dimensions of Development: Indigenous Knowledge Systems*. London: Intermediate Technology Publications.

Wilson, M. 2001. DFID renewable natural resources research strategy. *Tropical Agricultural Association Newsletter* 21(1): 6–9.

Wright, S. and S. Nelson (eds). 1995. *Power and Participatory Development: Theory and Practice*. London: Intermediate Technology Publications.

Chapter 2

Upsetting the sacred balance

Can the study of indigenous knowledge reflect cosmic connectedness?[1]

Darrell Posey

Anthropology is caught in an international policy and legal vacuum regarding protection of indigenous knowledge (IK) and traditional resources. Those who study indigenous knowledge must respond by overcoming the legacy of *terra nullius* and developing research programmes which respect the *cosmic connectedness* that permeates traditional knowledge and resource management systems. This chapter looks at some of the efforts to develop a new anthropology that leads in the creation and encouragement of genuine dialogue between those who would study, and those who hold, indigenous knowledge. It is this dialogue that will characterize and transform current studies of indigenous knowledge into a new interdisciplinary and intercultural science.

Rights and knowledge

European powers often found it expedient to deploy well-established legal doctrines and principles to legitimize their control over large expanses of the 'New World' (or perhaps, 'New Worlds', since related doctrines were frequently applied as colonies were established in other continents). One such doctrine was *terra nullius*. *Terra nullius* literally means *empty land*, referring to the imposed notion of the sovereign powers of Europe that land – and all the resources associated with it – was considered *empty* until their country's banner could be planted to proclaim legal ownership. The fact that peoples already lived on these so-called empty lands presented little problem to the colonizing powers. Anthropologists know the story all too well: natives were declared to be primitive savages – little more than beasts – who had no legal rights whatsoever. Supposedly the world has progressed well beyond this scenario. But has it?

The evidence seems to indicate that the concept of *terra nullius* is alive and well (and living in a research project near you), albeit enforced in different ways and through different mechanisms than in the sixteenth century. And basic rights for indigenous peoples remain tenuous in the international community of nation states.

It was not until 1957 that the world's first convention specifically on indigenous peoples was adopted by the International Labour Organization (ILO). ILO Convention 107 (Convention Concerning the Protection and Integration of Indigenous and Other Tribal and Semi-tribal Populations in Independent Countries) established basic rights for indigenous and tribal peoples, but only on the assumption that indigenous peoples would inevitably be integrated as modern citizens into the nation states that had usurped sovereignty over their communities, resources and territories. Integration almost always meant – and continues to mean – subjugation of indigenous cultures and resources to the presumed more advanced and developed national cultures.

In 1989 ILO Convention 107 was replaced by Convention 169 (Concerning Indigenous and Tribal Peoples in Independent Countries). The newer convention substituted the concept of integration for notions of self-government, cultural integrity and auto-denomination (i.e. the right of indigenous peoples to define themselves). Article 13(1) requires governments to

> respect the special importance of the cultures and spiritual values of the peoples concerned, of their relationship with the lands or territories, or both as applicable, which they occupy or otherwise use, and in particular the *collective* aspects of this relationship.
>
> (ILO Convention 169, Article 13(1), emphasis mine)

The recognition of collective rights was a significant advance for indigenous peoples.

However, ILO 169 offers only veiled protection of indigenous knowledge through its recognition of customary law (Article 9). It does call for states to consult with indigenous and tribal peoples when considering 'legislative or administrative measures which may affect them directly' (Article 6(1.a)). This at least paves the way (but provides no guarantees) for indigenous peoples to be involved in the drafting of new national laws regarding such things as, for example, intellectual property rights, and protection of and access to traditional knowledge and genetic resources. To date, however, only fourteen countries have ratified the ILO Convention, leaving indigenous peoples with little substantial international legal protection for their customs, languages, and cultures. Peru probably stands alone as the only country in the world actually to have involved indigenous peoples in the drafting of legislation to protect their knowledge or natural resources (although Venezuela involved indigenous peoples in discussion drafts of its new constitution which prohibits patenting of collective knowledge and resources of indigenous peoples).

Who are indigenous peoples?

Before plunging into indigenous knowledge issues, perhaps one should at least mention the 'minor' problem of defining what is *indigenous*, and who are indigenous peoples. ILO 169 defines indigenous peoples as:

peoples in countries who are regarded by themselves or others as indigenous on account of their descent from the populations which inhabited the country, or a geographical region to which the country belongs, at the time of conquest or colonisation or the establishment of present state boundaries and who, irrespective of their legal status, retain, or wish to retain, some or all of their own social, economic, spiritual, cultural and political characteristics and institutions.

(ILO 169, Article 1)

Such a definition is highly problematic in many parts of the world. As a result, the Special Rapporteur of the UN Economic and Social Council Sub-Commission on Prevention of Discrimination and Protection of Minorities has tried to clarify 'indigenous' in the following manner:

Indigenous communities, peoples and nations are those which, having a *historical continuity* with pre-invasion and pre-colonial societies that have developed on their territories, consider themselves distinct from other sectors of the societies now prevailing in those territories, or parts of them. They form at present non-dominant sectors of society and are determined to preserve, develop and transmit to future generations their ancestral territories, and their ethnic identity, as the basis of their continued existence as peoples, in accordance with their own cultural patterns, social institutions and legal systems.

(UN ECOSOC 1986, Addendum 4, Paragraph 625, emphasis mine)

The *historical continuity* central to this definition is characterized by:

- occupation of ancestral lands, or at least of part of them;
- common ancestry with the original occupants of these lands;
- culture in general, or in specific manifestations (such as religion, living under a tribal system, membership of an indigenous community, dress, means of livelihood, lifestyle, etc.);
- language (whether used as the only language, as mother tongue, as the habitual means of communication at home or in the family, or as the main, preferred, habitual, general or normal language);
- residence in certain parts of the country, or in certain regions of the world; and
- other relevant factors.

Utilizing this definition and these guidelines, the United Nations estimates that there are currently at least 300 million people worldwide who are indigenous. According to UNESCO (1993a) 4,000 to 5,000 of the 6,000 languages remaining in the world are spoken by indigenous peoples, implying that indigenous groups still constitute most of the world's cultural and linguistic diversity (Maffi 1999).

Knowledge, space and material

Despite these legal definitions and guidelines, however, determining who is 'indigenous' remains difficult and, in many places, is a highly charged political issue. The conundrum of defining 'indigenous' means that delimiting indigenous knowledge is no less complicated. To avoid incessant definitional arguments, most anthropologists now use local knowledge (LK) and traditional knowledge (TK) as synonymous with indigenous knowledge (IK). In effect, such terms accommodate the self-defining principle of ILO 169, according to which ethnic groups themselves can choose to designate themselves as indigenous.

But there are more entries in the forest of *what we study* acronyms, since there is also a large contingent of anthropologists who study TEK (traditional ecological knowledge). TEK includes those aspects of traditional knowledge that apply directly to local peoples' knowledge about and management of natural resources.

I must also mention an on-going and (in my opinion) often tedious debate as to whether knowledge should be seen as functioning *systems*. The systems or ethnosystematic anthropologists would add the 's' word to everything so as to indicate the internal logical matrix that underlies and links elements of knowledge systems. Thus we have IKS, LKS and TKS.

Jan Slikkerveer (1999), Director of Leiden Ethnosystems and Development Programme (LEAD), argues that the ethnosystems approach facilitates assessment of 'cognitive and behavioural components of particular groups or communities as "systems" in a holistic mode, and facilitates the elaboration of the concept of culture as the result of historical processes of acculturation and transculturation in a more dynamic way'. It follows that this will lead to a better understanding of indigenous knowledge, and 'at the same time enhance a non-normative, more realistic comparison between indigenous and global systems of knowledge and technology' (Slikkerveer 1999: 172).

But Arun Agrawal (1999) criticizes those IK scholars who are so 'preoccupied with using "scientific criteria" to show the validity of indigenous knowledge, with collecting, systematising, and storing indigenous knowledge, with proving the utility of indigenous knowledge to development initiatives' that they forget the question of power. Indigenous peoples, he points out (1999: 178), generally remain 'in positions of local resistance to the effects of domination produced by those who possess and apply scientific knowledge'. Thus, following Agrawal, efforts to document and *scientize* indigenous knowledge are doubly unfortunate since 'they channel resources away from the more vital political task of transforming the relations of power' and 'they provide a means for more powerful social actors to appropriate useful indigenous knowledges'.

Indigenous peoples and their knowledge

I must agree with Agrawal. But there is another problem with the study of IK. In the fury and fret of academic debate, a key factor is often ignored: what do indigenous peoples themselves think about their knowledge? In an eagerness to understand IK/LK/TK and TEK (not to mention IKS/LKS/TKS), an intellectual *terra nullius* takes over, leaving the *sources* of knowledge out of a process that – like planting imperial banners – transforms 'their' information into 'our' data or 'our' intellectual debate.

This process is highly problematic from the indigenous perspective. This is because, for indigenous peoples, knowledge is viewed as emanating from a spiritual – not a unilineal scientific – base. Thus, all *Creation* is sacred, and the sacred and secular are inseparable. Spirituality is the highest form of consciousness, and spiritual consciousness is the highest form of awareness. In this sense, traditional knowledge is not *local* knowledge at all, but rather an expression of *universal* knowledge as expressed through the local.

Experts (often labelled by anthropologists as shamans) exist who are peculiarly aware of nature's organizing principles, which are sometimes described as entities or spirits, or by cosmic laws. Knowledge of the environment, therefore, depends not only on the relationship between humans and nature, but also between the visible world and the invisible spirit world.

African religion, according to Opoku (1978), is:

> A way of life, [with] the purpose of … order[ing] our relationship with our fellow men and with our environment, both spiritual and physical. At the root of it is a quest for harmony between man, the spirit world, nature, and society.
>
> (Opoku 1978)

Thus, the unseen is as much a part of society as that which is seen – the spiritual is as much a part of reality as the material. In fact, there is a complementary relationship between the two, *with the spiritual being more powerful than the material.*

Indigenous peoples frequently view themselves as guardians and stewards of this *spiritual nature* or *nature of spirit*. Harmony and equilibrium are central concepts in most cosmologies, which also recognize linkages between health, diet, properties of different foods and medicinal plants, and horticultural/natural resource management practices – all, as Stephen Hugh-Jones (1999) reminds us, within a highly articulated cosmological-cum-social context.

Indigenous knowledge also embraces information about location, movements, and other factors explaining spatial patterns and timing in the ecosystem, including sequences of events, cycles and trends. Direct links with the land are fundamental and obligations to maintain those connections form the core of individual and group identity. Nowhere is this more apparent than in the Dreaming-places of the Aboriginal peoples of Australia. As James Yunupingu, Chairperson of the Northern Land Council, explains: 'My land is mine only because I came in spirit from that land, and so did my ancestors of the same land. My land is my foundation' (Yunupingu 1995; see also Bennett 1999).

The Aboriginal anthropologist Marcia Langton (2000) reminds us that land is a manifestation of symbolic environmental space or, to use her term, *spacialization*. This is expressed by Aboriginal Australians through the concept of *totem*, in which animal spirits define other dimensions of knowing that emerge from cosmic environments. These nonlineal manifestations may be thought of as spiritual clusters that, unlike the electron clouds that enshroud atomic nuclei, are literally grounded through sacred sites that define human landscapes marked by cultural mechanisms such as ceremonial/sacred sites and song lines. It is the *knowledge* of elders and spiritual specialists that concretizes, reconfirms and maintains this fundamental dynamic of human, spiritual and Earth life.

[margin note: Places & objects can connect spiritual w/ material]

Indigenous peoples around the world are said to share (albeit in very different ways) this view of the *cosmic connectedness* between knowledge, living things and the Earth. In some indigenous societies, human beings not only share life with all other living organisms, but, indeed, may be transformed into other living forms through transgenic processes of death, rebirth, ritual or shamanism. Thus, the plant, animal, artefact or crystal some anthropologist wants to collect, investigate or turn into data, may, in fact, encompass, contain or *be* the manifestation of ancestral spirits – or even the local elders' own progenitors. Again, it is knowledge of these transformations and manifestations that attaches the spiritual to the material – the culture to the land. Without that knowledge, there would be no connectedness. Or, more to the point, to remove knowledge breaks the connectedness.

The Cherokee of North America, for example, see knowledge as an integral part of the Earth. Thus a dam does not just flood the land, but destroys the medicines and the knowledge of the medicines associated with the land. As one healer explained:

> If we are to make our offerings at a new place, the spiritual beings would not know us. We would not know the mountains or the significance of them. We would not know the land and the land would not know us … We would not know the sacred places … If we were to go on top of an unfamiliar mountain we would not know the life forms that dwell there.
>
> (Whitt 1999)

The same is true for the Mazatecs of Southern Mexico, whose shamans and *curandeiros* confer with the plant spirits in order to heal. Successful curers must above all else learn to *listen* to their plants (Harrison 2000). For many groups, these communications come through the transformative powers of altered states or trances. Don Hilde, a Pucallpa healer, explains: 'I did not have a teacher to help me learn about [healing] plants, but visions have taught me many things. They even instruct me as to which ... medicines to use' (Dobkin de Rios 1972: 146; see Freedman 1999).

These links between life, land and society are sometimes identified as the 'Sacred Balance'. According to David Suzuki (1999), science can never adequately describe the holism of indigenous knowledge and belief. In fact, science is far behind indigenous knowledge because it still sees nature as only objects for human use and exploitation ('components' of biodiversity is the term used in the Convention on Biological Diversity).

Furthermore, the banner of scientific 'objectivity' tends to mask the moral and ethical implications that emerge from the functionalist anthropocentrism that informs much scientific research. Marilyn Strathern (1996) makes this clear when discussing the ethical dilemmas raised (or avoided) when embryos are treated in certain contexts as being no more than 'objects of knowledge' for scientific research. For indigenous peoples, removal of life forms and knowledge from their cosmic connections evokes moral indignation because it destroys the sacred balance.

Thus, for indigenous peoples, nature and knowledge are non-fragmental extensions of human society. As a consequence, landscapes can be energy-charged cultural expressions that are anchored to the physical Earth by embedded knowledge. Many so-called 'pristine' ecosystems are in fact *cultural* or *anthropogenic landscapes*, either created by humans or modified by human activity (such as through natural forest management, cultivation or the use of fire).

As Joseph Matowanyika (1997: 260) points out, 'in societies with no written language or edifices[,] hills, mountains and valleys become the libraries and cathedrals that reflect cultural achievement'. Such is the case, he says, for the Kagore Shona people of Zimbabwe, whose sacred *local* (burial grounds) and other sites of special historical significance are such inextricable elements of the landscape that they often cannot be recognized by outsiders. Indeed, it took years before my botanical colleagues or I realized that the widespread forest islands (*apêtê*) in the savannah lands of the Kayapó Indians of Brazil were, in fact, artefacts of indigenous ecological management (Posey 1996).

Unfortunately, scientists, including some anthropologists, continue to be careless in assuming cultural landscapes to be 'wild' or 'wildernesses'. These terms imply that the lands and their resources are the result of 'nature' and as such, have no original owners. This interpretation has proved convenient for those who would deny that local communities have ownership rights, and proclaim that their lands, territories and resources are 'free' to others for the taking. This is why indigenous peoples have come to oppose the use of 'wilderness' and 'wild' to refer to the regions in which they now or once lived. For example, an Aboriginal Resolution from the 1995 Ecopolitics IX Conference in Darwin, Australia states:

> The term 'wilderness' as it is popularly used, and related concepts as 'wild resources', 'wild foods', etc., [are unacceptable]. These terms have connotations of *terra nullius* [empty or unowned land and resources] and, as such, all concerned people and organisations should look for alternative terminology which does not exclude Indigenous history and meaning.
>
> (Quoted in Sultan *et al.* 1995: 3)

Significantly, since 1993 cultural landscapes have been recognized under the 1972 UNESCO *World Heritage Convention* (Convention Concerning the Protection of the World Cultural and Natural Heritage) under the category of 'combined work(s) of nature and of man'. This category is intended to recognize: 'the complex interrelationships between man and nature in the construction, formation and evolution of landscapes' (UNESCO 1993b: 14). The first cultural landscape World Heritage Site was Tongariro National Park, a sacred mountain and region for the Maori people of New Zealand.

Indigenous knowledge, innovations and practices

A major international catalyst for enhanced efforts to protect the knowledge of indigenous peoples and local communities is the 1992 Convention on Biological Diversity (CBD). The CBD has become a significant forum for discussions on indigenous rights and 'knowledge, innovations and practices' of indigenous and local communities 'embodying traditional lifestyles'. Article 8.j of the CBD requires that Member States:

> Subject to … national legislation, respect, preserve and maintain *knowledge, innovations and practices* of indigenous and local communities embodying traditional lifestyles relevant for the conservation and sustainable use of biological diversity and promote the wider application with the approval and involvement of the holders of such knowledge, innovations and practices and encourage the equitable sharing of the benefits arising from the utilisation of such knowledge, innovations and practices.
>
> (1992 Convention on Biological Diversity, Article 8.j, emphasis mine)

While indigenous peoples welcome this recognition of their relevance to biodiversity conservation, they are understandably sceptical that governments that have for the last five centuries tried so hard to destroy them and their habitats are now suddenly going zealously to defend their rights. Neither are they convinced that many benefits will ever trickle down to the source of both the knowledge and resources, i.e. their communities. Indigenous leaders are both frustrated and angry that while countries do little to protect their interests or guarantee even their most basic rights, governments are nonetheless now anxious to claim sovereignty over their resources and even the knowledge of their communities.

Is this nothing more than adapting old colonial policies to create *intellectual* or even *genetic terra nullius*? Could it be just another example of more powerful forces and institutions again usurping indigenous knowledge and genetic resources with impunity?

There is some evidence that such a sinister interpretation may indeed be justified. As yet, the only systems of 'protection' envisioned for indigenous knowledge innovations and practices seem to be intellectual property rights (IPRs) such as patents and copyrights. IPRs in general – and patents in particular – are problematic for indigenous, traditional and local communities for the following reasons:

1   They are founded upon a conception of individual authorship that does not suit community innovation. Indigenous knowledge may, for example, be attributed to ancestor spirits, vision quests or lineage groups, but rarely to individuals. A group of lawyers, academics and activists summed up the situation in a document known as the Bellagio Declaration:

> Contemporary intellectual property law is constructed around the notion of the author as an individual, solitary and original creator, and it is for this figure that its protections are reserved. Those who do not fit this model – custodians of tribal culture and medical knowledge, collectives practising traditional artistic and musical forms, or peasant cultivators of valuable seed varieties, for example – are denied intellectual property protection.
>
> (Quoted in Boyle 1996: 192–200)

2   They are intended to benefit society through the granting of exclusive rights to individuals and juridical persons (i.e. corporate entities). Indigenous peoples and local communities do not usually have a legal personality and cannot easily claim legal rights as a group.
3   They cannot easily protect information not resulting from a specific historic act of 'discovery'. Most indigenous knowledge is transgenerational, communally shared, and is usually considered to be in the public domain, and therefore unprotectable.
4   They are likely to conflict with customary systems of ownership, tenure and access.
5   They help owners to capture the *market* value of knowledge, but fail to reflect spiritual, aesthetic or cultural – or even local economic – values. Information or objects may have their greatest value to indigenous peoples because of their ties with cultural identity and symbolic unity, not because money can be made from selling them. In fact, indigenous

peoples may be concerned primarily to *prevent* commercialization and to restrict use and distribution. As a 1994 COICA (Coordinating Group of the Indigenous Peoples of the Amazon Basin, Posey and Dutfield 1996: 215) statement puts it:

> For members of indigenous peoples, knowledge and determination of the use of resources are collective and inter-generational. No indigenous population, whether of individuals or communities, nor the government, can sell or transfer ownership of resources which are the property of the people and which each generation has an obligation to safeguard for the next.

6 They are subject to manipulation by economic interests that wield the most political power. So while *sui generis* protection has been obtained for, say, semiconductor chips, indigenous peoples lack the legal means for protecting even their most sacred plants, places, songs, art or artefacts.

7 Most IPRs (especially patents) are expensive, complicated and time-consuming to obtain, and even more difficult to defend.

There are other good reasons why indigenous peoples are worried that intellectual property rights cannot protect their knowledge and resources. Take, for example, the three patent applications granted during the 1990s for human cell lines developed from blood 'donated' by indigenous peoples, including one from a member of a recently contacted group of hunter-cultivators in New Guinea, another from the Solomon Islands, and a third from the Guaymi Indians of Panama (Posey and Dutfield 1996: 25–27). The patent applicants in each case were US government agencies.

Another current case has led to something of a diplomatic row between Guyana and Great Britain. A British scientist (Conrad Gorinsky) is being sued in a British court over his patenting active medicinal compounds from the Greenheart tree *Ocotea rodiaei* and the Cunani bush *Clibadium sylvestre*.[2] Both have been used for centuries by the Wapishana Indians. It is clear from the patent application that initial 'leads' for the research came from indigenous knowledge. Yet nowhere are indigenous collaborators acknowledged in the patent – nor does there appear to be any provision for equitable benefit sharing.

Indigenous peoples in Latin America became acutely aware of how their plants were being patented when *ayahuasca*, a sacred, dream-inducing medicinal drink commonly used by Amazonian peoples of Ecuador, Colombia and Brazil, was patented by a US scientist/entrepreneur. At the request of indigenous peoples from Ecuador and Colombia – and facing worldwide pressure – the United States Patent and Trademark Office revoked the *ayahuasca* patent in November 1999.

There are numerous other examples of what has now become known as biopiracy. Anthropologists often unwittingly contribute to the unauthorized exploitation of indigenous knowledge as publications are gleaned by industry for leads for new products for medicines, hair and body products, dyes and a myriad of other uses. Indigenous groups and peasant communities are increasingly suspicious of researchers (of all disciplines) seeking information about local knowledge and practices. It is little wonder that patents (the main focus of IPR debates) have become a new war cry for indigenous rights.

Moratoria and criminals

Indigenous peoples have taken up the fight against biopiracy in well-articulated and sophisticated ways. They have also begun to demand that researchers acquire their prior informed consent and fully disclose information on all phases of research, database preparation and management, and publication of data. Some indigenous groups have even declared a moratorium on all research with commercial application until appropriate protection measures are in place.[3] Two examples are the 1994 UNDP Consultation on the Protection and Conservation of Indigenous Knowledge, organized by COICA, and the 1993 Mataatua Declaration, signed in New Zealand by indigenous groups from many parts of the world. The threat of a moratorium could well restrict the activities of anthropologists and other researchers.

Such an apparently extreme response is understandable in light of the fact that academics and public research institutions depend increasingly on the private sector for research funding. This situation makes it difficult for indigenous peoples to be sure they will not be exploited. It is also hard for academics, who must wear both the hat of their patrons *and* the mantle of their intellectual discipline. Increasingly, even public funding institutions and private foundations demand to hold the IPRs for the results of projects they finance. Thus, not even researchers have control over the data they collect. Recent legal decisions in the USA that all information obtained using public funds must be made available for public scrutiny deeply perturbs anthropologists whose work and credibility depend on confidentiality.[4]

Thus, and with good reason, many indigenous peoples lump scientists and industrial researchers into the same category. This means that negotiating access by anthropologists to indigenous and local communities – for whatever purpose – may take considerable time and energy and is now a profoundly political act (Posey *et al.* 1995).[5]

In spite of their scepticism, indigenous peoples retain some hope that the CBD will become the international vehicle to clarify terms of access for and transfer of genetic resources and appropriate technologies. Indeed, the CBD has advanced considerably towards the development of guidelines and principles for *sui generis* (i.e. specially developed) alternatives to existing IPRs. The Conference of the Parties to the CBD has established an 'ad hoc open-ended inter-sessional working group' to address IPR and issues related to Article 8.j.

Whatever the CBD recommends, it is up to governments to pass national legislation on indigenous knowledge. Many of them have little genuine interest in doing so. However, in a few countries legal measures to protect traditional knowledge have been enacted. For example, some Brazilian states have passed laws making the unauthorized collection of indigenous knowledge or genetic resources a *criminal* act. The State of Acre, tired of awaiting national action, enacted its own *Lei de Accesso aos Recursos Geneticos* (Projeto de Lei No 15/97) in 1997. The law regulates collection of genetic materials for 'research, bioprospecting, conservation, industrial application, commercial use, and other purposes', and requires equitable and adequate benefit sharing from such materials and collections. Infringements of the law carry criminal penalties.

In 1998 three Swiss scientists (one an anthropologist) were arrested for attempting to transport medicinal plant samples and research materials out of Acre without the appropriate authorizations. In October 1999 two German researchers were arrested at an international airport as they attempted to export without permission their fieldnotes, slides and specimens. Similar criminal legislation is under consideration in other Amazon Pact and Andean Community countries, as well as in some Asian countries.

On a more positive note, the 1998 Åarhus Convention[6] (Convention on Access to Information, Public Participation in Decision Making and Access to Justice in Environmental Matters) has set new standards of public participation on all aspects of decision and law-making that affect local peoples. The Convention is specifically aimed at environmental issues, but, as I have tried to show, 'environment' for indigenous peoples means land, resources, knowledge – and all living things. It will be interesting to see how indigenous peoples can use the four guarantees provided by the Åarhus Convention:

1   The right to a healthy environment.
2   The right to know.
3   The right to participate.
4   The right to access to justice.

The 'right to access to justice' is perhaps the most interesting advance in the Convention. Effective and affordable legal representation for individuals, their organizations and communities is guaranteed. Furthermore, the Convention provides for legal processes to be brought against governments and countries. The inability of indigenous peoples to sue the governments that rule them has always been a serious barrier to indigenous rights.

Promoting dialogue

It is clear that in such a climate of mistrust and in absence of clear international legal guidelines and laws, something must be done. Many scientific and professional organizations and institutions are beginning to understand and respond to the deep anxieties and concerns of indigenous peoples over the misuse of and lack of protection for indigenous knowledge. Codes of conduct and standards of practice have been developed in order to guide research, health, educational, and conservation projects with indigenous and local communities.[7]

One of the most extensive codes is that of the International Society for Ethnobiology, which undertook a ten-year consultation with indigenous and traditional peoples – as well as its extensive international membership – to establish 'principles for equitable partnerships'. The main objective of the process was to establish terms under which collaboration and joint research between ethnobiologists and communities could proceed, based upon trust, transparency and mutual concerns. The principles are:

1   *Principle of prior rights* – This principle recognizes that indigenous peoples, traditional societies, and local communities have prior, proprietary rights and interests over all air, land and water ways, and the natural resources within them that these peoples have traditionally inhabited or used, together with all knowledge and intellectual property and traditional resource rights associated with such resources and their use.

2   *Principle of self-determination* – This principle recognizes that indigenous peoples, traditional societies and local communities have a right to self-determination (or local determination for traditional and local communities), and that researchers and associated organizations will acknowledge and respect such rights in their dealings with these peoples and their communities.

3   *Principle of inalienability* – This principle recognizes the inalienable rights of indigenous peoples, traditional societies and local communities in relation to their traditional territories and the natural resources within them and associated traditional knowledge. These rights are collective by nature but can include individual rights. It shall be for indigenous peoples, traditional societies and local communities to determine for themselves the nature and scope of their respective resource rights regimes.

4   *Principle of traditional guardianship* – This principle recognizes the holistic interconnectedness of humanity with the ecosystems of our Sacred Earth, and the obligation and responsibility of indigenous peoples, traditional societies and local communities to preserve and maintain their role as traditional guardians of these ecosystems through the maintenance of their cultures, mythologies, spiritual beliefs and customary practices.

5   *Principle of active participation* – This principle recognizes the crucial importance of indigenous peoples, traditional societies and local communities actively to participate in all phases of the project from inception to completion, as well as in application of research results.

6   *Principle of full disclosure* – This principle recognizes that indigenous peoples, traditional societies and local communities are entitled to be fully informed about the nature, scope and ultimate purpose of the proposed

research (including methodology, data collection, and the dissemination and application of results). This information is to be given in a manner that takes into consideration and actively engages with the body of knowledge and cultural preferences of these peoples and communities.

7 *Principle of prior informed consent and veto* – This principle recognizes that the prior informed consent of all peoples and their communities must be obtained before any research is undertaken. Indigenous peoples, traditional societies and local communities have the right to veto any programme, project or study that affects them. Providing prior informed consent presumes that all potentially affected communities will be provided complete information regarding the purpose and nature of the research activities and the probable results, including all reasonably foreseeable benefits and risks of harm (be they tangible or intangible) to the affected communities.

8 *Principle of confidentiality* – This principle recognizes that indigenous peoples, traditional societies and local communities, at their sole discretion, have the right to exclude from publication and/or to have kept confidential any information concerning their culture, traditions, mythologies or spiritual beliefs. Furthermore, such confidentiality shall be guaranteed by researchers and other potential users. Indigenous and traditional peoples also have the right to privacy and anonymity.

9 *Principle of respect* – This principle recognizes the necessity for researchers to respect the integrity, morality and spirituality of the culture, traditions and relationships of indigenous peoples, traditional societies and local communities with their worlds, and to avoid the imposition of external conceptions and standards.

10 *Principle of active protection* – This principle recognizes the importance of researchers taking active measures to protect and to enhance the relationships of indigenous peoples, traditional societies and local communities with their environment, and thereby promote the maintenance of cultural and biological diversity.

11 *Principle of precaution* – This principle acknowledges the complexity of interactions between cultural and biological communities, and thus the inherent uncertainty of effects due to ethnobiological and other research. The precautionary principle advocates taking proactive, anticipatory action to identify and to prevent biological or cultural harms resulting from research activities or outcomes, even if cause-and-effect relationships have not yet been scientifically proven. The prediction and assessment of such biological and cultural harms must include local criteria and indicators, thus must fully involve indigenous peoples, traditional societies and local communities.

12 *Principle of compensation and equitable sharing* – This principle recognizes that indigenous peoples, traditional societies and local communities must

be fairly and adequately compensated for their contribution to ethnobiological research activities and outcomes involving their knowledge.

13 *Principle of supporting indigenous research* – This principle recognizes,
    supports and prioritizes the efforts of indigenous peoples, traditional soci-
    eties and local communities in undertaking their own research and
    publications, and in utilizing their own collections and databases.

14 *Principle of the dynamic interactive cycle* – This principle holds that research
    activities should not be initiated unless there is reasonable assurance that
    all stages of the project can be completed from (1) preparation and evalu-
    ation, to (2) full implementation, to (3) evaluation, dissemination and
    return of results to the communities, to (4) training and education as an
    integral part of the project, including practical application of results. Thus,
    all projects must be seen as *cycles of continuous and on-going dialogue*.

15 *Principle of Restitution* – This principle recognizes that every effort will be
    made to avoid any adverse consequences to indigenous peoples, traditional
    societies and local communities from research activities and outcomes,
    and that, should any such adverse consequence occur, appropriate restitu-
    tion shall be made.

Indigenous peoples themselves have become proactive and provide forums for
extraordinarily productive dialogue between indigenous leaders and the scientific community. Significant collaborative projects have been effected by the
Dene, the Saami, various Aboriginal Land Councils, numerous Maori groups
and organizations, as well as the Zuni, Kuna, Masaai, and Cree, to name but a
few. Indigenous organizations, such as the Indigenous Peoples' Biodiversity
Network, International Alliance of Indigenous-Tribal Peoples of the Tropical
Forests, and Keepers of the Treasures have led to initiatives that encourage
dialogue with non-indigenous peoples involved in research, business, development, and planning. In February 2000 the Union of British Columbia Indian
Chiefs hosted a major international conference on 'Protecting Knowledge',
which resulted, amongst other things, in one of the most useful web sites
available (along with our own WGTRR site, of course – http://users.ox.ac.
uk/~wgtrr) on all aspects of traditional resource rights and cultural property
(http://www.ubcic.bc.ca/protect.htm).

Concluding remarks

The study of indigenous knowledge is fraught with methodological, theoretical, political and practical difficulties. Today, anthropologists must operate in a
relative policy and legal vacuum that makes the study of indigenous knowledge a highly political act, especially given the highly charged atmosphere of
mistrust that has been generated by fears of biopiracy. On the one hand we
are accused of *scientizing* indigenous knowledge, while on the other we are
suspected of being criminals out to loot valuable national heritage. Some-

where in the middle we are even accused of romanticizing indigenous peoples and their knowledge to create (paraphrasing from Kent Redford) 'intellectual noble savages'.

But as imperfect as we are, anthropologists are still some of the only people, as the US anthropologist Miles Richardson said years ago, trying to tell the great epic myths of human struggle. And if we don't try to understand the knowledge systems of indigenous peoples, then who will? Increasingly, however, the nature of the *telling* has become one that results from dialogue and partnership with indigenous peoples, rather than observation and distant analysis. Gone are the days when anthropologists described 'their peoples' as objects of study. We are now more likely to be called on as advisors or helpers in efforts by local communities to record their own knowledge, inventory their own resources, and map their own lands and territories in ways *they* see most culturally and politically appropriate. That is, in fact, the only way that the study of indigenous knowledge can advance without fragmenting the cosmic connectedness between land, culture and knowledge.

Anthropologists do not have to abandon their most treasured theories or research topics, but rather learn ways to negotiate with local peoples on how 'our' research can benefit 'their' communities. And this negotiation process, as the Oxford anthropologist Tom Griffiths found when doing fieldwork with the Witoto of Colombia, should now be seen as an essential part of research. Indeed, one of the most productive phases of fieldwork is that which establishes collaborative research interests, boundaries of knowledge, sharing of benefits, and control over outcomes.

Unfortunately, too few anthropologists have experience with IPR, or even know about the CBD and the emerging new international norms of full disclosure, prior informed consent, and equitable benefit sharing. There is a steep learning curve for those conducting research on indigenous knowledge. But anthropologists can build upon the considerable experience we have – more than any other discipline – to *lead* the international processes that are now under way to transform the predatory legacy of *terra nullius* into the collaborative partnerships that are urgently needed to curb the dramatic loss of biological, cultural and language diversity.

I believe the desire is there, but institutional support is still lacking. Which research councils or foundations will fund research into IPR for indigenous knowledge? Or provide resources for the lengthy and tedious processes of negotiating the protocols necessary to effect the new kind of anthropology that is needed? How many students are told that collaborative arrangements for data distribution are essential as the initial phase of fieldwork? The answer to these questions is: 'too few'.

This must change. And with these changes will emerge a much more dynamic, responsive, and relevant anthropology. It will be an anthropology that *guides* the multidisciplinary and multicultural responses that are needed to solve global problems, while respecting what indigenous peoples call 'the Sacred Balance'.

Notes

1   The editors thank Graham Dutfield for generously undertaking substantial work revising Darrell Posey's contribution to this book following his sad death.
2   This was done without permission of either the country or the Wapishana Indians who provided him information. According to the patent application, the active ingredient of the plant is an efficient antipyretic, capable of preventing comeback cases of diseases such as malaria, and also useful in treating tumours and even HIV. The Greenheart extract was baptized as *rupununine*, a reference to the region's main river. The other active ingredient registered by the chemist, *polyacetylene*, was obtained from the Cunani bush *Clibadium sylvestre*. It is prescribed as a powerful stimulant of the central nervous system, as a neuromuscular agent capable of reverting cases of heart blockage.
3   The Statement is printed as Appendix 10, pp. 219–222, in Posey and Dutfield (1996).
4   A careful look at IPR ownership clauses in DFID, ESRC or EC grants reveals that the granting agency retains primary ownership over data collected as a result of their funding. University contracts likewise frequently hold IPRs for the University. At Oxford, for example, students cede all IPRs to the University; and even faculty and staff must negotiate a maximum of 75 per cent of any financial benefits from research or publications.
5   Significantly, some indigenous groups already have their own policies and regulations addressing the need to control access to their territories, to monitor the activities of plant collectors and researchers, and to become beneficiaries of plant collections and research. Examples in Latin America are the Kuna of Panama and the Awa of Ecuador (see Posey and Dutfield 1996).
6   The Convention was organized by the Economic Commission for Europe of the United Nations and was signed by forty countries of Europe and Central Asia at a Ministerial Conference in Åarhus, Denmark in June 1998.
7   A summary of some of these can be found in Cunningham (1993) and Posey and Dutfield (1996).

Bibliography

Agrawal, A. 1999. On power and indigenous knowledge. In D. A. Posey (ed.) *Cultural and Spiritual Values of Biodiversity* (pp. 177–180). Nairobi: United Nations Environment Programme; and London: Intermediate Technology Publications.

Bennett, D. 1999. Stepping from the diagram: Australian Aboriginal cultural and spiritual values relating to biodiversity. In D. A. Posey (ed.) *Cultural and Spiritual Values of Biodiversity* (pp. 102–105). Nairobi: United Nations Environment Programme; and London: Intermediate Technology Publications.

Boyle, J. 1996. *Shamans, Software and Spleens: Law and the Construction of the Information Society*. Cambridge, MA: Harvard University Press.

Cunningham, A. B. 1993. *Ethics, Ethnobiological Research, and Biodiversity*. Gland: WWF/UNESCO/Kew People and Plants Initiative.

Dobkin de Rios, M. 1972. *Visionary Vibe: Psychedelic Healing in the Peruvian Amazon*. San Francisco: Chandler Publications for Health Sciences.

Freedman, F. B. 1999. *Vegetalismo* and the perception of biodiversity: Shamanic values in the Peruvian upper Amazon. In D. A. Posey (ed.) *Cultural and Spiritual Values of Biodiversity* (pp. 277–278). Nairobi: United Nations Environment Programme; and London: Intermediate Technology Publications.

Harrison, K. 2000. Leaves of the shepherdess. *Awakened Woman: The Journal of Women's Spirituality* 1 June. http://www.awakenedwoman.com/leaves_of_shepherdess.htm.

Hugh-Jones, S. 1999. 'Food' and 'drugs' in north-west Amazonia. In D. A. Posey (ed.) *Cultural and Spiritual Values of Biodiversity* (pp. 278–280). Nairobi: United Nations Environment Programme; and London: Intermediate Technology Publications.

Langton, M. 2000. Indigenous concepts of connectedness and the new environmentalism. Paper presented at the Linacre Lecture Series on *Consciousness of Connections: Global Environments in the New Millennium*. Oxford, 3 February.

Maffi, L. 1999. Language and the environment. In D. A. Posey (ed.) *Cultural and Spiritual Values of Biodiversity* (pp. 22–35). Nairobi: United Nations Environment Programme; and London: Intermediate Technology Publications.

Matowanyika, J. Z. Z. 1997. Resource management and the Shona people in rural Zimbabwe. In IUCN Inter-Commission Task Force on Indigenous Peoples *Indigenous Peoples and Sustainability: Cases and Actions* (pp. 257–266). Utrecht: International Books.

Opoku, K. A. 1978. *West African Traditional Religion*. Lagos: FEP International.

Posey, D. A. 1996. Indigenous knowledge, biodiversity, and international rights: Learning about forest from the Kayapó Indians of the Brazilian Amazon. *Commonwealth Forestry Review* 76: 53–60.

Posey, D. A. and G. Dutfield. 1996. *Beyond Intellectual Property: Toward Traditional Resource Rights for Indigenous Peoples and Local Communities*. Ottawa: International Development Research Centre.

Posey, D. A., G. Dutfield and K. Plenderleith. 1995. Collaborative research and intellectual property rights. *Biodiversity and Conservation* 4: 892–902.

Slikkerveer, J. 1999. Introduction. In D. A. Posey (ed.) *Cultural and Spiritual Values of Biodiversity* (pp. 169–177). Nairobi: United Nations Environment Programme; and London: Intermediate Technology Publications.

Strathern, M. 1996. Potential property: Intellectual rights and property in persons. *Social Anthropology* 4: 17–32.

Sultan, R., P. Josif, C. Mackinolty and J. Mackinolty. 1995. *Ecopolitics IX: Perspectives on Indigenous Peoples Management of Environment Resources*. Darwin: Northern Land Council.

Suzuki, D. 1999. Finding a new story. In D. A. Posey (ed.) *Cultural and Spiritual Values of Biodiversity* (pp. 72–73). Nairobi: United Nations Environment Programme; and London: Intermediate Technology Publications.

UNESCO. 1993a. UNESCO General Conference: Amendment to the draft programme and budget for 1994–1995 (27 C/5). Submission of Hungary, Philippines, Republic of Korea and Japan. Paris: Unesco.

——. 1993b. Conserving outstanding cultural landscapes. *The World Heritage Newsletter* 2: 14–15.

UN Economic and Social Council. 1986. 'Study of the problem of discrimination against indigenous populations', Geneva: ECOSOC (E/CN.4/sub.2/1986/7), Addendum 4, paragraph 625.

Whitt, L. A. 1999. Metaphor and power in indigenous and Western knowledge systems. In D. A. Posey (ed.) *Cultural and Spiritual Values of Biodiversity* (pp. 69–72). Nairobi: United Nations Environment Programme; and London: Intermediate Technology Publications.

Yunupingu, J. G. 1995. Quoted from Australian Catholic Social Justice Council's 'Recognition: The Way Forward'. In *Native Title Report: January – June 1994*. Aboriginal and Torres Strait Islander Social Justice Commissioner, Canberra: Australian Government Publishing Service.

Chapter 3

Beyond the cognitive paradigm
Majority knowledges and local discourses in a non-Western donor society

John Clammer

The anthropology of development faces perennial problems in deciding its role in the world and its relationship to its two principal clients – its informants, whose interests it is supposed to serve on the one hand, and the states or organizations for whom it acts as a specialized 'probe' (and from which it is probably receiving its funding) on the other. Buffeted internally by the 'crisis of representation' and externally by the demise of the colonial structures which once gave much of anthropology its authoritative voice, a state of subdued crisis in the sub-discipline seems to be the norm. Development anthropology has undergone a number of transformations over its relatively brief history. The current one is that by somehow constructing a relationship with 'indigenous knowledge' (often by way of engagement with 'participatory research') development anthropology will (re)establish its credentials. (The literature on this is rapidly growing. For good examples, see Pottier 1997 and Sillitoe 1998).

What exactly this relationship is supposed to be is not always well defined. Is it to 'discover' that knowledge (which locals already have); or to conscientize the locals so that they recognize that their local knowledge is, after all, valuable (which they presumably know anyway); or to publicize that knowledge to those in ignorance of it (development agencies and governments, even other anthropologists) in the hope one assumes that it will be used to formulate better policy; or even (something which is almost professionally unspeakable) to criticize that knowledge and the practices that it generates (one thinks for example of persisting slavery, female genital mutilation or ethnocide)? Each of these possible approaches clearly has problems: the widespread dissemination of local knowledges in the form, classically, of ethnographies, or more recently as reports to development agencies, inevitably faces the possibilities of the commercial exploitation or misuse of that knowledge, even in its most extreme case for strategic or military purposes.

Development anthropology's problems

Anthropologists are clearly aware of these problems; a reading of most of the contemporary literature in the field reflects an acute self-consciousness. But I would nevertheless contend that this reflexivity does not go nearly far enough, and that 'discourses of development' in anthropology (to borrow the title of Grillo and Stirrat's recent (1997) collection) still reflect a self-limiting frame within which 'development' issues are discussed in a distinctive language constituted of an odd amalgam of the terminology of development economics, the 'reportese' of development agencies and the currently politically correct. Open almost any standard text in the field and it is immediately apparent that one is in the presence of *development anthropology*, and not some other kind; it reflects a language and thematic selection that one suspects began as a bid to funding agencies and has remarkably quickly been institutionalized as a tradition.

So how might the reflexive project be pushed forward, not just for its own sake, but to refine (or even to question altogether) the purpose of development anthropology? Here I will propose two arguments, separate on some levels, but intertwined on others. The first is that, despite its avowed concern with local or indigenous knowledges, development anthropology is still essentially Cartesian in its epistemological framework. Such a framework is significant, not for what is popularly believed to be its problem with the mind–body relationship, but rather for its prioritizing of the cognitive dimension of knowledge over other possible dimensions, and in particular the more somatic dimensions of perception, action and response, including of course the emotions. Even in the context of much of the newer participatory research the emphasis is still on the cognitive dimensions of knowledge, in the hope that if one appends the word 'indigenous' this will somehow dissolve the Cartesian model, which is still, however, the epistemological foundation of the whole enterprise. This, I shall go on to argue, is a view that needs to be contested. My second contention is that this primary framework, and the way in which it causes questions in development anthropology to be posed, conceals (paradoxically for anthropology of all subjects) a strong and continuing Western bias. This arises from two sources. The first is that concern with (indigenous) knowledge has led in anthropology, as suggested above, to a dominating involvement with 'participatory development' (despite the hazards of that model having been vocally pointed out: e.g. Rahnema 1995). The logic by which this move is made is interesting and disingenuous. In one sense everybody 'participates' in the development being visited upon them or which they have themselves initiated. But this particular anthropological model only really works if an opposition is created between 'indigenous knowledge' (which is *a priori* determined to be good), and other kinds of knowledge (foreign, universal, 'Western'?) often left undefined, but which must be bad. The problem here is that indigenous knowledge is being harnessed to a project or a grand narrative ('development') in which it is invited (or more probably obliged) to participate, despite the fact that agreeing to the master narrative at all is almost certainly the first step in undermining the integrity or social validity of the indigenous knowledge itself. In other words, except in the most radical of social movements for local autonomy, 'participation' actually almost always means not (except perhaps at a very local level indeed) empowerment to define goals, but rather the strategic uses of local knowledge in pursuit of aims not autonomously defined (Esteva and Prakash 1998). Anthropology nevertheless has tried to defend its position in the development field by arguing that it is uniquely positioned to overcome the dichotomies of indigenous/foreign knowledge. On this point, however, it may be deluding itself. As anthropology was once accused of being the handmaiden of colonialism, it may all too easily find itself in the dock again, this time as the unwitting servant of the West's newest 'civilizing' project – development itself – not least through its continued romanticization of the local knowledge of the Other.

The second source of the Western bias lies in Euro–American anthropology's ignorance, or sidelining where it does know that it exists, of indigenous and alternative anthropologies. There are two related forms of this, both equally interesting. One is the nature of 'native' anthropologies, which are a subject of interest because they reveal indigenous intellectuals struggling to rework methodologies, theoretical frameworks, relations between anthropologist and informants, and the uses of social knowledge so learnt. Two very different 'indigenous' formulations of the problem can be found, by way of examples, in the work of the Maori scholar Linda Tuhiwai Smith (1999) and the doyen of Chinese mainland anthropology Fei Hsiao Tung (1981). It is often local anthropology which leads the process of mediating and interpreting local knowledge (of which itself it is a part) and of finding solutions to the problem of representation by looking within, and in so doing creating models which may not be in accord with the cognitive assumptions of Western social analysis in their reflection of alternative ontologies. The other source of alternative anthropology comes from non-Western countries which both have flourishing indigenous anthropological communities and actively participate in international development activities through support of multilateral institutions, their own aid and development agencies and extensive networks of local NGOs, often devoted to domestic 'development' issues as well as to international ones.

Japanese indigenous anthropology

How then might this critique of development anthropology be put into practice? I will explore this here through the study of one such large non-Western donor country, namely Japan. It has a significant anthropological profession and an extensive network of NGOs. It also has its own substantial ethnic and social minorities who constantly call into question the developmental discourse of the state and enter into solidarity arrangements with other 'indigenous' peoples globally.

Japan is an interesting case since it has also, despite or because of the inroads of modernity and modernization, quite self-consciously attempted to develop, almost as its national project, its own 'indigenous knowledge' (or cosmology perhaps, since that 'knowledge' very much transcends the purely cognitive), very different from and based on opposing epistemological principles from most of the West (Clammer 1995). This sets up an intriguing dynamic: a non-Western society which is a major aid donor but which frames its relationship to the world and its understanding of other societies in different terms from those of the West, and which possesses a large and active NGO sector challenging both local and exported definitions of development. This sense of cultural autonomy fundamentally affects the way in which local development anthropology sees its mission and methodology.

Quite apart from the intrinsic interest of exploring the nature and content of alternative anthropologies, it is the case that such anthropologies also understand the relationship between indigenous knowledge and development rather differently from their Western counterparts – something not only true in Japan, but also amongst Maori anthropologists in New Zealand and Amerindian ones in Canada among others (see Croal and Darou, chapter 5). Their sometimes radical reframing of issues substantially changes the nature of debates about the role of anthropology in development. This is not only because of disagreements about the meaning or desirability or even reality of 'development', but equally importantly because such alternative anthropologies deconstruct any simplistic notion of 'indigenous' knowledge along three lines. The first is that what foreign anthropologists understand to be such knowledge, or its most significant expressions, may not in fact be at the centre of a culture's cosmological system; the classical example in the anthropology of Japan being Ruth Benedict's famous and misleading monograph *The Chrysanthemum and the Sword*, originally issued in 1946 and still in print (Benedict 1989). The second is that 'indigenous' knowledge turns out to have a rather complex relationship with other forms of knowledge. It may not be a minority knowledge at all, but a widely shared majority knowledge which is simply suppressed, unnoticed or disregarded by academics or politicians as not being knowledge at all, but belief, superstition or something similar. This point is tellingly made by Esteva and Prakash (1998) in their argument that, paradoxically, it is that which is known to most of us, rather than the esoteric knowledge of non-native specialists, which is devalued (not in practice since it informs our everyday social strategies, but in hierarchies of prestige) (De Certeau 1988; Bourdieu 1979).

The third is that much substantial 'knowledge' may turn out to be not cognitive after all, but affective, corporeal, mystical and/or deriving from cultural conceptions of nature, with its sources in experience, memory and suffering rather than in thought, and its expression mediated through material objects, mythology, religion, art and self-images. In short, ontologies lie at the core of conceptions of being, and ontologies are primarily lived, not thought. Failure to recognize this can only lead to endless replaying of the old rationality debates that have plagued anthropology at least since Evans-Pritchard's (1968) *Witchcraft Among the Azande*. This is not of course to deny that local knowledges exist, but to argue that, like everything else in social analysis, they must be seen in a larger and even a global context (e.g. Mills 1995).

Development thinking from a 'peripheral centre': the Japanese case

Japan is the society most often juxtaposed with the West, which the Japanese at least see as the primary 'Other' (rather than China or the rest of Asia). The basis for this, constantly repeated, is that Japan is the only Asian society to have industrialized indigenously and without ever being colonized. The rise of Japan to the status of the world's second biggest economy has naturally triggered intense debates within the country – about Japan's role in the international community, its possible position as maybe the only fully 'postmodern' society, and about the social and cultural sources of this economic success. While some of these debates have taken a nationalistic and even chauvinistic stance (e.g. in the writings of Ishihara Shintaro (1991), the current Governor of Tokyo, in his notorious book *'No' to ieru Nippon* or 'The Japan That Can Say "No"'), others have accepted that Japan's economic might should translate into international social responsibility. This latter perception has taken two main forms. At the level of the state, Japan has become in the last decade (depending on the year and yen–dollar exchange rate), either the biggest or second biggest aid (official development assistance, or ODA) donor in the world.

But at the level of wider society the response has mostly taken the form of a proliferation of NGOs engaged in a huge range of activities including the provision of emergency aid and technical expertise; the import and sale of Third World products in Japan; bringing small farmers to Japan for agricultural training; the promotion of small industries in developing countries; and the creation of collective farms in developing countries. An equally important activity has been the collection and dissemination of information about developing countries through publications, seminars, fairs, the bringing of cultural troupes to Japan and the promotion of speaking tours by leading indigenous intellectuals. Such NGOs are often explicitly critical of government-led development efforts, which are widely seen as wasteful, badly planned, as promoting Japanese big business interests (since the contracts for almost all large-scale infrastructure projects funded by ODA can only be bid for by Japanese companies) and, in line with critiques of aid elsewhere, as generally encouraging corruption, dependency and underdevelopment, rather than positive social and economic transformation.

Underlying this diversity of approaches is an even more fundamental distinction, commonly made by Japanese NGOs. Government, seen as being in collusion with and almost indistinguishable from big business interests, is perceived as promoting basically nationalistic and capitalist goals in which ODA, proffered as a sign of Japan's responsibility and benevolence, actually benefits the Japanese economy by creating both opportunities for expansion overseas and a net in-flow (in terms of contracts and interest on loans) into Japanese corporate bank accounts. The role of the NGOs is seen, in contrast, as exporting not just some form of practical aid, important as that is, but in promoting the values which they believe gives Japanese culture its distinctive qualities, including 'relationalism' as opposed to extreme forms of individualism (Hamaguchi 1982), a deep affinity for nature, a Buddhist-based ethic of selflessness and non-attachment, an essentially non-materialist understanding of what constitutes the good life and the good society and, since the disastrous experience of World War II and the nuclear bombing of Hiroshima and Nagasaki, an attachment to peace promotion and conflict resolution. Many Japanese NGOs are consequently not just technical agencies, but also (often tiny) centres of ideological production and reproduction, offering a non-statist alternative range of visions about what 'development' itself is all about, as well as in many cases, practical suggestions about how to achieve it.

Ethnic stratification and social exclusion in Japan

The NGOs in Japan, as anywhere else, do not operate in a social vacuum. On the contrary, they are organic to the society, or at least to sectors or strata of it, and of which they are a part or an expression. Furthermore the NGO sector is imbued with and seeking to internationalize values which are seen as being fundamental to Japanese civilization, values which themselves need defending against the onslaughts of consumer capitalism, 'McDonaldization' and the forces of alienation at large in society. The perception of mainstream Japanese society as exclusionary towards its minorities needs to be tempered with the recognition of these alternative voices, which are neither quiet nor few in number. In a global frame this itself is an example of 'indigenous knowledge' on a large scale: an entire society offering itself as an alternative to a homogeneous, universal history of modernity.

Thus, despite strenuous government- and nationalist-led attempts to argue that it does, Japan does not have a totally homogeneous culture. It contains not only class differences (which we should remember can constitute different indigenous knowledges), but also substantial ethnic minorities who have been unwillingly incorporated into the modern nation state by a variety of devices. The Korean community, the largest minority, originated mostly in forced labour introduced into Japan during the period when Korea was a Japanese colony, a status that only ended in 1945 with Japan's defeat in the war. The Chinese community is similar in origin (both Taiwan and Manchuria having also been colonies of Japan). The Ainu of the northern island of Hokkaido, who are in origin a Siberian people, were incorporated by the annexation of Hokkaido by Japan in 1869 At the other end of Japan are the sub-tropical

Ryukyu Islands (Okinawa), a formerly independent kingdom that was absorbed as a prefecture of Japan in 1879 and which was under US military occupation from 1945 until its reversion to Japanese control in 1972. In each of these cases, and to a lesser extent on the part of the socially excluded but ethnically Japanese Burakumin (Buraku 1992; De Vos and Wagatsuma 1966), there is the claim for a counter-hegemonic local knowledge vis-à-vis the dominant Japanese one. In the case of the Koreans and Chinese this has taken the form not only of a critique of Japanese colonialism and continuing discrimination in work, housing, marriage and social reputation, but of appeals to the original high cultures, from which their modern and local societies derive, and from which Japan itself has borrowed very heavily. The Okinawans and the Ainu do not have this option, although the Okinawans come closest to it by arguing both for the distinctive features of their culture (shamanism is a popular one) and for its uniquely syncretic form, derived from Chinese, Korean and Southeast Asian sources and synthesized into a culture quite different from that of mainland Japan. The Ainu cite their colonized status, the suppression of their language and culture, and their position as genuine aborigines inhabiting Hokkaido long before any Japanese showed up. Both have adopted interesting parallel strategies. One is to emphasize and to some extent reconstruct their indigenous religious traditions, taken to reflect the core of their respective cultures and the wellspring of their indigenous knowledge. Much as North American Indian religion has been rediscovered or reinvented as the source of difference and wisdom of the people possessing it, so a similar process has occurred in both Okinawa and Hokkaido.

A second strategy is the internationalization of their struggles, not so much for cultural autonomy (although that is the position of a significant minority in both cases), but for cultural recognition, the right to cultural expression (including the use of their languages) and an end to negative discrimination. This has been done by active participation in the Indigenous People's Movement worldwide, attendance at international conferences and gatherings of indigenous peoples, and input into UN deliberations on the rights of indigenous peoples. This strategy has both highlighted ambiguities in the Japanese government's approach to development (exporting development while ignoring national minorities), and forced Japanese NGOs (most of the members of which are ethnic Japanese) to clarify their own values and to question the extent to which their own overseas activities are actually a form of subtle Japanese cultural imperialism, morally earnest no doubt, but certainly not innocent of quasi-colonial undertones dressed up in a language of internationalization and globalization. For the ethnic minorities the real proof of Japan's much vaunted *kokusaika* (internationalization) is not the export of Japanese values and culture to others, but the acceptance within Japan of certain key 'universal' values, such as human rights, autonomous development, and the provision of space and resources for the practice of local cultures.

Here we find local cultures appealing to 'universal' values to support their own localism, while finding in the majority indigenous knowledge with which they have to live (and especially its claims to 'uniqueness') the source of their own oppression.

Japanese anthropology as local knowledge

A certain expert knowledge is needed to mediate the local and the global successfully, and it is here that anthropology enters the picture. Many Japanese anthropologists are students of their own society and particularly of its minorities. The single largest centre of anthropology in the country – the National Museum of Ethnology in Osaka – devotes much of its collections, research and publications to local and regional cultures. Anthropology is consequently perceived by the minorities as a discipline for recovering cultural information (much of it now lost to younger generation members), for presenting it to the public in a respectable and 'scientific' form (something of considerable significance in a society where scholarship is still highly respected and its results often widely disseminated and discussed in the mass media), and as a resource which enables them better to argue their case in international forums. Many anthropologists have willingly taken on a medi-ating role as channels of information or spokespersons for minority groups and many are members of NGOs promoting their interests, a strategic posi-tion since it allows for the funnelling of information both ways between minorities and universities, and between minority spokespeople and govern-ment. Many Japanese anthropologists choose to represent themselves as outsiders to their own society and often sport clothes, accessories, hairstyles and the beards that identify them more with their subjects than with the mainstream society, of which they are in fact respectable members.

Social issues in Japan are actively constructed and contested within the country, despite the public front of being a harmonious and conflict-free society (Mouer and Sugimoto 1986). This is achieved by an interesting inter-play between perceptions of responsibility to the wider world, the qualities of Japanese (majority) culture, and the ways in which local groups of the rela-tively dispossessed (ethnic minorities certainly, but also such groups as the differently abled and foreign workers) demand fulfilment of the claims of the majority culture by counterposing them with the claims of the non-local – mostly supposedly 'universal' knowledge and values couched in a language of rights and rationality. This places them simultaneously inside and outside purely Japanese discourses, insiders using the lever of the global to support their claims for localism.

This socially constructivist model of knowledge has two important impli-cations. The first is that it once again challenges any simplistic concept of 'indigenous' knowledge, since in practice and strategically that knowledge proves to be implicated in 'majority' knowledge (so-called, although as I have argued earlier, this is often nothing more than a popularized version of some specialist orthodoxy taken on trust rather than being a form of *knowledge* as such). Local knowledges actually draw from, and in turn contribute to, 'majority' knowledges, and in this instance both contribute to anthropology and utilize it. It is actually not at all uncommon in many parts of the world to meet 'natives' who have a remarkable grasp of anthropological language and procedures, who know just what an anthropologist is likely to be looking for, and know how to 'explain' their society in those terms. When the culture in question is a highly literate one (as in Japan) many people will actually have read what anthropologists have been saying about them, something which may be scary for anthropologists, but certainly has the function of diluting the authoritative voice of the 'expert' and willy-nilly promoting dialogue and arguments about interpretation between the anthropologist and the studied community. This in turn impinges on the implicit models with which many (mainly Western) anthropologists work about the sharing or even 'owning' of local knowledges. Hobart's (1993) idea of an opposition between Western scientific knowledge and local knowledges, in which the former must necessarily override and suppress the latter, is misleading. It fails to recognize the ways in which local cultures draw on, assimilate and transform varieties of this 'Western' knowledge (Tobin 1992), even as that knowledge appropriates elements of the local knowledges (in herbal medical research, for example).

'Asian values' and NGOs

When the boundaries between 'local' and 'non-local' 'knowledges' are blurred and fuzzy, the concepts through which such knowledge is expressed become open to debate and redefinition. This is especially true of those terms entering local discourses from more global ones or, as is more often the case, from other specific but powerful politically or conceptually hegemonic cultures. The concept of 'human rights' is one such term much fought over in the context of the 'Asian values' debate in Southeast Asia. Concepts of freedom in Asia have likewise recently come under scrutiny and debate (Kelly and Reid 1998), mostly in terms of separating their local meanings from hegemonic ones, although even this boundary may no longer be altogether clear, as indigenous movements themselves increasingly draw on a more universal human rights discourse and have greater recourse to a legal language to contest the law itself (Merry 1997). Concepts 'migrate' and are often reinterpreted in a new context in unexpected ways, an inevitable consequence of the globalized environment which generates and frames such flows (Featherstone 1997; Appadurai 1998).

In Japan this debate has revolved partly around the definition of such concepts as modernity and postmodernity (Miyoshi and Harootunian 1989), partly around the discussion of the indigenization of the social sciences, and partly around the cultural framing and use of such concepts in political practice, labour disputes and gender conflicts. A conventional view has long been that the Japanese do not seek rights in any abstract or absolute sense, but seek rather to be recognized in terms of their legitimate role in the social hierarchy. A chauffeur may not have the same rights as his boss, but he does have rights as a chauffeur and should be respected as such. This, the historian T.C. Smith (1989) has called the 'right to benevolence'. It is possible that this was true in the past and still colours contemporary conceptions of rights, but what has changed is that the participants in local systems of knowledge now have access to much wider ones on which they can and do draw selectively. Their activities, strictly speaking, may appear ambiguous, contradictory or syncretic, but that is in the nature of everyday culture, which is never 'finished' and is always strategic.

The same is true of local NGOs. They too draw on more universal 'knowledges' and professional expertise, particularly that of anthropologists in the case of those NGOs concerned primarily with minority or ethnic issues, while others, especially those focusing on environmental questions draw on an even wider range of 'scientific' input. But such NGOs and the wider social movements which they represent or reflect also draw on local knowledge, and in particular cultural values, ideas about relationships and social organization, and particular methodologies for social analysis and social action. Much of the current 'civil society' discourse, which tends to lump NGOs together as a unified social category defined primarily by the characteristic of not being part of the state apparatus (e.g. Clayton 1996), overlooks the actual complex ethnography of NGOs themselves. Again the assumed model is of major Western NGOs and their characteristic modes of operation, when in fact there is immense diversity not only in objectives and size, but in cultural style, ideology and ontological premises. These factors not only determine the relationship of NGOs to the society of which they are a part, but also the values and strategies which they project onto other societies in which they work or have interests. This also accounts for the range of vocabularies that Japanese (and other Asian and no doubt African and Latin American) NGOs use when addressing themselves to the world, many of which at first sight seem to have little to do with conventional 'development' discourses, a language often of values, religion or peace, rather than the economistic language of so much development discourse. The closest parallel to this might be feminist critiques of 'knowledge', which show that much of what passes for, or is represented as, the 'objective' is actually ideology and patterns of power, and as such must be displaced by an alternative mode of knowing and seeing.

Indigenous knowledge and social movements

A major shift, and in many ways a very positive one, in development thinking, has been away from seeing states and the big multinational actors, especially those closely identified with Western interests, as the key to social transformation towards seeing NGOs as playing a role. The expectation is, of course, that the values of sustainability, participatory activity and consciousness raising are best embodied in NGOs, which are seen as being not only the most efficient agencies for the 'delivery' of these desirables, but in many cases as their origi-nators. In much of the emerging civil society discourse NGOs are consequently seen as saviours, as embodying democracy and as filling the space rapidly being vacated by the shrinking state. There are numerous problems with this analysis, just one of which is the broad and undefined category 'NGO', which is in reality very varied in organization, objectives, size, financial stability, political position and role. Some NGOs are basically service organizations delivering a certain very limited product, some are global in scale, while others are single-issue focused. Many in fact are not or do not see themselves as agents of direct social change. This latter role is rather the prerogative of social movements. The line, however, between NGOs and social movements is fuzzy: in some cases they are the same thing, some may serve wider social movements, while others may even oppose them. Ethnographically, then, where does one look for manifestations of indigenous knowledge?

Debates about representation (Marcus and Fischer 1986) and feminist critiques have made it impossible any longer to locate such knowledge in the heads of village elders, or informants of only one gender, or of only one social class. The lesson of contemporary debates about the nature of culture itself (e.g. Friedman 1996) suggests that culture is rarely unified. Rather, it is frag-mented, partially grasped in different ways by different members of a society, and is used (and even invented) strategically and pragmatically. 'Knowledge' itself then cannot be an 'essence', but must be, to paraphrase Wittgenstein, revealed only in its usage. How 'knowledge' is to be recovered ethnographi-cally thus becomes a central question, since much of what can be obtained by conventional methods is almost certainly ideology (class-, gender- or posi-tion-specific) rather than shared, and much of what is shared is actually imposed by other patterns of authority (education, socialization, religion or hierarchies of power, for example). In the context of 'development' I would suggest that at least the beginning of an answer lies in the study of indigenous social movements because they encapsulate social knowledges in the process of their formation.

A social movement, including one of an activist orientation, is by its nature, a dialogic entity in which the views of organic intellectuals and those of other indigenes who constitute the actual or potential wider membership of the movement are in constant interaction and a process of mutual refine-ment. A social movement is also crucially one of the points in a society at which 'knowledge' is being translated into 'practice' or at which the distinction between these (conceptual) categories is being questioned and undermined. The classical sociological opposition of agency and structure is being wrestled within concrete terms in such movements. They represent a genuine source of social knowledge and a particular framing of that knowledge, not necessarily in intellectualist terms, but in terms of a language of ritual, imagination, nostalgia, memory or the utopian.

This makes it odd that social movements theorists (largely concentrated in sociology and political science) rarely address non-Western examples (the few exceptions coming from non-Western analysts, e.g. Wignaraja 1993) and rarely look beyond purely sociological factors (a language of resources, mobilization, class) to anthropological ones. It is also strange that anthropologists rarely talk explicitly about social movements and that in development discourses, where sociology and anthropology should most obviously inform each other, the whole topic is absent. Yet if development is about social transformation, then indigenous social movements are where it is happening – outside a purely economic paradigm and, indeed, as telling local critiques of that paradigm.

Japanese reframings of development discourse

To illustrate these points I will briefly discuss some empirical dimensions from Japan of such alternative views. This is a synthesis of much more extensive research that ranges across and attempts to relate five main areas of interest: (1) indigenous peoples' movements in Japan; (2) the situation of foreign workers, and the support groups that have grown up to provide legal, social and medical provision for such migrants, who are themselves largely of Asian origin; (3) Japanese NGOs and their organization and ideologies; (4) the nature and distinctive characteristics (including value orientation) of Japanese anthropology; and (5) new social movements in Japan. These interrelate with each other in complex ways and any one case study would fail to capture the network-like structure of linkages and mutual influences that characterize the situation. Rather than attempt an 'ethnography' of any one part of this complex system, I will attempt a more holistic sketch of the field of forces within which Japanese development debates take place.

Development debate in Japan is not simply concentrated in the two sectors of government and NGOs. It spills over into a much wider constituency, the main actors in which are (in no particular order) the *shin shukyo* or 'New Religions', some of Buddhist and some of Shinto and a few of Christian origins (Reader 1991); the aforementioned indigenous peoples' movements (e.g. De Vos and Wetherall 1983); professional anthropologists (AERA Mook 1995); and citizen's movements, particularly those of housewives (LeBlanc 1999). Others include groups concerned with environmental issues, recycling and social concerns, the feminist movement (Ueno 1988), and the organic food and farming movement and its more New Age fringes. Some elements in the 'old' religions, in particular Pure Land school Buddhists who have been influenced by Buddhist 'theologies of liberation' thinking from Thailand and Sri Lanka, should also be included, together with the very extensive peace movement and the quite self-consciously new social movements of which the anti-nuclear movement would be an example.

Many of these elements have links with each other. Many of the New Religions not only engage in evangelism and development activities in other parts of Asia, Latin America and even in Europe, but identify themselves very strongly with the peace movement (Kisala 1999). Other factions in the peace movement, many of them with decidedly socialist leanings and which arose from the experience of the atomic bombings of Hiroshima and Nagasaki, find themselves in dialogue with religious communities with which they would otherwise have no dealings.

The city of Hiroshima is itself a good case in point. The first of the two Japanese cities to be the target of atomic bombs in August 1945 and now completely rebuilt, it offers itself to the world as a 'Peace City'; numerous religious and secular peace organizations have offices there. The Peace Park and memorial, which now exists at what was the epicentre of the blast, is a national, and to some extent international, site of pilgrimage, together with the one remaining standing bombed building – the old Industrial Promotion Hall, which is now the 'A Bomb Dome' – a large museum and an international conference centre. The city is also the centre of numerous social activist movements, including vocal Korean and Burakumin defence groups and elderly-rights groups. The national university in the city is a major centre for the teaching of development studies and has many foreign (mainly Asian) students on its postgraduate course. One of the private universities is a major site of social activism and human rights studies, both within Japan and internationally, and independent activist scholars have created a development and research institute in the city to carry on work outside the constraints of university politics (the Institute of Urban Sociology). Hiroshima has turned its sense of victimhood, as the first city to be A-bombed, into a thriving peace and development industry, not only for export, but also for Japan itself; here the Japanese tensions and political conflicts on these issues are focused and magnified (Yoneyama 1999).

Many of the New Religions have international departments, and actively spread their peace message overseas. Other social movement organizations are beginning to do the same. The Seikatsu Club, a cooperative movement started by a man as an explicit social transformation movement but now with a large and overwhelmingly female (largely housewives) membership, both markets organic food on a nationwide basis and has a political wing (*Netto*) which operates mainly at the town and prefectural level. As Robin LeBlanc (1999) argues, such housewives' movements are interesting precisely because many, probably most, of their members reject politics as the way to change society. In keeping with many other movements in Japan, they see positive social change as emerging from the linking of the moral transformation of individuals through paths of self-cultivation to wider social structures. The organic food movement in general, and some of its communalist expressions such as the Yamagishi movement,[1] exemplifies many of these concerns which, whether applied at home or abroad, provide an interesting basis for 'development' (i.e. social transformation or, alternatively, a conservative vision of the good society that opposes development).

These concerns can be summarized as: (1) that knowledge is situational and, in the case of the majority of Seikatsu members, seen to be gendered; (2) that the individualism of Western liberal politics and social philosophy is false and, even if it were true, would be an inadequate basis for the construction of a desirable social order (from their point of view of the needs of human beings); and (3) that the goal of 'development' is to achieve moral coherence, not growth or other economically defined goals. From this perspective it is argued that (a) the strategic role of social movements is to mediate power and values, since both exist, but the failure of transformative thinking has been its inability to translate the latter into the former; (b) the alternative to seeing change through politics is not a withdrawal into privatized lifestyles, but the revitalization of the much talked about but rarely achieved desire for community; and (c) perceptions of the world as well as knowledge about it are crucial to effecting social change or to mobilizing people to act so that an 'aesthetics of development' rather than the economics of development is the desired goal. In this worldview development is not a positivist, materialist process but a drama of the human spirit, and in the last analysis such dramas are really the only interesting thing to human beings. Development is inherently value laden because it is essentially to do with the shaping of new subjectivities (or rediscovering old ones), rather than with material progress as such. It is a matter of one's *relationship* to the world that is at stake, and not the (to a great extent unchangeable) objective nature of that world (Irokawa 1988).

This brief sketch of some of the major elements in indigenous thinking and internal contestations about development of a rather significant non-Western culture highlights several key issues. Anthropologists who have looked at the 'developers' as well as the 'being-developed' have rightly noted that they come from many ideological persuasions and have quite varied philosophies of development (Kaufmann 1997). In this they are quite correct, except that their sample hitherto has been confined to Western agencies, all of which may share a certain Eurocentric view of the world. The Japanese case adds another dimension by asking how things might look from a non-Western donor country with both a huge official aid budget and an extensive range of NGOs, many of them religious and some of them cultural nationalists. It is also a society in which local anthropologists debate these issues as their Western counterparts do, but they do not necessarily come to the same conclusions, assume the same values, philosophical orientations or methodological procedures, ascribe to the same theories, or relate in the same way to their subjects either within Japan or abroad. Anthropologists occupy a structural position within Japanese society as a slightly exotic if not marginalized intellectual community often still identified with folklore and museums rather than with the dynamics of social change. This is reinforced by their links to indigenous peoples' movements within Japan, as well as to more academic research outside the country. Japanese society, as we have seen, has both an extensive NGO sector and an active indigenous people's movement, both of which are linked, often through their knowledge of international law, human rights issues or currents in contemporary development or anti-development thinking, to much wider networks and constituencies. Indeed, local struggles within Japan frequently attempt to force the majority to live up to its espoused values. When what is supposed to be a 'relational' culture excludes Others from its community or pays only lip-service to its traditional concern with ethical self-cultivation, then its first critics are understandably those within the political community who are not real members (they may be ethnic minorities, but can also just as well be Japanese housewives). If the postmodernity debate in Japan has shaded off into a discussion of post-materialist values (including the rights of nature), which many claim that Japan has always had, then it is reasonable for those who do not feel the practical benefits of this philosophy to protest, not against the philosophy itself or its ontological underpinnings, but against the failure to apply it equally.

Japan, development discourses and anthropological theory

A number of theoretical points of interest arise from this discussion. Anthropology is supposed to be an antidote to ethnocentrism, not a way through which new forms are smuggled in. Yet I would contend that academic discourses of development are still essentially Western in character, and that the study of non-Western varieties (not simply of ethnographic cases, but of actual rival or alternative discourses) points a way out of this continuing Eurocentric bias. Linked intimately to this by way of the fundamental 'cosmology' of Western knowledge (Sahlins 1996) is also its cognitive bias. This seemingly irreducible 'Cartesianism', while undoubtedly part of the local knowledge of the West, is not necessarily universal. If it leads to the construction of alternative knowledges in purely intellectualist terms then it is a damaging neocolonial virus that comes in part from the persistent tendency to compare the West with the 'non-West', rather than, in the context of this chapter, one part of Asia with other parts with which it might have far greater continuities of cosmology and social practice. The power of the cognitive model in Western anthropology is great (one thinks of examples such as Lévi-Strauss' contention that totemic categories are not constructed on ecological or dietary grounds, but because they are 'good to think'), and is reflected in attempts to define anthropology itself largely in terms of its being a cognitive science with a methodology drawn more from positivistic psychology than from anthropology itself (D'Andrade 1996). Yet at the same time the anthropology of the emotions has been relegated to a minor sub-field, rather as the related sociology of the body has been in sociology.[2] The major point of convergence between Western and Japanese anthropology has probably been in the area of the anthropology of self/personhood/identity (for the Western side, see Cohen 1994; Csordas 1994), but unfortunately as yet these potential resources have been left unexploited by development anthropologists, whose concept of 'development' is still largely techno-economistic rather than cultural and holistic.

In Japanese social thought the non-rational is given equal weight with the rational, the emotions are considered central to cultural analysis, and aesthetics is represented as being in many ways the central cultural value to which even ethics is subordinated or from which it is derived. A sophisticated form of animism lies at the basis of a large range of local social practices and beliefs and a totalizing cosmology in which Cartesianism is consciously rejected as the larger frame (e.g. Yuasa 1987). If one sees, as Sahlins does, the native cosmology of the West as relating to a particular epistemological configuration, then a parallel analysis could be undertaken not for the 'East' (surely an Orientalist category), but for the major cultures of Asia individually. Such an analysis would suggest very different epistemological configurations. The Buddhist aspects of this epistemology in Japan (a major knowledge tradition throughout most of East, Southeast and large parts of South Asia) contain amongst other things a very different understanding of the self, causality, the reality of the material, and the relationship between the individual and society, which pose a radical challenge to the cognitive assumptions of the West (Pickering 1997).

Part of the problem is the use of the word 'knowledge' itself. A better term might be 'ontology', since an ontology represents not so much knowledge itself as a theory or model of knowledge (which is actually what an epistemology is), and much more in addition, including that which implicitly as well as explicitly derives from that 'knowledge', such as ritual and religious activities. Ontologies are prior to knowledge, since they culturally frame knowledge itself and separate 'relevant' from 'irrelevant' knowledge in terms of the perspective of that cultural frame. They are the root of everyday 'practical knowledges' such as ideas of health, the body, emotions, gender, nature and law. Disputes between cultures are often the clash of ontologies focused on conflict over such issues as land, resources or hunting rights, which typically surface in indigenous people's responses to 'development' initiatives taken on their behalf (e.g. Dove 1988). Ontologies are consequently political in the widest sense, and a Foucauldian theory of knowledge as power only makes anthropological sense if it is understood that this 'knowledge' − presumably actually the creation of the categories through which 'reality' is framed and interpreted − far exceeds the mentalist model often implicit in the narrower concept of knowledge as cognition. People do not only 'think' with their minds. Ontologies are not (or only) metaphysical, but have a profound range of practical implications, not surprisingly as they are modes of being, not just modes of knowing, and as such embody alternative models of social order, including the 'relational epistemology' which while very characteristic of

Japan, is certainly not restricted to that country (Bird-David 1999). Indigenous 'knowledge' seen in this light is both constitutive of a 'culture' and may constitute a sociocultural critique of other cultures or of elements within that culture, which may, of course, include a critique of 'knowledge' itself.

Concluding remarks

First, a methodological comment: it is not at all clear that 'participatory development' does actually produce a new kind of understanding if 'participation' is still in reality managed or directed from above, or that autonomy results from participation in such development (for a literature that critically engages this problem, see Carmen 1996; Goulet 1989; Siamwisa 1995; Brohman 1996). The playing field of 'knowledge' is not level, and the expression of 'indigenous knowledge' is subject to the same hierarchical ordering as any other form of knowledge. Giving voice to the knowledges of the excluded is in a 'development' context as much a priority as the discovery of the knowledge of the local establishment.

Second, significant knowledge in a development context is rarely simply abstract knowledge, but is knowledge about *process* (hence my emphasis on social movements). People subjected to development naturally evolve a discourse about it, a dialectical procedure that inflects and changes what they themselves understand to be knowledge. Such knowledge as praxis becomes in fact largely a means of explaining and adapting to the changes being visited upon them.

Third, it was noted above that Japanese NGOs tend almost universally to be engaged in a dialogue, internally, with other organizations and with the societies in which they work, that is essentially about *values* rather than *knowledge*. While of ethnographic interest in itself, this should also alert us to the paradoxical situation that critiques of knowledge are often intellectualist themselves. This is not only philosophically unhelpful, but deflects attention from the fact that practical critiques of knowledge are most often couched in terms of morals, not alternative cognitive categories. A major recent study of North American social movements (Jasper 1997) sees them as driven by moral imperatives, not by knowledge concerns, and as movements to both reclaim and redefine culture as something beyond, and autonomous from, economics. They are the soil from which other concerns grow: 'Far from being the opposite of rationality, culture, including emotions, defines rationality' (Jasper 1997: 98). Moral communities rather than cognitive communities (if such things exist) consequently provide the basis for (or against) development, and moral communities are built on sympathy and emotion. A social ethic furthermore provides a stable structure of identity, while identities built on knowledge concerns soon crumble in the face of moral challenges (Bettelheim 1986). As recent scholarship on new social movements has suggested, most are actually based on expressivism and performativity, and are primarily forms of identity politics rather than 'rational' agents of change (Hetherington 1998). Unfortunately, however, in this respect anthropology and sociology continue their dialogue of the deaf, since not only do social movements represent participation in action, they also demonstrate the generation of new forms of knowledge in which intellectualism is subordinated to very old, but now re-emphasized, holistic conceptions of the human person, and philosophical and anthropological debates about rationality are reopened in fresh ways.

What finally drives development is not just the power of reason, but also moral goals and the power of desire. Anthropology, for the most part and despite its central concern with culture, is still largely wedded to a cognitive model of how culture works, and worse still a Cartesian one. As Stoller (1997) has so powerfully argued, what anthropology still lacks and what is so conspicuously missing from many of the most refined ethnographies is what he calls the 'sensuous' – smells, tastes and textures certainly, but also a wider suppression of the morality of everyday life and the way it is reflected in a myriad of little decisions. While a few anthropologists have belatedly turned to the analysis of morals (Howell 1997), they have done so largely in the frame of identifying ethical systems, rather than the dynamic contribution of morals to determining social goals (the higher meaning surely of development?). Ultimately, this means transcending a knowledge-infatuated approach, and the development of an anthropological language capable of adequately addressing fundamental human existential, ethical and social problems. As Stoller again puts it in his insightful discussion of rationality from an anthropological perspective:

> The key test for a future rationality, then, may well be whether its processes and procedures can lead us not only to increasingly insightful truths but also to wisdom. My own guess is that if we allow humility to work its wonders, it can bring embodiment to our scholarly practices and expression. It can also enable us to live well in the world.
>
> (Stoller 1998: 253)

Which is, after all, the acid test of 'development'.

Notes

1 A communal farming movement based in Mie prefecture, with communes and marketing outlets across Japan and now in several foreign countries.
2 Although the recent turn to both these crucial aspects of human identity in both anthropology and the more cultural studies varieties of sociology (e.g. Lutz and Abu-Lughod 1990; Featherstone *et al.* 1991) represents a belated catching up with the long-established, but rarely acknowledged, contributions of Japanese anthropology (e.g. Ichikawa 1993).

Bibliography

AERA Mook, 1995. *Jinruigaku ga wakaru* (Special Report 8). Tokyo: Asahi Shimbun.

Appadurai, A. 1998. *Modernity at Large: Cultural Dimensions of Globalisation*. Minneapolis: University of Minnesota Press.

Benedict, R. 1989. *The Chrysanthemum and the Sword: Patterns of Japanese Culture*. Tokyo and Rutland, VT: Charles E. Tuttle.

Bettelheim, B. 1986. *The Informed Heart*. Harmondsworth: Penguin Books.

Bird-David, N. 1999. 'Animism' revisited: Personhood, environment and relational epistemology. *Current Anthropology* 40(suppl.): 567–591.

Bourdieu, P. 1979. *An Outline of a Theory of Practice*. Cambridge: Cambridge University Press.

Brohman, J. 1996. *Popular Development: Rethinking the Theory and Practice of Development*. Oxford: Blackwell.

Buraku K. K. (ed.). 1992. *Zusetsu konnichino buraku sabetsu*. Osaka: Kaiho Shuppansha.

Carmen, R. 1996. *Autonomous Development*. London: Zed Books.

Clammer, J. 1995. *Difference and Modernity: Social Theory and Contemporary Japanese Society*. London: Kegan Paul International.

Clayton, A. (ed.). 1996. *NGOs, Civil Society and the State*. Oxford: INTRAC.

Cohen, A. P. 1994. *Self Consciousness: An Alternative Anthropology of Identity*. London: Routledge.

Csordas, T. J. 1994. *The Sacred Self: A Cultural Phenomenology of Charismatic Healing*. Berkeley: University of California Press.

D'Andrade, R. 1996. *The Development of Cognitive Anthropology*. Cambridge: Cambridge University Press.

De Certeau, M. 1988. *The Practice of Everyday Life*. Berkeley: University of California Press.

De Vos, G. and H. Wagatsuma. 1966. *Japan's Invisible Race: Caste in Culture and Personality*. Berkeley: University of California Press.

De Vos, G. and W. O. Wetherall. 1983. *Japan's Minorities: Burakumin, Koreans, Ainu and Okinawans*. London: Minority Rights Group.

Dove, M. R. (ed.). 1988. *The Real and Imagined Role of Culture in Development*. Honolulu: University of Hawaii Press.

Esteva, G. and M. S. Prakash. 1998. *Grassroots Postmodernism: Remaking the Soil of Cultures*. London: Zed Books.

Evans-Pritchard, E. E. 1968. (1937) *Witchcraft, Oracles and Magic Amongst the Azande*. Oxford: The Clarendon Press.

Featherstone, M. 1997. *Undoing Culture: Globalisation, Postmodernism and Identity*. London: Sage.

Featherstone, M., M. Hepworth and B. S. Turner (eds). 1991. *The Body: Social Process and Cultural Theory*. London: Routledge.

Fei, H. T. 1981. *Towards a People's Anthropology*. Beijing: New World Press.

Friedman, J. 1996. *Cultural Identity and Global Process*. London: Sage.

Goulet, D. 1989. Participation in development: New avenues. *World Development* 17(2): 165–178.

Grillo, R. D. and R. L. Stirrat (eds). 1997. *Discourses of Development: Anthropological Perspectives.* Oxford: Berg.

Hamaguchi E. 1982. *Kanjinshugi no Shakai.* Tokyo: Toyo Keisai Shimposha.

Hetherington, K. 1998. *Expressions of Identity: Space, Performance, Politics.* London: Sage.

Hobart, M. 1993. Introduction: The growth of ignorance? In M. Hobart (ed.) *An Anthropological Critique of Development: The Growth of Ignorance* (pp. 1–20). London: Routledge.

Howell, S. (ed.). 1997. *The Ethnography of Moralities.* London: Routledge.

Ichikawa H. 1993. *Mi no Kozo: Shintairon wo Koete.* Tokyo: Kodansha Gakujutsu Bunko.

Irokawa D. 1988. Popular movements in modern Japanese society. In G. McCormack and Y. Sugimoto (eds) *The Japanese Trajectory: Modernisation and Beyond* (pp. 69–86). Cambridge: Cambridge University Press.

Jasper, J. M. 1997. *The Art of Moral Protest: Culture, Biography and Creativity in Social Movements.* Chicago: University of Chicago Press.

Kaufmann, G. 1997. Watching the developers: A partial ethnography. In R. D. Grillo and R. L. Stirrat (eds) *Discourses of Development* (pp. 107–131). Oxford: Berg.

Kelly, D. and A. Reid. (eds). 1998. *Asian Freedoms: The Idea of Freedom in East and Southeast Asia.* Cambridge: Cambridge University Press.

Kisala, R. 1999. *Prophets of Peace: Pacifism and Cultural Identity in Japan's New Religions.* Honolulu: University of Hawaii Press.

LeBlanc, R. 1999. *Bicycle Citizens: The Political World of the Japanese Housewife.* Berkeley: University of California Press.

Lutz, C. A. and L. Abu-Lughod. (eds). 1990. *Language and the Politics of Emotion.* Cambridge: Cambridge University Press.

Marcus, G. E. and M. J. Fischer. 1986. *Anthropology as Cultural Critique.* Chicago: University of Chicago Press.

Merry, S. E. 1997. Legal pluralism and transnational culture: The *Ka Ho'kolokolonui Kanaka Maoli Tribunal, Hawaii, 1993.* In Richard Wilson (ed.) *Human Rights, Culture and Context* (pp. 28–48). London: Pluto Press.

Mills, M. B. 1995. Attack of the widow ghosts: Gender, death and modernity in Northeast Thailand. In Aihwa Ong and M. G. Peletz (eds) *Bewitching Women, Pious Men: Gender and Body Politics in Southeast Asia* (pp. 244–273). Berkeley: University of California Press.

Miyoshi, M. and H. D. Harootunian (eds). 1989. *Postmodernism and Japan.* Durham, NC: Duke University Press.

Mouer, R. and Sugimoto Y. 1986. *Images of Japanese Society.* London: Kegan Paul International.

Pickering, J. (ed.). 1997. *The Authority of Experience: Essays on Buddhism and Psychology.* Richmond: Curzon Press.

Pottier, J. 1997. Towards an ethnography of participatory appraisal and research. In R. D. Grillo and R. L. Stirrat (eds) *Discourses of Development* (pp. 203–227). Oxford: Berg.

Rahnema, M. 1995. Participation. In W. Sachs (ed.) *The Development Dictionary: A Guide to Knowledge and Power* (pp. 116–131). London: Zed Books.

Reader, I. 1991. *Religion in Contemporary Japan.* London: Macmillan.

Sahlins, M. 1996. The Sadness of sweetness: The native anthropology of Western cosmology. *Current Anthropology* 37(3): 395–415.

Shintaro, I. 1991. *The Japan that Can Say 'No'.* Trans. Frank Baldwin. New York: Simon & Shuster.

Siamwisa, R. 1995. Community participation and self-help: The Zambian case. In V. K. Pillai and L. W. Shannon (eds) *Developing Areas: A Book of Readings and Research* (pp. 345–357). Oxford: Berg.

Sillitoe, P. 1998. The development of indigenous knowledge: a new applied anthropology. *Current Anthropology* 39(2): 223–252.

Smith, L. T. 1999. *Decolonising Methodology: Research and Indigenous Peoples.* London: Zed Books.

Smith, T. C. 1989. *The Native Sources of Japanese Industrialisation 1750–1920.* Berkeley: University of California Press.

Stoller, P. 1997. *Sensuous Scholarship.* Philadelphia: University of Pennsylvania Press.

——. 1998. Rationality. In M. C. Taylor (ed.) *Critical Terms for Religious Studies* (pp. 239–255). Chicago: University of Chicago Press.

Tobin, J. J. (ed.). 1992. *Remade in Japan: Everyday Life and Consumer Taste in a Changing Society.* New Haven: Yale University Press.

Ueno C. 1988. The Japanese women's movement: The counter-values to industrialism. In G. McCormack and Sugimoto Y. (eds) *The Japanese Trajectory: Modernisation and Beyond* (pp. 167–185). Cambridge: Cambridge University Press.

Wignaraja, P. (ed.). 1993. *New Social Movements in the South.* London: Zed Books.

Yoneyama, L. 1999. *Hiroshima Traces: Time, Space and the Dialectics of Memory.* Berkeley: University of California Press.

Yuasa, Y. 1987. *The Body: Towards an Eastern Mind-Body Theory.* Albany: State University of New York Press.

Chapter 4

Ethnotheory, ethnopraxis

Ethnodevelopment in the Oromia regional state of Ethiopia

Aneesa Kassam

This chapter describes how a non-governmental organization (NGO) from the Oromia regional state of Ethiopia is attempting to apply an indigenous theory of development in order to bring about social and economic change from within the culture.[1] This ethnotheory is based on a model of development that was elaborated by experts of the oral traditions of the Boorana of southern Ethiopia, the most traditional of the Oromo territorial groups. The model was recorded as part of an anthropological study conducted by a 'native' scholar to reconstruct the system of knowledge that existed prior to the incorporation of the Oromo people into the Ethiopian empire state at the end of the nineteenth century (Megerssa 1993). The chapter discusses how this strategy of development has come to represent the ideological basis upon which the past and present problems of underdevelopment of the Oromo in Ethiopia are being addressed. It shows how the model offers an alternative approach, both to the dominant local and hegemonic Western views of development. The chapter hence brings to bear on issues of indigenous knowledge and development in the context of politicized ethnicity and nationalism in Ethiopia (Chanie 1998; Hassen 1996; Jalata 1993a, 1993b; Krylow 1994; Lata 1999; Ottaway 1999; Poluha 1998).

The attempt by a group of Oromo social activists to formulate a culturally appropriate theory and praxis of development constitutes a case of what Stavenhagen (1986, 1990) has termed 'ethnodevelopment'.[2] It thus forms part of a movement for the 'right to development' which is being led by a number of indigenous peoples in many parts of the world today (Stavenhagen 1986: 92). As Stavenhagen explains, these groups are demanding the right by which their future is discussed and decided; to political representation and participation; to respect for their traditions and cultures; to the freedom to choose what kind of development, if any, they want (Stavenhagen 1990: 90).

In this sense, the Oromo case belongs to a more general, worldwide phenomenon that involves a complex web of issues linking ethnicity and development. As Stavenhagen (1986: 77) points out, this ethnic problematic represents a 'paradigmatic blind spot' in development theory. The idea of ethnodevelopment, as conceptualized by Latin American theorists, was also significantly absent from papers presented at the Association of Social Anthropologists conference on *Participating in Development: Approaches to Indigenous Knowledge* in April 2000. In this chapter, ethnodevelopment is contrasted with recent indigenous knowledge and development approaches (as outlined by Sillitoe 1998) in that it is understood as an internally, rather than an externally, led movement. Methodologically, however, there are similarities between these etic and emic views, in that both stress a participatory grassroots approach to development, generally seek to empower (even if rhetorically) the poorest sectors of society and draw on cultural knowledge. The main differences lie in the identity of the 'originating agents' implementing participation and the question of whether the method serves as both an end and a means for establishing a true dialogue and exchange between the disseminators and users of knowledge (Goulet 1989: 166).

The chapter begins with an outline of the concept of ethnodevelopment as elaborated by Stavenhagen (1986, 1990). The 'colonial' situation of the Oromo in Ethiopia is then presented as an illustration of the premise that ethnicity and development are interrelated problems. This overview is followed by a description of how Boorana Oromo experts of the oral traditions conceptualize development, showing that other peoples also possess their own models of socioeconomic growth. The following section examines how an indigenous Oromo NGO from central Ethiopia is translating this traditional view into modern-day development practices. The chapter concludes with a discussion on the current ethnopolitics of development in Ethiopia. The issues raised in the chapter echo those of a number of other contributors to this volume, in particular those of Clammer (chapter 3), Croal and Darou (chapter 5), Schönhuth (chapter 7) and Posey (chapter 2). These authors also discuss how the very notion of 'development' is being challenged and dynamically reinterpreted by non-Western peoples, the indigenous knowledge systems from which the concept emanates, and the role being played by different actors in this process of redefinition.

The concept of ethnodevelopment

'Ethnodevelopment' refers to the right of ethnic groups to participate (or not, as the case may be) in the modern development process on their own terms. The concept was formulated within Latin American critical anthropology to address problems of unequal development of indigenous and other marginalized groups (Seymour-Smith 1986: 97). In the English-speaking world, this work is best known through the publications of Rodolfo Stavenhagen (1986, 1990). Hettne (1995) takes up some of the issues of ethnicity and development raised by Stavenhagen as part of his critique of Eurocentrism in development thinking. Two edited volumes, those of Dwyer and Drakakis-Smith (1996) and Salih and Markakis (1998), provide useful regional case studies illustrating the problems of ethnicity and development. The latter work focuses more particularly on the role played by the state in these processes. Generally, these contributions tend towards an instrumentalist view of ethnicity. They present ethnicity as one of the variables which interact with other factors, such as class, state and power (Doornbos 1998: 20), and show how it becomes politicized in the struggle over economic resources.

Stavenhagen's work lays particular emphasis on the *rights* of indigenous people to determine their own development. He therefore contrasts ethnodevelopment with the process of economic and cultural 'ethnocide'. Economic ethnocide, he shows, relates to the destruction of traditional systems of production, through the alienation of land and the incorporation of ethnic groups into national and global processes. Cultural ethnocide, on the other hand, arises out of linguistic, educational and other policies designed by the nation state to assimilate ethnic groups into the 'national' culture at the expense of their own traditional value systems (Stavenhagen 1990: 85–92).

As Stavenhagen points out (1990: 11), this 'national' culture is, in fact, usually a generalization of that of the dominant ethnic group, whose ruling elite controls the power of the state. Within such ethnocratic states, he argues, non-dominant groups find themselves in a situation of 'internal colonialism' in respect of the dominant group (1990: 15, 40).[3] This system of ethnic stratification results in the differential access to political power and to the allocation of economic resources, a point elaborated by Hettne (1995: 195–197). When such domination occurs, Stavenhagen (1990: 33) explains, subordinate ethnic groups will vie with each other and with the central state for political power and a greater share of these resources, as shown in the case studies presented by Dwyer and Drakakis-Smith (1996), and Salih and Markakis (1998). This subordination leads to situations of ethnic conflict, violence and civil war, in which the object of the struggle is either the state apparatus itself or secession from the state.

The analytical framework developed by Stavenhagen can usefully be applied to the consideration of the regionally and culturally specific case of the Oromo. As Stavenhagen (1990) emphasizes, it is important to take account of the concrete historical circumstances of each particular case and to understand how it relates to the given economic and social realities.

The 'problem' of the Oromo

The Oromo (formerly pejoratively known as 'Galla', a name they reject) are one of the most populous of the indigenous Cushitic peoples of the region, who constitute the major ethnic group in Ethiopia. Reliable demographic figures on the Oromo are not available due to the 'politics of number' practised by the state (Demie 1997). It is thought that they make up about 30–40 per cent of the total population of 62 million. Smaller numbers of Oromo live in northern Kenya, along the Tana River on the Kenyan coast and in parts of Somalia. Oromo speak a mutually intelligible language and share a common set of cultural values, despite their territorial dispersal, religious diversity and forms of livelihood. Traditionally, they exploited different ecological niches as part of a regional economic system, which included nomadic pastoralism, hunter-gathering and plough agriculture. Today, they also participate to a limited extent in the modern economy in various capacities.

From before its inception to the present day, the Ethiopian nation state has had to contend with what Baxter (1983) has termed the 'problem' of the Oromo. For Baxter (1983), however, it is rather the position of subordination of the Oromo within the Ethiopian state that has become a problem *for* the Oromo. This position has been described as one of internal colonialism (Neuberger 1986: 86). In effect, the Oromo have been subjected to the same forms of economic exploitation, political oppression and cultural domination by successive Ethiopian regimes that are characteristic of external colonialism (see Jalata 1993a, 1993b; Hassen 1994; Megerssa 1993). This subordinate position has resulted in the economic and social underdevelopment of the Oromo. Despite the various political transformations that have taken place in Ethiopia, from autocratic rule (1930–1974) to socialism (1974–1991) and currently, federalism, the crux of the problem as stated by Baxter remains basically unchanged. As he points out: 'If Ogaden or Eritrea were detached from it, Ethiopia would merely be diminished; but if the Oromo were to detach themselves, then ... the Empire, which Menelik assembled and Haile Selassie held together, would fall apart' (Baxter 1983: 146).[4]

The centre cannot hold because it is economically dependent on the peripheries it has forcibly created. As the largest of these, Oromia is the main 'granary' of Ethiopia and the source of most of its essential commodities. It is also the supplier of its principal exports of coffee, gold, pulses, incense, hides and skins. In short, as Baxter (1983: 146) suggests, the country would not be able to survive economically without the food and labour power provided by the Oromo peasantry. It is this dilemma that has historically been at the heart of the ethnic conflicts in Ethiopia.

Although Ethiopia was never colonized in the scramble for Africa (except for a short period by Italy from 1936–1941), Western European powers created a dependent ethnic bourgeoisie through which they controlled this strategically important region. This intervention changed the balance of power between the ethnic groups in the area (Holcomb and Ibssa 1990). To summarize at least three millennia of complex historical ethnic interactions, the firearms provided to the Semitic-speaking Christian Amhara kings enabled one branch of this feuding northern settler group to gain a technological advantage over the numerically and militarily stronger Oromo (Darkwah 1975). This alliance facilitated the southward expansion of the Amhara and their occupation of the central highlands of the region of Shawa (Tamrat 1972). The Oromo and other minority groups were conquered at the end of the nineteenth century and forced to submit to the dominant rule of the Shawan dynasty of Amhara kings.

Up to the sixteenth century, the Oromo had formed a confederation made up of five territorial groups (Megerssa 1993).[5] Each of these groups was organized according to its own variant of the *Gadaa* and *Qaalluu* institutions (Legesse 1973; Baxter and Almagor 1978). The *Gadaa* institution, which was based on a complex age and generation grading system, had economic, social, political, legislative, military and ritual functions (Legesse 1973). It operated on a highly democratic set of values (Legesse 2000). A leader (*Abba Gadaa*), elected for a term of eight years, exercised power through local assemblies. Each set of incoming and outgoing leaders was required to perform a pilgrimage (*mudaa*) to the central *Qaalluu* (or *Abba Mudaa*), who represented the highest religious and judicial authority of the Oromo. After the sixteenth century, a stratified monarchical (*moottii*) system also evolved among some of the northern and western Oromo groups (Hassen 1994).

The cultural unity of the traditional Oromo confederacy was undermined by the abolition of the pilgrimage to the *Abba Mudaa* by the Amhara Emperor Menelik in about 1900 (Hassen 1994: 8). Following the incorporation of the Oromo into the Ethiopian empire state, their most fertile lands were appropriated and allocated to Amhara armed settlers (*naftaanya*). The Oromo were reduced to colonial subjects on their own land. They were forced to adopt the dominant Christian Orthodox religion and culture to the detriment of their own traditional practices, which were denigrated (Baxter 1983; Megerssa 1993). As a form of protest, many Oromo converted to Islam (Baxter 1983: 133). Other policies of 'Amharization' included educational and linguistic assimilation (Bulcha 1994).

The Oromo movement for self-determination was created in the early 1970s as a response to this colonial rule, although local rebellions occurred prior to this date (Baxter 1983: 139–140). In 1991, the military junta, which had ruled from 1974, was overthrown through the combined efforts of a number of guerrilla movements, including the Oromo Liberation Front (OLF). The OLF leadership initially participated in the Transitional Government of Ethiopia (TGE) that was formed to oversee democratic elections during this period. The campaign carried out by the OLF to prepare the people to participate in this process contributed to the creation of a pan-Oromo national consciousness, transforming the movement from a small group into a mass one (Hassen 1996: 78). In 1992, when it became evident that the dominant Tigrean Peoples' Liberation Front (TPLF) was undermining the democratic process, the OLF withdrew from the TGE and boycotted the regional and national elections (Lata 1999). It has since continued its armed struggle against the new Tigrean-dominated state. The Tigrean minority is linguistically and culturally related to the Amhara, and the elites of the two groups have historically been rivals for power.

In 1994 Ethiopia became a federation made up of nine ethnic states, the largest of which is Oromia (see Figure 4.1). The Oromo are officially represented in both the regional and federal assemblies by the Oromo People's

Democratic Organization (OPDO). The majority of the Oromo people do not accept this pseudo party, which was established under the aegis of the TPLF in 1991 as a legitimate and independent political organ (Krylow 1994: 236). However, hitherto, none of the Oromo groups has been able to pose a credible challenge to the dominant minority. This is in part because the Oromo ethnonationalist movement is not a unified one. It is splintered into a number of factions, and is divided along regional and religious lines (Chanie 1998: 104; Jalata 1993b: 394). There are also political differences between those Oromo nationalists who are striving for an independent state of Oromia and those who are pursuing the struggle for self-determination within the existing Ethiopian state (Hassen 1996: 71).

It is against this background that the establishment of the indigenous Oromo NGO Hundee in Ethiopia in 1995 and its efforts to build on its own cultural roots should be understood.

An Oromo theory of development

'Development' as it is understood today is a Western concept, which does not reflect the social, cultural and historical realities of other peoples in the world

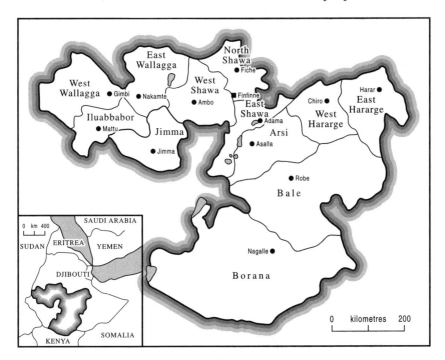

Figure 4.1   The Oromia regional state in Ethiopia

Note: Used with the kind permission of Ato Shifferaow Jammo.

(Hettne 1995). Since the 1970s, Third World intellectuals, who have sought to formulate theories and practices that are more relevant to their own social experiences and cultural aspirations, have challenged this Eurocentric view of development. The attempt by an Oromo social anthropologist, Gemetchu Megerssa (1993), to define an ethnotheory of development forms part of this 'indigenization' of development thinking. As Hettne (1995: 74) explains, indigenization refers here to the 'process in which transplanted ideas and institutions are more or less radically modified by the receivers to suit their own specific situation'. Such indigenization has arisen in reaction to the cultural imperialism of the West.

In trying to articulate this ethnotheory, Megerssa looked to the southern-most pastoral Boorana, who still practise many elements of the *Gadaa* system. The Boorana are perceived by other Oromo and view themselves as embodying the prototypical cultural traditions of the group. In 1987, as part of his effort to reconstruct the pre-conquest indigenous knowledge system of the Oromo, Megerssa asked one of his Boorana mentors, Dabassa Guyyoo, what he understood by the term 'development' and whether the Oromo possessed their own definition of this concept.[6] At the time of the interview, Megerssa's teacher, an expert on customary law, was in his early forties. He had been in exile in Kenya since 1984. He was trained from an early age in the historical traditions of the Boorana. Among the Oromo, such training is imparted selectively to certain groups of male children.[7] When they reach adulthood, such individuals are initiated into the ranks of the 'men of knowl-edge' of the group. As custodians of the oral traditions, these men possess a highly systematized form of knowledge that is not generally known to ordinary members of the group. Although the members of the community at large may know the constituent features of the model of development elaborated by Dabassa Guyyoo, their interconnections are not common knowledge. This model belongs, thus, to the field of expert knowledge.

According to Dabassa Guyyoo, the word 'development' can be rendered in the Oromo language by the term *finna* (or *fidnaa* in western Oromiffa). This term is a polysemous one and has a highly complex semantic structure. It can be derived from the verb *fidu*, meaning to bring, to give, or to hand down. It thus forms part of the cultural patrimony of the past (*finna durii*), which is transmitted from one generation to another. It can be translated loosely as 'cultural heritage'. The core meaning of the word can be said to refer to different forms of fertility, whether of a human, vegetal, animal, abstract or spiritual nature (Kassam 1986, 1994). This notion of fertility constitutes one of the underlying generative principles of the Oromo culture, through which all aspects of the productive and reproductive life are cognitively structured. It is, thus, a pervasive concept that can be found in all the Oromo groups, although the term *finna* itself may be used in slightly different ways.

In another of his teachings, Dabassa distinguishes between five types of fertility: *finna namaa*, 'human fertility'; *finna lafaa*, 'fertility of the earth'; *finna horii*, 'fertility of livestock'; *finna baraa*, 'fertility of the times'; and *finna durii*, 'fertility of the past'. For development to take place, Dabassa states, there must be concordance between all these forms of reproduction, which is ultimately brought about through the harmonious relationship (*finna Waaqaa*) of the people with their Supreme Deity.

In his model (Figure 4.2), Dabassa identifies seven interlocking phases leading to *finna*. Each one of these defines a form of growth: *guddinaa*, 'growth outwards, increase in height'; *gabbinaa*, 'growth outwards, gain in weight'; *balinaa*, 'coming into leaf'; *badhadhaa*, 'abundance, fullness'; *hormataa*, 'reproduction'; *dagagaa*, 'branching outwards'; and *daga-horaa*, 'expansion and prosperity'. *Finna* is an outcome of the preceding processes, which leads, at the eighth stage, to 'development'. Dabassa compares this transformative process to the unfolding of the spirals in the horn of a ram.

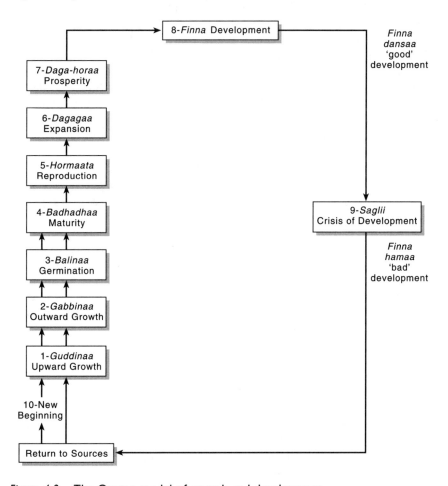

Figure 4.2 The Oromo model of growth and development

As Megerssa (1993) demonstrates, this synthesis is accomplished through a set of rules that form part of the Oromo system of knowledge. These classificatory rules are based on a set of numerical and temporal formulae (*ayyaana*) through which causality is explained. The order of development generated is founded upon custom or tradition (*aadaa*) and is regulated by the law (*seera*). It is predicated on an institutionalized social welfare system (*busaa gonoofaa*), through which wealth is redistributed. It is also based on a set of environmental rules (*aloof alollaa*) that protect the communal natural resources (Kassam and Megerssa 1994). Such usage is ultimately governed by an ethical code of practice (*safuu*) (Bartels 1983). For the Oromo, peaceful coexistence (*nagaa*) is also an essential prerequisite for development (Baxter 1978: 180–1).

Dabassa states that when development is based on the democratic principles enshrined in the *Gadaa* and *Qaalluu* institutions, 'it grows for everybody, for everybody in the land without leaving out any one individual, whether big or small, young or elderly' (see Megerssa 1993: 228). He contrasts this 'good' development (*finna dansaa*) of the past, with the 'bad' development (*finna hamaa*) of the present. For him, the model of development implemented by the Ethiopian state and the Oromo model are 'contrary and contradictory to each other' (Megerssa 1993: 246). Dabassa believes that such states of development and underdevelopment alternate, and that the Oromo will eventually emerge from the crisis in which they currently find themselves. This new beginning, he says, will entail a return to the sources of the Oromo culture and society.

As Stavenhagen (1990: 90) explains, ethnodevelopment does not necessarily imply the rejection of modern forms of development. Sahlins (1999) makes a similar point when he argues that what non-Western groups are seeking is 'the indigenization of modernity, their own cultural space in the global scheme of things' (1999: 410). The basis for Dabassa's hope may lie in the development work being carried out by the indigenous Oromo NGO Hundee. Significantly, the word *hundee* designates 'root(s)' and stands for the social and cultural origins of the Oromo. In particular, it refers to the primary or principal root, which the Oromo trace back to Horo, their apical ancestor. The term evokes the blood ties and the kinship affiliations that link the Oromo communities to one another in time and space. It stands, in short, for the people, their land and their culture.

Hundee's effort to translate this theory into practice through its work at the grassroots level of Oromo society serves as a bridge that dynamically links tradition with modernity. Dabassa's view of development has thus come to represent, in 'Geertzian' (Geertz 1973: 93) terms, not only a 'model of reality', but also a 'model for reality'. Gemetchu Megerssa, who worked on a part-time, voluntary basis with Hundee on his return from exile in 1996, has played an instrumental role in articulating the ethnodevelopment approach that has become central to Hundee's work.

An ethnopraxis of development

Hundee was established in early 1995, as part of the expansion of the voluntary sector that took place in post-revolutionary Ethiopia (Campbell 1996). It was founded by a group (sympathetic to the armed struggle) to address the fundamental problems of equity and poverty affecting the Oromo peasantry (Kassam, in prep.). Hundee was one of a number of Oromo NGOs that were established around this period (Campbell 2000). Hundee's development agenda is not a new one, in that aspects of it have long formed part of the OLF's socioeconomic reform programme (Jalata 1993b: 393–394). However, its approach, which draws on the knowledge of the Oromo culture, its social, economic, legal and religious institutions, as well as on modern participatory techniques, can be described as an innovative one in the Ethiopian context.

Hundee's philosophy of development is based on the view that culture represents a fundamental force for social and economic change. This approach is founded on the premise that if meaningful development is to take place, it must build on the roots that have given the Oromo society its unique cultural identity. It seeks, therefore, to revitalize the social institutions of the Oromo and to give them a new, modern-day meaning. Hundee's development programmes have, thus, been carried out within the parameters of the traditional institutions of welfare and assistance and of the customary laws governing gender and the environment. All its interventions are based on extensive consultation with the members of the community and are sanctioned by the traditional law-making assemblies (*chaffee*) of the elders. This development doctrine provides Hundee with an ethical code of conduct in all its work.

Hundee's long-term objective is to empower the Oromo communities to become self-reliant. Its development strategy consists in enabling the communities to understand the root causes of their problems and to take action to remedy the situation. This strategy is inspired by the method of 'conscientization' elaborated by the Brazilian pedagogue Paolo Freire (1974), whose work has become part of contemporary participatory approaches (Goulet 1989). This process is brought about through Hundee's Civic Education project, which aims at informing the communities of their rights and duties within the framework of the Ethiopian constitution. Hundee's participatory approach begins by facilitating a collective analysis of the social and economic problems faced by the community. This problem analysis is carried out in three stages: through groups of women, groups of men and finally in mixed gender groups which are representative of the whole community. This consultation allows Hundee to identify the felt needs of the communities. Second, Hundee takes practical measures to assist the community to deal with its problems by providing financial assistance through its revolving Savings and Loan credit scheme. To this end, it has established its own Micro Credit Association, which is named Busaa Gonoofaa, after the traditional welfare organization. Third, it addresses with the community the problems of environmental degradation and protection based on traditional laws. Fourth, it has established a Grain Bank project to combat the problem of recurrent food shortages and to deal with the price fluctuations faced by Oromo farmers on the open market.

Hundee's cultural approach was empirically evolved. In the initial stages of implementing its Civic Education project, the facilitators discovered that the customary law was being practised in parallel with the modern legal system in many parts of Oromia. It had generally been thought that this traditional system, which is still widely practised among the Boorana, had ceased to function in those regions most subjected to Amhara rule, such as in the central region of Shawa. It was found that like many other aspects of the Oromo culture, this system had survived by going underground. The organization realized that in order to help the communities to tackle their social problems, it would need to channel these issues through the traditional law-making bodies for legislation. It therefore presented the topics raised to the assemblies of *Gadaa* elders. In this way, Hundee has been able to involve these elders in the effort to bring about positive social change in the community. Such legislation includes the banning of harmful practices affecting young women, like female circumcision, early marriage and marriage by abduction, among other aspects. These practices are not considered to have formed part of the traditional Oromo culture, but are thought to have been adopted as a result of historical social interaction with the mainstream Christian and Islamic religions.

Hundee's overall development strategy has thus aimed to give the Oromo communities the impetus for self-growth from within their own cultural traditions. This development work marks a continuity with the democratic institutions of the traditional *Gadaa* system of governance and its mechanisms of consensus building and conflict resolution. This ethnodevelopment approach does not mean that Hundee is not open to new methods and practices. The organization believes, however, that such modern innovations should be integrated into the framework of the 'receiving culture'. It considers that the processes of social and economic change initiated through its work will eventually lead to transformative growth for the hitherto marginalized Oromo communities along the lines outlined in the model developed by Dabassa Guyyoo. This model is used implicitly, rather than explicitly. For instance, the facilitators of Hundee rarely employ the word *finna* to designate 'development', but usually use the more commonly known Oromo word *guddina*, 'growth', or the Amharic term *limmaati*, depending on the context. At other times, the term *misooma*, recently coined by OPDO cadres, may also be reluctantly employed. The model serves, nevertheless, as the ideology of development underlying all of Hundee's work.

This ethnodevelopment strategy has brought Hundee into conflict with regional and federal politicians and planners in Ethiopia. The organization has been seeking, however, to complement, rather than oppose regional and central development planning. Its work has also encountered opposition from

Oromo hardliners, in particular those in the North American and European diaspora. These Oromo critics have interpreted Hundee's policy of selective cooperation with the new regime as a betrayal of the Oromo ethnonational cause. The organization considers, however, that it is merely asserting, on behalf of the Oromo people, their collective right to participate in the development process on equal terms with other ethnic groups in the country.

Conclusion: the right to participate in development

This chapter has attempted to show how a model of development elaborated by experts of the southern Oromo oral traditions has come to inform the development praxis of an indigenous NGO in the central part of the Oromia state of Ethiopia. It has provided evidence in support of Stavenhagen's (1990) thesis that there exists an intrinsic link between ethnicity and development. As Clammer (chapter 3) points out, NGOs do not operate in a social vacuum. Hundee's ethnodevelopment approach has to be seen, thus, both in the context of the political changes that have taken place at the local level and the larger movement for the rights of indigenous peoples at the global level.

At the local level, the transition to democracy that was effected in Ethiopia in 1994 opened up a new space that allowed civil society institutions to re-emerge. This rebuilding of civil society is taking place as part of the move to federalism and as part of the devolution of power to the ethnic-based regional states (Ottaway 1999). This political change is still a very contentious one, in that Ethiopia has still not been able to resolve the dilemma of what Baxter (1983) has termed the 'problem' of the Oromo. As the largest of the regional states, Oromia has not gained real political representation in proportion to either its numbers or to its contribution to the federal economy. Until this problem is acknowledged and addressed, there will never be political stability and peace in Ethiopia. Nevertheless, the new federal structure *has* created a certain amount of political space for the practice of participatory democracy. This change, which was imposed by the international donor community as part of its policy of good governance (see Leftwich 1995), has enabled indigenous NGOs such as Hundee to begin the work of addressing the problems of the underdevelopment of Oromo communities. The difficulties faced by Hundee stem partly from the fact that it is viewed inside Ethiopia as being embedded within the Oromo movement for self-determination, which is still waging a guerrilla war against the present ethnocractic regime. Certain Oromo factions outside Ethiopia, on the other hand, see Hundee as betraying this ethnonational cause. As Clammer (chapter 3) notes, the line between some southern NGOs and the new social movements for democracy which are emerging in many parts of the world, is a fuzzy one. In this respect, Hundee can more properly be seen as a 'social and political force rather than a convenient mechanism for delivering aid' (Hulme 1994: 274).

The social activists that founded Hundee are making an ideological stance by choosing to build development on the indigenous knowledge system. They are employing culture as a political weapon in the struggle against the colonial experience undergone by the Oromo in Ethiopia over the past century. At the same time, they are making a statement against the Eurocentric view of development. This attempt to indigenize the Euro–American concept of development forms part of the movement for the decolonization of knowledge that is taking place in many parts of the world (cf. Croal and Darou, chapter 5; Schönhuth, chapter 7). Yet these choices are not merely tactical; they are also driven by moral imperatives. As Sahlins (1999: 409, 413) points out, 'cultures are meaningful orders' that derive from the sacred order of things (cf. Posey, chapter 2). In situations of crisis, modern native elites will strive to rearticulate authoritatively the charter myths of their societies. Campbell (2000) clearly misunderstands this position when he writes that such idealist 'fascination with culture' detracts from the more material problems of illiteracy and poverty in Ethiopia. On the contrary, for indigenous intellectuals such as Megerssa, culture represents a resource for tackling very real problems of equity and development. The revalidation of the indigenous knowledge system constitutes, thus, both an essentialist symbol of ethnic and/or national identity and an instrumental aspect of the struggle of the Oromo against the economic and cultural discrimination to which the Ethiopian state has historically subjected them. The reactivation of the indigenous knowledge system is not a mere luxury; it is a matter of the cultural survival of the group.

The case of the Oromo is not an isolated phenomenon. Stavenhagen (1990: 64–65) illustrates how numerous other indigenous groups in the world are similarly claiming their collective rights to exist as distinct entities and to pursue their own development. As elsewhere in the world (cf. Croal and Darou, chapter 5; Clammer, chapter 3; Stavenhagen 1990), the grievances of the Oromo are being framed in terms of their democratic *rights* to participate in development. In some parts of the world, such claims are based on the United Nations conventions giving collectivities the right to live according to their own cultural traditions and knowledge systems (Croal and Darou, chapter 5; Posey, chapter 2; Stavenhagen 1990). In Ethiopia, however, this demand is being made in the context of politicized ethnicity. As Poluha (1998: 31) explains, when Ethiopia became a federal republic in 1994, the map was redrawn according to ethnic lines and this situation has given rise to a process of 'ethnification'. The power struggle between the elites of different groups is thus being made using an ethnic idiom. As Chanie (1998: 103) suggests, such politicized ethnicity 'is an outcome of ethnic group interaction with the state'. In the Oromo case, Chanie proposes, this ethnopolitical struggle can be attributed to two interrelated factors that form part of the development of a pan-Oromo (as opposed to an earlier regional) consciousness. It stems, in the first place, from the competition of a now educated

Oromo elite for state power and resources. During the period (1991–1993) of transition to democracy, this elite 'challenged the entire distribution of resources and the division of power in society'. In the second place, the dominant elite 'denied the Oromo elite its right to be part of the highest state apparatus and confined it to a subordinate role'. It is these two sets of circumstances that led the former OLF leader Lata (1999) to warn that Ethiopia was 'at the crossroads'. If the Ethiopian state fails to accommodate the Oromo demands and to acknowledge the contribution of its people to the wealth of the nation, it faces the prospect of total disintegration and regional 'ethnochaos' (Dwyer and Drakakis-Smith 1996). The effort of an ethnic-based development NGO such as Hundee has been to find a middle way between those elite who advocate the need to control state power and those members of the OPDO regional government who have compromised this stance by 'sharing' power in a subordinate capacity. It has taken advantage of the window of opportunity that was created by ethnic federalism, which gives the different groups the rhetorical right to cultural self-determination, to address the urgent problems of grassroots development. As Goulet argues:

> When people are oppressed or reduced to the culture of silence, they do not participate in their own humanization. Conversely, when they participate, thereby becoming active subjects of knowledge and action, they begin to construct their properly human history and engage in processes of authentic development.
>
> (Goulet 1989: 165)

Whatever its constraints and shortcomings, Hundee has taken a positive step in this direction.

Knowledge, then, is situational and processual (Clammer, chapter 3). It reflects shifting political realities. It is also never neutral (Sillitoe 1998: 247). By translating theory into practice and by drawing on both the Oromo model of development and on Western development ideas and methods, Hundee is in the process of transforming the indigenous knowledge system. As the organization grows and its staff become more preoccupied with the practicalities of development and less with its ideological principles, it is important that they be critically aware of the potential dangers to which their actions may be contributing. Some questions that need to be asked are: To what extent are alternative development 'interventions' such as those being made by Hundee and other indigenous NGOs modifying the cultural knowledge system? In what ways are these insider applications, like outsider ones before them, tampering piecemeal with aspects of a culturally embedded system? What will be the consequences of promoting certain types of social changes, advocated by Western donor communities, on traditional gender relations and age groups such as the elderly? These and other concerns voiced by critics of the indigenous knowledge and development approach also apply to ethnodevelopment.

If ethnodevelopment is to be distinguished as an internally, rather than an externally defined praxis, it is vital that its practitioners uphold and retain the 'sacred balance' and 'cosmic connectedness' (Posey, chapter 2) upon which indigenous knowledge as a whole is founded.

Notes

1   I am grateful to the director and staff of Hundee for sharing with me their experiences of establishing the organization. I am thankful to the organization and to Dr Gemetchu Megerssa (Department of Sociology and Anthropology, University of Addis Ababa) for encouragement and support in my research on the links between tradition and modernity. I acknowledge my intellectual debt to Dr Megerssa (and through him to Dabassa Guyyoo) in the preparation of this chapter. I would also like to thank Sam Hickey, a postgraduate student at the University of Staffordshire, who is studying the Mbororo Fulani of Cameroun, for having provided me with the key references on ethnodevelopment.

2   The notion of praxis is employed here in the two interconnected meanings given by Marx: (1) as practical activity through which human beings engage in the world and transform social reality through their actions; and (2) as the actualization and advancement of theory (see Bottomore 1983: 384–389; Habermas 1973). Bernstein (1976) provides an excellent discussion of the work of the Frankfurt School of critical theory on the links between theory and practice, and notes that critical theory 'seeks a genuine unity of theory and revolutionary praxis where the theoretical understanding of the contradictions inherent in existing society, when appropriated by those who are exploited, becomes constitutive of their very activity to transform society'. It 'aspires to bring the subjects themselves to full self-consciousness of the contradictions implicit in their material existence, to penetrate the ideological mystifications and forms of false consciousness that distort the meaning of existing social conditions' (1976: 182). Freire's (1974) method of 'conscientisation', used in many recent participatory approaches to development, can be seen as an application of this theory of praxis at the popular level.

3   'Internal colonialism', a concept formulated by Hechter (1975), refers to the structural relationship that exists between subordinate and dominant ethnic groups in which the former find themselves in a position similar to that of peoples who have undergone external colonialism. This relationship reproduces the global centre–periphery model at the local level through a dependent bourgeoisie (Stavenhagen 1990: 40).

4   Eritrea seceded and became an independent state in 1993, but in 1998 Ethiopia was again at war with her former 'colony'.

5   In the dominant narrative of Greater Ethiopia, Oromo are represented as barbaric hordes that invaded the Ethiopian space in the sixteenth century, bringing destruction in their wake (see Hultin 1996: 81–90). Oromo intellectuals have contested this view and have been engaged in rewriting their own cultural history. In this ethnohistory the Gadaa political system is portrayed as a cultural ideal. For some writers on Ethiopia, this historical reconstruction is viewed as an 'invented tradition', in the sense elaborated by Hobsbawm and Ranger (1983). As Sahlins (1999) and other writers point out, however, this debate does not take into account the cultural logics of such accounts, their epistemological bases and their continuities with the past. It is the alternative, Oromo perspective of history that is followed here.

6   This study formed a component of a research project based at the University of Stockholm to explore local notions of development in different parts of the world (see Dahl and Rabo 1992). A translation of the interview recorded by Megerssa (1993) is reproduced in his doctoral dissertation. Dahl and Megerssa (1992) and Kassam (1994) also provide interpretations of this data.

7   These children belong to the *dabbaallee* grade in the Oromo *Gadaa* generation-set system. Legesse (1973) and Megerssa (1993) have described this process of knowledge transmission.

Bibliography

Bartels, L. 1983. *Oromo Religion. Myths and Rites of the Western Oromo of Ethiopia: An Attempt to Understand*. Berlin: Dietrich Reimer Verlag.

Baxter, P. T. W. 1978. Booran age-sets and generation-sets: Gada, a puzzle or a maze? In P. T. W. Baxter and U. Almagor (eds) *Age, Generation and Time: Some Features of East African Age Organization* (pp. 151–182). London: C. Hurst.

——. 1983. The problem *of* the Oromo or the problem *for* the Oromo? In I. M. Lewis (ed.) *Nationalism and Self-determination in the Horn of Africa* (pp. 129–150). London: Ithaca Press.

Baxter, P. T. W. and U. Almagor (eds). 1978. *Age, Generation and Time: Some Features of East African Age Organization*. London: C. Hurst.

Bernstein, R. J. 1976. *The Restructuring of Social and Political Theory*. Oxford: Basil Blackwell.

Bottomore, T. (ed.). 1983. *A Dictionary of Marxist Thought*. Oxford: Blackwell Publishers.

Bulcha, M. 1994. The language policies of Ethiopian regimes and the history of written afaan Oromoo 1884–1994. *Journal of Oromo Studies* 1(2): 91–115.

Campbell, J. R. 2000. The charitable impulse: NGOs and development in East and Northeast Africa. In D. Barrow and M. Jennings (eds) *Faith, Hope and Charity* (pp. 282–310). London: James Currey.

Campbell, W. 1996. The potential for donor mediation in NGO–state relations: An Ethiopian case study. Brighton: Institute of Development Studies, Working Paper 33.

Chanie, P. 1998. The rise of politized ethnicity among the Oromo in Ethiopia. In M. A. Salih and J. Markakis (eds) *Ethnicity and the State in Eastern Africa* (pp. 95–107). Uppsala: Nordiska Afrikaininstitutet.

Dahl, G. and G. Megerssa. 1992. A Booran elder's view of development. In G. Dahl and A. Rabo (eds) *Kam-ap or Take Off: Local Notions of Development* (pp. 157–173). Stockholm: Stockholm Studies in Social Anthropology, 29.

Dahl, G. and A. Rabo (eds). 1992. *Kam-ap or Take Off: Local Notions of Development*. Stockholm: Stockholm Studies in Social Anthropology, 29.

Darkwah, R. H. K. 1975. *Shewa, Menilek and the Ethiopian Empire, 1813–1889*. London: Heinemann.

Demie, F. 1997. Population growth and sustainable development: The case of Oromia in the Horn of Africa. *Journal of Oromo Studies* 4(1–2): 153–178.

Doornbos, M. 1998. Linking the future to the past – ethnicity and pluralism. In M. A. Salih and J. Markakis (eds) *Ethnicity and the State in Eastern Africa* (pp. 17–29). Uppsala: Nordiska Afrikaininstitutet.

Dwyer, D. and D. Drakakis-Smith (eds). 1996. *Ethnicity and Development: Geographical Perspectives*. Chichester: John Wiley and Sons.

Freire, P. 1974. *Pedagogy of the Oppressed*. Harmondsworth: Penguin.

Geertz, C. 1973. *The Interpretation of Cultures*. New York: Basic Books.

Goulet, D. 1989. Participation in development: New avenues. *World Development* 17(2): 165–178.

Habermas, J. 1973. *Theory and Practice*. Trans. John Ciertel. Boston: Beacon Books.

Hassen, M. 1994. *The Oromo of Ethiopia: A History, 1570–1860*. Trenton, NJ: Red Sea Press.

——. 1996. The development of Oromo nationalism. In P. T. W. Baxter, J. Hultin and A. Triulzi (eds) *Being and Becoming Oromo: Historical and Anthropological Enquiries* (pp. 67–80). Uppsala: Nordiska Afrikainstitutet.

Hechter, M. 1975. *Internal Colonialism: The Celtic Fringe in British National Development, 1536–1966*. London: Routledge and Kegan Paul.

Hettne, B. 1995. *Development Theory and the Three Worlds* (2nd edition). Harlow: Addison Wesley Longman Ltd.

Hobsbawm, E. and T. Ranger. 1983. *The Invention of Tradition*. Cambridge: Cambridge University Press.

Holcomb, B. and S. Ibssa. 1990. *The Invention of Ethiopia*. Trenton, NJ: Red Sea Press.

Hulme, D. 1994. Social development in research and the third sector: NGOs as users and subjects of social enquiry. In D. Booth (ed.) *Rethinking Social Development: Theory, Research and Practice* (pp. 251–275). Harlow: Longman.

Hultin, J. 1996. Perceiving Oromo: 'Galla' in the great narrative of Ethiopia. In P. T. W. Baxter, J. Hultin and A. Triulzi (eds) *Being and Becoming Oromo: Historical and Anthropological Enquiries* (pp. 81–91). Uppsala: Nordiska Afrikainstitutet.

Jalata, A. 1993a. *Oromia and Ethiopia. State Formation and Ethnonational Conflict, 1868–1992*. Boulder: Lynne Rienner.

——. 1993b. Ethiopia and ethnic politics: The case of Oromo nationalism. *Dialectical Anthropology* 18: 381–402.

Kassam, A. 1986. The fertile word: The Gabra concept of oral tradition. *Africa* 56(2): 193–209.

——. 1994. The Oromo theory of development. In E. Osaghae (ed.) *Between State and Civil Society* (pp. 16–40). Dakar: CODESRIA.

—— (in prep.) Grasping the opportunity for change: A study of an indigenous NGO from the Oromia region of Ethiopia.

Kassam, A. and G. Megerssa. 1994. *Aloof alollaa*. The inside and the outside: Booran Oromo environmental law and methods of conservation. In D. Brokensha (ed.) *A River of Blessings: Essays in Honor of Paul Baxter* (pp. 85–98). New York: Maxwell School of Citzenship and Public Affairs.

Krylow, A. 1994. Ethnic factors in post-Mengistu Ethiopia. In A. Zegeye and S. Pausewang (eds) *Ethiopia in Change: Peasantry, Nationalism and Democracy* (pp. 231–241). London: British Academic Press.

Lata, L. 1999. *The Ethiopian State at the Crossroads: Decolonization and Democratization or Disintegration?* Lawrenceville, NJ: Red Sea Press.

Leftwich, A. 1995. Governance, democracy and development in the Third World. In S. Corbridge (ed.) *Development Studies. A Reader* (pp. 427–438). London: Edward Arnold.

Legesse, A. 1973. *Gada: Three Approaches to the Study of African Society*. New York: Free Press.

——. 2000. *Oromo Democracy: An Indigenous African Political System*. Lawrenceville, NJ: Red Sea Press.

Megerssa, G. R. 1993. *Knowledge, Identity and the Colonizing Structure: The Case of the Oromo of East and Northeast Africa*. Unpublished Ph.D. dissertation, University of London, School of Oriental and African Studies.

Neuberger, B. 1986. *National Self-determination in Postcolonial Africa*. Boulder, CO: Lynne Rienner.

Ottaway, M. 1999. *Africa's New Leaders: Democracy or State Reconstruction?* Washington, DC: Carnegie Endowment for International Peace.

Poluha, E. 1998. Ethnicity and democracy – a viable alliance? In M. A. Salih and J. Markakis (eds) *Ethnicity and the State in Eastern Africa* (pp. 30–41). Uppsala: Nordiska Afrikaininstitutet.

Sahlins, M. 1999. Two or three things that I know about culture. *Journal of the Royal Anthropological Institute* 5(3): 399–421.

Salih, M. A. M. and J. Markakis (eds). 1998. *Ethnicity and the State in Eastern Africa*. Uppsala: Nordiska Afrikainstitutet.

Seymour-Smith, C. 1986. *Macmillan Dictionary of Anthropology*. London and Basingstoke: The Macmillan Press.

Sillitoe, P. 1998. The development of indigenous knowledge: A new applied anthropology. *Current Anthropology* 39(2): 223–251.

Stavenhagen, R. 1986. Ethnodevelopment: A neglected dimension in development thinking. In R. Apthorpe and A. Kráhl (eds) *Development Studies: Critique and Renewal* (pp. 71–94). Leiden: E. J. Brill.

——. 1990. *The Ethnic Question: Conflicts, Development and Human Rights*. Tokyo: United Nations University Press.

Tamrat, T. 1972. *Church and State in Ethiopia, 1270–1527*. Oxford: Clarendon Press.

Chapter 5

Canadian First Nations' experiences with international development

Peter Croal and Wes Darou

The indigenous peoples of Canada refer to themselves under the term *First Nations* or *Native People*. This group includes the Inuit (i.e. Eskimo), Dene, Métis, and forty-nine distinct Amerindian cultures such as the Dakota, Cree and Haida (INAC 2000). The term *aboriginal* is not acceptable in parts of Europe; *indigenous* is not acceptable in China or South Africa; and the term *Indian*, while acceptable in the USA, is not in Canada. We follow the nomenclature in use in Canada because we believe that it is an inherent right of peoples to choose their own name. Although the cultures are diverse, the late Clare Brant★[1] (1990), a Mohawk psychiatrist, points out that most share certain values. These include non-interference, sharing, respect for elders, harmony with the land, and social responsibility. There is, however, much diversity between First Nations cultures, such that the difference in values between some is larger than the difference between First Nations and Caucasians (Trimble *et al.*★ 1996).

There are over 630 First Nations communities in Canada with a total population of about 1 million (INAC 2000). They account for about 3 per cent of Canada's population of 30 million. The link between international development and First Nations is not immediately obvious. To some First Nations leaders, international development has ignored their situation while favouring countries half a world away. From the point of view of some in the international development community, First Nations show little interest in developing countries, and their cultural dynamics are foreign. In 1989 Amazonian Indians protested in front of Canada's embassy in Washington regarding low-level military flights over the Innu hunting territories in Labrador. The Crees of Quebec were major per capita contributors to Ethiopian famine aid. The international political dimension is evident. First Nations provide a unique pool of experience. In our own back yard we have 630 developing countries to observe and cooperate with in their efforts for development.

The challenges faced by these 630 *developing nations* relate to questions about rural life, urbanism, health, education, women in development, private sector implication, infrastructure, good governance, poverty reduction, and the environment. In addition, there are a variety of models and innovations among these nations from an independence-oriented approach, such as the James Bay and Northern Quebec Agreement, to an integrationist one, such as the Nisga'a treaty. Some of these communities have produced important learnings based on their own principles and social structures. Various mixtures of this indigenous knowledge with Euro–American approaches have produced some spectacular successes, greatly improving some communities in twenty-five years. The lessons learned from these activities should be of interest to the development community, and the First Nations themselves may be enriched by involvement with it.

This chapter aims to give a sense of the value of First Nations approaches to international development, or alternatively, what in international development might be of interest to First Nations. It begins with an explanation of the relevant aspects of the culture and history of First Nations. This accounts for the apparent reticence of First Nations to become involved in international development, due to lack of capacity, interest, and cultural factors. Next, it outlines a series of development principles adopted by First Nations, along with some cases, followed by examples of international development projects undertaken by First Nations. Finally, we suggest what First Nations offer the majority culture in terms of their learning about development, and indicate aspects of international development that might potentially interest First Nations.

Canadian society is not uniformly open to First Nations issues. For example, Canada experienced the Oka crisis, where Mohawks in Kahnesatake, a small indigenous community on the fringes of Oka near Montreal Quebec, were trying to block the expansion of a golf course because they said it would be built on an ancestral burial ground. The local mayor opposed the barricade erected by the Mohawks and asked the Quebec provincial police to intervene. In the early hours of 11 July 1990, police stormed the barricade and engaged in a gun battle with masked Mohawk warriors. When the tear gas and smoke had cleared, one police officer, Corporal Marcel Lemay, was dead. The stand-off among the Mohawks, Quebec police and the Canadian army, who were eventually called in, lasted a further seventy-seven days.

There are those who share the following views from a letter to the editor of *Time* magazine:

I really do not like what is happening these days with the Indians. They seem to have forgotten that we conquered this land centuries ago. The fight was not easy, but they lost and we won. Period. I do not see why we should give them what they are asking for. We civilized this place and they are enjoying the comforts of that civilization. The Canadian government should firmly stop all their claims and cancel all their tax advantages. These people should be punished in a court of law for any unlawful actions they undertake, just like any regular citizen.

(*Time*, 23 November 1992: iv)

Historically, Canada's approach to First Nations has been one of paternalism and assimilation, compromising their autonomy and reducing many to poverty (Mercredi★ 1999). Before White contact, the population in the region today called Canada was between 500,000 and 2 million; after contact the indigenous population was reduced to about 200,000. One nation, the Beothuk of Newfoundland was brutally extinguished; several other nations across Canada and the USA were also lost (Dickason★ 1993; Larsen 2000). In the eighteenth century, First Nations became the first recorded victims of what in effect may be considered to be *germ warfare* when they were given smallpox-infected blankets. There were unfathomable abuses in the residential schools. Aboriginals fought in both world wars in larger numbers per capita than any other group in Canada. Yet they were denied democracy – no vote, no benefits, no social security on their return from overseas (Jenish 2000). Of the sixty Native languages that were spoken in Canada at first contact, seven have disappeared, and another fifty are not expected to survive (York 1992). Language is key to the application of indigenous knowledge and cultural survival. Language expresses culture. For example, Tuktoyakyuk in Canada means *crossing place of the caribou*; Ottawa (*odawa*) means *meeting place* (i.e. of three rivers).

Nevertheless, over time, the pattern in Canada has become one of negotiation, collaboration and partnership. On 1 April 1999, the Northwest Territories of Canada divided into two parts: the Eastern portion is now known as Nunavut (which means *our land* in Inuktitut). Nunavut has a population of about 24,000 of whom 85 per cent are Inuit. The Nunavut agreement took twenty years to negotiate!

First Nations worldview

European-based cultures have a hierarchical, individualist worldview, in which an elite has mastery over the majority. Humans master the animals; living beings exploit the land. A First Nations worldview (from western Canadian sources) comprises concentric circles with the land in the middle, followed by plants and then animals, and with humans in the outer circle (Figure 5.1). Humans serve the animals and plants, and the land is central to all (Arthur Blue,★ pers. comm. October 1999; McCormick★ 1996). The model is based on equality, connectedness, and harmony between humans and nature.

The unity and balance of life are represented by the *medicine wheel* (Figure 5.2), a symbol that is found in several North American indigenous cultures (Bopp *et al.* 1984). It reflects life as a whole and is helpful for maintaining a

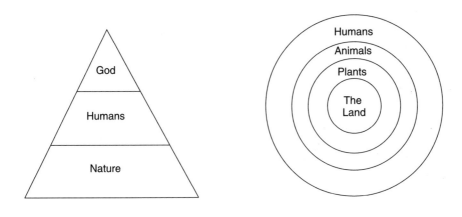

Euro-Western model   **First Nations model**

Figure 5.1   Two different models of creation

balance between various aspects of existence. The medicine wheel can structure problem solving. The eagle of the East represents the vision (identifying issues), the mouse of the South represents relationships (what exists now for the group), the bear of the West represents knowledge and feelings (reactions to the current situation), and the buffalo of the North represents action (what can be done) (Blue,* pers. comm., October 1976; Chevrier* 1998). Even today, medicine wheels made of rocks aligned and placed in circles can be found all over western Canada, particularly on promontories and other prayer sites. These sites were used traditionally, and are still sometimes used today, for a ceremony of self-discovery and rite of adulthood called the *vision quest*.

In most traditional First Nations societies, status was gained by giving, not by hoarding. It was not the person who collected the greatest amount of goods who was respected, but the person (or family or clan) who *gave away* the most. This is seen today in the Sundance ceremony, illegal for most of the twentieth century, where participants and their families give away large amounts of goods, even if they are of meagre means. It is the central act of the west coast Potlach, another ceremony that was illegal for decades. The *giveaway* is an aspect of the egalitarian social structure.

Contact between First Nations and Euro–Americans has brought and continues to bring about changes at both the group and individual levels. The process of psychological acculturation describes the new behaviours and strategies of individuals in such situations (Berry 1997, 1999). These can be categorized by the degree to which (1) people wish to maintain their cultural distinctiveness and identity, and (2) they desire contact with the other culture or are accepted by it. These can be represented in a two-by-two grid (Figure

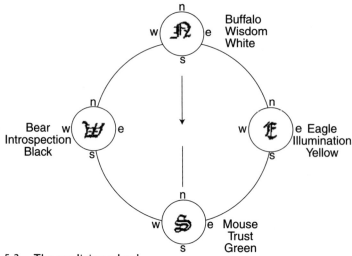

Figure 5.2   The medicine wheel

5.3), showing four general acculturation strategies. If individuals wish both to maintain identity and accept the new culture, their approach is called *bicultura-tion*, or in earlier configurations, *integration*. Research suggests that some people, particularly those in relatively good mental health, are able to and may prefer to choose this approach. If someone rejects their own culture and seeks relationships with the other culture, this is *assimilation*. If a person rejects or refuses the other culture seeking to maintain their own cultural identity, the option is *segregation* or *separation*. If the person rejects or is rejected by both cultures, the result is *marginalization*, accompanied by confusion, anxiety, and sometimes aggression.

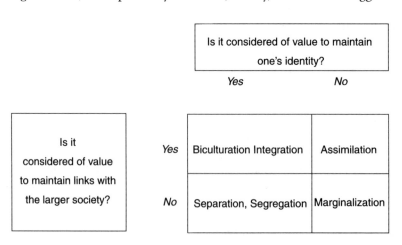

Figure 5.3   Acculturation strategies

A large number of studies indicate that First Nations generally prefer the bicultural strategy (Berry 1997). However, when a society is under particular acculturative stress, there is a tendency towards *differentiation* i.e. to close ranks and withdraw, and reject the outside culture (Kurtness★ 1991, pers. comm., February 2000). When people feel strong enough to resist acculturation, they become more open to outside communities, in a state of *biculturalism* or *integration*. When First Nations are comfortable with their own development, they will show interest and involvement in international development.

First Nations historical precedents

Colonial history

A review of First Nations history places international development in a Native perspective. While Europeans settled permanently in America only 500 years ago, the First Nations have been here at least 10,000 years. In fact, several studies suggest it could be as long as 50,000 years (Zazula★ 1999).

A brief description of the Métis of Manitoba is instructive for understanding attitudes to international development. Until very recently, mainstream Euro–Canadian school textbooks presented a biased image of First Nations history. For example, the Métis uprising of 1869 and the North West Rebellion of 1885 were described as resistance to the legitimate colonization efforts of the newly formed Canada. The Métis were a decent if somewhat primitive people who were taken in by a charismatic, insane leader, Louis Riel. In 1869 the French-speaking Riel savagely executed an innocent English-speaking settler. Troops were brought in to restore order and Riel fled to the USA. He later returned to lead the North West Rebellion of 1885, defeated by superior British troops, and he was hanged for treason. The same events look very different from a Métis point of view (Sealey★ and Lussier★ 1975). The Métis lived a yearly cycle according to which they would plant crops in Manitoba and then move west for the buffalo hunt, drying meat for sale to the fur traders. The pattern was broken when Canada decided to open the area to settlers. They sent in survey teams, which laid out land holdings in grid form, whereas the Métis, who needed access to the river, saw their land stretching from the river. The Canadians disregarded their land ownership and issued title according to the surveys. When the Métis returned for the winter to harvest their crops, they discovered that the new settlers, granted deeds to their land, had destroyed them.

Louis Riel was democratically elected as leader of the Métis Nation in 1868. In 1869 the Métis tried and convicted a violent, racist immigrant and hanged him. Riel tried to dissuade the court from executing him. The (English) Canadian government sent in troops to control the Métis Nation and Riel fled to Montana.

In 1885, after the Canadians had intentionally destroyed the buffalo to weaken the Métis, the people of Manitoba went to Montana and asked Riel to return to lead them. Again Riel attempted to get the government of Canada to recognize the illegal occupation of Métis land, but it refused and opened up more settlement. The government even refused to recognize their duly elected members of parliament in Ottawa. When the Métis and other people of the territory resisted the intrusion, the government sent an army. It overran the Métis nation and jailed the leaders. The Métis, under the military leadership of Gabriel Dumont, lost to the Canadians only because of the acts of clemency of Riel and the Cree chiefs in refusing to massacre defeated enemy troops. Riel was later arrested, wrongfully accused, and hanged as a traitor in 1885. According to Dickason* (1993):

> The Red River crisis and the subsequent question of amnesty were the first serious racial controversies to be faced by Canada. Although the English–French confrontation took centre stage, the underlying Amerindian–Métis–White division had been the major factor
>
> (Dickason* 1993: 272)

It is understandable that First Nations, because of their history with Europeans, may take a dim view of development programmes that exploit natural resources in a non-sustainable manner or involve what may be perceived as colonization, assimilation, or exploitation. To maintain levels of autonomy, there may be interest in development using their own private-sector capacity. Because of the long history on their ancestral territories, they could be expected to show interest in programmes that are consistent with cultural identification with *mother earth*.

Residential schools

Education has featured as a tool in the colonization of Native North Americans. It is anticipated that with their negative experiences of European education, First Nations are likely to regard critically educational programmes in developing countries. They are likely to show more interest in indigenous education movements, particularly in higher education. The British, French and Canadian educational systems have not been kind to First Nations. Indian residential schools began in 1620 and ended in 1976, a 350-year history of violence, hunger, loneliness and abuse. The objectives were at first to convert and educate students. By the nineteenth century, elders actively tried to establish schools for their children, seeing the advantages of communication in writing and access to professions. By the 1950s a malicious sense of driving out their Indianness had set in. The children were beaten, underfed and forced to work more than they studied to maintain the underfunded institutions

(Millar 1996). Chrisjohn★ and Young (1997) maintain that aspects of the system can still be found in contemporary education. They recommend, for example, a moratorium on intelligence testing of First Nations students. They are sceptical of any schools run by non-Natives for the education of Natives.

Women in development

Women have come to occupy an important place in international development. According to Clarkson *et al.*:

> The status of indigenous women has been dramatically altered as a result of assimilating education, government policies, introduction of production for exchange and loss of traditional lands, and as a result of the marginalization of indigenous communities and men. Their knowledge, political influence, role of producer and caretaker have been systematically devaluated, with the consequence that they have nowadays to fight against both the wider society, and the male-dominated political structures for their survival … Colonialism, the early integration into the global economic system, and the ongoing application of inappropriate development strategies have eroded the strength of traditional societies and radically transformed the indigenous way of life.
>
> (Clarkson *et al.* 1992: vii)

First Nations were historically more gender egalitarian than European cultures, although the status of women varied between societies. In Iroquoian culture, for example, women had a level of control over their lives unheard of in Europe (Viau 2000). Although there was a distinct separation of roles by gender, this did not translate into hierarchical relations. Several groups, such as the Iroquois and the Sioux, were matriarchal and matrilineal. Several historical documents cite the role of women in community decision making, a fact found curious by first-contact white explorers and missionaries (Dickason★ 1993).

Today, the most contentious issue around gender concerns *An Act to Amend the Indian Act Bill C-31 (1985)*. As part of the assimilation aims of the *Indian Act of 1876*, women lost their Indian status when they married a non-Native. Native People were also considered *emancipated* by exercising a profession or even by voting, thus losing their ancestral rights for themselves and their descendants. When this aspect of the law was judged unconstitutional for reasons of equity, corrections were made applying back two generations. As a result, 105,000 people regained their Native status, including their fair share of First Nations assets (Forest and Rodon 1995; INAC 2000). This was welcomed by many, but strongly resisted by others. The result is on the one hand, some hostility to some women's new status, but, on the other hand, a recognition of human capital, particularly regarding the areas of educational resources.

First Nations reticence about international development assistance

It is expected that Native Peoples may show limited interest in international development, given their experiences of assimilation stress, a history of exploitation and colonization, their strong sense of identity with their lands, and acceptance of development only if it is sustainable. Exceptions may involve cooperating with other indigenous peoples, offering mutual help, or expressing solidarity with peoples experiencing problems they themselves have survived. Forest and Rodon (1995) argue that, although Canada's First Nations have developed a distinct international image, and have consistently reached out to the international community, they have little sympathy for international development activities.

We generally consider that First Nations entered the national political area with the 1969 publication of the ironically named *White Paper on Indian Affairs* (Government of Canada 1969). From this time, the Canadian government commissioned a series of studies of the political and social situation of First Nations. These studies have attempted to understand grievances resulting from colonization and to combat racist and paternalistic structures. More cynical observers believe this work was undertaken to create conditions more favourable to resource exploitation (Forest and Rodon 1995).

The *Constitution Act of 1982* and the *Constitutional Amendment Proclamation of 1983*, dealing with aboriginal rights, better protected the rights of First Nations, but the distribution of power remained unchanged. The various First Nations remain sceptical about protection of their rights by constitutional powers, despite such successes as the Mohawk gaining recognition of their own passports in seventeen countries, based on the 1664 *Two-row Wampum Treaty*.

It is understandable that First Nations may see little relevance in international development. There are, however, benefits to international engagement. They can give assistance to others seeking various administrative powers, based on their experiences of over a century. They can work mutually for territorial rights and environmental protection. There is international work for political identity and recognition. There are more radical and ideological movements arguing for a return to traditional tribal government. Economic development has led to a few Native businesses tapping international markets. In all, First Nations look outward to resolve various international problems that touch them.

International recognition came in 1974 when George Manuel had the National Indian Brotherhood recognized as an official non-governmental organization at the UN. Today, international activities fall in four categories: (1) participation in organizations such as the UN; (2) participation in international aboriginal organizations; (3) relations between First Nations and foreign governments; and (4) relations with foreign aboriginal communities. Some of these activities, such as Inuit circumpolar relations, put into doubt the logic of territorial integrity.

Indigenous peoples and international development

The indigenous peoples' movement is gaining strength around the world. As indigenous peoples' issues become more prevalent, established models and methods of development are being challenged and rethought. The preference for open markets, technology, urban expansion and individual rights is not in juxtaposition with indigenous values of rights to ancestral lands and resources, the drive for self-determination and the maintenance of respective cultures. Governments focusing on supposed modernization are being challenged by indigenous peoples who do not share the same development paradigm.

For much of the world's recent development history, indigenous peoples have been viewed by the dominant culture as primitive, backward and perhaps uncivilized. As a result, indigenous peoples have not been part of the development agenda. Regardless, as globalization advances and countries reach ever more into the forests, mountains, deserts seas and lakes for natural resources, contact with indigenous peoples is guaranteed. And, with sustainable development the goal of many of the more enlightened countries, working with indigenous peoples in a more respectful and cooperative way offers many opportunities and benefits for countries to realize their development objectives in a more substainable way. The use of indigenous knowledge and practice can provide more realistic evaluations of environmental, natural resource and production systems for long-term management and use.

There is a growing understanding in the development community that the poverty issue needs to be re-examined to answer the questions: 'Who is poor?' and 'How do the poor describe their own situation?' (Dunnet 2000). When these questions are discussed, the plight of indigenous peoples and their vulnerability becomes apparent.

To address the poverty issues among indigenous peoples, governments must make choices that provide as many benefits to its citizenry as possible. The challenge is to reduce negative effects of progress on indigenous peoples and ensure that they can share in the opportunities of development to the extent that they freely choose to do. This demonstrates a government's respect for self-determination. A priority of development is that it must recognize and respond to the unique relationships that indigenous peoples have with their lands and the ecosystems which sustain them. Change, of course is inevitable; the pace of change, however, should be within the control of the indigenous peoples and not the outside interveners.

The argument posed by Arizpe with respect to using local knowledge in development is compelling:

The present conditions of the international system are not only making peoples in the countries of the South poorer in economic resources, but they are also making them poorer in knowledge. And what is perhaps even worse, poorer in the confidence with which they can continue to create knowledge ... Mobilization, self reliance and initiatives for poverty alleviation have to be backed by confidence in what peoples know and have learned to do. This is why focusing on culture and the preservations of people's knowledge is central in the fight against poverty.

(Arizpe 1988: 18)

Ignoring indigenous peoples and their knowledge systems is not a sound economic strategy. A massive, 7-million hectare, groundnut project in Tanzania for the production of edible oils was originally budgeted to be $US940 million. But after ten years and a final cost of $US1.3 billion the project was deemed a complete failure. Rainfall was not accurately predicted, soil chemistry was not appropriate to the crops, and soil texture was high in clay, which quickly ruined the farm machines. Throughout the life of the project, only Western scientific methods of analysis and data gathering were used. All of these factors, and how to deal with them, were well known to the indigenous farmers of the area, who were deliberately ignored. Fuglesang (1984: 51) noted, 'ignorance, apparently is evenly distributed'.

The development model based on macro-economic approaches, nested in a framework of exclusion of local and indigenous peoples, is no longer a sustainable option. Economic systems, patterns of trade and sociopolitical institutions must be better aligned with local and indigenous requirements. In doing so, indigenous characteristics such as simplicity, functionality, holism and cooperative integration will help ensure that development is more culturally and ecologically sensitive, while at the same time maximizing the benefits of a natural resource base that is in jeopardy. The following points (Obomsawin* 2001) summarize well why indigenous knowledge is important in the planning, execution and evaluation of development projects:

- Indigenous knowledge remains a valuable resource for strengthening development efforts locally, nationally and internationally. Perhaps of greatest importance is that its very existence and multiple uses can become a source of pride and ownership to local beneficiaries in development efforts. Furthermore, its practical employment encourages and intensifies participatory decision-making processes, and aids in the formation and effective functioning of local organizations.
- Indigenous knowledge also includes practical concepts that can be used to facilitate communication among and between peoples coming from diverse backgrounds such as development researchers, extension workers and project beneficiaries. Familiarization with indigenous knowledge can assist outside change agents in both understanding and communicating

with clientele groups. This factor is also important in facilitating genuinely participatory approaches to local decision making.

- The appropriate employment of indigenous knowledge helps to assure that the end users of specific development projects are more intimately involved in developing technologies that are best suited to their needs. By working with and through existing local knowledge systems, change agents can more effectively facilitate the transfer of technology generated through the international research networks (both conventional and indigenous) in order to improve local systems.
- Indigenous knowledge is highly cost-effective since it directly builds on locally existing cultures and development efforts, thus enhancing local capacity building and sustainability.

Around the world, indigenous peoples are deeply involved in development. In Costa Rica and Belize indigenous groups provide interpretative tours of their culture (Pleumarom 1999). In Guyana, the Macusi Amerindian communities benefit from a nature reserve and ecotourism on their traditional lands (Shackley 1998). Indigenous communities are working towards regional autonomy and self-government in eastern Nicaragua, fighting intentionally restrictive laws. The Kuna and the Miskito fought for and attained a higher degree of autonomy (Sherrer 1994). The Wichi, Toba and Chorote of northern Argentina have successfully made agreements covering environmental restoration and control over natural resources (Hanson 1996).

In Canada, the following three examples demonstrate how indigenous peoples are taking charge of their own development agenda and priorities for economic as well as cultural gain.

James Bay and Northern Quebec Agreement

According to the Quebec government, the James Bay project to harness the power of the principal rivers flowing into James Bay would produce 10,000 megawatts of electricity and 120,000 jobs. A *National Geographic* article referred to it as the most monumental hydroelectric project ever undertaken in North America (Kohl 1982). To date, it has cost 15 billion dollars, and the first phase alone has resulted in the construction of 208 kilometres of dams. It has affected about 155,000 square kilometres of land, approximately the area of England. The project has had a profound effect on the peoples living in the James Bay region. In October 1974, after lengthy negotiation, the Cree chief, Billy Diamond announced that an agreement had been reached between the Quebec government, the federal government, the Grand Council of the Crees, and the Northern Quebec Inuit Association. The Crees would relinquish all aboriginal claims in the territory of James Bay in return for 225 million dollars and control of a smaller and clearly defined area, and partial control over a larger region. The Agreement established a series of Cree institutions, such as Cree health services and a Cree school board, giving autonomous control of these previously problematic services. These institutions also allowed the Crees to undertake major development activities by establishing a construction company, producing outfitting camps, founding their own airline and engaging in ecotourism.

The Cree of Quebec, the Eeyou Istchee, are one of a dozen aboriginal groups to obtain consultative status with the United Nations Economic and Social Council. This is a status that enables the Cree Grand Council representatives to speak and take part in debates held by the UN Commission on Human Rights. Their experience at the UN quickly showed them that indigenous peoples throughout the world are suffering the same disadvantages as in Canada, in many places greater ones. They began to collaborate with others from around the world in an effort to establish a permanent international role for aboriginal peoples, and to obtain recognition of rights. The Crees have participated in a number of international cooperation activities. For example, they have had representatives at the Coalition against Large Dams in Vienna. They have worked with indigenous peoples of Australia, Chiapas and Guatemala, among others. They have also been major donors to disaster relief situations such as the Ethiopian famine of 1982, a policy founded on their beliefs.[2]

Kitgan-Zipi sugar bush

A sugar bush is an installation for collecting and reducing maple sap to maple syrup and sugar. It is generally a small cottage industry. The Anishinabek community of Kitgan-Zipi near Maniwaki, Quebec, is developing a commercial sized sugar bush. It has substantial impact on both the Native and non-Native communities nearby, supporting the infrastructure for other agro-industry activities. It is likely to be the first of a series of similar projects because of the expanding market for maple sugar products. It is also part of a larger plan that has seen the construction of a day-care centre, extensions to the local school, etc. The project becomes the focus for various spin-offs that benefit the whole population (Millar 2000).

Nisga'a treaty

On 4 August 1998 the Nisga'a treaty was signed in New Aiyansh, a village in British Columbia's Nass Valley. The treaty is expected to increase economic development because of its formalization of rights and opportunities. Tenures have been granted to back country recreation facilities including bed-and-breakfasts, tourism facilities and restaurants. There are also sustainable opportunities to sell water. The Nisga'a believe that their ability to govern themselves will greatly increase their chances of advancing economic development (Weir 2000).

There are also many problems for indigenous peoples regarding development of the countries in which they live. The Masai were evicted from their traditional lands in the 1950s to encourage ecotourism, and even today their pastoral lifestyle is discouraged (de Chavez 1999). Resource development can produce inequality in otherwise egalitarian societies (O'Faircheallaigh 1998). In Madagascar, ecotourism has marginalized indigenous peoples from their tribal lands that are now private property (Mulligan 1999). Ecotourism has promoted ethnic conflict in Central America as indigenous groups have lost land (Van Cott 1996).

First Nations principles of development

In Panama, in 1984, the World Council of indigenous peoples (WCIP) ratified a Declaration of Principles acknowledging their rights (Anderson 1999). The principles include the following:

1 All human rights of indigenous peoples must be respected.
2 All indigenous peoples have the right to self-determination.
3 Every nation-state within which indigenous peoples live shall recognize the population, territory and institutions belonging to said peoples.
4 The culture of indigenous peoples is part of mankind's cultural patrimony.
5 The customs of the indigenous peoples must be respected as legitimate sources of rights.
7 All indigenous peoples have the right to determine the form, structure and jurisdictions of their own institutions.
10 Indigenous peoples have inalienable rights over their traditional lands and resources.
15 All indigenous peoples have the right to be educated in their own language and to establish their own education institutions.[3]

These principles largely agree with various expressions of First Nations' ideas of development. They could however come into conflict with certain development activities. The Canadian International Development Agency's mandate concentrates on six priorities: basic human needs, women in development, infrastructure services, good governance, private-sector development and the environment. The Organisation for Economic Cooperation and Development (OECD) supports three major goals: economic well being, social development (including education, infant mortality and health services), and environmental sustainability.

If the customs alluded to in principle 5 are a strict but benevolent patriarchy, these could conflict with the demands of women in development. Some of these principles even seem to be written to protect the indigenous peoples from certain aspects of (indigenously poorly conceived) development.

It is evident that exploiting forest resources will conflict with principle 10, regarding traditional lands, unless the indigenous peoples living there are deeply involved in developing the forest management plan and its implementation. Even the declaration of national parks intended to protect the environment can run foul of the principles, for example principle 7, which states that indigenous peoples have the right to determine jurisdictions.

Indigenous peoples also recognize that Western and indigenous knowledge systems may complement each other with respect to providing goods and services that a community has defined as appropriate for itself. The combination of Western and indigenous knowledge is proving to be a powerful symbiotic relationship to address development challenges that would otherwise be less successful if approached using only one knowledge system. But they are saying that there must be respect for the cultural values behind their knowledge and that their rights to maintain these values must be acknowledged and protected in the development process.

Economists see indigenous knowledge as social capital because it represents generations of learning about how to organize productivity. It is one of the most valuable forms of capital any peoples possess for formulating their development goals. The key problem for indigenous peoples has been their lack of control of how the knowledge is accessed and used outside their communities. It is ironic that the poorest and often the dispossessed peoples on the planet are suddenly being recognized as holders of knowledge that is critically important to global human well being, sustainable development and environmental conservation. The following example from the Yukon Territory of Canada demonstrates how an indigenous community can gain control over the use of indigenous knowledge.

The community of Old Crow in Canada's northern Yukon illustrates how a small indigenous community of 300 people manages the integration of indigenous knowledge and environment assessment. The region is under constant pressure from primary industry development, particularly the oil and gas industries. Previous environmental assessments interpreted their culture and indigenous knowledge in inappropriate and skewed ways. For example, comments were made to the effect that if peoples were not using the land, then it must not be of any value to them. Old Crow turned this around. It developed its own community-based environmental assessment system. The community defines its own goals and objectives, and asks the government and industry to define their goals and objectives to see where there are potential areas of collaboration or issue resolution. The community also stipulates that scientific methods and knowledge must be defined in a way to fit into their traditional views of land and cultural survival. For example, a local goal is to ensure the recognition of traditional ways of harvesting. The value that underpins this is the custom of respect. An indicator that these goals and values are being upheld by all parties is the number of community-based agreements on co-management of resources that have indigenous knowledge, controlled by the community, as a key element.

In North America, the Four Worlds International Institute for Human and Community Development (2000) has built its foundation on a consultation with elders from forty different North American First Nations. The Institute was born out of intense deliberations and prayers at a gathering of Native elders and community leaders held on the Kainai First Nation on the high plains of Alberta in December 1982. Distinguished representatives of the tribes involved met to search for a solution to the social devastation brought by alcohol, poverty and an increasing sense of powerlessness sweeping across tribal communities. The Institute is involved in training, health issues and funding international humanitarian work. Its four strategic foundation principles are:

1   Development comes from within: others may help and assist, but the driving force for change, healing, learning, growth and progress must come from within the communities themselves.
2   No vision, no development: the peoples need to be able to visualize health and well being for themselves in order to be able to create it in their world.
3   Individual and community transformations must go hand in hand: the healing, learning and growth of individuals, and the transformations of community relationships and conditions are mutually interdependent.
4   Holistic learning is the key to deep and lasting change: Learning is at the heart of sustainable change processes. Human beings are multidimensional learning beings, physically, emotionally, intellectually, spiritually and volitionally.

The elders in their worldview believe that:

1   The spiritual and material aspects of life are inseparable and interdependent.
2   Indeed everything is related to everything in this universe.
3   Healing ourselves, our communities, our nations and mother earth depends on our capacity to understand our own selves.
4   Human beings have within them, as a gift of the Creator, the power to transform and heal the world.

These principles reflect themes such as a global conception of creation, a search for vision, generosity and a preference for introspection. Clarkson *et al.* (1992) point out several further aspects of First Nations' thoughts about development. In Algonkian thought, all actions must take into account consequences for seven generations, an excellent base for sustainability. The Algonkian state that there is a sacred aspect to their relationship with the earth: We are placed on the earth, our mother, to be caretakers of all that is here (Clarkson *et al.* 1992: 4). Their key principles for development include:

1   Respect for the earth and all creation.
2   To relearn history from an indigenous peoples' perspective. 'Western peoples must realize that by defending indigenous peoples and their lands, they are working to secure their own future as well' (Clarkson *et al.* 1992: 65).
3   The expansionist/materialist Western society will eventually collapse under its own weight.
4   Traditional forms of social, economic and political organization have a great deal to contribute to understanding the requirements of socially sustainable societies.
5   First Nations societies are built on the foundations of true democracy. The American Constitution only incompletely replicated the true democracy of the Iroquois Confederacy.

The Meadow Lake Tribal Council in Saskatchewan is an example of the new approach to economic development emerging among First Nations, according to which they create profitable businesses which compete in the world market. Development activities include forestry and transportation. The very successful economic development activities of the Meadow Lake Tribal Council are based on the following principles (Anderson and Bone★ 1999):

1   Attainment of economic self-sufficiency.
2   Preservation and strengthening of traditional culture, values and languages.
3   Improvement of socioeconomic circumstances.

Another example is the assertively pragmatic approach encompassing the following principles from the Tahltan Tribal Council:

1   Assurance that development will not pose a threat of irreparable environmental damage.
2   Assurance that development will not jeopardize outstanding land claims.
3   Assurance that a project will have more positive than negative social impacts on the First Nations peoples.
4   Provision for the widest possible opportunity for education and training.
5   Provision for the widest possible employment opportunities for the peoples.
6   Provision for substantial equity participation.
7   Provision for the widest possible development of First Nations business opportunities.

Collective development experience between indigenous and non-indigenous groups in the Northwest Territories has resulted in the following advice (Myers 1999):

1   Earlier approaches tried to assimilate northerners into the mainstream Canadian economy.
2   Evidence proves the viability of modern development based on traditional resources, skills and values.
3   Earlier approaches were short lived and drew peoples away from traditional land-based livelihoods, leaving them unemployed and unskilled when projects closed down.
4   The traditional, land-based Native economy is not viable. Harvesters in the Northwest Territories earned on average $10,000 to $15,000 in food and fuel in 1988 (by comparison, the family income of the James Bay Crees included the equivalent of $40,000 per year from hunting; Darou 1989).
5   Out of 473 projects that developed locally-based commercial enterprises, the success rate in terms of two-year survival was 73 per cent, comparable to southern businesses.
6   Success factors included use of traditional resources and skills, use of traditional and innovative approaches together, management structures that suit indigenous culture, use of small and seasonal projects, focus on local markets, and including all resource users in resource management.

Regarding development, Billy Diamond, the first Grand Council Chief of the Crees of Quebec, has taken the vision issue as central (Diamond* 2000). He argues that the priority of all aboriginal leaders should be to ensure that the human, physical and financial resources available to their peoples are used wisely. There must be continued benefit to future generations. He believes that Canadian society has failed the peoples by assuring a welfare culture and frowning on indigenous economic activities: 'The situation was compounded by the pervasive problems of racism, remoteness, lack of adequate infrastructure to support business and generate jobs, and the serious lack of adequate training and relevant education' (Diamond 2000: 4). Diamond believes that politicians should be kept away from economic development projects, and suggests that young people receive culturally relevant business education, in the face of the 'flourishing business of aboriginal training' (Diamond 2000: 6).

First Nations international involvement

Realizing that they were not listened to by their nation states, indigenous peoples have sought to make their voices heard at the international level for hundreds of years. For example, in the past, Canadian First Nations made representations to the Queen, who sent them back to their respective colonial governments. To regain basic economic and political rights they founded associations. They explored the possibility of League of Nations support for their grievances. Deskaheh, a representative of the Iroquois Confederacy, travelled to Geneva in 1923, where he succeeded in having a resolution introduced in the forum, but failed to have it debated and submitted for voting. In the late 1960s the National Indian Brotherhood was created in western Canada. During the next decade the association took shape and began to be seen as an organization which could exercise pressure on the federal government for early settlement of land titles and treaty issues. The Chairman of the Indian Brotherhood, Chief George Manuel, travelled extensively. He visited New Zealand and Australia in 1971. In 1972 he was an advisor to the Canadian delegation to the United Nations Conference in Stockholm. Following the Stockholm conference, he visited the International Labour Organization's International Working Group for Indigenous Affairs in Copenhagen. There he announced his plan for a world conference of indigenous peoples. He was committed to the principle that indigenous peoples must organize and control the conference themselves. The international conference was held in Port Alberni, British Columbia in 1975. Two hundred and sixty persons participated. The programme included drafting a charter for the creation of a World Indigenous Council. Chief Manuel achieved his goal when the World Council of Indigenous Peoples (WCIP) came into existence. The Council has received a total of $4.9 million in funding from the Canadian International Development Agency since 1976. Its development activities are concentrated in Central and South America where it coordinates and supports projects of local indigenous organizations and communities.

There are some examples of First Nations engaging in international development activities. There is even a scholarly journal devoted to First Nations economic development (*Journal of Aboriginal Economic Development*). History has demonstrated to First Nations that development in the sense of becoming rich does not resolve their problems of self-determination. They have found that a more successful strategy is to build self-governance. The experience of First Nations peoples of outside-imposed development and domination make them active partners to peoples elsewhere suffering from similar imposed programmes as they have aroused sympathy for their protests borne of bitter personal events. The following examples, chosen from many hundreds, illustrate the development involvement of First Nations.

The Assembly of First Nations undertook a demarcation project in Venezuela to establish the boundaries of the ancestral territory of the Ye'kuana peoples. It works in partnership with Otro Futuro, a Venezuelan NGO that provides technical support and legal counsel to indigenous communities of Venezuela. Mamo Atoskewin Atikamokw Association, which promotes the use of traditional aboriginal knowledge, works in collaboration with Resources Kitaskino XXI Inc., an aboriginal company specializing in geomatics and environment. These two organizations undertook a technical assistance project in partnership with indigenous communities in Northern Thailand. In 1998 the 86-year-old William Commanda, an elder from Kitigan-Zipi First Nation near Maniwaki in Quebec, also organized Elders without Borders, a gathering of elders and spiritual leaders from North and South America and Thailand. The organization brings together elders to share information and strategies, with the ultimate objective of 'saving the earth'.

The Meadow Lake Tribal Council, cited above, through its MLTC Investment Company has a joint venture project with Corporación Indigena Para El Desarrollo Económica SA (CIDESA), a Miskito Indian company, for social development projects. Seaku Fisheries, an indigenous company responsible for the development and management of commercial fishing in the Nunavik region of northern Quebec, also has a joint venture project with CIDESA for the creation of a company that will produce commercial fishing products.

The Centre canadien d'étude et de coopération internationale (CECI) (Canadian Centre for International Studies and Cooperation) has organized several exchanges between the Innu of Maniuténam in Northern Quebec and the Quéchua and Aymara of Bolivia, beginning in 1992. One of the outcomes of this project was an agreement for exchanges with the Société de Communication Attikamech–Montagnais (The Attikamech–Montagnais Communications Corporation). It also involved youth exchanges, and discussion of hunting and wildlife management issues. The Innu report that the greatest mutual benefits were contact with a different group facing the same challenges, and exchanges of information between the elders on issues of cultural values and well being. They have established a Committee for Quebec Bolivian Solidarity. The Turtle Island Earth Stewards, a Canadian indigenous peoples' group, held an international youth camp entitled Listening to the Voice of the Elders, bringing together indigenous youth from around the world.

The Anishinabek Educational Institute (AEI), part of the Union of Ontario Indians, is involved in several international activities. For example, it is in the process of developing an exhibition in conjunction with the Landesmuseum in Hanover, Germany. The exhibition, entitled 'From the Heart of Turtle Island', describes the Woodland peoples living around the Great Lakes, and includes migration stories, archaeological artefacts and current activities. Of more direct interest to international development, the AEI has connections with indigenous peoples of Panama. They are involved in the delivery of accredited educational programmes with the Kuna, which involve training courses in aboriginal small business, early childhood education and English as a second language. In addition, they are helping the Kuna with curriculum development for other courses, and are supporting the transfer of skills so that the Kuna can ultimately do the work themselves. The advantage of this programme for the Anishinabek is that it helps them build capacity and supports international relationships. The Kuna have chosen to cooperate with the Anishinabek because they felt they would be sensitive to their legitimate concerns about being exploited. Through several visits, both parties gradually developed a relationship based on trust and mutual sympathy.

What First Nations have to contribute to majority culture development: the other view

The use of indigenous knowledge by Europeans in North America has a history of hundreds of years. The first medical prescription from Canada involved Vitamin C from spruce needles given to European explorers as treatment for scurvy. There is also aspirin, the canoe, lacrosse and several agricultural practices, to name a few of the one thousand named by Côté *et al.* (1992). The US system of government is even based on the Iroquois system of confederacy.

Douglas Cardinal, the Blackfoot architect who designed the award-winning Canadian Museum of Civilization in Gatineau, Quebec, has written about what First Nations can offer White society (Cardinal 1990). In the development of First Nations culture, he foresees a salvation of all peoples, not just First Nations. Cardinal refers to the individualistic Euro–American culture as *ego society*, and maintains that it cannot teach balance because it is based on an obsession with power. Cultural balance comes from efforts of indigenous peoples to retain their identities. European knowledge must be communicated in the indigenous way so that indigenous peoples can assimilate it as appropriate to their own cultural tradition. After his global vision, Cardinal urges that First Nations not restrict themselves to being Canadian or American citizens.

Their alternative collective wisdom is needed for a number of reasons:

1 Some green revolution technology is associated with ecological degradation and poorer diets.
2 Some development concepts have not proven appropriate or sustainable.
3 Rapid growth of the *life* industries such as medical research and biotechnology.
4 Local peoples tend to abandon technical interventions that have come from the outside.
5 Top-down planning fails to promote effective natural resource management at the local level.
6 Communities that receive much aid may become less able to handle their own affairs.

Today even hard-nosed business is recognizing the importance of indigenous approaches and is responding to them. Take, for example, the comment of Voisey's Bay Nickel Company President, Dr Stewart Gendron (1997): 'In today's mining industry having access to traditional knowledge is so important because it allows companies to put in place more successful mitigation strategies to address the environmental and socio-economic impacts of mining operations.' Dr Thomas Alcoze★, a Navajo biologist from Arizona, puts it this way:

> The environmental crisis must be addressed at the practical, functional and scientific level. However, a major aspect of the new environmental relationships between human society and the earth must incorporate ethics. That is one of the most fundamental and important aspects of what Native traditions and values can provide our global society. Credibility needs to be given to those teachings ... Science is not just a white man's thing.
>
> (Greer★ 1992: 24)

Compared with many modern technologies, traditional techniques have been tried and tested, are effective, inexpensive, locally available and in many cases based on preserving and building on the patterns and processes of nature. Traditional approaches usually examine problems in their entirety, as opposed to the Western way of looking for individual solutions to discrete problems. For example, in Canada the health industry is now starting to realize that good health is a mix of physical, spiritual and psychological well being, and not just good blood chemistry. Indigenous healers have known this for countless years. Sometimes there is a practical reason for favouring traditional knowledge. In the north of Canada dog teams are becoming popular again, because if you are lost, they know the way home, unlike a snowmobile.

What First Nations might find interesting in international development

It is clear that First Nations peoples report conflicting feelings about development. On the one hand, they are suspicious of development because they see themselves as its victims, as marginalized by it, even today. In addition, they may see themselves as being in no position to help others because they are too needy themselves. On the other hand, when they have the resources, involvement in development gives First Nations an opportunity to share the experiences of their own struggles, affording them an opportunity to build their own and others' capacity. It may also offer First Nations invaluable international political links. Many times, as we have seen, their motivation is altruistic; when First Nations become aware of a problem they generally wish to help.

It is clear why First Nations may be suspicious of, or disinterested in, international development activities. But, many projects exist, indicating that there is interest in some aspects. Those wishing to involve First Nations in international development might consider the following possible directions:

- social exchanges that allow First Nations to share a common cause such as threats to territorial integrity;
- opportunities to help others who are facing problems First Nations have dealt with;
- opportunities to share surplus resources with other indigenous peoples in need, thereby expressing the *give-away* ethic, and to devise poverty-reduction strategies (e.g. the Crees of Quebec do not use a welfare system);
- sharing of collective knowledge that may be poorly understood by the majority Canadian culture;
- businesses built on other cultural foundations;
- ecotourism, teaching respect for nature and sharing indigenous knowledge about the land or resources;
- ecological interventions meant to 'heal the earth';
- indigenous education; or
- activities resisting assimilation or colonization.

We need a long-term approach to capacity building. It is important to focus on respectful partnerships and not just on development activity or on factual indigenous knowledge. Respectful approaches will depend on better use of participatory development methodologies. Development practitioners realize that development will have greatest success when the beneficiaries of the development have more opportunities to participate in the planning, implementation, operation and monitoring of development projects. Within most indigenous societies, one of the defining characteristics of the cultures is the high degree of participation in all community decisions. By including indigenous communities in development efforts and by creatively combining these with external resources, the chances of project success and community benefit would surely increase.

Many Native leaders seem to look at development in the way a hunter kills prey with compassion, and yet fears offending the animal's spiritual essence (Arthur Blue*, 2001, pers. comm., March 2001). Six elements of such a partnership might be:

1   Indigenous peoples, Canadian and otherwise, identify what is important and why.
2   A consensus is reached to identify objectives of development.
3   Developers and indigenous peoples work together to respect each other's needs.
4   Indigenous peoples have a key role in project monitoring and follow-up.
5   Project planning gives scope to using indigenous knowledge to specify the aims and benefits of projects.

6   Indigenous peoples are allowed to practise their indigenous knowledge rather than simply talk about it. The richness of indigenous knowledge is in the doing and not the telling.

This chapter closes with two questions:

1   How can First Nations, who hold indigenous knowledge and experience, communicate effectively with governments and industry, who are seldom properly trained to conceptualize human development in the way that indigenous peoples do?
2   How can indigenous peoples be effective in international development if the process in Canada is itself managed and controlled by non-Native North Americans?

In conclusion, the development community can benefit from First Nations involvement in several ways. First Nations have a wealth of experience of successful (and less successful) development activities, often analysed in detail and published in professional journals. In addition, because of common experiences discussed here, First Nations have been able to develop trust relationships with aid recipients that would be difficult for other development workers to achieve. The North American aid community could exploit this resource more effectively, and with the full involvement of the First Nations. Finally, such a strategy would allow institutions to conduct very effective double-edged development. The resulting projects could generate highly effective multifaceted development, helping international organizations, NGOs and international indigenous peoples build their capacity to deliver aid – in concrete, achievable ways.

Notes

1   Native authors are indicated by an asterisk after their name.
2   For further information on the Crees' international activities, see their website at http://www.gcc.ca/Political-Issues/international/international_menu.htm.
3   Note that the complete list is available at http://www.anatomy.usyd.edu.au /danny/anthropology/anthro-l/archive/may-1994/0046.html.

Bibliography

Anderson, R. B. 1999. *Economic Development Among the Aboriginal Peoples in Canada: The Hope for the Future.* Toronto: Captus Press.

Anderson, R. B. and R. M. Bone. 1999. First Nations economic development: The Meadow Lake Tribal Council. *Journal of Aboriginal Economic Development* 1(1): 13–34.

Arizpe, L. 1988. Culture in international development. *Journal of the Society of International Development* 1: 17–19.

Berry, J. W. 1997. Immigration, acculturation and adaptation. *Applied Psychology: An International Review* 46(1): 5–68.

—— 1999. Aboriginal cultural identity. *The Canadian Journal of Native Studies* 19: 1–36.

Bopp, J., M. Bopp, M. Brown and P. Lane. 1984. *The Sacred Tree*. Lethbridge, Alberta: Four Worlds Development Press.

Brant, C. 1990. Native ethics and rules of behaviour. *Canadian Journal of Psychiatry* 35: 534–539.

Cardinal, D. 1990. How Indian culture can heal White society. *Ottawa Citizen*, 20 January: D1.

Chevrier, M. 1998. Niijaanhzinaanig–Waaniniigaanhzijig Anishinabek youth gathering 1998: Final report. North Bay (ON): Anishinabek Educational Institute.

Chrisjohn, R. and S. Young. 1997. *The Circle Game: Shadows and Substance in the Indian Residential School Experience in Canada*. Penticton, B.C.: Theytus Books.

Clarkson, L., V. Morrissette and G. Regallet. 1992. *Our Responsibility to the Seventh Generation*. Winnipeg, Manitoba: International Institute for Sustainable Development.

Côté, L., L. Tardivel and D. Vaugeois. 1992. *L'Indien généreux: Ce que le monde doit aux Amériques* (The Generous Indian: What the World Owes to the Americas). Montreal: Boréal.

Darou, W. 1989. *Obstacles to Effective Experimentation: A Study Among the James Bay Cree*. Unpublished Ph.d. dissertation, McGill University: Montreal.

de Chavez, R. 1999. Globalisation and tourism: Deadly mix for indigenous peoples. *Third World Resurgence* 103: 17–19.

Diamond, B. 2000. For the benefit of all: Challenges of community economic development. *Journal of Aboriginal Economic Development* 1(2): 3–6.

Dickason, O. P. 1993. *Canada's First Nations: A History of Founding Peoples from Earliest Times*. Toronto: McClelland and Stewart.

Dunnet, J. 2000. *Being Indigenous in Asia: An Overview*. Internal CIDA draft discussion paper.

Forest, P.-G. and T. Rodon. 1995. Les activités internationale des autochtones du Canada (The international activities of Canada's Native Peoples). *Études Internationales* 26(1): 35.

Fuglesang, A. 1984. The myth of people's ignorance. *Development Dialogue. Dag Hammarskjold Foundation*: 51.

Gendron, D. 1997. Media release, 6 September. Voisey's Bay Nickel Company, Canada.

Government of Canada, Department of Indian and Northern Affairs. 1969. Statement of the Government of Canada on Indian Policy (The White Paper). Ottawa: Queen's Printer.

Greer, S. 1992. Science: It's not just a white man thing. *Winds of Change* 7(2): 23–34.

Hanson, I. 1996. The flowers of the earth: Argentine Indians win land-claim dispute. *New Internationalist* December: 4.

INAC. 2000. Hull: Indian and Northern Affairs Canada. http://www.inac.gc.ca/.

Jenish, D. 2000. *Indian Fall: The Last Great Days of the Plains Cree and the Blackfoot Confederacy*. Toronto: Penguin Canada.

Kohl, L. 1982. Quebec's northern dynamo. *National Geographic* 162: 123–142.

Kurtness, J. 1991. Trois phases-clés dans l'acculturation des Montagnais du Québec (Three Key Phases in the Acculturation of the Montagnais of Quebec). In M.

Lavallé, F. Ouellet and F. Larose (eds) *Identité, culture et changement social* (pp. 72–81). Paris: L'Harmattan.

Larsen, C. S. 2000. Reading the bones of La Florida. *Scientific American* June: 80–85.

McCormick, R. 1996. Culturally appropriate means and ends of counselling as described by the First Nations of British Columbia. *International Journal for the Advancement of Counselling* 18: 163–172.

Mercredi, O. 1999. Un Canada uni: Comprendrait-il les autochtones? (A united Canada: Will it include Native Peoples?). *Policy Options*, December: 25–32.

Millar, C. 2000. Un impact important (An important impact). *La Gatineau*, 10 March: 4.

Millar, J. R. 1996. *Shingwauk's Vision: A History of Native Residential Schools.* Toronto: University of Toronto Press.

Mulligan, P. 1999. The marginalization of indigenous peoples from tribal lands in southeast Madagascar. *Journal of International Development* 11: 649–659.

Myers, H. 1999. Culturally sensitive development for Northern Peoples: Canadian experiences, Russian opportunities. *Journal of Aboriginal Economic Development* 1(1): 49–57.

Obomsawin, R. 2001. Indigenous knowledge systems: Harnessing the wisdom of the ages for sustainable development. Unpublished discussion paper.

O'Faircheallaigh, C. 1998. Resource development and inequality in indigenous societies. *World Development* 26: 381–394.

Pleumarom, A. 1999. Tourism, globalisation and sustainable development. *Third World Resurgence* 103: 4–7.

Sealey, D. B. and A. S. Lussier. 1975. *The Métis: Canada's Forgotten Peoples.* Winnipeg: Manitoba Métis Federation Press.

Shackley, M. 1998. Designating a protected area at Karanambu Ranch, Rupununi Savannah, Guyana: Resource management and indigenous communities.

Sherrer, C. 1994. Regional autonomy in eastern Nicaragua (1990–1994). In W. Assies and A. Hoekema (eds) *Indigenous People's Experiences with Self-government* (IWGIA Document no. 76). Copenhagen: IWGIA and University of Amsterdam.

Trimble, J., C. Fleming, F. Beauvais and P. Jumper-Thurman. 1996. Essential cultural and social strategies for counselling Native American Indians. In P. B. Pedersen, J. G. Draguns, W. J. Lonner and J. Trimble (eds) *Counselling Across Cultures* (4th edition) (pp. 177–249). Thousand Oaks, CA: Sage.

Van Cott, D. 1996. Prospects for self-determination of indigenous peoples in Latin America: Questions of law and practice. *Global Governance* 2: 43–64.

Viau, R. 2000. *Femmes de Personne: Sexes, Genres et Pouvoirs en Iroquoisie Ancienne* (Nobody's Wife: Sex, Gender and Power in the Early Iroquois Lands). Montréal: Boréal.

Weir, W. I. 2000. Economic development and the Nisga'a treaty: Interview with Dr. Joseph Gosnell Sr., President of the Nisga'a Nation. *Journal of Aboriginal Economic Development* 1(2): 7–13.

York, G. 1992. *The Dispossessed: Life and Death in Native Canada.* Toronto: McArthur.

Zazula, G. 1999. The role of linguistics within a multidisciplinary framework for studying the initial peopling of the Americas. *Pimohtewin.* http://www.ualberta.ca/~pimohte/pimohtewin.html.

Chapter 6

Globalizing indigenous knowledge

Paul Sillitoe

What is indigenous knowledge? I have heard this question many times since becoming directly involved in international development work, asked both by sceptical social scientists and curious natural scientists, not to mention puzzled bureaucrats, technocrats and policymakers. The sceptics ask if there is such a field, and some even argue that it is improper to suggest there is. This questions the existence and propriety of the discipline of anthropology, as I understand it. Can it be that we have not only been engaged in a thoroughly dubious enterprise but have even been deluding ourselves by giving credence to the non-existent? It sounds like the ultimate postmodern denouement. The large number of terms vying for prominence as the more correct to label this field, whatever it is, are symptomatic of the confusion voiced: local knowledge, citizen science, traditional knowledge, folk science, people's knowledge, among others (DeWalt 1994; Antweiler 1998; Purcell 1998).

The following ideas come from working with natural and social scientists on development-funded environmental research projects in South Asia in trying to agree what we understand by the concept of 'indigenous knowledge'.[1] They reflect an on-going personal struggle to come to terms with tangling in development, a struggle captured in the indigenous knowledge debate. The intention of the conceptual model advanced here is therefore to clarify the discussion, notably for development personnel and natural scientists working on constraints to technical interventions among poor populations, and to explore further the relevance of this knowledge to their work.[2] It has evolved not only in interaction with scientists, borrowing from their atomic models and chaos theory (Feynmann 1998a, 1998b),[3] but also from my engagement with South Asia and its literature as I struggled to contextualize our work both culturally and historically (McGreal 1995). The model's intellectual roots reflect equally the two strands of my experiences with international science and Asian philosophy.

Whatever term we take, and I have advocated the use of indigenous knowledge as the one of widest currency in development discourse (Sillitoe 1998a; Purcell 1998), we have not only to define it but also to clear away misconceptions and justify its use, if we are to make it acceptable and globalize its implementation across disciplines. A problem with several terms, including indigenous knowledge, is that they conjure up and reinforce in the minds of development practitioners the idea of research into some sort of unique traditional sociocultural heritage (Sillitoe 2000). Some current definitions of indigenous knowledge encourage this image:

> Indigenous knowledge – the local knowledge that is unique to a given culture or society – contrasts with the international knowledge system which is generated through the global network of universities and research institutes.
>
> (Warren *et al.* 1995: xv)

> The unique, traditional, local knowledge existing within and developed around specific conditions of women and men indigenous to a particular geographic area.
>
> (Grenier 1998: 1)

This is the image that apparently comes to the minds of some anthropologists too, to judge from their negative reactions to the term 'indigenous knowledge'. Tradition suggests timelessness, whereas knowledge is ever changing and dynamic.

In some senses we need to engage ourselves, to use the development jargon, in an 'extension exercise', bringing others 'up to speed' with changes in our discipline. Further to informing them about changes of perspective, we have to advance methods appropriate to their demands, going beyond a social critique to engage with urgent problems. It is hardly surprising that for many the idea of researching local communities amounts to understanding something about largely unchanging traditional orders, for this after all is what anthropology has been about for most of the twentieth century, speaking as it was in the ethnographic present tense. This image is likely to define the discipline for the twenty-first century, as the nineteenth century's interests in stone-age to civilized evolution remained for many what anthropology was about throughout much of the twentieth century. This is probable because the subject is having considerable difficulty, along with others, in deciding what it is, as subliminally reflected perhaps in a subjective fascination with identity. The ethnographic present may come to stand as a golden age, from functionalism to structuralism, before the diaspora, a time when we knew what the subject was about.

Whatever future interpretations of the past, we cannot put anthropology's traditional ethnographic Humpty Dumpty back together again. The world has moved on and we can no longer use the conventional ethnographic present to talk about people – the forces of globalization have shaken the wall to its foundations. The notion that we ever could has been thoroughly criticized in anthropology on the grounds that people already had, of course, some documented history, however brief, by the time any fieldworker arrived (whatever the status of peoples' oral history about events before that time, and ethnographers did face problems going back beyond their memories). Furthermore, change is, and always has been, pervasive in all human societies. Our problems are compounded when we try to differentiate one society from another, because unlike nation states, they run continuously into and ever influence one another. Given the contemporary scale of worldwide communications and associated rapid change, and the accelerating forces of 'globalization' now loose, we can no longer employ the ethnographic present without qualification – even despite justifying it as an heuristic device in documenting other cultures or prior understandable reasons for its use (Cvetkovich and Kellner 1996; Kiely and Marfleet 1998; Tomlinson 1999).

The first dimension: lines of knowledge

International development in considerable part comprises a search for scientifically researched technical solutions to some of the pressing problems facing the poorest people in the world, such as promoting food security and health. It is understandable that the more enlightened scientists involved should be interested in indigenous knowledge as something that might inform and complement their own work. Consequently, in development contexts it is common to see indigenous knowledge as something possessed by those who are subject to development, and distinguished from science as something that will inform any development intervention. It is usual to find two-column tables listing comparable traits, and contrasting them between indigenous knowledge and science (Table 6.1; see also Whickam 1993: 31; Wolfe et al. 1992: Figures 2 and 3; Chambers 1986: 14; DeWalt 1994: 124).

Anthropologists have learnt to be sceptical of such cut-and-dried binary discriminations between 'us' and 'them', reminiscent of the structuralists' simplistic representations of human thought according to contrasting pairs of

Table 6.1   Indigenous knowledge compared with science

Features	Indigenous	Scientific
Relationship	subordinate	dominant
Communication	oral	literate
	teaching through doing	didactic
Dominant mode of thought	intuitive	analytical
Characteristics	holistic	reductionist
	subjective	objective
	experiential	positivist

Source: After Wolfe et al. (1992).

opposites.[4] The stark polar discrimination between the scientific and indigenous, in the two-column tables that characterize current development
literature, is not only inadequate (Antweiler 1998: 484) but also misleading,
even pernicious as to the relationship and distinction between them. It tends
to depict science as more rational, better integrated, having a strong theoretical model, and better grounded in evidence with controlled experiments and
so on. It may even suggest differences in thought processes and intellectual
capacity between scientists and non-scientists, a disappointing conclusion after
a century of anthropological research that we might assume had conclusively
demonstrated the error of this view. The relationship between them is considerably more complex. We are not talking about two tenuously connected
knowledge traditions separated by a cultural–epistemological gulf, but rather a
spectrum of relations.

In the context of our South Asian research we have come to conceive of
the relation between scientists and farmers as comprising a continuum
(Sillitoe 1998b; Dixon *et al.* 2000). At one end of the spectrum we have poor
farmers who have no formal education, whom we may take to have what is as
close as we might hypothetically come to 'real' indigenous knowledge, derived
from their own cultural tradition. At the other end of the continuum we have
Western scientists, who are trying to incorporate some empathy with local
perceptions and practices into their work, wrestling with the problems of
interdisciplinary research (Figure 6.1). In between, we have various intergra-
dations of local insider and global outsider knowledge depending on
community of origin and formal education. Each potentially influences the
other, in which process indigenous knowledge research tries to mediate. As
we pass along the continuum, starting from those whose entire experience is
of their local region, and its cultural heritage, we come to persons who have
received some formal schooling, and have some passing acquaintance with
science, which they will blend with their locally derived knowledge and
cultural heritage. Their education informs not only their own understanding
but also that of their uneducated relatives and neighbours, to whom they will
in some measure impart their foreign-derived knowledge. All of them will
also be subject to extension advice, either first or second hand, received from
government agencies, non-governmental organizations and so on – messages
based on scientific advice, and received increasingly through the mass media.

When we pass further along the continuum we come to the more advan-
taged members of communities who may progress through school to college
and university (some to study agricultural subjects, environmental science,
geography and so on). We have our national collaborators on research and
development projects, whom we might take to be mid-way in some senses
along the continuum. They have an extensive formal scientific background,
with higher degrees, and some occupy senior university posts, but they also
have a familiarity with the indigenous culture, as native-speaking members of
its metropolitan society. This gives a unique perspective, with its own potential

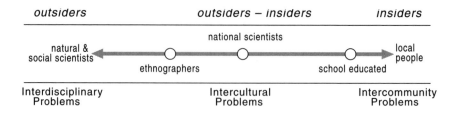

Figure 6.1   The knowledge continuum (R_i)

insights and blind spots. Some of these persons may be landowners, coming from farming families, a further conduit of scientific understanding into local communities. They inevitably pass on some of their learning to relatives and friends when they return home to rural areas, even if they do not themselves engage in cultivation. Those who are trained as scientists tend to accept the international paradigm of science and seek to apply it to their country's problems. Others trained in the humanities are increasingly critical and are using their cultural heritage to question the notion of development, in the manner of some anthropologists (Dallmayr 1996; Das 1995; Kothari 1988). Social scientists researching local communities, particularly anthropologists, may also fall somewhere near the centre of the continuum, often, though not exclusively, attempting to connect the two poles and facilitate understanding between them (Sillitoe 1998a). But we should not overlook the importance accorded currently to local people brokering for themselves, as promoted by the participatory development movement (Chambers 1997).

Hierarchical relations

A worrying criticism of those of us who try to relate indigenous knowledge and practices to science and technology is that we reinforce the idea that the former is somehow inferior. We are not talking about nasty imputed ethnic inferiority because we find indigenous knowledge everywhere – it is frequently called citizen science in Europe, and includes such knowledge as my father's about the management of his allotment to maximize its productivity. But it concerns me greatly to think that talking about indigenous knowledge may weaken others' rights as non-scientists to be treated as equals and for their views and position to count (Agrawal 1995; Smith 1999; Goonatilake 1999), particularly when awareness of and access to scientific knowledge vary between countries, reflecting literacy levels, extent of formal education and so on.

There is something slightly disingenuous about this politically correct criticism. We need, first, to agree what development is about. If we agree that in part it attempts to promote the use of scientifically informed technology to help improve the lives of the poor, then we unavoidably accord some status to scientists' knowledge, as significant contributors to this process (Bhaskar 1986). The reductive approach of science has proved very successful in tackling life's everyday problems, in advancing our technological management of the environment, and may likewise assist others. If we do not think that science and technology have anything to offer, on what grounds are we presuming to interfere in others' lives (Escobar 1995; Fergusson 1994; Mehmet 1995; Grillo and Stirrat 1997)? I do not subscribe to the view that my job as a foreign academic and knowledge broker is to involve myself overtly with their political problems, amounting at worst to experiments in social engineering, although it would be naive to assume that our work can proceed in a vacuum. The relationship between power and knowledge brokering is becoming increasingly problematic as we engage in development-related work and is something that currently occupies many minds. It is a difficult subject, with an awkward ethical dimension, giving rise to the critical field of enquiry 'anthropology of development', which contrasts with 'development anthropology' or direct practical engagement as in indigenous knowledge research (Tierney 1998).

We need, second, to agree that we find a rich variety of knowledge traditions around the world. I assume that an audience of anthropologists will take this as read, or else I have been working for years under a gross misunderstanding about the discipline. We think that cattle station owners in the arid Australian outback have a different body of knowledge and understanding of agricultural issues from Bangladeshi peasants struggling to manage their floodplain rice paddies, and arable farmers in England from swidden cultivators in New Guinea. These different knowledge traditions not only concern different environments and address varying farming problems, but emanate from different cultural traditions and histories, frequently encoded and expressed in different languages. It is unhelpful to suggest otherwise, even with the best of chauvinism-knocking intentions. This returns to the opening question about definition, and I shall take as an initial working answer, against which to refine a model of indigenous knowledge's relationship with science, that indigenous knowledge is a unique formulation of knowledge coming from a range of sources rooted in local cultures, a dynamic and ever changing pastiche of past 'tradition' and present invention with a view to the future.

We need, third, to acknowledge the problems that scientific technology brings – such as environmental pollution, unsustainable production, social anomie, etc. – to moderate any superiority and power assumed by science. One of the central tenets of the indigenous knowledge movement is that scientists have something to learn from local practices too; we should have a two-way flow of information, drawing on the combined strengths of different cultural traditions in this cosmopolitanizing world (Sillitoe 1998a). We have to combat the tendency for development and globalization to amount to the imposition of Western values on the rest of the world. According to the emerging Asian critique of development, the rational scientific view that dominates our society and the development agenda is unhealthy (Sen 1992; Shiva 1993; Goonatilake 1999). We need to listen, to get the balance right. The mechanistic and reductionist worldview denies nature's complex harmony at its peril. There is a deeper reality behind the empirical concerns of day-to-day life. The Oriental view is that we need to move towards a more dynamically balanced view (Giri 1997; Kothari 1988). The parallels with the current participatory methods in development are intriguing, which suggests, when harnessed to an indigenous knowledge perspective, that we have to encourage not only the participation of beneficiaries, but also the reciprocal participation of the outsider 'experts', or at least their celebration of local intellectual achievements and worldviews.

One of the problems with tables such as Table 1 above is that they set up science in contrast to indigenous knowledge in such a way that many readers will accord superiority to science. Others may, of course, do the reverse. So we have, on the one hand, hard-nosed scientists advocating high-tech innovation, and on the other, romantics of tradition praising sustainable human–scale lifestyles. The continuum idea better reflects the current position, and takes us to the heart of the debate over the definition of indigenous knowledge, its correctness and the complexity of associated relations. Its linear perspective extending from poor local resource managers to research scientists attempts to overcome the pernicious side of the effective/destructive science versus ineffective/benign local practices polarity by uniting the two poles. Nonetheless, the poles remain, with the attendant danger that one may be thought positive and the other negative.

It has been suggested that the problem is largely one of labels and their contents, a view reflected in the battle for prominence between the many terms used to label the indigenous/local/traditional, etc. knowledge field. One suggestion is that we use more similar terms for the two poles, for example 'disciplinary experts' and 'regional experts'. Another suggestion is that we talk more neutrally about 'outsider' scientific knowledge and technology, and 'insider' local knowledge and practices. But are there such entities as insider and outsider knowledge traditions, when we have, as the continuum idea tries to convey, a blend of customary and locally generated knowledge (informed possibly by a wider historico–cultural tradition, such as the Hindu, Muslim or Buddhist worldview) mixed with other knowledge, much of it scientific, increasingly incorporated through education and extension? Other candidates currently coming into favour in politically influenced development discourse have the ring of the mysterious 'third way' about them, with local populations labelled as primary stakeholders. We may take their national governments and administrations as secondary stakeholders, aid agencies such as the Department for International Development (DFID) as tertiary stakeholders, and scientists as quaternary stakeholders. But whatever terms we adopt, there remains scope for hierarchical perceptions, and primary stakeholders may be taken as either first in the sense of leading and senior (i.e. primary party over others) or first in the sense of beginning or junior (i.e. primary school versus higher education).

The second dimension: wheels of knowledge

Playing with terms is unlikely to solve the problem of hierarchical relations. We need a conceptual model that better reflects equal relations and offers the potential to allow all a fair voice (Smith 1999). The problem with the continuum is that it is a flat one-dimensional model. It has two ends, science and indigenous knowledge, inviting hierarchical discrimination. And actors are dotted along it, when in some regards their positions may overlap, although their knowledge may be quite different (e.g. ethnographers and national scientists). Furthermore it is static, with no sense of the dynamism that characterizes knowledge. While puzzling about this I read Capra (1983), who explores parallels between modern physics and Eastern philosophy, an entertaining forerunner of the science and indigenous knowledge debate (see also Rothman and Sudarshan 1998; Goonatilake 1999). While Asian philosophy recognizes differences, it sees these as existing within an all-encompassing unity. It sees opposites (such as life and death, hot and cold, happiness and despair, light and dark, male and female) as extreme aspects of the same reality – not separate experiences, for they cannot exist without each other, cannot be experienced except in contrast with one another.[5] It maintains that these polar relationships are relative, intellectual constructs. The aim is to see them as one: 'Be in truth eternal, beyond earthly opposites', as Krishna says in the *Bhagavad Gita*. This is incomprehensible in our normal state of consciousness and puzzling to the Occidental mind (or my mind anyway). The experience of reality beyond opposites requires freeing of the mind from the rigid bonds of conventional logic, to flow constantly and to change perspective seamlessly. When *sadhu* transcend these abstract ideas in meditation they realize their relativity. It is, by all accounts, a vivid experience.

The unity of opposites is suggestive regarding reformulation of the continuum model of indigenous knowledge and science. In the manner of the ancient mystics, we can ask how we might turn a one-dimensional linear representation with two opposite ends into a two-dimensional one. What structure viewed end-on looks like a line with movement along it appearing like a ball oscillating to and fro? The mystics turned to the circle, the symbol of a seamless and endless whole (Figure 6.2). There is the Buddhist wheel of life, comprising the teaching of one of Buddha's foremost disciples, Maudgalyayana, which depicts the *samsara* cycle of life, with its different realms of existence and underlying *karma*-related forces (Kennedy 1985).[6] The Chinese sages elaborated on the circle symbolism to link their polar concepts of *ying* and *yang* – the one representing feminine, earthly, intuitive and the

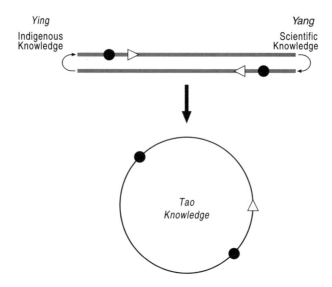

Figure 6.2   The Oriental two-dimensional unification of one-dimensional opposites

Figure 6.3   The *T'ai-chi T'u* Supreme Ultimate

other male, celestial, rational – into the *Tao* unity, giving the famous *T'ai-chi T'u* symbol of the Supreme Ultimate (Figure 6.3).

The complementarity and interdependence of opposites means that neither pole can achieve dominance; virtue is to achieve a dynamic balance in the interplay between the two. The circle is more inclusive than a line, having no separate ends. We have the two separate poles united with no beginning or end, no superior and inferior knowledge, everything informing all else endlessly. It seems a promising metaphor for indigenous knowledge research in development, symbolizing the mutuality of all knowledge and subverting notions of hierarchy; we can see that science may cycle to indigenous knowledge, and indigenous knowledge in turn cycle to science (Figure 6.4). We can spin points anywhere around the circle; none occupies a privileged position.

The circle also shows knowledge potentially passing equally in both directions. We have a sense of movement. To know the unity of opposites is not a static experience, it is to maintain a state of dynamic tension between the poles. The derivation of the word *Brahmin* from the Sanskrit root *brih* (growth) captures the dynamism. Any knowledge has the potential to pass into the local pool and merge with what is known to inform today's understanding and practice. Local understanding is a blend of knowledge from various sources, which is difficult to disentangle. It is syncretic. There is no repository of agreed knowledge; it is in a constant process of change, being continually influenced by outside ideas. In indigenous knowledge research we are trying to facilitate some communication around the circle, and to promote it as a more overtly two-way learning process, extending beyond scientists to

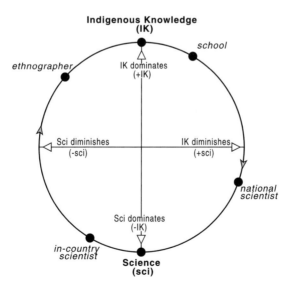

Figure 6.4   Relative dominances of science and indigenous knowledge (R_2)

policymakers and so on. We all have something to learn from one another. We recognize here the process currently called globalization (Waters 1998; Jameson and Miyoshi 1998; Scholte 2000), leading in some quarters to calls for the study of hybridization rather than culture (Latour 1993; Clifford 1988, 1992). While knowledge systems are not the same whatever the culture, the current trend towards global society and history is constantly modifying distinctions between them.

The third dimension: globes of knowledge

The circle may advance on tables and continua as a representation of the relationship between indigenous and scientific knowledge, helping to subvert dominance, but it has drawbacks. It is flat and lifeless. The potential for hierarchical thinking remains with the existence of two poles customarily seen top and bottom of the circle, or on the right and left. This two-dimensional model also suggests that some categories of persons know less than others about their fields – for instance that a national scientist or one living in-country will know less science than a visiting foreign scientist, who will be situated at the science pole. The national scientist is shown at approximately the same latitude as the anthropologist, who may well know less natural science. This model also continues to represent the indigenous and scientific as two monolithic knowledge traditions, when in fact they are comprised of many strands. For example, the specialist knowledge of a soil chemist is different from that of a crop breeder and both differ markedly from that of a veterinary surgeon, and we likewise know that the knowledge held by persons making up a local community is not uniform, being structured according to gender, age, occupation, caste, class, etc.

It is perhaps inevitable that we should move on to three-dimensional representations, curved space and the sphere (Feynmann 1998b). We can imagine large numbers of the above circles comprising meridians on a globe. Each one can represent a different domain of knowledge: for example, in natural resources management we can distinguish various fields, such as crops, soils, water resources, livestock and so on (Figure 6.5). We can now accommodate variations in knowledge according to disciplines at the science pole, and life experience at the indigenous one. The meridians can represent any knowledge domain relevant to enquiries, so we can have religious ones (e.g. Islam, Hinduism, Buddhism and Christianity in a South Asian context), political ones (e.g. regional government, non-governmental organizations, village power structures, etc.), economic ones (e.g. markets, credit suppliers, cooperatives, etc.), and so on. Ethnographic experience teaches us the importance of including these domains, of setting enquiries within a broad cultural context, and not merely considering technical issues, as done in development work focusing on 'indigenous technical knowledge' (Sillitoe 1998c). We do not have to envisage the meridians arranged like lines of longitude, all crossing at the

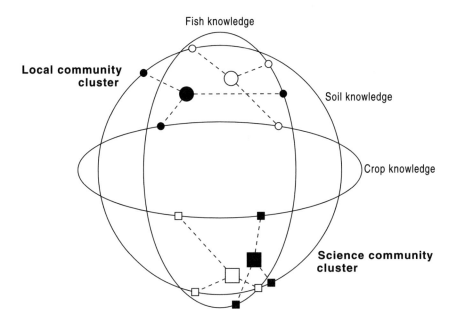

Figure 6.5 The global plotting of knowledge $(\mathbb{R}_3)$

same two polar points. They could be arranged more randomly about the globe, obviating any tendency to polarize knowledge into a hierarchy of capable science versus less effective indigenous knowledge.

The globe represents an interaction domain. In indigenous knowledge research contexts this will likely be thought of as a region where some local tradition pertains, in the classic anthropological sense of a culture (although in reality, given the problems that attend the working definition of such an entity, it will probably be a local community defined geographically). An interaction domain does not have to be so regionally defined: it could be an institution (e.g. a development agency) or an academic discipline (e.g. anthropology). We can think of plotting within the globe the positions of individuals who interact within a domain, according to their knowledge of the meridian issues. We plot them onto each knowledge meridian and then extrapolate from these where they fall within the globe. We have the meridians acting together as force fields to pull any person into a certain location. In effect this allows us to plot individuals for a range of knowledge continua.

If we intend to make this model operational, as opposed to academic, we face much methodological research, as we do generally if we are to make indigenous knowledge research a real force in development. We should have to devise, check and refine ways of plotting individual knowledge for any meridian field, perhaps devising sophisticated questionnaires to probe and score them consistently and rigorously. It is a large task. Some recent advances in qualitative software applications for use in indigenous knowledge research suggest possible ways forward, such as the Agroforestry Knowledge Toolkit, an iteratively created knowledge base which can be interrogated using formal reasoning procedures (Sinclair and Walker 1998; Walker and Sinclair 1998; Barr and Sillitoe 2000). What is the point? The plotting of knowledge coordinates is not advocated to define knowledge traditions alone, which would scarcely justify the labour. It should serve as a methodology to structure the comparison and correlation of different knowledges, which is central to the indigenous knowledge endeavour.

Knowing it all: the culture concept

We should not expect any one person's configuration to be identical to anyone else's, but we anticipate more overlap between some persons than others (Simpson 1997). Those who overlap tightly might be taken to comprise a culture in anthropological terms. If we imagine plotting global coordinates to investigate interaction with respect to natural resources knowledge in a local community visited by a team of scientists on a development research project, we should find our points forming clusters within the globe. These clusters will equate with our points on the continuum/circle, with foreign scientists comprising one cluster, local people another, and so on.

If we take the cluster of scientists, we can enquire into the nature of interdisciplinary research, its facilitation being a major methodological challenge facing indigenous knowledge research in development (Dixon et al. 2000). We can research the interaction of knowledge meridians when those specializing in the subjects they represent come together. On the other hand, if we take the cluster that represents the knowledge of a local community, we can enquire into its distribution. The global model is apt for conveying to the development community that local knowledge is not monolithic but individually variable (Scoones and Thompson 1994; Simpson 1997). In Bangladesh, for example, all persons with their faculties know that fish live in water, that their availability varies with the seasons (monsoon floods swelling numbers, etc.), and that people may catch them using various nets. But if you wish to know how to erect one of the elaborate static net structures, or about the behaviour of different fish species, or the ecology of their preferred habitats at different times of the year, it is necessary to approach a professional fisherman. When we talk about scientific and indigenous knowledge we are referring to the overlapping yet variable understanding of individuals taken as bearers of these traditions, in some circumstances linking them together.

Anthropology must bear some responsibility for those in development thinking of indigenous knowledge as some static and uniform tradition. It has purported to write in the ethnographic present voice about entire cultures as normative structures, talking, for example, about Trobriand, Nuer or Tikopia society. When we write about such cultural entities we have in mind a collection of persons who share much the same knowledge. A considerable part of this is encoded and transmitted by language, although an ill-defined proportion is non-verbal, experiential, tacit, etc. (and difficult for outsiders convincingly to access at all). We customarily take language as a defining feature of culture, and assume that the majority of members of a speech community apply words to agreed categories, holding a certain ill-defined overlapping core of knowledge in common, while we know that as individuals they each have an idiosyncratic understanding of the world, sharing some of the things they know with some others, but not all.

The implications of the global model are intriguing for the discipline. We need to give some attention to gauging the extent of internal variation to assess what anthropology has achieved, to see what it is that we think we know and have put down on the record – the epistemology of our largely normative heritage. When we concede that a society comprises individually variable knowledge we question the status of twentieth-century anthropology, in much the same way as the assessment of evolutionary history as speculative guesswork undermined nineteenth-century anthropology. This is why I have written about the indigenous knowledge revolution. It brings to mind the social structure versus social process debate of the past three decades, of social inculcation informing persons' behaviour versus self-will guiding individual actions. The global model suggests one way to proceed. It is to plot the knowledge of individuals, which comprises a complex dynamic network, and take the resulting clusters as amalgamations representing community understanding. By plotting the extent of interactional domains, the meridian model might further understanding of the elusive culture concept.

The problem with representing the knowledge of any social group relates in part to claiming a privileged perspective, to seeing it all in assuming to write about culture. We can discern this further in the venerable distinction between those who live close to and with nature, our indigenous knowledge bearers, and those who live distanced and separate from nature, our scientists. This relates to the idea that 'they' live with and accommodate to nature whereas 'we' struggle to dominate and control it. This difference in worldviews may be taken by some to account in part for the mismatch between indigenous and scientific knowledge, for the problems that we experience in relating one to the other. They are based on fundamentally different ideas about the world and the place of humans in it. They are opposites in some senses (Vayda 1996). A reformulation of this dichotomy is to contrast people living in the world with those living on it, or to contrast a view from inside the globe with a view from above it as if from a spaceship (Ingold 1993). According to the model presented here no one can escape beyond the globe. We are all at the same level, with no privileged view accorded to one knowledge tradition above another. We cannot escape from our global place and the particular perspective it gives us.

This accords further with the postmodern critique, the model assuming that each individual occupies a different place within the globe depending on cultural heritage, personal history, life experiences and so on. We cannot, as a consequence, entirely share each other's views, even if we have much background in common. The plotting of individuals' knowledge positions will place them somewhere off-centre towards a particular region of the globe's surface, in their knowledge/culture cluster. The centre of the globe is the axis about which all their dynamic knowledge relationships articulate. A more appropriate analogy than space travel is to envisage voyaging to the centre of the world. It is from here that one might aspire to see equally how all the knowledge represented in the interactional domain interrelates – a truly interdisciplinary and cross-cultural perspective.

According to the Eastern sages we can gain access to this absolute all-aware realm, but only in a meditative state, through contemplation, not intellectual reflection on reality. Its ultimate form for Buddhists is *nirvana*. These philosophies talk about experiencing oneness with the world, appreciating an undifferentiated unity. The *sadhu's* transcendental triumph is to apprehend personally that everything we perceive, the self included, comprises a connected whole of mutually interrelated phenomena and events. Some teachers have tried to convey this in diagrams, frequently featuring circles (Figure 6.6). Meditative discipline results in a deep contact with things integrated into an infinitely complicated, beautiful web of relations. The implications are profound for our aspirations to know other cultures and how they interrelate, and suggest that whatever the methodology, any understanding that we achieve of relations both between indigenous knowledge and science, and within these cultures will be inescapably limited, subject to contradictory checks and balances as predicted by the transcendental view of the world.

Universes of knowledge

The sages' view of being, that all is interwoven and interdependent, prompts the observation that, regarding our sphere model, no interactional global domain exists in isolation. Many persons are players in more than one interactional domain. The natural scientists visiting overseas communities, for example, are members of institutions elsewhere; likewise the staff of aid agencies. We have to consider the linking together of several global domains. The visualization of the links is difficult, as Asian philosophy predicts. We can envisage a series of interrelated global domains centred on a local community differentiated according to indigenous and scientific knowledge. Each additional globe may be differentiated according to any appropriate interactional domains, such as a development domain (perhaps comprising several agencies such as DFID, the World Bank, the Food and Agriculture Organization, etc.), a government and non-governmental organizations domain, a university globe, and so on.[7]

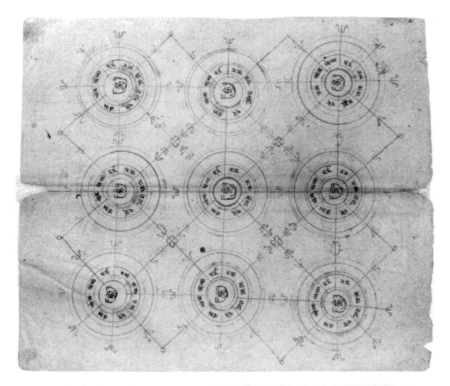

Figure 6.6   Asian cosmological diagrams featuring circles. Both written by Jain
scribes. The upper one features circles with paired vowel sounds
(one short, one long) with a mantra (probably *hum*) in the centre.
The lower one, in the Prakrit language (probably Ardhamagadhi
dialect) and written in Jaina Nagari script, refers to the moon, sun,
stars and cardinal points

Note: Both reproduced by kind permission of the Oriental Museum, Durham University
– manuscript catalogue nos 1974.105 and 1974.117. I am grateful to Dr Mahbub
Alam and Dr Dominik Wujastyk for assistance with provenancing and translation.

It is necessary to enter multidimensional space to represent the resulting complex galaxy networks. We can appreciate this if we take a group of colleagues who are collaborating on the same research project and are members of the same university. They share many interests in common, in addition to discussing their work – they may lunch together regularly in college, use the same bar, and so on. But they may be in different departments and will have different circles of colleagues, may come from different parts of the country (even different countries) and will be members of different families, and so on. While they are clustered players within the research project's interactional domain, focused on the community overseas where they work, they will find themselves in quite different locations in other situations, even different globes, clustered with other members of their social networks, such as family members, colleagues in their departments, etc. They are simultaneously connected to all. Although at any instant one may have their attention (e.g. the research project while overseas), the others are not switched off but inform their understanding of the world continuously.

Beyond this we have indirectly linked interactional domains. We can imagine this if we think of several local communities in different countries, even different continents, each with their own unique ensemble of indigenous knowledge and globe of relations, and each having development projects funded by the same agency (e.g. DFID). These projects and their personnel will serve indirectly to connect the communities. We could go on multiplying such links endlessly, and have only to think of their modern communication agents, particularly radio, television, and now the Internet. We live in a global age, as the media likes to tell us. We cannot represent all such galaxy connections at once in conventional three-dimensional space. We have many globes interacting with one another where they have points of connection. We can only plot these multiple connections multidimensionally, which requires computers to calculate principal component analyses, etc. No more diagrams, only equations. When we contemplate the possibility of representing the complex networks of interactional domains in mathematical equations we have a condensed representation of knowledge that again recalls the teaching of Eastern philosophies that talk of reducing knowledge and experience to a single meditative utterance, such as *om*. A mathematical equivalent is $\mathbb{R}_n$. According to philosophies such as Hinduism, these devices help access the ultimate reality of the multidimensional natural world where events occur simultaneously and mutually affect one another endlessly, giving infinite complexity and variety.

The fourth dimension: time and knowledge

The complexity increases further when we add the fourth dimension of time. No individual or cultural constellation remains static. The complex multidimensional connections between global domains are not rigid structures, but loose and constantly changing sets of relations. We are always moving as we learn new things and forget others. All social systems are dynamic, the behavioural interaction of individuals generating and sustaining them, as affirmed in the contemporary notion of social process. Any methodology seeking to advance the incorporation of indigenous knowledge research into development will have to accommodate this dynamism. The aim of development after all is to promote such change, or at least that judged by funding agencies to be positive, currently defined as reducing poverty. There are many other sources of change, prompting us to ask what constantly generates it. Many commentators, often with Marxist backgrounds, argue that it centres on power relations, which returns us to hierarchies of knowledge. It is domination over other communities, they argue, that is at the heart of development.

When one interactional domain interacts with another we have change promoted. In terms of the conceptual model advanced here, we can think of individuals' ever-moving knowledge points as analogous to electrons making up an atomic cloud, comprising the cluster around the ineffable nucleus of their sociocultural core. We can visualize the interaction that occurs when such a knowledge-bearing community is approached by another – for example, when scientists employed by a development agency interact with a local community and its indigenous knowledge heritage – as similar to the behaviour of atoms in chemical reactions. They disturb each other's electron clouds, which shift into new combined configurations. Instead of thinking of them as comprising spheres, we can imagine that the forces result in distorted figures, the extent of the distortion experienced reflecting the relative power balance between the knowledge traditions (Figure 6.7). From this perspective we can denote science as coming from the more politically and economically powerful society and exerting a major distorting influence on the weaker local one, through education, development interventions, extension activity, etc. Domination is forcing others' global clustering of knowledge to comply with our own configuration and understanding of the world. Indigenous knowledge research aims to redress this imbalance somewhat, obliging scientists to review their understanding in the light of local know-how. Multidimensional representations of relations, for example, completely defeat the idea of ranking any one knowledge tradition above another; there is no privileged position where individuals occupy many different points simultaneously. We all belong somewhere, where we draw on an indigenous knowledge tradition.

We can extend further on the chemical bonding analogy. Interactions at the atomic level involve the particle–wave duality concept (Feynmann 1998a). The parallels with our global knowledge domains are informative.[8] If we focus on knowledge points in globes, as we do in fieldwork when we work largely in the ethnographic present, this is analogous to plotting sub-atomic particle positions. In so doing we lose sight of social change and dynamic multidimensional connections, just as one cannot simultaneously follow the movement of particles if one focuses on their position. When we focus on

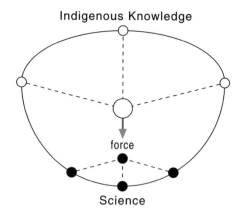

Figure 6.7   Power distortions of knowledge domain

points, we lose sight of their direction, namely the complex interactional forces resulting in changed states. The particle–wave duality theory of contemporary physics rests on a contradiction: sub-atomic matter behaves as both a particle and a wave, but both manifestations, essential to its existence, are not observable together. When you see one, you are ignorant of the other.

The correspondence with Eastern philosophy is again intriguing in its plays with the resolution of opposites (Capra 1983). The mystics teach that we can only experience the dynamic union of opposites on a higher plane of consciousness. There are many ways to achieve this liberation, some of which strike the mechanistic occidental mind as baffling and contradictory.[9] But contradiction is not worrying because the Divine is beyond concepts, which spawn paradoxes. The dissolution of distinctions, the interpenetration of opposites, has to be experienced. It is beyond any form and cannot be specified, and is sometimes described as a limitless void. This does not imply nothingness. Indeed the reverse for it is to experience the essence of everything: life's source. The objective of meditative techniques is to switch off the thinking mind. The moment we try to capture the experience in a structured sequential concept – to describe reality – we lose it. It cannot be known by reasoning, being beyond our intellect which uses language to play with concepts that trap thinking and expression on an everyday plane. It concerns higher dimensions of reality that transcend language and thought. It is literally past words:

> While describing the uncommon activities of Krsna before Uddhava, Nanda Maharaja gradually became overwhelmed and could not speak anymore. As for mother Yasoda she sat by the side of her husband and heard the pastimes of Krsna without speaking. She was simply crying incessantly, and milk was pouring from her breasts.
>
> (Bhaktivedanta 1982: 294)

In some fundamental senses analysis is impossible, as some Eastern philosophies try to demonstrate through brainteasing, frequently humorous paradoxes designed to reveal the logical limitations and contradictions, even the absurdity, of verbal communication. They also attempt to show it in paradoxical designs, such as the Hindu *kolam*, Vedic *yantras* and Buddhist *mandala*, signifying cosmic forces (Figure 6.8), whose influence is evident in the interlinking global domains presented here (Tucci 1974; Powell 1979; Khanna 1997). These bring to an abrupt end attempts to represent and reduce complex sociocultural knowledge domains to diagrams. They seek, in their contradictory visual play, to demonstrate the ultimate futility of attempts to understand that which is beyond everyday three-dimensional comprehension and our limited logic. So from the perspective of this written chapter, we cannot aspire to journey to the centre of any world of knowledge. It is indescribable, which puts academic exercises, such as the one related here, whose currency is language and diagrams, in a quandary.

It is difficult initially to see how we might relate analytical scientific thinking to the mystical truth of meditative experience – to come to terms with the Asian critique (Bhaskar 1986; Kothari 1988; Dallmayr 1996; Giri 1997). How can we compare science, with its sophisticated technical and mathematical language, with meditative philosophies that insist that they can only communicate insights experientially and not through discussion? The two knowledge traditions reflect the rational and the intuitive aspects of the human intellect. The rational depends on abstraction, selecting a few key features to represent, and think about, the infinite variety 'out there', put together as a linear series of symbols and concepts to structure reality intellectually. It is always incomplete and inaccurate, never entirely capturing any aspect of reality but only symbolizing it in a limited way, a point laboured by postmodernists. According to transcendental teaching, nature cannot be understood and experienced, which is quite different from being manipulated and engineered, reductively, as so many elementary parts of which the system is merely a contingent arrangement. It has to be understood as an interconnected whole of relative parts.

But from an occidental operational point of view, that seeks to extend some control over the mundane world occupied by the majority of people (which is at the heart of the development agenda) the idea that everything is interconnected and that to understand any phenomenon we must understand all the others is an impossible injunction. We cannot know it all at our everyday level of existence, and one of the successes of scientific method has been to demonstrate that approximations and our partial intellectual constructions can give us an understanding sufficient to exert considerable control over nature through technology. The transcendental worldview of a harmonious, seamlessly integrated, cosmic whole experienced in a state of non-ordinary meditative consciousness is not appropriate to tackling technical problems of feeding adequately an increasingly populated world, ensuring its health and advancing environmentally sustainable production.

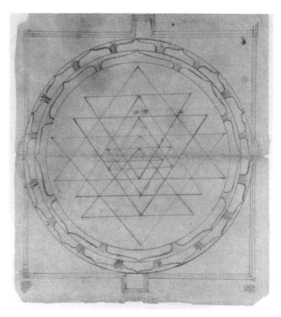

वेयंत्रकष्टकोल्लुटेसद॥

Figure 6.8   Above: the celebrated *Sri Yantra* comprising interpenetrating male
and female principles, contemplated to envision the totality of
existence and one's unity with the cosmos (set within the sacred
chakra 'wheel' design depicting earthly elements and human
senses). Below: a sacred battle *chakra* taught by Drnacharjo (of the
Moha Bhanot) which constantly changes shape, confusing an enemy.
'This *tontro* is perfect' reads the Hindi caption.

Note: Reproduced by kind permission of the Oriental Museum, Durham University –
catalogue nos 1978.15E and 1974.122. I am grateful to my colleague Mahbub Alam
for assistance with provenancing and translation.

We cannot reduce one understanding to the other; each leads to an entirely different apprehension of the world. It would be misguided to seek a synthesis, as neither can be comprehended in the other. Instead we can anticipate a dynamic coming together of scientific analysis and mystic intuition to achieve a fuller and deeper understanding. This reflects the objective of indigenous knowledge research in development. These are complementary understandings. They both have a place, the mechanistic scientific one for solving technical problems encountered in everyday life – even *sadhu* have to feed themselves – and the mystical meditative one for achieving spiritual harmony and fulfilment – even satellite scientists seek peace of mind. We should not strive to subsume other ways of understanding under scientific analysis, but seek to optimize the insights of all perspectives, to aim for balance and synergy. For many natural scientists, who may readily think in terms of monolithic knowledge traditions, particularly when presented with tables (Table 6.1) that give this idea, and who subscribe to powerful theories of proven effect 'out there', these are ideas of a different order. Nonetheless there is a receptive audience, as increasingly apparent in some contemporary scientific debates.

The ideas of chaos and complexity theory currently emerging in science (Gelick 1988; Hall 1992) resonate with Eastern philosophy, unlike previous mechanistic scientific theories rooted in ancient Greek philosophy which attempt to explain complex structures by breaking them into smaller parts. These new theories view the world as a complex interrelated web of properties, none of which are fundamental but depend on their variable relations with others for their expression. According to one theorist,

> The complex approach is total Taoist. In Taoism there is no inherent order … The universe in Taoism is perceived as vast, amorphous and ever changing. You can never nail it down. The elements always stay the same but they are always arranging themselves.
>
> (B. Arthur cited in Sardar and Abrams 1998: 165)

The idea of eternal rhythmic movement recurs repeatedly in Asian myths and philosophy, such as the image of the dancing four-armed Shiva personifying the universe's dynamic unity, gathering together all things in the ceaseless rhythm and infinite balance of his dance, and symbolizing the never-ending flow of energy in an infinite variety of patterns, eternal creation and destruction. The cosmos is impermanent, growing organically and ever mutating without end. There are no fixed structures and it is folly to resist the flow of life.

The constant shifting of peoples' knowledge and practices with time complies with this interpretation of the world. The inappropriately named chaos theory seeks to understand the process of spontaneous self-organization exhibited by such complex systems as collectivities of human beings balanced on the 'edge of chaos' (Kiel and Elliot 1996). These manifest emergent properties lead to order, as seen in the outcome of market behaviour. The theory allows for unpredictable small events to amplify and have large effects, as in the apoc-ryphal butterfly's wing flaps triggering a cyclone. We have countless episodes of such potential butterfly-wing-flapping behaviour in human societies which can magnify under particular imperfectly understood conditions to great effect, illustrating why the search for science-like mechanical laws of society proved so futile (Radcliffe-Brown 1952; Malinowski 1944). Chaos accommo-dates for the time dimension. Irreversible time is the source of order: it stops everything happening at once, it allows constructive interaction and form (Prigogine and Stenger 1985).

It is no wonder that time has proved a problematic dimension for social theorists. According to Asian philosophers, it is a superficial reality, a construct of the mind. In meditation such philosophers go beyond conventional time and enter another temporal dimension, sometimes contemplating symbols of cosmic unity (Figure 6.9). They experience an infinity, a dynamic timelessness, the 'eternal now' in which past and future are concentrated in the present ever-moving moment. The state is utter tranquillity, a release from the constraints of *karma* cause and effect. It may be difficult to so conceive of oneself as part of the cosmos, transcending our limited, mundane worldview of causation, but no more difficult than trying to get one's head around the scientific assertion that time can vary with velocity and that planet Earth is hurtling through space-time at an amazing 20 km/sec., and our Milky Way galaxy at a mind-numbing 604 km/sec., so constituting our experience of time (Feynmann 1998b).

Figure 6.9   The symmetrical *Sri Yantra* classic cosmic diagram meditated upon to connect with the totality of creation and the eternal present

Local to global and back again

Accommodating the fourth dimension of time to our model puts in perspective the opening comments about the inadequacy, even distortion of the ethnographic present voice in indigenous knowledge enquiries. Time is history's vehicle. And a historical perspective is now expected in anthropological work – the subject is even a sub-discipline of history for some.[10] This is a change from previously, when anthropology eschewed history as pointless speculation in non-literate cultures with no record extending back beyond living memory. When the intensive fieldwork tradition came of age it revealed the conjectural status of historical accounts, largely presented as racially biased social evolution. It supported the emergence of the ethnographic present tense, avoiding any historical pretence. Its use may in some instances have been taken too far, some ethnographers overlooking recent, often historically documented colonial events, but few probably wished to convey an equally bogus image that they were studying uncontacted, maybe Stone Age people. It was not, as some suggest, the tense of deliberate ethnographic pretence.

The convention of the ethnographic present also fed on another important principle that came to inform ethnographic fieldwork, and that is that when we go to study other communities we try so far as possible not to interfere in their lives – the 'fly on the wall' methodology. The present tense confirmed this non-interference ethic, an ethnographic 'now' that belonged to the people. While again there is something specious in this perspective because just by being there ethnographers unavoidably interfere to some extent in peoples' lives – probably supplying elementary medical assistance, changing perceptions of the world and so on – the important point is that ethnographers are not there to effect changes and what they do contribute is of miniscule significance compared to other agencies; for example what government officers and missionaries stationed in the next valley do in the New Guinea Highlands. More importantly, the non-interference ethic itself is an aspect of a wider principle that remains central to anthropological enquiry, namely an unswerving belief in cultural relativity, that whatever other people may do we are not there to judge their behaviour, but to study, document and, so far as possible, come to some understanding of it.

Indigenous knowledge research to inform development challenges this fieldworking tradition, central to the discipline for the past century and represented in the ethnographic present voice. For an anthropologist raised on the established ethnographic principles of field engagement, this is, personally speaking, disconcerting, as reflected in these musings on the meaning and legitimacy of indigenous research in development. The historical critique is of small moment compared to the challenge to the cultural relativity ethic. While it would be naive to imply that anthropologists never interfered, and the discipline's professional bodies may be indicted for failing consistently to establish what was morally acceptable, the pressures are increasingly growing to involve ourselves in intervention research. It is a response in part to contemporary demands that publicly funded university teaching and research address issues relevant to society. Development is one field where anthropology can do this and maintain some integrity as a discipline.

Any involvement in research to inform development implies intervention. It demands judgements about what constitute advances for a population. This is evident, for example, when trying to inform people of the possible consequences of accepting certain scientific knowledge and adopting foreign technologies. We must beware of compromises to our culturally relative stance, of appearing judgmental. On the other hand, the indigenous knowledge movement is part of the contemporary participation drive in development, which seeks to extend a voice to local stakeholders. I imagine that most anthropologists would support these efforts to assist the 'poorest of the poor' by better informing the development process. They inspire this chapter's modelling exploration of hierarchical knowledge relations that subvert meaningful participation and its quest to advance more egalitarian relations.

All anthropologists know how time consuming and painful it can be to achieve a sympathetic and informed understanding of another way of life, and the temptation for development personnel, with the political pressures on them to achieve quick results, is that they may turn to anthropologists to tell them what they wish to know, instead of engaging in long-term, expensive enquiries to encourage and facilitate people to communicate their own ideas and problems. This may increasingly become a problem as the shortcomings of current participatory methods become evident. The methodological implications for anthropology as a discipline are considerable. There is a danger that we may be manoeuvred into presuming to speak for others. There is the problem of not only representing the knowledge of a community or cultural region (however we struggle to define/fudge it), but also of deciding whose voices should be heard, for, as the global model seeks to convey, anthropology's continuing normative stance may be inadequate. We face the contentious issue of deciding whose knowledge should count, whose views should be put forward, for it is unlikely that a scientist, policymaker, etc. will wish to know all shades of opinion.

The global domains model tries to convey, in accommodating the effects of globalization on knowledge, that we are increasingly implicated anyway, and inevitably drawn into the process of change (Cvetkovich and Kellner 1996; Kiely and Marfleet 1998). If we are all becoming members of a global community, we might ask does this impute/infer an expectation that we might interfere? This question relates to contentious issues such as global environmental management, international policing of human rights and so on, and which nations should set these agendas. The implications for intellectual and cultural property rights, hotly debated currently, are also considerable. If the globalizing process is resulting in a mish-mash of knowledge, to what extent can any society lay claim to owning any knowledge exclusively or using it to direct change, as opposed to having a particular combination of knowledge?[11] It appears that we cannot avoid condoning some sort of interference. We find ourselves confronted by a paradox of the sort beloved by Asian philosophers.

If we side with those who argue that we should have no truck with the idea of indigenous knowledge (Agrawal 1995), we may inadvertently support not only interference but also top-down modernization. The non-compliance with the indigenous knowledge argument is frequently put forward in a laudable attempt to reduce ethnic chauvinism of one culture, here the scientific, assuming superiority over others, namely the local. But it unmindfully strengthens the case for scientific- and capitalist-dominated approaches to development. If we eschew indigenous knowledge, we have presumably to agree that people everywhere possess the same understanding and have the same perceptions of problems. In this event, the imposition of scientifically informed technological solutions from above is valid, for these will extend on what people already know and not clash with their expectations. Few of those who argue against the notion of indigenous knowledge would be comfortable with this conclusion.

If, on the other hand, we support those who advocate the incorporation of indigenous knowledge research into development, we face other contradictions. We have to exercise caution in arguing that there are important differences between knowledge traditions around the world, and that we need to know about these, to inform development positively. We have to avoid unhelpful reification of indigenous knowledge, interfering to defend it and subverting development opportunities. While cultures may not be similar, they are increasingly interpenetrated and influencing one another. We have the globalization of knowledge spheres. There is, on this opposite tack, not only a danger of outsiders wishing to see the 'other' as different, and voyeuristically seeking exotic customs, but also one of insiders, eager to bolster their identity in a rapidly changing, globalizing world, seizing on, even reinventing, indigenous knowledge to this end. The balance between the local and the global means that we have communities wishing to embrace aspects of the global order while at the same time paradoxically defending their local identity (Sillitoe 2000). While we have academics debating globalization issues, we frequently find local people seeking their identity in the ethnographic present, emphasizing custom and indigenous knowledge.

The wish of people to globalize their local knowledge while simultaneously retaining its identity illustrates well the irony of indigenous knowledge research informing development. We have paradoxes to resolve, in the spirit of Asian philosophy, in addition to problems to solve, in the tradition of scientific research. The geometries of knowledge and associated political agendas become infinitely complex and we need to advance on models such as that of interrelated global knowledge domains to assist us not only in definition, to see the issues more clearly, but also in action, to promote the meaningful integration of indigenous knowledge research into development policies and programmes.

Notes

1 Department for International Development funded projects in Bangladesh and Sri Lanka. The views expressed are those of the author and not necessarily those of the DFID. I thank all those colleagues who have collaborated on the projects for many stimulating discussions, and particularly Julian Barr and Peter Dixon for their unstinting support.

2 The comments address themselves to the natural resources field – covering agriculture, forestry, fisheries and the environment, etc. – as that with which I am familiar, but the model should apply equally to other fields prominent in development, such as health and population.

3 This drawing on theories familiar to scientists is also a ploy to promote parity, and to further acceptance of indigenous knowledge as relevant to their work.

4 The symmetry concepts of chemistry also come to mind here, featuring sophisticated mathematical modelling not drawn upon in structuralist debates.

5 The combination of *ha* (sun) and *tha* (moon) in the name of the *hatha* school of *yoga*, which aims to unite such opposites, catches this belief in balanced unity (Khan 1985: 36). There are clear parallels with structuralist thinking in anthropology, which borrowed heavily from similar duality notions expressed by Amazonian Indians (Lévi-Strauss 1968a).

6 It has six spokes, the segments between depicting states of existence (hell's denizens, hungry ghosts, animals, humans, titans and deities), and a central hub with cock (greed), snake (hatred) and pig (ignorance) locked in a tail-biting circle to symbolize the 'three unwholesome roots' that underlie human misery and life's evils. The rim of the wheel comprises twelve segments representing the different stages and dispositions of life (birth, being, consciousness, death, etc.).

7 The representation of human interaction and knowledge transmission by turning to network theory is not new to anthropology, and dates back at least to the Manchester School's discussion of these ideas in the 1960s (Barnes 1969; Epstein 1961; Mitchell 1969). Anthropology has a wealth of experience to draw upon in furthering understanding of such relations from its knowledge of acephalous social orders where cross-cutting ties are central to the political order. We have only to think of the complex moiety and sub-section systems that intellectually structure marriage alliances, initiation rituals, totemic relations and so on in Australian Aboriginal society for a rich ethnographic analogy.

8 The particle–wave view of science contrasts with the planetary one employed so far in this paper, which depends on planets orbiting in equilibrium (seen in human, not cosmic time spans: Feynmann 1998a). The sub-atomic view is analogous to the social process perspective, while the astronomic one is reminiscent of the structural and functional theories of society that dominated in the past.

9 Probably the best known in the West is *yoga* (uniting) of the *Atman* to the *Brahman* through physical and mental exercises to reach the requisite spiritual plane.

10 As argued some time ago by Evans-Pritchard (1962) and Lévi-Strauss (1968b), among others.

11 This is not a new phenomenon. The *neem* tree, for example, is commonly exploited throughout South Asia and elsewhere, primarily for its medicinal insecticidal qualities. Who should benefit from any increasing commercial interest shown in the tree: the 'original' owners now numbering, thanks to the process of generations-long diffusion, hundreds of millions of persons? Or should it be those whose particular use of it is first documented by commercial concerns? Is the free operation of the global market the most equitable way to sort out these issues, or is this an unfair, culturally biased mechanism?

Bibliography

Agrawal, A. 1995. Dismantling the divide between indigenous and scientific knowledge. *Development and Change* 26: 413–439.

Antweiler, C. 1998. Local knowledge and local knowing: An anthropological analysis of contested 'cultural products' in the context of development. *Anthropos* 93: 469–494.

Barnes, J. A. 1969. Networks and political process. In M. J. Swartz (ed.) *Local-level Politics* (pp. 107–130). London: University of London Press.

Barr, J. J. F. and P. Sillitoe. 2000. Databases, indigenous knowledge and interdisciplinary research. In P. Sillitoe (ed.) *Indigenous Knowledge Development in Bangladesh: Present and Future* (pp. 179–195). London: Intermediate Technology Publications; and Dhaka: University Press.

Bhaktivedanta Swami Prabhupada, A. C. 1982. *Krsna: The Supreme Personality of Godhead* (2 vols). Sydney: The Bhaktivedanta Book Trust.

Bhaskar, R. 1986. *Scientific Realism and Human Emancipation*. London: Verso.

Capra, F. 1983. *The Tao of Physics: An Exploration of the Parallels between Modern Physics and Eastern Mysticism*. London: Fontana (Flamingo).

Chambers, R. 1986. Normal professionalism, new paradigms and development. Discussion Paper no. 227. Institute of Development Studies, Sussex University.

——. 1997. *Whose Reality Counts? Putting the First Last*. London: Intermediate Technology Publications.

Clifford J. 1988. *The Predicament of Culture: Twentieth Century Ethnography, Literature and Art*. Cambridge, MA: Harvard University Press.

——. 1992. Travelling cultures. In L. Grossberg, C. Nelson and P. Treichler (eds) *Cultural Studies* (pp. 96–116). New York: Routledge.

Cvetkovich, A. and D. Kellner (eds). 1996. *Articulating the Global and the Local: Globalization and Cultural Studies*. Boulder, CO: Westview Press.

Dallmayr, R. 1996. Global development? Alternative voices from Delhi. *Alternatives* 21: 259–282.

Das, C. 1995. Politics of theorizing in a postmodern academy. *American Anthropologist* 97(2): 269–281.

DeWalt, B. R. 1994. Using indigenous knowledge to improve agriculture and natural resource management. *Human Organization* 53(2): 123–131.

Dixon P. J., J. J. F. Barr and P. Sillitoe. 2000. Actors and rural livelihoods: Integrating interdisciplinary research and local knowledge. In P. Sillitoe (ed.) *Indigenous Knowledge Development in Bangladesh: Present and Future* (pp. 161–177). London: Intermediate Technology Publications; and Dhaka: University Press.

Epstein, A. L. 1961. The network and urban social organisation. *Rhodes-Livingstone Journal* 29: 29–62.

Escobar, A. 1995. *Encountering Development: The Making and Unmaking of the Third World*. New Jersey: Princeton University Press.

Evans-Pritchard, E. E. 1962. Anthropology and history. In *Essays in Social Anthropology*. London: Faber.

Fergusson, J. 1994. *The Anti-Politics Machine: 'Development', Depoliticization and Bureaucratic Power in Lesotho*. Cambridge: Cambridge University Press.

Feynmann, R. P. 1998a. *Six Easy Pieces: The Fundamentals of Physics Explained*. London: Penguin.

——. 1998b. *Six Not-So-Easy Pieces: Einstein's Relativity, Symmetry and Space-Time.* London: Penguin.

Gelick, J. 1988. *Chaos.* London: Sphere.

Giri, A. 1997. Transcending disciplinary boundaries: Creative experiments and the critiques of modernity. Madras Institute of Development Studies Working Paper no. 150.

Goonatilake, S. 1999. *Toward a Global Science: Mining Civilizational Knowledge.* New Delhi: Vistaar.

Grenier, L. 1998. *Working with Indigenous Knowledge. A Guide for Researchers.* Ottawa: IDRC.

Grillo, R. D. and R. L. Stirrat (eds). 1997. *Discourses of Development: Anthropological Perspectives.* Oxford: Berg.

Hall, N. (ed.) 1992. *The New Scientist Guide to Chaos.* London: Penguin.

Ingold, T. 1993. Globes and spheres: The topology of environmentalism. In K. Milton (ed.) *Environmentalism: The View from Anthropology* (pp. 31–42). ASA Monograph no. 32. London: Routledge.

Jameson, F. and M. Miyoshi (eds). 1998. *The Cultures of Globalization.* Durham: Duke University Press.

Kennedy, A. 1985. *The Buddhist Vision: An Introduction to the Theory and Practice.* London: Rider and Co.

Khan, F. A. 1985. *Practical Yoga.* Karachi: Oloom-e-Makhfi.

Khanna, M. 1997. *Yantra: The Tantric Symbol of Cosmic Unity.* London: Thames and Hudson.

Kiel, L. D. and E. Elliot (eds). 1996. *Chaos Theory in the Social Sciences.* Ann Arbor: University of Michigan Press.

Kiely, R. and P. Marfleet. 1998. *Globalisation and the Third World.* London: Routledge.

Kothari, R. 1988. *Rethinking Development: In search of Humane Alternatives.* Delhi: Ajanta.

Latour, B. 1993. *We Have Never Been Modern.* Trans. C. Porter. London: Harvester Wheatsheaf.

Lévi-Strauss, C. 1968a. *Structural Anthropology.* London: Allen Lane.

——. 1968b. Introduction: History and anthropology. In *Structural Anthropology* (pp. 1–27). London: Allen Lane.

Malinowski, B. 1944. *A Scientific Theory of Culture.* University of North Carolina Press.

McGreal, I. P. (ed.). 1995. *Great Thinkers of the Eastern World: The Major Thinkers and Philosophical and Religious Classics of China, India, Japan, Korea and the World of Islam.* New York: Harper Collins.

Mehmet, O. 1995. *Westernizing the Third World: The Eurocentricity of Economic Development Theories.* London: Routledge.

Mitchell, J. C. (ed.). 1969. *Social Networks in Urban Situations.* Manchester: Manchester University Press.

Powell, J. N. 1979. *Mandalas: The Dynamics of Vedic Symbolism.* New Delhi: Stirling Publishers.

Prigogine, I. and I. Stenger. 1985. *Order out of Chaos.* London: Fontana.

Purcell, T. W. 1998. Indigenous knowledge and applied anthropology: Questions of definition and direction. *Human Organization* 57(3): 258–272.

Radcliffe-Brown, A. R. 1952. *Structure and Function in Primitive Society.* London: Cohen and West.

Rothman, T. and G. Sudarshan. 1998. *Doubt and Certainty*. London: Perseus.

Sardar, Z. and I. Abrams. 1998. *Chaos for Beginners*. Duxford: Icon Books.

Scholte, J. A. 2000. *Globalization: A Critical Introduction*. Basingstoke: Macmillan.

Scoones, I. and J. Thompson. 1994. Knowledge, power and agriculture: Towards a theoretical understanding. In I. Scoones and J. Thompson (eds) *Beyond Farmer First: Rural People's Knowledge, Agricultural Research and Extension Practice* (pp. 16–32). London: Intermediate Technology Publications.

Sen, G. 1992. *Indigenous Vision: Peoples of India, Attitudes to Environment*. New Delhi: Sage.

Shiva, V. 1993. *Monocultures of the Mind: Perspectives on Biodiversity and Biotechnology*. London: Zed Books.

Sillitoe, P. 1998a. The development of indigenous knowledge: A new applied anthropology. *Current Anthropology* 39(2): 223–252.

——. 1998b. Defining indigenous knowledge: The knowledge continuum. *Indigenous Knowledge and Development Monitor* 6(3):14–15.

——. 1998c. Knowing the land: Soil and land resource evaluation and indigenous knowledge. *Soil Use and Management* 14(4):188–193.

——. 2000. Introduction: The state of indigenous knowledge in Bangladesh. In P. Sillitoe (ed.) *Indigenous Knowledge Development in Bangladesh: Present and Future* (pp. 3–20). London: Intermediate Technology Publications; and Dhaka: University Press.

Simpson, B. M. 1997. Towards a conceptual framework for understanding the structure and internal dynamics of local knowledge systems. Paper presented at *Creativity and Innovation at the Grassroots* Conference, Ahmedabad, January 1997.

Sinclair F. L. and D. H. Walker. 1998. Acquiring qualitative knowledge about complex agroecosystems. Part 1. Representation as natural language. *Agricultural Systems* 56(3): 341–363.

Smith, L. T. 1999. *Decolonising Methodologies: Research and Indigenous Peoples*. London: Zed Books.

Tierney, A. 1998. Studies in the anthropology of development: Their relevance for social policy. Poverty Research Unit at Sussex Working Paper no. 5.

Tomlinson, J. 1999. *Globalization and Culture*. Oxford: Polity.

Tucci, G. 1974. *The Theory and Practice of the Mandala*. Trans. A.H. Brodrick. London: Rider and Co.

Vayda, A. P. 1996. *Methods and Explanations in the Study of Human Actions and their Environmental Effects*. Jakarta: Center for International Forestry Research and World Wide Fund for Nature.

Walker, D. H. and F. L. Sinclair. 1998. Acquiring qualitative knowledge about complex agroecosystems. Part 2. Formal representation. *Agricultural Systems* 56(3): 365–386.

Warren, D. M., L .J. Slikkerveer and D. Brokensha (eds). 1995. *The Cultural Dimensions of Development: Indigenous Knowledge Systems*. London: Intermediate Technology Publications.

Waters, M. 1998. *Globalization*. London: Routledge.

Whickam, T. W. 1993. Farmers ain't no fools: Exploring the role of Participatory Rural Appraisal to access indigenous knowledge and enhance sustainable development research and planning: A case study, Dusun Pausan, Bali, Indonesia. MA thesis, University of Waterloo. Ann Arbor: University Microfilms International (1996).

Wolfe J., C. Bechard, P. Cizek and D. Cole. 1992. Indigenous and Western knowledge and resource management systems. *Rural Reportings, Native Canadian Issues Series 1.* Canada: University of Guelph.

Chapter 7

Negotiating with knowledge at development interfaces
Anthropology and the quest for participation[1]

Michael Schönhuth

Whose participation, whose development?

'Participating in Development', the title of the 2000 ASA Conference, contains an intentional ambiguity and leaves room for interpretation: Who will participate here and in whose development? Is it the anthropologist, for whom 'exciting events' in the development scene have opened opportunities 'to engage practically as never before', as the call for papers suggests? Is it the local communities, for whom 'a revolution in anthropological method and theory in the new millennium' might open the door to be 'no longer research subjects but participants' (*ibid.*)? Even if many anthropologists seem happily unaware of it, Sillitoe recognizes 'a revolution in the pursuit of ethnography' (1998b: 204, also 1998a) in an article published several years ago. This revolution comes together with the recent participatory approach in development circles, namely the interest in local knowledge/indigenous knowledge[2] in bottom-up approaches. With the expertise needed here, Sillitoe sees a chance for anthropologists to consolidate their place in development practice as implementing partners.

In the early 1990s Johan Pottier (1993) in his *Practising Development* noted an increased emphasis on research informed by ethnography. The discovery of the 'human factor' and participatory approaches to development has provided several openings for qualitative, contextual research, and Pottier sees a new generation of social analysts emerging. 'This new generation of (mainly) social anthropologists has gained relevant experience by eking out autonomous positions at the interface between local-level agency personnel and targeted beneficiaries' (Pottier 1993: 2). A combination of participatory and anthropological research in the project context should help us to escape the dilemma of conventional anthropological research, 'so often criticised for being isolationist and unrelated to community needs', and at the same time exploiting the advantage of ethnographic understanding, reducing the risk 'that false assumptions creep into the design of development programmes' (Pottier 1993: 3).

I would, however, doubt both assumptions: that of a revolutionary new era for the practice of anthropology with development,[3] and that of new opportunities for local communities through the marriage of participatory and anthropological research. My reservations towards the first assumption come from academic anthropology's unresolved relationship with development and applied research; the reservations towards the second from fundamental inconsistencies between participatory and academic anthropological research traditions.

Though empirical in view, an actor oriented theoretical perspective informs the chapter. It seeks to understand social action at development inter-faces. Here people from the academy, development agencies and 'local communities' shape processes and outcomes in ways that are both creative and constrained.[4] It accepts but goes beyond the discourse oriented 'deconstruc-tion of development approach' offered by Escobar, Ferguson or Hobart in the 1990s (Escobar 1991; Ferguson 1990; Hobart 1993). Modernity, development and knowledge from this perspective are not only categories imposed by a Western discourse to discipline and transform local realities. They are also features that are reworked from within by local actors to shape and enhance their room for action, in a field where power and resources are limited and unevenly distributed.[5] This holds true for local actors in places where develop-ment practitioners work and anthropologists undertake research. It also holds true in the institutions that employ developers and anthropologists, where they earn their living, seek approval and power, and advance their careers.

Opportunities for anthropology to engage practically in development as never before

As the national institutional settings are different, in order to assess anthro-pology's opportunities to engage in development, I take the German scene as an example, and only then take a look abroad to countries sharing the same development discourse.[6]

Many anthropologists in Germany, some in prominent positions, oppose the discipline's engagement with development. This is reflected in the at times uneasy position of the Working Group on Development, Anthropology/ Arbeitsgemeinschaft Entwicklungsethnologie (AGEE) with its mother organi-zation, Deutsche Gesellschaft für Völkerkunde (DGV). In 1987, when the informal working group asked for recognition as an official working group of the DGV, there were massive protests by members, some of whom even threatened to resign, leading to a rejection of the application. Basically the criticism was connected with three positions which I will label as 'the purists', 'the innocents' and 'the ethically correct'. Their arguments are characterized in Figure 7.1.

The argument of the purists, reflected in a testimony attributed to the famous American cultural anthropologist Clyde Kluckhohn in the 1950s, reflects an old but still existing conflict between those paid by and working for an institution, and those who earn their money beyond the halls of

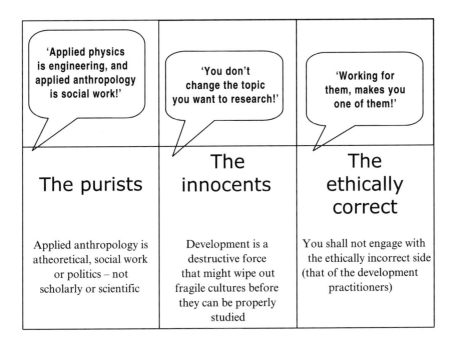

Figure 7.1   Positions within the discipline against the participation of anthropology in the development arena

academe who are dependent on market rules. As a result of discussions with the faction of the ethically correct – representatives of a Working Group on 'Ethics' in Anthropology in Germany (cf. Amborn 1993) – the AGEE has developed 'Ethical Guidelines' for anthropological work (AGEE 2000). The strength of their position in the debate has somehow declined in recent years. However, the positions of the purists – those who look down on practical anthropology as being non-scientific – and of those whom I named the innocents – for whom development is a destructive force that might wipe out fragile cultures before they can be properly studied (Ferguson 1996) – are still prominent in Germany. Most practice oriented development researchers with an anthropological background have left the halls of academe and are engaged within development agencies or non-governmental organizations. Although AGEE received official 'accreditation' in 1989, it is still not advisable to be either an anthropologist in development (i.e. to be engaged practically) or to work and publish at the interface (i.e. an informed anthropology of development) if you do not wish to lose academic credibility (cf. Antweiler 1998a; Bliss 1988; Schönhuth 1998a).

Looking abroad

In Germany there is only a loose connection between anthropologists and development, whether as distinguished representatives of anthropology,[7] through institutional cooperation agreements, or through research institutes that work at the interface.[8] To my view, the absence of anthropological institutions at the interface is one major obstacle to further anthropological engagement in this field.

This applies beyond Germany, as Prudence Woodford-Berger observes regarding the six anthropologists employed in the Swedish Development Unit (DSU) in the 1990s:

> Few is the number of those, who look back on a qualified anthropological education, who understand themselves as anthropologists and who work at the same time as anthropologists in development co-operation … Actually, not one of us succeeded in linking these two worlds successfully in our personal careers to any extent.
>
> (Woodford-Berger 1996: 118)

A review and comparison of development anthropology in five countries (the USA, Great Britain, Norway, Sweden and The Netherlands; cf. Schönhuth 1998a) reveals that the arguments put forward against the establishment of the AGEE in the 1980s exist in the wider anthropological community. Even for the United States, where work on social change (development, modernization) increased in status after the Second World War, Ferguson describes anthropological work on development as becoming more and more adjusted to the bureaucratic demands of development agencies at the expense of intellectual rigour and critical self-consciousness, 'leaving behind a low-prestige, practice-oriented sub field of "development anthropology"'(1996: 159). I won't presume to judge this argument for American development anthropology in general,[9] but looking at the excellent work of the Institute of Development Anthropology in Binghamton, for example, one can hardly find proof of this testimony.[10] On the other hand, it is remarkable that out of eleven commentators of an overview article on indigenous knowledge and applied anthropology (Sillitoe 1998a), only one (Brokensha 1998) admits that many academic peers are sceptical or even hostile towards any involvement of anthropology with development.

In my view, the prejudices and arguments against development oriented anthropology also seem to work abroad. Perhaps the fact that during the ASA 2000 Conference the 'pure academic faction' of British anthropology, with its prominent representatives, was hardly to be seen was also not accidental, but due to this circumstance. I agree with Sillitoe that, from the point of view of development, the prospects for integrating anthropological competence are quite good.[11] It is the tirade of reservations from the discipline of the purists, the ethically correct and the innocents that makes me sceptical about anthropology's opportunities to engage practically in development as never before.

Combining academic anthropology with the participatory approach: new opportunities for local communities?

Anthropological research can often be a vehicle for the appropriation – not the protection – of indigenous knowledge (Posey 1998). Bridging the gap between observer and observed, and making local people active partners in research is therefore the request of anthropologists who combine participant observation and participatory research.[12] For Wright and Nelson in their comparison of both approaches, a synthesis would hold the possibility 'of combining an approach constructing people as active agents in research with new theoretical understandings of wider processes of domination, in which both researcher and participants are located and which they are in different ways seeking to change' (1995: 59). The approaches are compatible to a great extent. Local/indigenous knowledge[13] and realities lie at the heart of both, and both seek expression of local perceptions, categories and classifications. Both stress the importance of the emic perspective (from within). In both approaches building a good rapport with the group is a necessary precondition. The attitude is one of 'learning', or even 'learning to unlearn', to be open to local systems, strategies and values. The aim is to establish a dialogue – in ethnography usually with informants, in participatory research with a community group. In both approaches methods such as observation (from unobtrusive to participant), interviews (from non-structured to semi-structured) and forms of focus group discussion play a prominent role and all work (at different levels) with maps, tables and diagrams to visualize local history, physical and social relationships.

Through the principal overlaps new approaches developed in the 1980s and 1990s which try to integrate the advantages of the ethnographic view into action oriented programmes.[14] Participatory methods, on the other hand, have also enriched the sociocultural research agenda. The National Association of Practicing Anthropologists (NAPA), a subsidiary of the American Anthropological Association, delivered as early as 1991 a brochure in which the advantages of Rapid Rural Appraisal (RRA) methods were introduced to an anthropological audience (van Willigan and Finan 1991). So the preconditions for anthropologists to engage practically in development in the last few years have been quite good.

But there are fundamental inconsistencies between participant observation and participatory research, which have to do with their different traditions. The first, from Malinowski's day onwards, takes indigenous knowledge (IK) as a resource for describing and translating sociocultural reality according to scientific standards. The second takes local knowledge as a resource to act on and change sociocultural reality together with people in a world of domination and unjustified distribution of resources. It is these different traditions that make the combination a difficult task, in which the researcher faces unsuspected dilemmas, and the actors may lose as much as they can win by negotiating with knowledge in a participatory mode.

The prerequisites of participatory research

To illustrate my point, a look at the origins and prerequisites of participatory research is helpful. Participation of local communities in research and action is far from being new. Its origins can be traced back as far as the early work of Engels (in his alignment with the working class of Manchester) or Marx (in his use of 'structured interview' with French factory workers; cf. Hall 1981: 8). In more recent times, the liberation movements in Latin America and the work of theorists on the mechanisms of cultural and economic dependency in the 1960s advanced the political participatory research agenda.[15]

Participatory research became a prominent methodological concept when the 'Participatory Research Network' was created through the International Council of Adult Education in 1977. It brought together social scientists but also literacy teachers, community organizers, administrators, factory workers and urban activists. Owing much to the work of Paulo Freire, participatory research was described as 'an integrated activity that combines *social investigation, educational work* and *action*' (Hall 1981: 9; emphasis added).

Only one side of this triangle, the social investigation process, has its roots in a scientific tradition. The *educational mandate* of academics towards a liberated knowledge of ordinary and marginalized people and the *striving for political transformation for the better* demand an explicit value position from the researcher, who sees him or herself as an agent of change in a world where social justice is still to be reached. The emphasis on action and educational work in participatory research can be seen as a reaction from Third World activists to the dominant Western research paradigm of empiricism and positivism.[16]

This also involves the process of social science investigation. Not only is the methodology action oriented, the research process itself is informed and partly controlled by local communities, now partners in research and analysis. The researcher becomes a facilitator in this process, who does not control the research agenda or own the results any more. This is a process 'by which the "raw" and somewhat unformed – or, at least, unexpressed – knowledge of ordinary people is brought into the open and incorporated into a connectable whole' (Hall 1981: 12). Participatory research has, on the one side, socially and politically deprived communities, and on the other, activist researchers with certain theories of change in mind, ideally as equal counterparts. The *activist* researchers are accountable to the communities they are working with, and of course to the social or political theory which guides the researcher's activities. The problem for the activist researcher is how to avoid imposing alienating, elitist concepts of reality or preconceived theoretical constructions on the community, a charge sometimes made against approaches inspired by the Marxist models of society.

Problems combining academic and participatory research: evidence from practice

The problems for the researcher who tries to implement participatory research methodology within an academic research design are different from those of an activist researcher. A workshop at the Institute of Development Studies (IDS) in 1996 noted several dilemmas (cf. Attwood 1997) regarding time, ownership and frames of reference:

- How should the interests of researcher and local community be reconciled? (Even if community and researcher agree on a common interest, their agendas will differ, the first aiming for local action and development, the second for a Ph.D. or other academic outcome.)
- How can time frames be matched? (The pace at which community members and the researcher want the project to unfold may differ considerably, the first having a lifetime perspective, the second time restrictions due to funding or reporting of research results.)
- Who should own and who should be allowed to communicate research results? (While the topic of 'intellectual property rights for indigenous groups' is discussed among anthropologists,[17] field research results are most credited by the academic community if they are validated, interpreted and controlled by a single author.)

I want to address some of these problems empirically. The field examples mainly come from a GTZ[18] project in the Rukwa region in Tanzania, where I was engaged as a short-term consultant on a three to four weeks per year basis from 1995 to 1997, from numerous field workshops between 1993 and 2000 with different groups, and from a field research training programme in 1999 with students of anthropology in a Siberian village with an ethnic German population.

Finding the 'right' representatives

Finding the 'right' representatives who are legitimate counterparts within the community, and not creating a biased relationship right from the start, can be a problem. In a participatory one-week field workshop we facilitated in an East German village shortly after German reunion in 1993, the first official contacts where made through the village mayor with an active group around the village pastor. Informal talks during the field stay and results of some of the participatory instruments revealed that this group, and especially the pastor, were marginalized in village life to a great extent because of their change orientation, the symbol of which being the modern windmill in the pastor's garden that could be seen from every point in the village. What seemed to have been a good start (having official and interested counterparts) came to be one of the main obstacles to a trusting research partnership with the rest of the village (cf. Schönhuth 1994; for similar experiences, see Botes and van Rensburg 2000).

In another participatory research project with students of anthropology in a Siberian village in 1999, which had the situation of ethnic Germans as a research focus, the preparations had also been made through official channels together with the local teacher of German. We asked her to arrange housing for the research team of thirteen people in at least four different families to get different household perspectives and family strategies into view. It was only at the end of the week, while trying to generate a kinship village diagram, that we realized that the whole research team was lodged in one and the same big family clan (cf. Schönhuth et al. 2000). Although marginalized informants and biased field access are classic ethnographic research problems (cf. Stocking 1983), in participatory research the questions of who biases the information and to whose end are much more prevalent because of the active part local people play in the research process.

At the end of the field workshop we presented a video taken in Trier, our University town in Germany. It showed interviews with German emigrants (Aussiedler) from Russia regarding their partly problematic integration into German society. We wanted to confront the idealistic imaginations of those who wanted to migrate with the reality of those who already had migrated. It was remarkable that not one of the participants wanted to comment on the testimonies in the film, and even more so that there was little enthusiasm in the village for discussing the outcomes of the one-week appraisal with us. Of course we didn't force our research partners to share more of their reality with us than they wanted to. But it was also obvious that in spite of contacts made beforehand and a commonly agreed field contract with the participating villagers, our reference frames in the end did not match (cf. Schönhuth et al. 2000). Local research partners have their own research interests, and their own, sometimes hidden, agendas that may differ greatly from those of scientific researchers.

Authorship

Research normally starts with a research proposal. It is unlikely that the researcher will have the time and money to tune and negotiate the proposal with the local community beforehand. Even if this is possible, the representations of community members might be difficult to translate into the scientific aims and demands of the funding agency. However interactive the research process, in the end, the scientist must also validate his understanding and interpretation to the academic community. At the time of writing, representations become controlled by the author, whose voice is privileged (Wright and Nelson 1995: 150). They pass over into the property of the Western world, becoming part of their 'truth regimes' (Foucault 1980) or 'world ordering knowledge' (Hobart 1993). The academic establishment expects academically authored pieces. But 'does the anthropologist need to be an author?' asks Jain (2000) in her paper submitted to the ASA conference, 'Can't there simply be a dialogue where the erstwhile objects become subjects and anthropologists follow the leads given by them' (Jain 2000: 1)? If an author expects academic peers to recognize and credit their work, the answer seems to be 'no', although this is not in line with the philosophy of participatory research where information should be collectively owned (cf. Attwood 1997: 3).

Expectations raised

Engaging in participatory research implies interfering in a community where change will affect people's lives and not that of the researcher. This relates to the different time frames of the actors. Time restrictions on the side of the researcher concerning funding or the reporting of results collide with the life-time perspective of local people. This has consequences for the pace at which the respective parties would like the project to unfold, how they decide on explicit or implicit research strategies, and how they allot their resources and energy. On the other hand, people usually identify much more with their own research results than those produced for them by external experts. This raises expectations for action. If the researchers lack the resources to meet these expectations or to assist the processes triggered by the research, they face practical and ethical problems. Veronika Ulbert's experience in her participatory study with women in Ecuador is typical:

> When the author withdrew from group work at the end of the PRA research process, many women reacted with indignation. Their expectations of continued 'animation for problem analysis' had been disappointed. Moreover it lay beyond the competence of the author to implement the solutions developed together with the women into concrete action for change.
>
> (Ulbert 1995: 87)

Participatory research within an academic setting needs backing within an institutional context that allows longer time involvement and action orientation – preconditions often not found within academic institutions.

Reliability of data

Another problem comes with reliability standards of data. Whenever you try to explain the methodological principles of 'optimal ignorance' and 'appropriate imprecision' in Participatory Rural Appraisal (PRA)[19] to academic audiences, you can find yourself in discussions about the reliability, not to say seriousness, of the whole approach. Some of the harshest critics come from anthropology.[20] It is the methodological pragmatism, which in case of doubt sacrifices scientific rigidity and depth of data to appropriateness for action that makes the participatory approach suspect for pure academics. Those who work at the interface face a classical dilemma here.

In one of my first PRA exercises in Tanzania the project team wanted to determine categories of vulnerable households in the village for whom special funds had been reserved in the project budget. We used a participatory method called 'wealth ranking', by which villagers could define wealth categories according to their local criteria and then rank the households. To ensure reliable results, the leading social scientist in the team not only wanted to select village participants according to random sampling criteria,[21] she also made sure that the participants did not know why they were playing the game and to what ends. To guarantee confidentiality, the work had to be done in a closed setting.

At the end of the village workshop in Tanzania the local participants in the wealth-ranking game faced strong interrogation from their fellow villagers: all other PRA instruments had been facilitated and shared in the open, they asked, why not this one? When specific households got their material inputs some weeks after the village workshop, we could be quite sure that the participants of the wealth-ranking game had selected them without any biasing interest. But at the same time we had generated envy, gossip, uncertainty and distrust in the village, and between village and project.

The reliability of data problem in participatory approaches not only concerns contemporary researchers. Wright and Nelson (1995: 52f.) report how a professor of sociology trained three thousand 'mass observers' in the 1930s to work all over Britain, to collect information on various topics to create an 'anthropology of ourselves' by the people of Britain.[22] Anthropologists at that time disapproved of this method of collecting data and representing 'everyday life'. In a critique of such mass observation, Marshall (1937: 49) pointed out that 'observations of ordinary citizens are shot through with selection and interpretation', and Raymond Firth (1939) argued that an inquiry should be informed by a clearly established theory of society to define a particular problem on which facts will be collected. Firth was a student of Malinowski, who in his classical work *Argonauts of the Western Pacific* stated that the 'natives obey the forces and commands of their tribal code but they do not comprehend them' (1922: 11). For him, as for generations of students after him, it is the authoritative task of the ethnographer to collect 'concrete data of evidence … drawing the general inferences for himself' (Malinowski 1922: 12). The central message of the mass observation approach – to aspire to bridge the gap between observer and observed in order to make the understanding of society a task of society itself – was not apprehended by any of the anthropological critics of that time.

Scientific, expert, local knowledge

Negotiating with knowledge elicited in a participatory way can also become a problem when the anthropologist feeds back participatory research results to decision makers in development. Anthropologists who have done consultancy work for government organizations or NGOs know about the difficulties involved in integrating 'soft', 'local' or 'indigenous', or even anthropological knowledge into executive summary reports. The anthropologist has to have a leading position in an evaluation team to give these topics relevance. Otherwise their arguments can often be found buried in the appendices of such reports. This sort of negotiating within power structures is a quality urgently needed if anthropological competence is to have a stronger influence in development.

In relation to this, if anthropologists are part of multidisciplinary teams, they have to translate the knowledge and constraints of indigenous people to foresters, hydrologists, nutrition or agricultural specialists in a way compatible with the language of those sciences. The experience of the German Development Service (Deutscher Entwicklungsdienst, DED)[23] with the anthropologists employed in the organization in the 1990s shows that intercultural competence did not automatically enable them to communicate successfully with team members of other disciplines. Heidt summarizes:

> They [the anthropologists] sometimes don't find it easy to illustrate the anthropological and social science insights and findings in a way that local and German team members can find in it an aspect essential for the success of the program.
>
> (Heidt 1997: 97)

(For this argument, see also Cleveland 1998; Sillitoe 1998a.)

When it comes to planning with local people following participatory appraisals, experts often find it difficult to plan on the basis of pictures and models that the people have created. The results are often criticized as being childish and not to be taken seriously – a problem we faced in Tanzania more than once. Even if the results are translated in a format compatible with administrative structures, layperson's knowledge and expert's knowledge might not fit. A review of experiences during the implementation of a participatory approach in German village planning in the 1990s (Boos-Krueger 1998) showed that the most critical point in the process was reached at implementation: when the ideas and plans of local people were to be executed by planning authorities or implementing agencies. For local people who have given days and weeks of their leisure time in participatory village planning, it is demoralizing when they learn that for technical, legal or administrative reasons their proposals are dismissed by the authorities. I agree with Brokensha (1998) that it is the integration of local or indigenous knowledge into administrative structures which may cause the most critical and demanding communication gaps to close.

How to balance expert knowledge, scientific knowledge and local/indigenous knowledge in participatory processes is a demanding challenge, requiring a lot of communication skills right from the start. In the participatory processes in the Rukwa region of Tanzania, from the second year onwards we made sure that the political and administrative branches of the regional development office were integrated from the very beginning. The project submitted information workshops or invited the decision makers on exposure days in the field. Even though some of them found it a strange experience to be exposed to village life, others were impressed by the capacities and knowledge of people elicited by participatory methods. These are valuable and easily interpretable tools to demonstrate the richness of local knowledge to outsiders. Those of the decision makers who understand the potential of these processes are the best brokers when it comes to channelling local people's knowledge into administrative planning schemes.

Anthropology's reservations towards participatory approaches

In spite of the features they have in common and the positive encounters they have had with anthropology it is a remarkable fact that participatory approaches have been mainly developed by other disciplines and that the most explicit critiques do come from anthropology.[24] Anthropological reservations mainly come from two directions:

- In their effort to produce timely and action oriented results, approaches such as rapid rural or participatory appraisal (RRA/PRA) fade out crucial parts of local reality as well as the sociocultural dimension.
- Participatory approaches contain implicit or explicit assumptions that relate to a Western discourse, but not the cognitive structures and decision-making processes of local cultures.

Participatory methods should inform external researchers but they should also give local people the opportunity to analyse their situation. For the anthropologist, the question arises as to whether the smallholder in rural Africa or South America structures and analyses experience in this way. Classic anthropological studies (Bourdieu 1977; Richards 1985) suggest that structure in these societies develops above all from experience. Knowledge is very much transferred by traditions (Sillitoe 1998a; Ellen 1998). Decisions are derived from practice, not from counting and analysing tables or matrices. Vokral (1994) and

Ulbert (1995), for example, doubt the value of PRA methods on the basis of their experiences in Ecuador in the Andean context. Vokral finds these methods much more appropriate 'for the public, often aggressive discourse in the North American culture [than] for the relatively taciturn and ritualized one of the Andean society' (1994: 42). To put it in the words of a local team member, reviewing the first year of our Tanzanian PRA village approach, 'I have the feeling that the PRA toolbox is not culturalized into the setting of the village. In identifying problems [for outsiders], it's good. But in action and problem solving [for people themselves] it's still dependency' (Schönhuth and Müller 1998: 127). Rew takes up this point in his critique of the PRA approach and adds:

> The PRA method emphasizes intensive interrogation and the use of role reversals and visual techniques in public settings. Each of these emphases can be problematic. First, the information is elicited in a social situation where the influence of power, authority and gender inequalities are great and highly likely to bias the PRA results ... Secondly there is a high bias towards verbalized information in PRA ... Thirdly, an important part of practical cultural knowledge remains encoded in technical routines and everyday experience and cannot easily be elicited verbally.
>
> (Rew 1997: 100)

(See also Becker *et al.* n.d.: 2ff. for these arguments.)

Rew refers here to contexts that rapid/participatory approaches have tended to fade out until recently: the social, the political and the cultural. Richards (1995: 15) asks: 'Was it ever realistic to think that a discourse-oriented PRA/RRA would evade co-option by local politics?', and he continues, 'any confidence that PRA/RRA operates independently of established local structures of political discourse ... is based on faith, not science' (1995: 16).

In applying a participatory methodology, the anthropologist faces a 'which power do I want to serve?' dilemma. Twenty years ago it was called 'pedagogy of the oppressed' or 'liberation anthropology'. Its promoters worked within an anti-imperialist movement against the Western development apparatus, seeking to effect a structural change in the power system. Nowadays it is called 'empowerment': seeking mainly to extend room for individual or local action, but not seriously questioning existing power structures. It was RRA and PRA, which have almost no political connotations, and not the approaches based on a 'liberation of the oppressed philosophy' of people such as Huizer (1989) or Freire (1970), which entered the development arena so easily in the 1990s. PRA and its successor PLA (Participatory Learning and Action approaches) today use a more political rhetoric (cf. Blackburn and Chambers 1996; Holland and Blackburn 1998), but still they are locked in existing hierarchies, facing the danger of only supporting improved data collection for Western world-ordering knowledge.

From my experience, if used in a culturally suitable way, visualizing tools can be extraordinarily useful for the outsider as a means of gaining a quick picture of the local situation and people. Far from being objective, these pictures provide an excellent basis and act as a catalyst for elucidating discussions on local features, local knowledge and local views of reality within homogeneous groups, and between different groups. But as these visualizations are process results, highly situational and context specific, they require interpretation and explanation by knowledgeable experts (i.e. local people and members of the facilitating team). Many participatory approaches such as GRAAP, DELTA, SWAP, PRA and others make strong use of the visual principle. Ranking, mapping and modelling draw their theoretical value, among others, from the 'projective' element contained in the visualization. The strength of these projective methods depends on weak pre-structuring by the facilitator. But because of this loose pre-structuring, projective methods (Lindzey 1961) need experience, training and theoretical knowledge to be interpreted correctly – a sort of expertise refuted by its proponents in the participatory development context ('everyone can do it'), but at the same time often very easily missed by participants of RRA/PRA trainings (cf. Holthusen and Paulus 1998).

Participatory diagrams are by no means an analytically deduced portrayal of local knowledge, which can be handed over to decision makers as a basis for development decisions, or bound into the analytic part of so-called 'participatory' scientific studies – a misunderstanding unfortunately sometimes produced in field reports and publications. The tools are also only rarely a good basis for local people's decisions. Local decision structures often run along other pathways than those of official village decision meetings organized by external personnel at the end of participatory village workshops.

An example from Rukwa in Tanzania (cf. Schönhuth and Müller 1998), where the ethnic Fipa constitute the majority of the local population, illustrates this point. At the end of one of the PRA village workshops we wanted the villagers to decide on possible projects. To minimize biases of power and gender, we enabled a differentiated voting process. Women voted with beans, men used corn. The seeds were cast into gourds passed round – one for each project – so that everyone could participate in voting secretly. When counting the votes, the local health worker, who was integrated into the PRA workshop, took me aside, telling me: 'Mr. Michael, this is not the Ba-Fipa way.' He pointed out that in this area village decisions were made in the responsible men's and women's committees in a process that lasted up to one week. After a controversial discussion the PRA team agreed to quit the democratic and gender-sensitive decision-making process and met with village officials to find a compromise: projects related to the village were to be decided in accordance with local structures of decision making. The PRA team, however, retained the option to support certain groups independently (e.g. women and vulnerable households for which special programmes in the project budget had been designed).

Conclusions: opportunities at the interface

I have dealt with only some of the dilemmas faced when working at the interface, touching upon others or leaving them aside: for example, the sometimes problematic consequences of empowering people (see n.28) or the question of sustainable solutions, which sometimes run counter to the immediate interests of local groups and their knowledge (Ellen 1998). Nevertheless, empirical evidence allows some conclusions.

What is positive in the encounter between anthropology and participatory development? First, on an ethical level, working also with and for people, and not only 'on' them helps us to come to terms to a certain extent with the ethnographic fieldworker's dilemma mentioned by Pottier (1993) and described vividly by Elizabeth Koepping in her article on trust and its abuse in long-term fieldwork:

> To what extent is it proper to use information gained almost by chance, that is during the conduct of an everyday life with friends, to clarify and expand one's anthropological understanding? ... When one grasps enough to write the whole, one has also reached the point where silence is a more decent response, a bizarre situation which perhaps offends the positivist as much as the voyeurist ... Then is the time to give back more than before to the other, to the source of one's own knowledge and success.
>
> (Koepping 1994: 115)

This is where anthropological appropriation of indigenous knowledge can give way to facilitation and brokerage.

Second, on a methodological level, anthropology could profit from making more use of visual cues to focus group discussions, and to elicit cultural maps of reality.[25] Research results, which are normally analysed at home by the anthropologist after fieldwork, could be discussed and corrected in the field with the local people. The perspective of the outsider, communicated through discussion of research results, can help to generate new insights and new momentum for change in the community, even where there are no funds or project. For example, a villager in Mecklenburg-Vorpommern, an area of the former German Democratic Republic, reflecting on the impact of PRA training with GTZ personnel in his village in 1992, commented, 'we can't say whether the workshop will initiate change here, but it was the first time since the reunion in 1989 that we as a community talked to each other about village problems' (cf. Schönhuth 1994). The empowering aspects of research do happen through interaction during the fieldwork itself, not so much through claiming to give people a voice, or through representations in texts afterwards (cf. Cameron in Wright and Nelson 1995: 49).

Third, at an operational level, ethnographic research and the PRA approach could profit from one another. Anthropological theory and field practice could contribute to a better understanding of how knowledge is created and used at the local level ('studying down'), at the interfaces and in development institutions ('studying up'; cf. Shrijvers 1995). It could help bring into focus competing local perspectives and decision making.[26] It could function with Western decision makers as a broker for the rationality and functionality of indigenous knowledge by returning to the roots of anthropological fieldwork.[27] It could help deconstruct and localize concepts of empower-ment, participation, community, human rights, democracy and partnership.[28]

This chapter has questioned two assumptions, that of a new era for the practice of anthropology with development, and that of new opportunities for local communities through the marriage of participatory and anthropological research. The reservations towards the first assumption are to do with academic anthropology's unresolved relationship with development and applied research. The reservations towards the second assumption are concerned with fundamental inconsistencies between participatory and academic anthropological research traditions, and the problem of integrating indigenous knowledge into scientific and administrative structures.

Nonetheless, anthropologists have a role to play at the interface between knowledge, participation and development. To illustrate this, I offer a last example from the Philippines. Here patron–client relationships occur primarily through the institution of 'owed gratitude' (*utang na loob*), part of a hierarchical system of reciprocal and often lifelong relationships of goodwill and obligation not backed up by contract. The clients use this system as a network for support and help during times of crisis. Apart from the local political leaders there are also other influential members of society who provide resources such as loans, or who enable access to patrons who are important for providing certain strategic resources. In community develop-ment processes the local political leaders are usually assigned responsibility for the project. They tend to select the beneficiaries of projects from their own group of clients according to the *utang na loob* principles. The motivation of 'beneficiaries' for participating in programmes depends much more on strategic decisions within the *utang na loob* system than external sponsors and experts might realize. Without intending it, such persons will be integrated into the cultural system of dependence, owed gratitude and lifelong obliga-tions as modern 'patrons', including all the misunderstandings and disappointments that derive from this situation on both sides when the devel-opment intervention finishes and the departing expatriates take their resources with them (Schönhuth *et al.* 2001; cf. Teves 2000).

Where indigenous knowledge is woven into the fabric of the local world order, and people localize global concepts, it is the anthropologist who has the professional skills to translate this for outsiders. On the other side, the anthropologist should also take the opportunity to translate Western world-ordering knowledge in a way that empowers local people so that they can negotiate more successfully at development interfaces.

Cancian (1993) in her research on conflicts between activist research and academic success evaluated three successful strategies of her interview partners: participating in an organization that is accountable to both academia and activists; employing a 'two career' strategy that enhances scientific credibility through research and mainstream publishing for academic colleagues, whilst at the same allowing participatory research; and working in an academic department that values activist research. If the anthropologist is aware of the dilemmas inherent in participatory research and has got the institutional backing, this is the place where he or she can contribute most to development – as a two-way translator or a mediator at the interface.

Notes

1   Thanks go to Christine Bald, Christoph Antweiler and Paul Sillitoe for valuable comments and critique to earlier versions of this contribution.
2   Following Ellen (1998), I take indigenous knowledge (IK) to describe knowledge that is 'local, orally transmitted, a consequence of practical engagement, reinforced by experience, empirical rather than theoretical, repetitive, fluid and negotiable, shared but asymmetrically distributed, largely functional, and embedded in a more encompassing cultural matrix' (Ellen 1998: 238; see also Ellen and Harris 1997). Concerning development in resettlement schemes for example, cultural identity can sometimes be found to be bound to specific symbolic places in the old area. Here anthropological expertise on culturally bound IK is mostly needed, because people may not adapt even to a physically similar environment (cf. Cernea 1999; Sillitoe 1998a for IK in situations of rapid change). Local knowledge in a broader sense fits with 'situated knowledge', where practices of (different kinds of) people living together in an environment draw on locally available resources.
3   For other critical comments on this assumption, see Brokensha (1998), Ferradás (1998) and Posey (1998).
4   Cecile Jackson, in a comment to Crewe and Harrison's (1998) inspiring book *Whose Development? An Ethnography of Aid.*
5   Regarding the aspect of knowledge and power in this approach, on a theoretical level, see Long and Long (1992), and on a methodological level, see Smith *et al.* (1997). Regarding development and power, see Nelson and Wright (1995); on 'counter development strategies', see Arce and Long (2000). Regarding the construction of multiple modernities, see Comaroff and Comaroff (1993) and Arce and Long (2000).
6   Namely the Western donor countries with an anthropological tradition. For a totally different development discourse of a non-Western donor country (Japan), see John Clammer's remarkable contribution to this volume (chapter 3).
7   Such as Fredrik Barth in Norway, Roger Bastide and George Balandier in France, Raymond Firth, Polly Hill and Scarlett Epstein in England, Elizabeth Colson, David Brokensha, Michael Horowitz and Thayer Scudder in the USA.
8   Postgraduates interested in the field have to move to other faculties where anthropological topics in the field of development are touched upon, such as

development sociology in Bielefeld, agrarian (Berlin, CATAD) or economic courses of intercultural communication (Munich, for example).

9 Regarding the situation for practising and development anthropologists in the USA, see Baba (1994), Hess (1997) and Horowitz (1994); regarding anthropological careers in general, see http://www.ameranthassn.org/careers.htm.

10 The Institute was founded by David Brokensha, Michael Horowitz and Thayer Scudder in 1974, and is mainly engaged in the side-effects of dam projects. Scudder is one of the world's leading experts on relocation effects. For a recent assessment of IDA's research, see Postel (1999). The homepage of the institute is http://www.devanth.org/index.htm.

11 This also has to do with an increasing interest in culture and development. In 1997 the 'world decade for cultural development' came to an end, and a flood of publications and conferences accompanied this event, the last one being the conference of the World Bank and UNESCO on culture and development held in Rome in October 1999. Internationally, the most influential may have been the World Commission on Culture and Development Report *Our Creative Diversity* (1995). The latest development in Germany was the delivering of a 'cross-sectional participation concept' in September 1999, which obliges BMZ's administrative branches to make target group participation and consideration of the sociocultural dimension of development central to projects and programmes (see BMZ 1999).

12 I confine my focus to the combination of research oriented anthropology with participatory approaches in the 1980s and 1990s. I will therefore not follow the much older strands of applied anthropology, action anthropology and advocacy anthropology (Read 1906; van Willigen 1993; Seithel 2000).

13 For a long time the richness of local knowledge was not mentioned in the participatory research paradigm. The focus was powerless people's awareness of their oppression. It is only in recent years that it has given more credence to local perspectives (Sillitoe 1998a: 224; Biot *et al.* 1995).

14 The Rapid Assessment Procedures (RAP), invented by Scrimshaw and Hurtado (1987) for the UN and subsequently spread by UN universities, understood themselves as anthropological methods for the improvement of the effectiveness of health programmes. The Rapid Ethnographic Assessment (REA) approach of Bentley *et al.* (1988) stands as part of this tradition too. 'Listen to people' was the central message of Lawrence Salmen's (1987) 'Beneficiary Assessment' approach, which brought the method of participant observation into the evaluation programme of the World Bank's development projects. At the Development Studies Unit of the Swedish development authority SIDA, anthropologists worked on the inclusion of anthropological fieldwork methods into SIDA's 'Community Baseline Studies' in the 1990s (Rudqvist 1991).

15 Other strands can be found in the sociology of work, organizational psychology and the organizational management traditions of the 1930s and 1940s, and the political participation of civil society in community planning such as advocacy planning, community control, neighbourhood government in USA or the German 'Planungsbeirat' and 'Planungszelle' (cf. Rucht 1982).

16 As Hall observes, 'The Third World's contribution to social science research methods represents an attempt to find ways of uncovering knowledge that work better in societies where interpretation of reality must take second place to the changing of reality' (Hall 1981: 8).

17 Cf. Greaves (1994) for an overview, and Strathern *et al.* (1998) for a controversial debate.

18 GTZ (Deutsche Gesellschaft für technische Zusammenarbeit). The German Development Agency is the implementing agency for personnel cooperation of the national ministry of Development (BMZ).

19 Chambers (1991: 522) called this the concept of 'optimising tradeoffs'. It relates the costs of collection and learning to trade-offs between quantity, relevance, timeliness, truth and actual beneficial use of information. This means knowing what is not worth knowing or when enough is known and then ceasing to try and to find out more; and avoiding measurement or precision that is not needed.
20 cf. Richards (1995) for example; on the other hand, see Brokensha (1998) for an anti-critique.
21 The problem of reliability of data is also noted by other facilitators. Vietnamese PRA trainers, reflecting their experiences, complained in a workshop: 'A small sample size, and lack of control over sampling procedure can lead to highly unreliable results [especially] as local leaders and guides have had a considerable effect on the sampling process' (Danish Red Cross 1996: 34).
22 Sillitoe, in a comment on an earlier version of this chapter, remarks that this type of 'mass observation' is still reported to continue in Britain.
23 The German Development Service (DED) is the development service of the Federal Republic of Germany for personnel cooperation. Almost 1,000 development workers are currently working in approximately forty countries.
24 cf. Becker *et al.* (n.d.); Mosse (1994); Richards (1995); Rew (1997); Pottier (1997); Nelson and Wright (1995). For an overview, see Cornwall and Fleming (1995) and other articles in PLA Notes 24 (1995).
25 For the universal usefulness of formal cognitive methods, if they are adapted to the local cultural setting, see Antweiler (1998b) with an example drawn from the Indonesian urban setting.
26 See Goebel (1998: 254f.) for competing local perspectives; Pottier (1997) for cultural differences in the 'openness' and participation of decisions.
27 See Elwert (1996) for this argument; also Sillitoe (1998a), who sees one of anthropology's main contributions being to challenge ethnocentrism.
28 The sometimes dangerous side-effects of empowerment and the question of the protection of the empowered poor are described in Shah and Shah (1995) or Appleton, who asks: 'Do facilitators and researchers have the skills to deal with such situations?' (1995: 47); on democracy and participation cf. Beckmann (1997); on the cultural relativity of human rights see Schönhuth (1998b), Said (1978).

Bibliography

AGEE. 2000. *Ethical Guidelines for Development Anthropologists*. Cologne: AGEE (Arbeitsgemeinschaft Entwicklungsethnologie).
Amborn, H. (ed.). 1993. *Unbequeme Ethik: Überlegungen zu einer verantwortlichen Ethnologie*. Berlin: Reimer.
Antweiler, C. 1998a. Ethnologie als gesellschaftlich relevante Humanwissenschaft: Eine Systematisierung praxisorientierter Richtungen und eine Position. *Zeitschrift für Ethnologie* 123(2): 215–255.
——. 1998b. Local knowledge and local knowing. An anthropological analysis of contested 'cultural products' in the context of development. *Anthropos* 93: 469–494.
Appleton, J. 1995. PRA, social tremors and rolling heads: Thoughts on PRA and empowerment. *PLA Notes* 24: 43–47.
Arce, A. and N. Long (eds). 2000. *Anthropology, Development and Modernities: Exploring Discourses, Counter-tendencies and Violence*. London and NewYork: Routledge.
Attwood, H. 1997. Introduction. *IDS PRA Topic Pack: Participatory Research* (pp. 2–5). Brighton: Institute of Development Studies.

Baba, M. 1994. The fifth subdiscipline: Anthropological practice and the future of anthropology. *Human Organization* 53(2): 174–186.

Becker, L., O. Benoit, J. Fairhead, P. Gatter, M. Leach and P. Sikana. n.d. *Can Rural Appraisal Really Be Rapid? A Critical Assessment by a Group of Slow Researchers and Practitioners.* Mimeo. 9pp.

Beckmann, G. 1997. *Partizipation in der Entwicklungszusammenarbeit. Mode, Methode oder politische Vision?* Hamburg: LIT.

Bentley, G., G. H. Pelto, W. L. Strauss, O. Adegebola, E. de la Pena, G. Oni, K. Brown and S. Huffman. 1988. Rapid ethnographic assessment: Applications in a diarrhoea management program. *Social Science Medicine* 27(19): 107–116.

Biot, Y., P. M. Blaikie, C. Jackson and R. Palmer-Jones. 1995. *Rethinking Research on Land Degradation in Developing Countries.* World Bank Discussion Paper no. 289. Washington, DC: World Bank.

Blackburn, J. and R. Chambers. 1996. *The Power of Participation: PRA and Policy.* IDS Policy briefing, Issue 7. Brighton: IDS, 4 pp.

Bliss, F. 1988. The cultural dimension in West German development policy and the contribution of ethnology. *Current Anthropology* 29(1): 101–121.

BMZ. 1999. Übersektorales Konzept Partizipative Entwicklungszusammenarbeit. Partizipationskonzept. *BMZ Aktuell* 102(September): 5–6.

Boos-Krueger, A. 1998. *Bürgerbeteiligung in der Hessischen Dorferneuerung: Beteiligungsstandards zur Sicherung des partizipativen Programmansatzes in einer zivilgesellschaftlich begründeten Planungs- und Handlungsperspektive.* Kassel: Gesamthochschulbibliothek.

Botes, L. and D. van Rensburg. 2000. Community participation in development: Nine plagues and twelve commandments. *Community Development Journal* 35(1): 41–58.

Bourdieu, P. 1977. *Outline of a Theory of Practice.* Cambridge: Cambridge University Press.

Brokensha, D. 1998. Comment. *Current Anthropology* 39(2): 236–237.

Cancian, F. M. 1993. Conflicts between activist research and academic success: Participatory research and alternative strategies. *The American Sociologist* spring: 92–105.

Cernea, M. M. 1999. *The Economics of Involuntary Resettlement: Questions and Challenges.* Washington, DC: The World Bank.

Chambers, R. 1991. Shortcut and participatory methods for gaining social information for projects. In M. M. Cernea (ed.) *Putting People First: Sociological Variables in Rural Development* (2nd edition) (pp. 515–537). New York: The World Bank.

Cleveland, D. A. 1998. Comment. *Current Anthropology* 39(2): 237–238.

Comaroff, J. L. and J. Comaroff (eds). 1993. *Modernity and its Malcontents: Ritual and Power in Postcolonial Africa.* Chicago, IL: University of Chicago Press.

Cornwall, A. and S. Fleming. 1995. Context and complexity: Anthropological reflections on PRA. *PLA Notes* 24: 8–12.

Crewe, E. and E. Harrison. 1998. *Whose Development? An Ethnography of Aid.* London and New York: Zed Books.

Danish Red Cross. 1996. *Vietnamizing PRA: Reflections of a Group of Vietnamese PRA Trainers and Trainees.* Hanoi. Draft version.

Ellen, R. F. 1998. Comment. *Current Anthropology* 39(2): 238–239.

Ellen, R. F. and H. Harris. 1997. *Indigenous Environmental Knowledge in Scientific and Development Literature: A Critical Assessment.* Canterbury: University of Kent at Canterbury.

Elwert, G. 1996. Kulturbegriffe und Entwicklungspolitik: Über soziokulturelle Bedingungen der Entwicklung. In G. Elwert and W. Rudolf (eds) *Kulturen und Innovationen: Festschrift für Wolfgang Rudolph* (pp. 51–87). Berlin.

Escobar, A. 1991. Anthropology and the development encounter: The making and marketing of development anthropology. *American Ethnologist* 18(4): 658–682.

Ferguson, J. 1990. *The Anti-politics Machine: 'Development', Depoliticization and Bureaucratic Power in Lesotho*. Cambridge: Cambridge University Press.

——. 1996. Development. In A. Barnard and J. Spencer (eds) *Encyclopaedia of Social and Cultural Anthropology* (pp. 154–160). London: Routledge.

Ferradás, C. 1998. Comment. *Current Anthropology* 39(2): 239–40.

Firth, R. 1939. An anthropologist's view of mass-observation. *Sociological Review* 31: 166–193.

Foucault, M. 1980. Truth and power. In C. Gordon (ed.) *Power/Knowledge: Selected Interviews and Other Writings, 1972–1977* (pp. 109–133). New York: Pantheon.

Freire, P. 1970. *Pedagogy of the Oppressed*. New York: Continuum.

Goebel, A. 1998. Process, perception and power: Notes from participatory research in a Zimbabwean resettlement area. *Development and Change* 29: 277–305.

Greaves, T. (ed.). 1994. *Intellectual Property Rights for Indigenous Peoples: A Source Book*. Oklahoma City: Society for Applied Anthropology.

Hall, B. 1981. Participatory research, popular knowledge and power. *Convergence* 14(3): 6–17.

Heidt, G. 1997. Ethnologen in der Auslandsmitarbeit des Deutschen Entwicklungsdienstes (DED). (Anthropologists within the cooperation programs of the German Development Service (DED)). *Entwicklungsethnologie* 6(2): 93–99.

Hess C. 1997. Becoming a development anthropologist. *Entwicklungsethnologie* 6(2): 77–92.

Hobart, M. (ed.) 1993. *An Anthropological Critique of Development: The Growth of Ignorance*. London: Routledge.

Holland, J. and J. Blackburn. 1998. *Whose Voice? Participatory Research and Policy Change*. London: IT Publications.

Holthusen, B. and I. Paulus. 1998. Ein Venn-Diagramm ist noch keine Lösung *DED-Brief* 4: 39–41.

Horowitz, M. 1994. Development anthropology in the mid-1990s. *Development Anthropology Network* 12(1–2): 1–14.

Huizer, G. 1989. *Action Research and People's Participation. An Introduction and Some Case Studies*. Third World Centre: Catholic University of Nijmegen.

Jain, S. 2000. An anthropologist's experience of working with development practitioners. Paper given at the ASA 2000 conference *Participating in Development*, 2–5 April 2000, SOAS, London.

Koepping, E. 1994. Trust and abuse in long-term fieldwork. *Anthropological Journal on European Cultures: Anthropology and Ethics* 3(2): 99–116.

Lindzey, G. 1961. *Projective Techniques and Cross-cultural Research*. New York: Appleton.

Long, N. and A. Long. 1992. *Battlefields of Knowledge: The Interlocking of Theory and Practice in Social Research and Development*. London: Routledge.

Malinowski, B. 1922. *Argonauts of the Western Pacific*. London: Routledge.

Marshall, T. H. 1937. Is mass-observation moonshine? *The Highway*, December, 48–50.

Mosse, D. 1994. Authority, gender and knowledge. Theoretical reflections on the practice of participatory rural appraisal. *Development and Change* 25: 497–525.

Nelson, N. and S. Wright (eds). 1995. *Power and Participatory Development. Theory and Practice.* London: Intermediate Technology.

Posey, D. A. 1998. Comment. *Current Anthropology* 39(2): 241–242.

Postel, S. 1999. *Pillar of Sand: Can the Irrigation Miracle Last?* New York: W.W. Norton and Co.

Pottier, J. (ed.). 1993. *Practising Development: Social Science Perspective.* London and New York: Routledge.

——. 1997. Towards an ethnography of participatory appraisal and research. In R. D. Grillo and R. L. Stirrat (eds) *Discourses of Development: Anthropological Perspectives* (pp. 203–227). Oxford and New York: Berg.

Read, C. H. 1906. Anthropology at the universities. *Man* 38: 56–59.

Rew, A. 1997. The donor's discourse: Official social development knowledge in the 1980s. In R. D. Grillo and R. L. Stirrat (eds) *Discourses in Development: Anthropological Perspectives* (pp. 81–106). Oxford and New York: Berg.

Richards, P. 1985. *Indigenous Agricultural Revolution: Ecology and Food-crop Farming in West Africa.* London: Hutchinson.

——. 1995. Participatory Rural Appraisal: A quick and dirty critique. *PLA Notes* 25: 13–16.

Rucht, D. 1982. *Planung und Partizipation: Bürgerinititativen als Reaktion und Herausforderung politisch-administrativer Planung.* Munich: Tuduv.

Rudqvist, A. 1991. Fieldwork methods for consultations and popular participation. PPP Working Paper no. 9. Stockholm: Development Studies Unit (DSU).

Said, A. A. (ed.). 1978. *Human Rights and World Order.* New York: Praeger.

Salmen, L. F. 1987. *Listen to the People: Participant-observer Evaluation of Development Projects.* New York: Oxford University Press.

Schönhuth M. 1994. *Participatory Rural Appraisal. Dokumentation einer Trainingswoche mit praktischem Anwendungsteil in einer mecklenburgischen Gemeinde.* GTZ, Gruppe 6013 Aus- und Fortbildung. Berichterstatter: Michael Schönhuth.

——. 1998a. Entwicklungsethnologie in Deutschland. Eine Bestandsaufnahme aus Sicht der AG Entwicklungsethnologie und ein Vergleich mit internationalen Entwicklungen. *Entwicklungsethnologie* 7(1): 11–39.

——. 1998b. Was ist des Menschen Recht? Ein ethnologischer Diskurs zum Universalitätsanspruch individueller Menschenrechte im globalen Dorf. In W. Berg (ed.) *Globalisierung und Modernisierung: Kräfte und Gegenkräfte, Ängste und Perspektiven* (pp. 37–47). SSIP texts no. 5. Hilden: SSIP.

Schönhuth M. and H. Müler. 1998. Capacity building for whom? Paths of learning within the Integrated Food Security Programme (IFSP) Rukwa, Tanzania. In R. Scherler, R. Forster, O. Karkoschka and M. Kitz (eds) *Beyond the Tool Kit: Experiences with institutionalizing participatory approaches of GTZ supported projects in rural areas* (pp. 113–131). Eschborn: GTZ.

Schönhuth, M., F. Bliss and S. Wentzel. 2001. *Ethical Guidelines of the Working Group Development Anthropology (AGEE e. V.): Explanations and Advice.* Trierer Materialien zur Ethnologie 3. Trier. See also http://www.uni-rier.de/uni/fb4/ethno/Leitlinien .pdf.

Schönhuth M., F. Kupper and D. Horn. 2000. *Hätt' ich Fliegel, würd ich nach Deutschland fliegen: Eine partizipative Feldstudie bei Angehörigen der deutschen Minderheit in einem sibirischen Dorf.* Trierer Materialien zur Ethnologie 1. Trier.

Scrimshaw, S. C. M. and E. Hurtado. 1987. *Rapid Assessment Procedures for Nutrition and Health Care: Anthropological Approaches to Improving Programme Effectiveness.* Tokyo: The United Nations University.

Seithel, F. 2000. *Von der Kolonialethnologie zur Advocacy Anthropology: Zur Entwicklung einer kooperativen Forschung und Praxis von Ethnologinnen und indigenen Völkern.* Münster: LIT.

Shah, P. and M. K. Shah. 1995. Participatory methods. Precipitating or avoiding conflict? *PLA Notes* 24: 48–51.

Shrijvers, J. 1995. Participation and power. A transformative feminist research perspective. In S. Wright and N. Nelson (eds) *Power and Participatory Development* (pp. 19–29). London: Intermediate Technology Publications.

Sillitoe, P. 1998a. The development of indigenous knowledge: A new applied anthropology. *Current Anthropology* 39(2): 232–252.

——. 1998b. What know natives? Local knowledge in development. *Social Anthropology* 6: 203–220.

Smith, S., D. G. Willms and N. A. Johnson (eds). 1997. *Nurtured by Knowledge: Learning to do Participatory Action Research.* Ottawa: IDRC.

Stocking, G. W. (ed.). 1983. *Observers Observed: Essays on Ethnographic Fieldwork.* Madison, WI: University of Wisconsin Press.

Strathern, M., M. Carneiro da Cuhna, P. Descola, C. Alberto Alfonso and P. Harvey. 1998. Exploitable knowledge belongs to the creators of it: A debate. *Social Anthropology* 6: 109–126.

Teves, L. B. 2000. Patron–client relationship and participation: The case of the Philippines. *Entwicklungsethnologie* 9(1): 43–59.

Ulbert, V. 1995. Erfahrungen mit partizipativen Erhebungsmethoden in der wissenschaftlichen Forschung und in der entwicklungspolitischen Praxis. *Entwicklungsethnologie* 4(2): 75–99.

UNESCO (World Commission on Culture and Development). 1995. *Our Creative Diversity: Report of the World Commission on Culture and Development.* Paris: UNESCO.

Van Willigen, J. 1993. *Applied Anthropology: An Introduction.* Westport, CT: Bergin and Garvey.

Van Willigen J. and T. L. Finan. 1991. Soundings: Rapid and reliable research methods for practising anthropologists. *Napa Bulletins,* 10.

Vokral, E. 1994. Partizipative Methoden und Gruppenzusammenhalt. Erfahrungen mit Frauen im Andenhochland Ecuadors. *Entwicklungsethnologie* 3(1): 26–45.

Woodford-Berger, P. 1996. Schweden: Sozial anthropologisches Fachwissen ist gefragt. *E+Z* 37(4): 116–118.

Wright, S. and N. Nelson. 1995. Participatory research and participant observation: Two incompatible approaches. In N. Nelson and S. Wright (eds) *Power and Participatory Development: Theory and Practice* (pp. 43–60). London: Intermediate Technology.

Chapter 8

Indigenous knowledge, power and parity

Models of knowledge integration

Trevor Purcell and Elizabeth Akinyi Onjoro

Responding to Sillitoe (1998a) on indigenous knowledge development as a 'new applied anthropology', Posey noted that 'there will be nothing "new" if we do not develop new methodologies for dialogue with local knowledge holders. And those will not emerge', he notes, 'until indigenous peoples have political and economic parity with development forces – and anthropologists' (1998: 241). This call for parity raises many questions, one of which is: how can indigenous peoples assert their traditional cultural values – which may promote a sort of minimalist, sustainable adjustment with their environment – and achieve economic and political parity with those dominating forces whose guiding values promote maximalist, unsustainable development? Parity, taken at face value, in a globalized world, must involve more equal relations with the local state, as well as with the international industrial order. Furthermore, given the nature of those relations, parity for indigenous peoples is likely to engender their sociocultural shift within the global political-economic hierarchy toward the state and the industrial West, rather than those entities (the West) shifting towards the position of the indigenous peoples. Were this to occur, political, and particularly economic, parity would seem to be counter-productive to the aims of the integration of indigenous knowledge,[1] given the nature of the structure of power relations within states and within the global community. Theoretically, parity would pull indigenous culture toward a Western, less sustainable way of life – against which most indigenous knowledge traditions position themselves.

One answer to this dilemma might be to define parity less in material (economic) terms and more according to political power, notably increased autonomy. Parity is seen as the ability of a group to make autonomous decisions about its future based on a set of principles derived from its own collective ontology – its own 'truth'. Local judgments about the integration of 'outside' knowledge must derive from people's understanding of the world rather than from imposed assumptions. Parity, in this sense, is inherent in self-determination and consistent with cultural relativity. Sidney Mintz once defined exploitation as the inability of a people to determine their life chances in accordance with their own culture (1961: 579–587). This notion of exploitation, doubtless, is cognizant of Karl Marx's idea of producers producing goods, but under conditions not of their own choosing. Parity, then, embodies, as a priority, the absence of cultural exploitation, and, of necessity, also control of the material means of existence.

In this sense, this chapter endorses Posey's call for parity. It advances a methodology to achieve parity in the integration of multiple, socially unequal knowledges in planned change (or development). It proposes a procedural model for knowledge integration, focusing on how knowledges are applied in a context of material and cultural inequality. However, since the analytical and theoretical literature on the use of indigenous knowledge in applied settings is in its infancy (Agrawal 1995a; Antweiler 1998; Béteille 1998; DeWalt 1994; Dove 1999; Purcell 1998; Sillitoe 1998a), we offer a brief comparative review of earlier model building efforts.

The chapter compares two models of knowledge integration which have emerged in recent years. We select a uniform set of comparative variables we consider crucial to equitable application of knowledges. Our model builds on earlier models, emphasizing problematic areas of integration overlooked by them. To that end, we explore two interlinked arenas in the struggle for equity in knowledge integration: the nature of legitimate knowledge, and the unequal power relations within which multiple knowledges function. We treat both problematic areas not only as essential to integration, but also as areas which must be addressed if social scientists are to engage our sceptical colleagues (natural as well as social scientists) in the debate about competing knowledges and their legitimacy.

Why problematize knowledge and power?

The epistemological and functional status of indigenous knowledge is an issue today not because it lacks recognition and value to its holders, but because it is under threat from Western scientific based knowledge and its supporting sociopolitical relations. An integral aspect of the competing scientific knowledge is its built-in claim to universal authority, and, by implication, the inferiority of traditional knowledge. It follows that indigenous knowledge finds itself in an epistemological power struggle. The struggle is dialectically linked to the material: indigenous communities have historically occupied positions of relative privation, and their desire for material 'improvement' has become a vehicle for the incursion of scientific and technological knowledge.

In the attempt to achieve parity, neither the proponents of scientific nor indigenous knowledge can ignore the cultural, material or epistemological basis of the other's knowledge. There is need for mutual understanding and change on both sides. The investigation of indigenous knowledge and outside knowledge with social-philosophical analytic concepts presents proponents of each with a discourse that is comprehensible to both. Scientists are likely to view large segments of indigenous knowledge as *beliefs*, not subject to the testing standards of legitimate knowledge. Many indigenous knowledge bearers, on the other hand, are likely to view scientific knowledge as 'truth', as a marker of modernity and civility, and therefore a necessary vehicle for 'development'. The perceptual rift must be made transparent and bridged if the unequal power between the two knowledge systems is to be reduced.

The literature considering integration of indigenous knowledge implicitly recognizes the attendant power relations. Nowhere, however, is it made central to the discourse. Yet the consequences of the unequal power relations that structure interactions between these knowledges touch on every aspect of planned social change. The social relations in which power inhere are often those between the representatives of indigenous knowledge and Western scientific knowledge – including outside funding agencies. But we must treat the power relations that enmesh project planning and implementation as part of the larger universe of unequal relations – which themselves are products of, and in turn reproduce, a defined, though relatively heterogeneous, universe of understanding: economic rationality and the treatment of nature as capital – hence the idea of 'development'.

The problem of knowledge integration occurs mainly in the context of development projects. And the notion of development[2] almost always involves inequality between those receiving development and those from which ideas about the process and goal emanate. It matters not whether the actors are insiders or outsiders – the movement from condition A, the need for development, to condition B, the achievement of development, involves a vector of change which presupposes improvement of condition A. In almost all cases in the modern world, the standard for B originates from outside the community, often from outside the country and culture. Indeed, the perceived need for development, as well as its achievement, is usually a function of social-political-economic forces which inhere in the local and the global relationship. But even if the perception of a need for development originates locally, the ideas about what is required typically have roots outside the local sociocultural context. Those who have been exposed to those ideas are perceived to be higher on the social scale than others. The link between the community and the origin of the development model defines the power scale, even if all the actors are local or indigenous. The development of casino gambling on several Native American reservations illustrates the point. The casino concept originates from outside the native community, and commonly there are factions who object to it, yet the deprivation experienced in such communities preconditions them to grant more power to those who bring increased material resources. The majority may benefit materially, but power relations are nevertheless expanded and intensified. This is exacerbated when the principal actors, such as casino managers, are outsiders. All planned change conceived of as development involves unequal power, and that power largely resides in control of the resources for change: knowledge and capital.

It stands to reason, given the embeddedness of inequality in the concept of development, that we should not take it for granted in social processes that involve knowledge integration. The mere integration of indigenous knowledge in the development process does not by itself lead to parity. We must problematize power in its manifold manifestations and make it transparent at all levels of planning and implementation. We propose two related strategies to accomplish this: (1) a context of discourse in which all stakeholders and knowledge representatives may be interrogated; and (2) the open interrogation of roles, to make transparent their biases.

Current models of integration

Early efforts to integrate indigenous knowledge in development form the foundation for what we do today (see, for example, Brokensha *et al.* 1980; Warren 1991a, 1991b). However, they betray the dominant influence of the paradigm that makes conscious, concerted knowledge integration necessary: that of development based on material maximization and technological modernization. They are biased toward the technical, the scientific, the efficient, that which advances the material (Bastien 1992; DeWalt 1994; Jordan 1997; Kurin 1983; Lemley 1999). We cannot say with confidence that advances made in recent years have permeated 'mainstream' applied social science (see Sillitoe, this volume). Indeed, there is not even a stable language of knowledge integration. Social scientists refer to the process in sundry ways: *incorporation* (Sillitoe 1998a), *blending* (DeWalt 1994; Millar 1999), *fruitful accommodation* (Jordan 1978), *articulation* (Bastien 1992), *integration* (Emery 2000; Lemley 1999; Ortiz 1999; Weil 2000), and *empathic learning and action* (Millar 1999). Nor have we agreed on the terminology for referring to the knowledges we consider (Antweiler 1998). Not surprisingly, knowledge integration – both planned and unplanned – has been a defining feature of colonialism, imposed in a context of domination. Current social science attempts represent a radical ideological and epistemological break with that tradition.

The models we review here have made some advances away from biases of technique and efficiency, towards a more phenomenological view of knowledge. The two models we review offer varying opportunities for generalization. They are the Emphatic Learning and Action (ELA) model (Millar 1999), and the IWCK model (Emery 2000) (acronym explained on p. 168). We use a set of eight criteria to assess each model, critically comparing the following: level of recognition/inclusion of indigenous communities; articulation of clear and encompassing goals and objectives; respect for cultural relativity and the promotion of self-determination; problematization of knowledge; promotion of bilateral transfer of knowledge; consideration of power relations; interrogation of the roles of project principals; and the generalizability of each model (see Table 8.2 below). Space limitations prohibit addressing each comparative criteria in as much detail as we would like.

Furthermore, this review has a built-in bias: it devotes essentially the same space to the ELA model, which is a sixteen-page article, as it does the IWCK model, which is a 159-page manual.

We limit our selection to two models which do not just document knowledge integration, but also consider general processes and procedures of integration. Our interest is not in particular projects, but in general models of the integration process. Although project principals have been integrating knowledges for many decades, they focus on the particulars of their own projects; they have not given much thought to generalized ways in which they carry out the process (see, for example, Bastien 1992; Haverkort and Hiemstra 1999; Whiteford et al. 1999).

The Emphatic Learning and Action (ELA) model

The Emphatic[3] Learning and Action model focuses on small-scale agriculture. Native Ghanian agronomist, David Millar, developed it in and for his own region. In spite of this narrow focus, the model is more paradigmatic than procedural, and therefore shows a high generalizability potential. ELA is based on a keen, intuitive understanding of cultural relativity in development, and a conviction that all indigenous knowledge (empirical knowledge, as well as beliefs) is essential to a sustainable world. Its key criteria implicitly grant local people broad scope for self-determination: bilateral transfers of knowledge in a context of mutual relative autonomy; recognition of differences in roles by gender; joint experimentation led by local 'cosmovision' (local cosmology, in a broad sense); in-depth study of local cosmovision; and development based in cosmovision and redistribution of power.

The goal of ELA is integrated change guided by the preservation of local culture, to be achieved through: (1) reconstruction of the local cosmovision; and (2) joint experimentation based on what local knowledge determines to be worthwhile. Millar does not only want indigenous people to be involved in all aspects of a project, he wants them to ' "process us" (outsiders) within their cosmovision' to determine if our presence is desirable (1999: 153). This position shows an appreciation for cultural relativity and the value of traditional epistemology – evidenced by its promotion of cosmovision as a set of ideals and understandings that define what is the 'social good'. But not all scientists share this understanding, and Millar fails to engage in discourse with sceptics.

To achieve the incorporation of outside knowledge, the model proposes a set of parallel, complementary processes of experimentation and 'dialogue platforms' rather than a synergetic integration (Figure 8.1). The drawback of the parallel framework is that it does not allow for a close, interrogative, ongoing interchange of knowledge that might, through engaging sceptics, attenuate the unequal relations that inhere in conventional integration processes. Isolating and interrogating each role might also help to address unequal relations, but the model does not directly address specific roles; it treats actors collectively, using terms such as 'they', 'we', 'them', etc. The only role bias recognized, implicitly, is that of the extension officer toward 'modern agriculture and extension methods'.

While the parallel framework of experimentation and intermittent dialogue may work in differing projects, it is doubtful that it is the most productive pathway to knowledge transfer and integration. Nevertheless, its key concepts go to the heart of issues involved in knowledge integration and its link to sustainability.

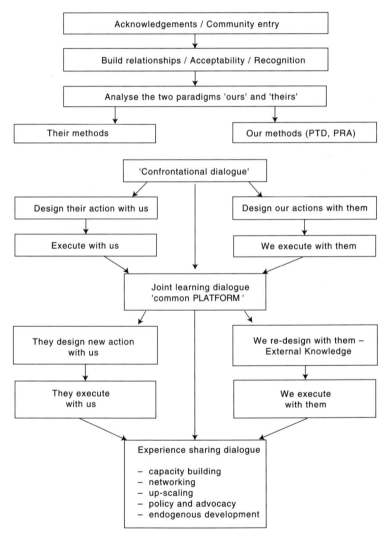

Figure 8.1   Emphatic Learning and Action
Source: Millar 1999

The International Labour Organization, World Bank, Canadian International Development Agency, KIVU Nature, Inc. (IWCK) Model

The IWCK model, referred to by its author as the 'Guidelines', is more comprehensive than its predecessors. The first draft, published in 1997, was developed for the World Council of Indigenous Peoples. The current version is jointly published by the International Labour Organization (ILO), the World Bank (WB), Canadian International Development Agency (CIDA), and KIVU Nature, Inc. – hence the acronym, IWCK (Emery 2000).

IWCK lists three broad goals: (1) all development initiatives should strive for sustainable projects; (2) all development projects should strive to benefit all; and (3) all development projects should strive to have the broadest possible knowledge base (Emery 2000: iv). Achievement of its goals is guided by a set of five principles, which, together, constitute its underlying conceptual framework. Foremost among these is the principle that indigenous people must be involved in all stages of planning and implementation to achieve sustainability. The model is distinguished for explicitly promoting integration within a framework of rights, guided by International Labour Organization Convention 169. IWCK's 'Best Practice Principles' for working with indigenous peoples make its position on recognition clear: gain indigenous people's consent; encourage them to choose their own representatives; include indigenous knowledge by including its 'holders' as part of the team of experts; and empower them (Emery 2000: 1).

The IWCK guidelines do not explore the concept of cultural relativity. They do, however, invoke the idea of *cultural integrity* in a manner that implies some appreciation for relativity. But such innovations alone do not provide adequate theoretical footing for full appreciation of the inherent conflict between cultural relativity and outside intervention. IWCK's author takes for granted that scientific and technical knowledge will pass into indigenous communities. The model, however, strives to ensure equity and respect for relativity. 'Traditional Guidelines' numbers 8 and 9 (Emery 2000: 77–81) suggest that indigenous people share traditional knowledge with outsiders but safeguard their rights. And 'Guidelines for Proponents' (pp. 82–107) suggest that outsiders 'work with indigenous experts as equals'.

In considering the nature of knowledge, IWCK suggests distinguishing between *ancient* and *modern* traditional knowledge – *ancient* is defined as that which has been 'passed down from generation to generation', and *modern* as 'that which has been acquired in present-day circumstances, and will be handed down in generations to come'. Ancient knowledge is said to be more spiritually oriented. A further distinction is made between spiritual knowledge – acquired through spiritual teachings – and empirical knowledge – acquired from experience. Spiritual aspects are non-scientific and 'cannot be tested' (Emery 2000: 77–78). The author notes that the distinction can lead to disagreements between science oriented actors and indigenous or local people, but fails to probe the implications of that disagreement for challenging power.

IWCK recognizes the absence of parity in the relations between indigenous people and some outside development forces, but it fails to analyse power relations. The guidelines aim to give indigenous groups 'empowerment' and 'individual rights', but the idea of A empowering B brings to mind the idea of A granting freedom to B. Nor does IWCK address roles in a manner that questions power relations. It lists four sets of 'Key Players' involved in development projects: government regulatory agencies; proponents of projects (which appears to mean international agencies); indigenous peoples and local communities; and non-governmental organizations (NGOs) (Emery 2000: 6). It does not explicitly suggest the interrogation of roles, but it offers specific guidelines to regulate the activities of the Key Players. There is, unfortunately, the assumption that projects originate from the outside, an assumption which casts local peoples as perhaps more dependent than they are. Nevertheless, the IWCK model is intended to apply to all types of projects which involve indigenous or local peoples, and in which unequal power relations are at work.

Towards a model of 'Equitable Integration' (EI)

Recent integration models have recognized some key conditions without which parity is unachievable. Yet, considerable weaknesses remain. The legacy of the perceived superiority of scientific knowledge lingers. Also, too much is taken for granted in two related, crucial areas of practice: relations of power and the nature of knowledge.

The model proposed in this chapter focuses on areas left unexplored by earlier ones. First, its procedural guidelines are based on a set of explicit theoretical and epistemological assumptions. Second, it suggests a strategy (which we call *contexts of planned discourse*) for the interrogation of roles and areas of responsibilities in the translation of indigenous and non-indigenous knowledges. Third, although interdisciplinary, this model explicitly privileges the ethnographer – as agent and facilitator.

Theoretical assumptions

Our first theoretical assumption addresses the conflict between cultural relativity and outside intervention (see Figure 8.2).[4] Although anthropologists who engage in applied work have not always recognized it, their work comes into direct conflict with the cherished idea of cultural relativity (Escobar 1995: 212–217; Hatch 1983). We acknowledge the idea as an unavoidable issue where planned social change involves outside agents. We do so, however, with the proviso that global political-economic processes mediate relativism in such a manner that the local culture has to find a sustainable social place in a world that features multiple knowledge systems. In such a context, local autonomy – cultural or otherwise – has its relativity already compromised by global forces. There are, therefore, firm grounds for the intervention of friendly outside knowledge brokers, as suppliers of information and material resources, and as co-interpreters of knowledge – indeed, as *real* collaborators.

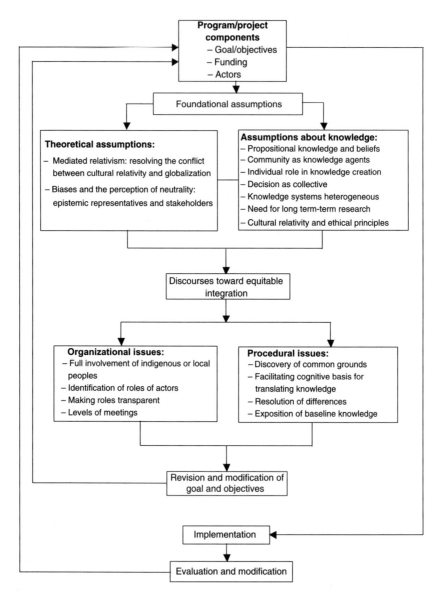

Figure 8.2   Schematic outline of the process of knowledge integration

We do not agree with scholars who argue that indigenous or local people should be left to figure things out on their own (Escobar 1995). Instead, we argue that they should be facilitated in making the best decisions they can, and that doing so requires, in most cases, in-depth knowledge of alternative strategies and of the wider world – information that outside collaborators have an ethical obligation to provide. In many situations, the outsider, especially the ethnographer with their cross-cultural knowledge and experience, is well positioned to expand on knowledge of outside alternatives which may affect a project. Many of the issues faced are likely to concern *ill-structured* problems (Turner 1989). Where such problems occur, the wider the information informing discourse and decision, the more viable the decisions. The decision as to whether local people should be left to their own devices should be theirs to make. Recognizing the central place of self-determination[5] to most indigenous groups' political stance, and their already compromised autonomy under globalization, we refer to our position as *mediated relativity*. We accept the intensified process of cultural hybridization as a given, but at the same time, underscore the right of indigenous peoples to the highest level of self-determination consistent with community viability under global conditions at any time.

Our second assumption addresses biases or subjectivities inherent in project actors' roles as agents and stakeholders. It also touches on misperceptions across epistemic borders. Hybrid knowledge must be produced by a syncretic community of *knowers*, in which all actors – funding agents, researchers, state representatives, etc. – are treated as representatives of knowledge systems (epistemic agents), in addition to being stakeholders. Both roles have their particular sets of biases, and these biases manifest themselves at different levels of social reality. The biases contained in the role of the expert, particularly the scientist's, are complex. Most 'outside' experts – scientists and non-scientists alike – are likely to base their expertise on one form or another of knowledge based in Western science, even if the basis derives from indirect exposure through Western-style education.

To begin with, local people – if less so the outside experts themselves – may innocently, but wrongly, assume a substantial degree of neutrality on the part of outside experts – as transmitters of 'objective' scientific knowledge. Many scientists may agree with that assumption, and the failure of a scientist to recognize the inherent biases in their position underscores the depth of that bias. Not only is science itself a cultural domain – a discourse, in Foucaultian language – with scientific and non-scientific values that its practitioners are inclined to deny, but by its nature it positions itself as the arbiter of 'truth' about the world. Furthermore, it buttresses its position by establishing purported universal criteria of exclusion-inclusion: examinations, certifications, institutionally legitimized employment, etc. As a standard of legitimate knowledge that has built a structure of self-protection, its practitioners are disposed to reject other knowledges that do not conform to its standards.

Perhaps the most ensnaring aspect of science is that indigenous people may be inclined to accept its position because of its universal status as *the* legitimate knowledge, rather than because of its truth value in local contexts (Jordan 1997).

There are biases inherent, too – although perhaps less beguiling – in the position of local epistemic representatives. Outsiders may assume local epistemic representatives to be acting selflessly in the interest of their community, mistakenly assuming the local community to be homogeneous. Communities are typically conflict ridden, although such conflicts may not be immediately evident to outsiders. Indeed, the prospect of 'development' may create new biases and conflicts. Viewed in terms of stakeholders, the bias in the role of the local actor is more obvious. It is commonsensical to assume that each individual will have some special stake. However, since both inside and outside epistemic representatives are also likely stakeholders, this further compromises their role as epistemic representatives. Indeed, there is an inherent conflict in the position of stakeholder versus epistemic representative. These built-in biases, stakes and conflicts make it necessary to provide a context during project planning and implementation in which all roles and positions can be made transparent, exposing conscious agendas (Sillitoe 1998a: 225) and unconscious biases. We outline ways in which this transparency can be achieved in what we call *contexts of planned discourse*.

Assumptions about knowledge

Aside from a few attempts at definitions, recent social science literature has largely neglected the question of whether indigenous knowledge meets standards of legitimacy set by Western epistemological canons. Common sense tells us that an adequate test of legitimacy is whether a knowledge system is effective. Yet, there are many sceptics in the scientific community and the public. As such, the question of legitimacy must be confronted in order to address sceptics and begin to set a basic foundation for common understanding (Agrawal 1995b; Sillitoe, this volume). As Nader (1996a: xi) points out, 'We need a perspective on how to regard different science traditions because public controversies over science should not be reduced to polemics.' The epistemological status of indigenous knowledge – often in relation to Western science-based knowledge – has been hotly debated for many decades, without resolution (Evans-Pritchard 1937, 1980; Horton 1967; Masola 1994; Nader 1996b; Tambiah 1990).

There is abundant evidence of indigenous knowledge of particular cultural domains which, although formed by worldviews that differ from that of conventional Western science, complements the largely theoretical literature on the debate and compares favourably with scientific standards. A small sampling of such domains include health (Adler 1999; Barsh 1997; Berlin 1995; Chapin 1994; Green 1999; Trotter and Chavira 1997), ecology and environment (Blackburn and Anderson 1993; Ellen *et al.* 2000; Granfelt 1999;

Posey *et al.* 1984; Posey 1999; Scott 1989), food and agriculture (Dove and Kammen 1997; Moock and Rhoades 1992; Rajasekaran and Whiteford 1993; Warren 1993; Warren *et al.* 1989), ethnopharmacology (Elizabetsky 1986; Etkin 1986, 1994; Stoffle *et al.* 1999), agronomy (Dove 1999; Kurin 1983; Msanya *et al.* 1998; Sandor and Furbee 1996; Sillitoe 1998b), astronomy (Goodenough 1953, 1996) and disaster management (Hassan 2000). Further, anthropologists have made respectable gains in mapping expert systems in indigenous knowledge (Benfer *et al.* 1991; Furbee 1989; Reed and Behrens 1989; Schoenhoff 1993) and ethnomathematics (Ascher 1990; Eglash 1997).

It is worth reiterating that the Western bias towards scientific knowledge as the *a priori* standard for all 'true' knowledge is as old as science itself. This notion of knowledge, which relegates much of indigenous oral tradition to the status of beliefs, has increasingly been challenged in anthropology (Claeson *et al.* 1996; Dove 1996; Nader 1996b; Pfaffenberger 1992; Sayer 1984; Sillitoe 1998a, this volume; Turnbull 2000). It has been challenged perhaps even more vigorously by feminist and African philosophers (Alcoff and Potter 1993; Harding 1991, 1993; Keita 1985; Masola 1994; Wiredu 1980). Feminist philosophers Dalmiya and Alcoff (1993), for example, have convincingly argued for new epistemological standards of justification that admit traditional knowledge as legitimate knowledge – building on ideas such as Ryle's (1949) concept of the cognitive process as a *capacity* or *disposition*, Nagel's (1979) idea of *point of view* and Harding's (1993) *stand point theory*. For their part, African philosophers have challenged ossified views of Africa, and by implication, conventional Western views of all oral traditional knowledge. They have mobilized, with different results, the concepts of *rationality, transla-tion, relativism* and *commensurability* to challenge an epistemology based on a non-contextual, universal logic of cause and effect, scientifically discoverable. In its place, some Anglophone African scholars offer a relativistic under-standing based on the distinction between knowledge (amenable to analytic causal logic) and beliefs (or *theory*) needing no external validation (contextual and internally consistent with starting premise(s)). They argue that both knowledge and theory are complementary. According to Masola (1994: 146), Francophone scholars, on the other hand, take a phenomenological approach, treating systems of thought and utterances as discourse. With few exceptions, both groups conclude that whether divided into knowledge and beliefs or not, such systems of thought form a whole that is necessary to practical life.

For our purpose, we will treat indigenous knowledge as a phenomenolog-ical whole, historically/culturally contingent, internally logical, and relative. The following points are central to our model's conception of knowledge:

1   Indigenous knowledge is taken to include propositional knowledge (which is accessible through representation) as well as beliefs and taken-for-granted understandings. By beliefs and understandings we are referring to that body of historically evolved assumptions and statements that Heidegger

refers to as the collective being, which informs social action, but which cannot be observed, only inferred. This knowledge includes theological and cosmological *beliefs* that can be justified according to some epistemological canons (such as *standpoint epistemology* – Dalmiya and Alcoff 1993), but not necessarily by empirical scientific methods. It forces the ethnographer to go beyond technical knowledge to consider the body of unobservable knowledges that informs group and individual self-definition and social action.

2   Single individuals (researchers, state representatives, etc.) involved in a social change project are infrequently *primary* producers of knowledge. The individual is merely a representative of a community of knowledge; it is the community that is the primary producer of knowledge.

3   The individual may be an agent (or producer) of knowledge under specific conditions: for example, when an individual persuades the collectivity to act on his/her unique interpretation of reality – to the good or detriment of the collectivity. The relationship of each individual to a project must therefore be open to challenge.

4   The second point logically implies that decisions regarding the process and product of integration should rest with a community rather than with individuals.

5   Local knowledge systems and their embodying communities are not typically homogeneous, even though project goals may be based on consensus. We should therefore anticipate competing and/or conflicting knowledge domains within a culture. Conflict resolution, then, must be a central part of knowledge integration.

6   The above points suggest that, ideally, knowledge integration should be based on long-term research with the beneficiary population. Research is frequently shortened in the interest of containing cost and conforming to politically imposed time objectives. Two strategies to counter this are: (1) engage the services of ethnographers who have prior in-depth research experience in the population; and (2) ensure *full* participation (if not leadership) of indigenous people.

7   The concept of cultural relativity implies that universal objectivity in dealing with human knowledge and social adjustment is not possible, arguments about cultural universals notwithstanding (Wiredu 1996). Each culture constructs its own standards. Therefore, decisions about project goals should be fully consistent with locally defined, moral and ethical standards.

Treating project actors as stakeholders and community representatives

Since different knowledge systems as well as different group and individual interests presuppose the likelihood of conflicting goals and methods, we need to devise an organized *context of discourse* to promote resolution. This may be achieved through planned democratic workshop-like forums in which epistemic representatives expose and interrogate specific issues.[6] The planned discourse is based on the recognition that project planning and implementation occur in contexts of evident, as well as hidden, power relations, and that such contexts can be arenas for the further production and reproduction of relations of power – in Foucault's (1980) terms, the context of the 'how' of power. The process of planned discourse has three objectives: (1) to sift out 'truth' from the relations of hegemony and thereby foster less unequal knowledge integration; (2) to expose power relations and biases, and thereby facilitate empowerment; and (3) to resolve conflicts that are developed or are uncovered by objectives 1 and 2 (Sillitoe 2000; Warner and Jones 1998).

In the following section we suggest a number of phases in establishing *contexts of planned discourse* (see Figure 8.2). In conceptualizing the phases and their content, we recognize that project organization may range from simple, locally conceived and funded projects to complex, internationally funded ones. Implementation must therefore be case-specific.

Penetrating power: contexts of planned discourse (COPD)

COPD 1: organizational issues

The contexts of planned discourse call for democratic workshop-like gatherings to discuss and challenge all actors, plans, goals, objectives, positions, and assumptions. Organizational issues may include but are not limited to:

A   A project idea or plan may originate from indigenous people or from 'outsiders'. Regardless of its origin, all epistemic representatives should have the opportunity to be involved at all levels of planning and implementation.

B   Indigenous representatives should be encouraged to freely critique and interrogate all aspects of the plan as well as the positions of other representatives – even though conflicts will likely be exposed.

C   All goals and objectives should be identified to the satisfaction of all representatives.

D   Systematically expose (i.e. make transparent) the following through discourse:[7]

   1   What does each representative know about the other representatives' cultural knowledge relevant to the project (e.g. if the project aims to reduce infant malnutrition the questions that might be posed, as a starting point, might pertain to what foods each culture considered appropriate for infants?);

2   The professional and relevant personal and employment background of each representative;

3   The representatives' personal interests, if any, in the project, using a simple neutrality-stake index (e.g. the interests of local community members differ vastly from those of the paid consultants);

4   The potential benefit of a project to epistemic representatives and/or employers, the community, or the country;

5   The funding and accounting processes.

E   Identify the roles of epistemic representatives (i.e., those stakeholder-knowers who represent bodies of knowledge) with their position in the project and their respective occupational, professional, and cultural groups.

Table 8.1 and the section 'Roles and their definitions' represent a guideline and explanations of some of the key considerations. The specifics of each cell in the table, or the number of categories and content of information, will vary with the specific project. The table represents only a partial list of the possible actors and roles that may be involved in a project.

Roles and their limitations

Funding agencies   Funding agencies are prime determinants of project outcomes, constituting the senior in the unequal relations that characterize projects. How their representatives perceive the project community is crucial. Yet, in many cases, funding representatives have no direct contact with or knowledge of the target community. The probability of funding representatives being available to participate in the context of planned discourse depends on many factors, the most obvious of which are whether funding is local or international and the cost of participation. This will, in turn, affect the degree of knowledge and appreciation funders have of local conditions, and the influence they have on the outcome.

Whether funding is public (i.e. state controlled) or private is important. Public funding agencies, while they may be relatively strict regarding their criteria of qualification for funding, may assume a more detached role regarding project planning and implementation. Such agencies may allow greater autonomy to social scientists, other professionals and community representatives.

The local representatives   When a project proposal originates from the 'outside', an important first task is the identification of indigenous representatives. This is a delicate endeavour, for in an heterogeneous local community a careless choice could cause or exacerbate conflict. We endorse the suggestions proffered in the IWCK guidelines discussed earlier. Perhaps the single most

Table 8.1   Project actors' roles and their limitations

Representative/actors	Roles	Primary limitations
Indigenous representative(s) – may be socially homogeneous or heterogeneous depending on the project	• Conveyer of local knowledge • Experiential knower • Articulator of local needs • Definer of moral basis for action • Student of non-local knowledge and alternative changes • State-community broker	• May not have adequate knowledge of non-local influences on project • Limited knowledge of alternative change models • Difficulty of transcending local cultural biases
Ethnographer(s) – may differ with respect to class and nationality from locals	• Propositional knower of local culture • Experiential knower of non-local culture • Interpreter/mediator between local and non-local epistemic representatives • Facilitator of indigenous/local people's understanding of implications of and alternatives to carrying out plan in the context of global conditions	• Knowledge of indigenous/local people may be largely propositional • Difficulty of transcending own cultural knowledge • Ethnographic time constraints • Limited independence from employer and/or funding agency
Non-ethnographic scientist(s) – may differ with respect to class and nationality from locals	• Conveyer of scientific research • Experiential knower of science culture • Collaborator with ethnographer in knowledge translation and integration • Collaborator with ethnographer as mediator	• May be accepting of unequal power between scientific and non-scientific knowledge • May not recognize the cultural embeddedness of knowledge • May not understand or support cultural relativity
Govt. representative(s) – multi-levelled: - international - national - regional - local	• Representative of state's interest • Interpreter of state policy • Student of local culture (ideally)	• Livelihood depends intimately on carrying out state interests • Potential incompatibility between political imperatives and indigenous or local needs
Funding representative(s): - international - national - regional - local - private or public	• Funding organization-community mediator • Interpreter of funding policy • Student of local culture	• Standard of success/progress may differ radically from that of local group • Inadequate knowledge of project goals and temporal frame of IP (indigenous people) • Biased towards cost efficiency
NGO - international - national - regional - local	• Will depend on type of NGO and should be determined case by case	• Limitations will depend on NGO type and role

empowering suggestion is that indigenous people should select their own representatives, using their own methods. To the extent that outsiders partici-pate in the selection process, two cautions are in order. First, it should be recognized that the indigenous representative is a potent agent of cultural and structural transformations, some of which will be unintended. Second, outside experts should be careful not to have unrealistic expectations of indigenous representatives – they should be aware of the boundaries of their expertise and experience.

The ethnographer   The ethnographer, assuming the role of *broker*, should make all efforts to ensure the participation of indigenous people in as much planning and implementation as possible. Achievement of these goals depends on numerous factors: the degree to which planning takes place locally; coordi-nation among local representatives and other project principals; the time frame allowed for project preparation and implementation; and the availability of funds and other facilities to allow for effective contexts of planned discourse.

Typically, the ethnographer may be the only epistemic representative who is not a direct stakeholder and who is trained to reach for cultural objectivity. Training, however, tempers biases; it does not remove them. And to the extent that the ethnographer is pursuing a career, earning a livelihood and advance-ment, the ethnographer is an indirect stakeholder. Yet, they are still likely to: (1) be the most neutral participant; (2) have the greatest command of both local and outside knowledges; and (3) be best able to mediate the knowledge (and other) conflicts. Where the political climate allows, the ethnographer should expect to play key mediatory roles between the following: funding agency and local people; funding agency and local government representa-tive(s); other scientists and the local people; and between the government representatives and local people. A project's methodology will require consid-eration of the knowledge and wishes of local people, but government representatives or funders may not support this requirement. It is the duty of the ethnographer to assist in *negotiating* the terms of the methodology.

The conventional role of the ethnographer is to gather information. But another important role – especially if the ethnographer is from or was trained in the West – is to inform locals regarding 'outside world' social, political and economic forces and processes which may impinge on planning, implementa-tion and long-term viability. If local peoples are to make the best decision they can, then they must have adequate information about the globalized world in which they participate with ever-greater intensity. The role of the ethnographer should not be simply to obtain but also to impart information. Typically, in addition, the ethnographer should strive to ensure effective steps be taken towards equity in knowledge integration. This includes responsibility for taking the 'local' to the 'outside', that is to funders, state representatives and so on (Whiteford, pers. comm.).

Government representative(s)   Representative(s) of government within whose jurisdiction a project falls may have a sincere interest in the welfare of the indigenous population. Simultaneously, they represent state, regional and/or local government interests – carrying out what Foucault (1980: 92–98) calls the 'King's right'. Multiple government representatives may be involved at multiple levels: international, national, regional or local. And funding agency and government representatives may be the same individual(s) in cases where a project is state-funded. The complex logistics of arranging for a government representative to engage in discourse with indigenous people may be daunting, and in some cases impossible. The government–indigenous relationship may potentially, if not actually, involve conflict, but it is crucial. Understanding between the two is imperative for long-term viability.

Non-governmental organizations (NGOs)   Since NGOs, as interest groups, are so varied ideologically, politically and economically, it is difficult to generalize about their role in projects. What they do, and the limitations inherent in their role(s), should be determined case by case, consistent with this model's general principles. It should be recognized that non-governmental, as well as governmental representatives, might be innocently inclined to favour science and thereby devalue indigenous knowledge.

COPD 2: discovering grounds for common understanding

Much frustration and many failures originate with the inability to find common ground on which to build mutual understanding (Sillitoe 2000). One way to begin bridging the cross-knowledge communication gap is to identify common (and in the process, also unique) elements of knowledge relevant to the project. For example, in evaluating soil and land resources among the Wola of the Southern Highlands Province of Papua New Guinea, Sillitoe (1998b) observed that the Wola use soil classification terms which, with caution, could be correlated or matched with US Department of Agriculture (USDA) and Food and Agriculture Organization (FAO) categories (i.e. in a Western soil sciences manner). The recognition of correlatable (if not commensurate) categories might be a good place to begin the discourse about common knowledge. However, as Sillitoe demonstrates, it would be misleading to stop there, for this surface appearance of common knowledge rests on a differing deeper cultural understanding which has political ramifications. The Wola soil categories are discontinuous representations of soil types with no concept of classes that relate to one another sequentially as in Western soil profiles. This discontinuous representation is, according to Sillitoe, related to the Wola 'aggressively egalitarian' sociopolitical organization (1998b: 190–91). Here, we have an example of areas of commonality embedded in a unique cultural context.

COPD 3: facilitating understanding and resolving differences

Scientists trained in one discipline often have difficulty communicating their ideas to those trained in others (DeWalt 1994: 129; Nader 1996a). Achieving understanding between scientists and people with minimal or no formal education is even more difficult. It is particularly important to identify outside knowledge that matches no similar pre-existing knowledge in the community and work to facilitate its understanding and integration. For example, in implementing an Integrated Pest Management programme among farmers plagued by Andean potato weevil and potato tuber moth in the Peruvian Andes, the limitations of pre-existing knowledge of biological principles caused confusion among farmers when presented with scientific information about pest propagation. They thought that the larvae and adult weevil were different insects (Ortiz 1999). The ethnographer (using knowledge of both science and local culture) and other scientists have a duty to supply the necessary background information to render knowledge comprehensible across discipline and cultural boundaries, i.e. to facilitate cognitive participation.

The Indu Basin Master Planning Project's (IBMPP) attempt to increase rice and wheat production in Pakistan's Indu Basin is instructive here (Kurin 1983). Project planners introduced high yielding variety (HYV) wheat and rice to be cultivated with technology available under the Green Revolution scheme. A survey soon showed that the plan was not achieving near its potential. As part of their cosmology, Chakpuri farmers classify all material objects according to the Greco–Arabic humoral system, attributing qualities or dispositions of *hot, cold, dry, wet* and *moderate* to all things in nature. In this system, all life can exist only if the proper balance of innate hot/dry and cold/wet occur. As it turns out, the farmers thought that conditions the IBMPP specified for HYV cultivation, based on the use of organophosphate fertilizers and piped (as opposed to well) water, were generating excess heat, thereby depleting the soil and resulting in less nutrition per unit than their native seeds and methods. Clearly, had the project principals been familiar with Chakpuri cosmology, they could have supplied strains of HYV seeds perceived as cooler and wetter, promoting a higher adoption rate.

Where knowledge incompatibility poses problems, we suggest the following steps:

1   The ethnographer should adopt the role of mediator/translator, using concrete ethnographic examples to illustrate points (e.g. acting as the link between empirical knowledge and cosmology, or to drive home points regarding cultural relativity and its implications for social change).

2   To facilitate cross-cultural understanding, substitute local understandings (not just terminology) for scientific ones where both refer to the same phenomenon. For example, the Luo of southern Kenya recognize a

condition in pregnant women called *rariuw*, characterized by pain in the lower back and abdomen (Onjoro 2001). They therefore successfully treat it with indigenous medicine. Biomedical medicine, however, recognizes no such illness. In such cases, clinicians should be cognizant of the native diagnosis so that they can refer patients to native healers.

3   Assess whether local understanding of phenomenon and/or solution of a problem is more consistent with project goals than a 'scientific' understanding.

4   Compare goals in relation to non-local and local cultural/moral imperatives (e.g. the IBMPP plan to increase production of high yield rice among Punjabis was consistent with the wishes of the national government, the scientists involved and perhaps even some farmers, but the majority were not willing to jeopardize the long-term viability of the soil, their idea of sound nutrition and their cosmology to achieve increased production: Kurin 1983).

5   Resolution of differences in understanding – as well as in other areas of conflict – should not exclusively concern the technical requirements of the project. Resolution will often require what Sillitoe (2000: 6) calls 'knowledge negotiation'. Priority should be given to the cultural and moral dictates and rights of the indigenous population, in keeping with the provisions of International Labour Organization Convention 169.

COPD 4: evaluating the project plan's progress, revising and proceeding to implementation

Discourses towards the resolution of organizational, procedural, and epistemological problems will lead to modification of the original project plan (see Figure 8.2). The logistics of modification will vary. All project epistemic representatives should have an opportunity to ratify the revised plans and make last-minute reflections. It is necessary to convene one or more fora to discuss the end product. The ethnographer, as mediator/facilitator, plays a key role.

Conclusion

At this early stage in the advancement of systematic knowledge integration, no single model will fulfil all the needs of practitioners. Emphatic Learning and Action (ELA), the IWCK guidelines, and our Equitable Integration (EI) are not the only models that address multiple knowledge integration; but others focus on specific limited areas of practice (see, for example, Bastien 1992; Haverkort and Hiemstra 1999; Whiteford *et al.* 1999). The proposed EI model addresses areas not explored by others; it stresses the importance of making transparent the power relations that surround knowledge, employing particularly the stratagems of interrogating roles in contexts of planned

discourse. It endorses the importance ELA places on a holistic, phenomenological view of knowledge to guide locally appropriate sustainable social
change, and the specificity and thoroughness of the IWCK guidelines.

Of the three models, the conceptual contours of ELA and EI are most
similar. The EI model, like the ELA, calls for structured discourse between
representatives of outside and inside knowledges. It expects interaction
between epistemic representatives at all phases of planning, implementation
and evaluation. The special *contexts of discourses* interrogate roles, ideas, interests, etc. One noteworthy difference between EI and ELA is that EI calls for
continuous discourse and interaction while ELA suggests parallel, discontinuous processes of experimentation with intervals of dialogue (see Figure 8.1).

Table 8.2 provides a rated comparison of the models by eight key criteria
of integration. The models vary in how they treat them. The rating scale is
1–5, with 5 the highest. The scale is subjective, but may serve as a rough-and-
ready guide for project planners.

The pioneer efforts in knowledge integration have emphasized what
Brokensha *et al.* (1980) have called 'indigenous technical knowledge' rather
than indigenous knowledge, broadly defined. They gave scant attention to
power issues and, of equal importance, what David Millar (1999) so aptly calls
cosmovision – the local view of the good society. Consideration of power and
cosmovision suggest alternatives to unsustainable development. The focus on
the technical, the efficient misses the more profound implications of knowledge integration as a strategy for social change. Beyond efficiency, technically
conceived, there is the more encompassing issue of the maintenance of an
inhabitable planet, which is not merely a technical issue. We must allow space
for other ethical and philosophical knowledges to question the scientific,
technological and political-economic practices which have brought us to our
current crisis. In other words, there must be room for alternative conceptions
of the world and how we live in it.

Table 8.2 Comparison of models using eight criteria of integration

Comparative criteria of integration	Models and their rating		
	ELA	IWCK	EI
Recognition/inclusion of indigenous community	5	5	5
Clear encompassing goals and objectives	2	5	3
Respect for cultural relativity and self-determination	4	5	5
Problematization of knowledge	2	3	5
Bilateral transfer of knowledge	4	3	4
Consideration of power relations	2	2	4
Definition and interrogation of roles	2	3	5
Generalizability of model	2	5	5

Radical alternative understandings can occur only through the preservation of a diversity of knowledges that maintain their integrity. In evolutionary terms, this epistemic diversity may be correlated with ecological diversity, thereby opening our eyes to the fact that just as the health of the planet depends on the preservation of ecological diversity, its sociopolitical health depends on epistemic diversity. Other knowledges raise questions and suggest answers in the form of alternative modes of existence. They do not exist as purely technical formations but as part of entire cultural heritages. Aside from respect for cultural diversity, aside from the desire for efficiency, and aside from the desire for achieving epistemic equity, we see integration posing critiques of dominant but destructive modes of existence and reviving practices which can ensure a sustainable and humane future.

Notes

1   The term 'indigenous' has different meanings to different scholars (Purcell 1998; Semali and Kincheloe 1999; Sillitoe 1998a; DeWalt 1994). We use 'indigenous' here in accordance with the definition sketched by Purcell (1998). He defines the term as the product of a particular historical moment, and, for the purpose of study, makes a distinction between *indigenous people* and *indigenous knowledge*. The new social science centred around the study and application of indigenous knowledge, the *indigenous perspective*, now addresses the way we treat planned social change not just among indigenous people but also among local people in communities which may not qualify as indigenous under certain definitions. We therefore use the terms 'indigenous' and 'local' here to reflect that reality, and we often combine them in the form, *indigenous/local*. We should also note that we have deliberately avoided use of the word 'development', because of its less than laudable historical and ideological legacy. We have chosen to use the term *planned social change* instead.

2   We use the term development here in the conventional sense, meaning growth or 'improvement' in economic, technological, social institutional conditions. We recognize, however, that in recent years the concept has taken on a more humanitarian meaning (i.e. attention to social, cultural and spiritual needs), in recognition of the failure of earlier processes of development to address local, culturally defined goals.

3   Called 'emphatic' because the 'outside' project principals assumed a posture of empathy in relation to local culture.

4   We do not explicitly discuss every cell or every item in each cell of Figure 8.2. Those cells and items not specifically addressed are self-explanatory in the context of the chapter.

5   Self-determination is at times reconceptualized by some activists as *reconciliation* (*Cultural Survival* 1999).

6   We suggest using the concept of *discourse* for such forums because it embodies the idea of critical, even irreverent interrogative discussions that lead to change in ways that workshops – very domesticated, hierarchical contexts – do not.

7   The idea of interrogating the various representatives was inspired by anthropologist Kay Warren's experience with a Mayan linguistic workshop in Guatemala in 1989, in which Mayans, who were building an indigenous Pan Mayan movement towards relative autonomy, raised disturbing questions regarding Warren's motives (see Warren 1998: Appendix 2).

Bibliography

Adler, S. R. 1999. Complementary and alternative medicine use among women with breast cancer. *Medical Anthropology Quarterly* 13(2): 214–222.

Agrawal, A. 1995a. Indigenous and scientific knowledge: Some critical comments. *Indigenous Knowledge and Development Monitor* 33(3): 3–6.

——1995b. Dismantling the divide between indigenous and scientific knowledge. *Development and Change* 26: 413–439.

Alcoff, L. and E. Potter. 1993. *Feminist Epistemologies.* London and New York: Routledge.

Antweiler, C. 1998. Local knowledge and local knowing: An anthropological analysis of contested 'cultural products' in the context of development. *Anthropos* 93: 469–94.

Ascher, M. 1990. *Ethnomathematics: A Multicultural View of Mathematical Ideas.* Pacific Grove, CA: Brooks/Cole.

Barsh, R. 1997. The epistemology of traditional healing systems. *Human Organization* 56(1): 28–37.

Bastien, J. W. 1992. *Drum and Stethoscope: Integrating Ethnomedicine and Biomedicine in Bolivia.* Salt Lake City: University of Utah Press.

Benfer, R. A., E. E. Brent Jr and L. Furbee. 1991. *Expert systems. Newbury Park.* London: Sage.

Berlin, E. A. 1995. Aspects of fertility regulation among the Aguaruna Jívaro of Peru. In L. F. Newman and J. M. Nyce (eds) *Women's Medicine: A Cross-cultural Study of Indigenous Fertility Regulation* (pp. 125–146). New Brunswick: Rutgers University Press.

Béteille, A. 1998. The idea of indigenous people. *Current Anthropology* 39(2): 187–189.

Blackburn, T. C. and K. Anderson. 1993. *Before the Wilderness: Environmental Management by Native Californians.* Menlo Park: Ballena Press.

Brokensha, D., D. M. Warren and O. Werner. 1980. *Indigenous Knowledge Systems and Development.* Lanhan: University Press of America.

Chapin, M. 1994. Recapturing the old ways: Traditional knowledge and Western science among the Kuna Indians of Panama. In C. D. Kleymeyer (ed.) *Cultural Expression and Grassroots Development: Cases from Latin America and the Caribbean* (pp. 83–101). Boulder, CO: Lynne Reinner Publishers, Inc.

Claeson, B., E. Ahern, W. Richardson, M. Schoch-Spana and K. Taussig. 1996. Scientific literacy, what it is, why it's important, and why scientists think we don't have it: The case of immunology and the immune system. In L. Nader (ed.) *Naked Science: Anthropological Inquiry into Boundaries, Power, and Knowledge* (pp. 101–116). New York: Routledge.

Cultural Survival. 1999. *Visions of the Future: The Prospect for Reconciliation.* Cambridge: Cultural Survival.

Dalmiya, V. and L. Alcoff. 1993. Are 'old wives tales' justified? In L. Alcoff and E. Potter (eds) *Feminist Epistemologies* (pp. 127–244). New York and London: Routledge.

DeWalt, B. R. 1994. Using indigenous knowledge to improve agriculture and natural resource management. *Human Organization* 53(2): 123–131.

Dove, M. R. 1996. Process versus product in Bornean augury: A traditional knowledge system's solution to the problem of knowing. In R. E. and K. Fukui (eds) *Redefining Nature, Culture and Domestication* (pp. 557–596). Washington, DC: Berg Publishers.

——. 1999. The agronomy of memory and the memory of agronomy: Ritual conservation of archaic cultigens in contemporary farming systems. In V. Nazarea (ed.)

Ethnoecology: Situated Knowledge, Located Lives (pp. 45–70). Tucson, AZ: University of Arizona Press.

Dove, M. R. and D. M. Kammen. 1997. The epistemology of sustainable resource use: Managing forest products, swiddens, and high-yielding variety crops. *Human Organization* 56(1): 91–102.

Eglash, R. 1997. When math worlds collide: Intention and invention in ethnomathematics. *Science, Technology & Human Values* 22(1): 79–98.

Elizabetsky, E. 1986. New directions in ethnopharmacology. *Journal of Ethnobiology* 6: 121–128.

Ellen, R. F., P. Parkes and A. Bicker (eds). 2000. *Indigenous Environmental Knowledge and its Transformations*. Amsterdam: Harwood Academic.

Emery, A. 2000. *Integrating Indigenous Knowledge in Project Planning and Implementation*. Ontario: KIVU Nature, Inc.

Escobar, A. 1995. *Encountering Development: The Making and Unmaking of the Third World*. Princeton, New Jersey: Princeton University Press.

Etkin, N. L. (ed.). 1986. *Plants in Indigenous Medicine and Diet: Behavioral Approaches*. Bedford Hills, NY: Redgrave Publishing Co.

——. 1994. *Eating on the Wild Side: The Pharmacologic, Ecologic, and Social Implications of Using Noncultigens*. Tucson, AZ: University of Arizona Press.

Evans-Pritchard, E. E. 1937. *Witchcraft, Oracles and Magic Among the Azande*. London: Oxford University Press.

——. 1980. (1965) *Theories of Primitive Religion*. Oxford: The Clarendon Press.

Foucault, M. 1980. *Power and Knowledge: Selected Interviews and Other Writings, 1972–1977*. New York: Pantheon Books.

Furbee, L. 1989. A folk expert system: Soils classification in the Colca Valley, Peru. *Anthropological Quarterly* 62(2): 83–102.

Goodenough, W. H. 1953. *Native Astronomy in the Central Carolinas*. Philadelphia, PA: University Museum, University of Pennsylvania.

Goodenough, W. H. 1996. Navigation in the western Carolines: A traditional science. In L. Nader (ed.) *Naked Science: Anthropology Inquiry into Boundaries, Power, and Knowledge* (pp. 29–42). New York: Routledge.

Granfelt, T. (ed.). 1999. *Managing the Global Environment: Local Strategies to Secure Livelihoods*. London: Intermediate Technologies Publications.

Green, E. C. 1999. *Indigenous Theories of Contagious Disease*. Walnut Creek, CA: Altamira.

Harding, S. 1991. *Whose Science? Whose Knowledge?* Ithaca, New York: Cornell University Press.

——. 1993. Rethinking standpoint epistemology: What is strong objectivity? In L. Alcoff and E. Potter (eds) *Feminist Epistemologists* (pp. 49–82). New York and London: Routledge.

Hassan, S. 2000. Indigenous disaster management culture: A comparative study between the cyclone affected people of Bangladesh and Japan. Paper presented at the Association of Social Anthropologists Conference 2000, London, February.

Hatch, E. 1983. *Culture and Morality: The Relativity of Values in Anthropology*. New York: Columbia University Press.

Haverkort, B. and W. Hiemstra (eds). 1999. *Food for Thought: Ancient Visions and New Experiments of Rural People*. London: Zed Books.

Horton, R. 1967. African traditional religion and Western science. *Africa* 37(1&2): 50–71; 155–187.

Jordan, B. 1997. Authoritative knowledge and its construction. In R. E. Davis-Floyd and C. F. Sargent (eds) *Childbirth and Authoritative Knowledge* (pp. 55–88). Berkeley: University of California Press.

Jordan, B. 1978. *Birth In Four Cultures: A Cross-cultural Investigation of Childbirth in Yucatan, Holland, Sweden and the United States.* Canada: Eden Press.

Keita, L. 1985. Contemporary African philosophy. *Praxis International* 5(2 July): 145–161.

Kurin, R. 1983. Indigenous agronomics and agricultural development in the Indus Basin. *Human Organization* 42(4): 283–294.

Lemley, B. 1999. Alternative medicine. *Discover* August: 56–63.

Masola, D. A. 1994. *African Philosophy in Search of Identity.* Bloomington and Indianapolis, Indiana: Indiana University Press.

Millar, D. 1999. When the spirits speaks. In B. Haverkort and W. Hiemstra (eds) *Food for Thought: Ancient Visions and New Experiments of Rural people* (pp. 139–154). Leusden and London: Zed Books.

Mintz, S. W. 1961. Review article: Elkings, Stanley's slavery. *American Anthropologist* 63(3): 579–587.

Moock, J. L. and R. E. Rhoades (eds). 1992. *Diversity, Farmer Knowledge, and Sustainability.* Ithaca: Cornell University Press.

Msanya, B. M., D. Mwaseba, D. J. Ole-Meiludie, G. G. Kimbi, A. R. Massawe and D. N. Kimaro. 1998. Indigenous knowledge in soil classification: The case of the Mbulu and Karatu Districts in Tanzania. *Journal of Management Development* 10(2): 237–260.

Nader, L. 1996a. Introduction: An anthropological inquiry into boundaries, power, and knowledge. In L. Nader (ed.) *Naked Science: Anthropology Inquiry into Boundaries, Power, and Knowledge* (pp. 1–25). New York: Routledge.

—— (ed.). 1996b. *Naked Science: Anthropology Inquiry into Boundaries, Power, and Knowledge.* New York: Routledge.

Nagel, T. 1979. *Moral Questions.* Cambridge: Cambridge University Press.

Onjoro, E.A. 2001. *Knowledge Integration in development: the relative autonomy of Western and indigenous knowledge in traditional birth attendants health practice in rural Kenya.* Dissertation, Department of Anthropology, University of South Florida.

Ortiz, O. 1999. Understanding interactions between indigenous knowledge and scientific information. *Indigenous Knowledge and Development Monitor* 7(3): 7–9.

Pfaffenberger, B. 1992. Social anthropology of technology. *Annual Review of Anthropology* 21: 491–516.

Posey, D.A. 1998. Comment. *Current Anthropology* 39(2): 241–242.

—— (ed.). 1999. *Cultural and Spiritual Values of Biodiversity. A Complementary Contribution to the Global Biodiversity Assessment.* London: Intermediate Technologies Publications.

Posey, D.A., J. Frechione and J. Eddins. 1984. Ethnoecology as applied anthropology in Amazonian development. *Human Organization* 43(2): 95–107.

Purcell, T. W. 1998. Indigenous knowledge and applied anthropology: Questions of definition and direction. *Human Organization* 57(3): 258–272.

Rajasekaran, B. and M. B. Whiteford. 1993. Rice-crab production in South India: The role of indigenous knowledge in designing food security policies. *Food Policy,* June 1993.

Reed, D. W. and C. Behrens. 1989. Modelling folk knowledge as expert system. *Anthropological Quarterly* 62(3): 107–120.

Ryle, G. 1949. *The Concept of the Mind.* New York: Harper and Row.

Sandor, J. A. and L. Furbee. 1996. Indigenous knowledge and classification of soils in the Andes of Southern Peru. *Soil Science Society of America Journal* 60(5): 1502–1513.

Sayer, A. 1984. *Method in Social Science: A Realist Approach.* London: Hutchinson.

Schoenhoff, D. M. 1993. *The Barefoot Expert: The Interface of Computerized Knowledge Systems and Indigenous Knowledge Systems.* Westport, CT: Greenwood Press.

Scott, C. 1989. Knowledge construction among Cree Hunters: Metaphors and liberal understanding. *Journal de la Société des Américanistes* 75: 193–208.

Semali, L. M. and J. L. Kincheloe (eds). 1999. *What is Indigenous Knowledge? Voices from the Academy.* New York: Falmer Press.

Sillitoe, P. 1998a. The development of indigenous knowledge: A new applied anthropology. *Current Anthropology* 39: 223–252.

———. 1998b. Knowing the land: Soil and land resource evaluation and indigenous knowledge. *Soil Use and Management* 14: 188–193.

———. 2000. Indigenous Knowledge, Science and the 'Poorest of the Poor.' *Anthropology Today* 16(6): 3–7.

Stoffle, R. W., D. B. Halmo and M. J. Evans. 1999. *Puchuxwavaats uapi* (To know about plants): Cultural significance of southern Paiute plants. *Human Organization* 58(4): 416–429.

Tambiah, S. J. 1990. *Magic, Science, Religion, and the Scope of Rationality.* Cambridge: Cambridge University Press.

Trotter, R. and J. A. Chavira. 1997. *Curanderismo: Mexican American Folk Healing* (2nd edition). Athens: University of Georgia Press.

Turnbull, D. 2000. *Mason, Trickster, and Cartographers: Comparative Studies in the Sociology of Scientific and Indigenous Knowledge.* Amsterdam: Harwood Academic.

Turner, S. P. 1989. Truth and decision. In D. Chubin and E. Chu (eds) *Science of the Pedestal: Social Perspectives on Science and Technology.* Belmont, CA: Wadsworth Publishing Company.

Warner, M. and P. Jones. 1998. Assessing the need to manage conflict in community-based natural resource projects. Overseas Development Institute National Resource Perspective no. 35.

Warren D. M. 1991a. *Using Indigenous Knowledge in Agriculture Development.* Washington, DC: World Bank.

———. 1991b. *Indigenous Systems: The Cultural Dimension of Development.* New York: Colombia University Press.

———. 1993. Indigenous knowledge and sustainable agricultural and rural development in Africa: Policy issues and strategies for the twenty-first century. Paper presented at the Annual Meeting of the African Studies Association. Boston, December.

Warren, D. M., L. J. Slikkerveer and S. O. Titilola (eds). 1989. *Indigenous Knowledge Systems: Implications for Agriculture and International Development.* Studies in Technology and Social Change no. 11. Ames: Iowa State University,.

Warren, K. B. 1998. *Indigenous Movements and Their Critics: Pan-Mayan Activism in Guatemala.* Princeton, NJ: Princeton University Press.

Weil, A. 2000. *Dr. Andrew Weil and Integrative Medicine,* http://www.family-friendly-fun-.com/health/alternative-Weil.htm.

Whiteford, L., A. Arata, M. Torres, D. Montaño, N. Saurez, E. Creel and K. Ramsey. 1999. *Diarrheal Disease Prevention Through Community-based Participation Interventions.* Washington, DC: US Agency for International Development.

Wiredu, K. 1996. *Cultural Universals and Particulars: An African Perspective.* Bloomington and Indianapolis: Indiana University Press.

——. 1980. *Philosophy and an African Culture.* Cambridge: Cambridge University Press.

Chapter 9

Interdisciplinary research and GIS

Why local and indigenous knowledge are discounted

John R. Campbell

The debate between proponents of 'hard' (i.e. quantitative) and 'soft' (i.e. qualitative) social science research which extended to the merits of different research methods (e.g. surveys, ethnography, interviewing, etc.) has generated a huge amount of hyperbole regarding the qualities of 'good' research. Phrased in terms of the distinctiveness and ability of one methodology to offer a better explanation of 'reality' than the other, the debate has proved impossible to resolve. The resulting polarization has resulted in a failure to see that good research combines methods and forms of explanation from both 'paradigms' (Bryman 1988). In addition, some of the claims made by proponents of a methodology lack substance because they do not reflect the way in which research was actually conducted. For example, Sechrist and Sidani (1995) argue that misunderstandings arise partially from the failure of researchers clearly to distinguish between the precise manner in which field research was conducted and the reconstructed version of an ideal to which a researcher adheres.

A further complication arises from the manner in which disciplinary knowledge is taught, and the manner in which professional identities are internalized and valued. Entrenched professional identities contribute to a situation in which the debate between qualitative and quantitative methodologies resurfaces in interdisciplinary research and in the assessment of 'new' forms of knowledge. In particular, the idea of local or 'indigenous knowledge' challenges professional and disciplinary thinking in fundamental ways, and, naturally enough, its status and value are contested. Despite differences in the way that natural and social scientists have been taught, there is general agreement that 'good' research depends upon a pragmatic approach to research methodology which draws upon all relevant traditions including the use of multiple methods to triangulate findings (e.g. Jick 1979; Booth *et al.* 1998). This common ground provides a useful foundation on which to build interdisciplinary research, just as it provides an ideal platform for a technology like Geographic Information Systems (GIS) to assist research by managing large, diverse datasets.

However, viewed against a backdrop in which professional identities and bureaucracy dominate development research, we should not be surprised to find that a technology like GIS may be used to reinforce 'narrow' disciplinary thinking and foreclose possibilities for interdisciplinary research that challenges established ways of thinking. The challenges confronting interdisciplinary research are explored by examining an internationally funded and supported GIS project operated by the government of Botswana. First, I outline the promise and limitations of GIS for interdisciplinary research in the context of work on Renewable Natural Resources (RNR) and poverty alleviation on the southern African rangelands. Next, I examine the institutional and policy context in which the GIS was situated and its impact on research. Then I look at contending discourses about environmental change that revolve around the disputed value of different forms of knowledge, some of which was privileged and used while other knowledge was blocked. Finally, I explore the need to agree a common methodological focus for interdisciplinary research. Given the problems that arise between scientific and social science research, I briefly explore the possibility of combining research methods in research on indigenous knowledge.

I argue that while designated project outputs were completed, they contributed little to the wider objective of developing an interdisciplinary methodology capable of evaluating changing environmental conditions and their impact on rural poverty. The reasons behind this failure relate to institutional politics, the bureaucratic management of the GIS project, entrenched disciplinary thinking, and donor failure to insist that a project objective should be agreement on a research methodology. Without such an objective, project management directed research towards institutional goals and objectives, and away from a concern for sustainable natural resources. In short, without prior agreement on the reason for access to better data, the GIS reinforced disciplinary divisions at the expense of developing an interdisciplinary methodology.

Geographic Information Systems: promise and problems

A GIS is a sophisticated database management system designed to acquire, manage, manipulate, visualize and display spatially referenced (geographic) forms of data. Originally developed from work on computer-assisted mapping, it can handle a wide range of data and generate new information by manipulating existing databases (Aldenderfer 1996). In particular, datasets take the form of layers or themes; each layer is a specific natural, cultural or derived variable that describes the environment of the study. In addition, depending on the format in which a dataset is referenced, it is possible to juxtapose or 'overlay' different datasets to produce a visual representation or map. For example, spatially referenced data from the national census, on local infrastructure, and on the provision of government services might be overlaid to identify the population with least access to education, etc.

More importantly, a GIS has been successfully used to manage very large datasets for a diverse range of research applications including: archaeological data to map regional settlement patterns (Goodchild 1996); integrating aerial photography (Goodchild 1996); managing remotely sensed satellite data (Moran 1992); managing data on the interrelationship between land degradation, settlement, poverty, and vegetation (Stonich 1996; Loker 1996; Ringrose et al. 1996); and designing and implementing development projects (Weiner et al. 1995).

To date, very little has been written about the problems that arise in using a GIS in interdisciplinary research. In the past, the cost of these systems (computer hardware, software and training) was so great that only government's or government-supported institutions could afford them. However, costs have dropped considerably, to the extent that the private sector[1] now utilizes GIS systems. Acquisition costs aside, training and systems support for a GIS remain expensive and difficult to obtain, a fact which has led some critics to suggest that it is an inappropriate technology to transfer to less developed countries. Nevertheless, a number of international aid agencies now provide the technology as part of their strategy to promote regional environmental research.

From an anthropological point of view, a concern with GIS arises in overlaying datasets to create 'maps' that purport to show the way space is utilized. Such maps are essentially based on Western cultural perceptions that 'see' human activities as occupying or occurring in discrete and non-overlapping spaces. Notions of individualism and private property lie at the heart of such representations, regardless of longstanding anthropological critiques of their inappropriateness. In short, such ideas misrepresent and misinterpret non-Western cultures. African land tenure provides an excellent example of the interpretive problems involved because the variety and fluidity of cultural conceptions and social arrangements negate simplistic spatial maps. Thus, semi-nomadic or transhumant herders may think of routes traversing a piece of land as more important than the grazing potential of the land itself. Farming people may or may not conceive of their own persons as inseparable from particular pieces of land, or from the right to farm in particular areas. Moreover, they may understand their rights as attaching not to fixed points on the ground but to elastic spaces on a 'rubber map', defined in relation to the rights of other kin or neighbours (Shipton and Goheen 1992: 309).

However, a more fundamental problem with mapping/inscribing indigenous knowledge concerns the nature of indigenous knowledge and the relationship between indigenous peoples and the 'natural' world. Indigenous knowledge (IK) can be understood as a form of local knowledge that is dynamic and context specific, and which is intimately related to the livelihoods of a people (Agrawal 1995). Significantly, IK is communicated orally and is not inscribed/written; indeed, some forms of IK knowledge are not widely available but are 'owned' by specific individuals or social groups who have the right to possess such knowledge (e.g. shamans). In contrast to the knowledge of local agricultural communities whose adaptation to their environment is relatively recent in historical terms, IK has sustained indigenous peoples (like the San/Basarwa of southern Africa) for hundreds of years (Purcell 1998; Hitchcock 1995). Intimately linked to a conception of relatedness between the environment and a culture, IK differs fundamentally from science in its holistic character, which is linked explicitly to a culture (e.g. through symbolic meaning systems, religion and ritual, morality, etc.), and through a sense of 'kinship' that establishes an on-going relationship between a people and an environment. This relation is often based upon a cyclical concept of time that interconnects social, personal, environmental and spiritual processes and events (Rundstrom 1995). As such, IK represents a different epistemology from science not only in terms of its understanding and knowledge about the natural world, but also because of its central role in sustaining a culture and its natural resources.

If the cultural conceptions which underlie land tenure and IK are not enough to confound map making, we have to consider the range of social relationships and affiliations – via social groups (e.g. lineage, village, household), social networks (e.g. patrons, religious leaders, bond partnerships, friendships) and social categories (e.g. gender, age, status, etc.) – that feature in gaining access to land. Indeed, it is impossible to incorporate into a map the principles which inform land tenure, the contested nature of access to land, and the extent to which rights to or duties over land are socially contingent on things like changing livelihoods, population density, labour migration (and access to remittance income). Additional difficulties arise in taking into account the changing effect of state policy, of deepening rural poverty, or processes of land concentration (Downs and Reyna 1988; Hitchcock 1985). Equally importantly, even where Western land law operates or private land markets are promoted, 'traditional' institutions and customary law continue to play a central role in gaining access to land[2] (Freudenberger 1998). A key issue in the Kalahari concerns the extent to which policy has displaced hunter-gatherer/foragers by reducing and altering patterns of seasonal mobility, in effect ending their entitlement to range resources which have increasingly disappeared behind fences (of ranches, national parks, etc.). The 'fuzzy' social nature of nested rights to land and resources in Africa cannot be captured by GIS representations depicting clearly bounded social groups or clearly demarcated rights to or use of natural resources.

Furthermore, qualitative socioeconomic data which explore the fuzzy nature of rights to land and resources, and which are spatially referenced, are rare and expensive to produce, and their use on a GIS may entail important ethical questions (i.e. confidentiality, disclosure, etc.). On the other hand, the data that are available may be of poor quality and of limited value (assuming that they are geo-referenced; Dunn et al. 1997). Obtaining suitable data requires the development of a methodology which identifies data that can be modelled using a GIS – a methodology to guide research in collecting relevant and spatially referenced data. In short, data collection and data capture are time consuming and expensive (Daplyn *et al.* 1991; Campbell 1999).

While various provisos have been made about the uncritical use of GIS – i.e. poor training, unethical use of data, reliance on poor quality data, etc. – it remains the case that GIS maps and data must be critically evaluated to prevent their use in destructive 'developmentalism' (Weiner *et al.* 1995). Misuse may arise from the legitimacy the GIS gives to expert 'knowledge', and because the technology is seen as an unproblematic means of planning and implementing government policies without being subject to accountability or consultation. Apart from concerns about the technology, some geographers have criticized GIS as 'a techno-representation readily controlled by the powerful', a tool that reinforces and legitimates state authority (Dunn *et al.* 1997). It is pertinent to examine the politics and policies of the institutions that utilize GIS and the role the technology plays in policy formulation.

Botswana and the Range Inventory and Monitoring Project

The Botswana GIS is located in the Range Ecology Section of the Ministry of Agriculture (MoA). It was funded by the UK Department for International Development (DFID) in a three year £1 million project which sought to establish a pilot system to provide reliable and regular information on changing environmental conditions on the southern African rangelands, and which would assist the MoA in formulating sustainable land management and grazing policies, strengthen the land use planning process, and aim to generate rational utilization and management of the range (DFID 1994: 2).

The rationale for the project arose out of a 1992 review of Overseas Development Agency (ODA)[3] support for the RNR sector, which recommended that 'assistance should be focussed on addressing poverty alleviation and environmental management'. This objective was explicitly linked to the task of developing a better database for sustainable land use policy and to improve institutional linkage and cooperation within the Ministry of Agriculture (DFID 1994: 5).

The rangelands play an important role in Botswana's political economy. First, the source of power and wealth of the Tswana elite comes from owning cattle and controlling the range. This process was accomplished via the *metse* (ward) system which legitimated and organized Bamangwato[4] control over land (pasture), cattle and the labour of *malata* (serfs) to herd cattle (Hitchcock 1985). Access to borehole technology and moves to privatize tenure meant that by the 1940s the Bamangwato had moved their cattle west into the Kalahari transforming local hunter-gatherers and their territories into the property of powerful Tswana individuals. This transformation ordered socioeconomic inequality between the elite, commoners and serfs (among the latter were the San/Basarwa hunter-gatherers and the Bakgalagadi peoples). The growth in cattle herding correlates with the deterioration of the rangelands. A decline in the wildlife population, formerly an important component of rural livelihoods, also occurred with the rise of the cattle industry, along with severe drought in the 1980s, individuation of tenure, and the use of fencing (to 'manage' the range) which displaced the local population and transferred rights over land to the elite.

By the 1960s ecological deterioration was a serious concern and land shortage was contributing to conflict over land use for cattle grazing or cultivation; this conflict remains central to contemporary land privatization today (Peters 1994). The policy driving privatization was the implementation in 1975 of the Tribal Grazing Land Policy (TGLP), whose objective was to remove large cattle owners from overgrazed communal areas to the western sandveld.[5] This policy did not work because the areas zoned for grazing already contained sizeable populations, because there was insufficient space for expansion into the sandveld, and because no effort was made to consult local people whose livelihoods were affected. In effect, TGLP contributed to greater competition over land, and to continuing overgrazing and land degradation (Tsimako 1991). At the same time the fencing of leasehold lands has further reduced access to the land, water and natural resources that local people depend upon.

While there is considerable debate about the extent of land degradation (e.g. Abel 1993; Abel and Blaikie 1990; Adams 1996; Behnke et al. 1993), understanding the problem involves consideration of social and physical processes including: (1) the dynamic ecological conditions of the arid and semi-arid lands of the Kalahari; (2) range management issues arising from the failure of previous policies (i.e. rising livestock densities and poor land management; White 1992); and (3) the socioeconomic consequences of the transformation of the Kalahari into a rangeland, especially the displacement and impoverishment of rural households.

Two different estimates indicate the extent of rural poverty and, by implication, the role of rangelands policy in the transformation of the Kalahari:

1   Poverty – nationally, poverty declined between 1985 and 1994 from 59 per cent to 47 per cent of the population. However, 55 per cent of rural households as compared to 29 per cent of urban households remain poor or very poor (BIDPA 1997).
2   Ownership of cattle – the number of those owning livestock dropped sharply: in 1981 about 51 per cent of rural people neither owned nor had access to cattle; however, by 1991 this figure had risen to 74 per cent. Simultaneously, a concentration of ownership occurred between the mid-1970s, when large cattle owners (15 per cent of the population) owned 75 per cent of the national herd, and the early 1980s, when very large herds were owned by just 5–10 per cent of all farmers (Good 1999: 190).

Government and the ruling political party have decisively transformed rural Botswana – a country whose mineral resources make it the fourth wealthiest country in Africa – into a society with one of the highest levels of rural poverty in southern Africa. Policy – particularly the TGLP but also land use strategies, taxation and drought relief – have disproportionately aided large cattle owners (White 1992; Hitchcock 1985; Peters 1994; Valentine 1993; Hay 1988). At the same time, government has consistently refused to adopt a minimum wage for rural labour, and has continued to dispossess Basarwa by refusing to recognize their right to land and moving them to marginal areas, where, along with other 'Remote Area Dwellers', they face certain destitution (Good 1999).

The MoA occupies a central role in rangeland management where it is concerned to promote beef production for export (heavily subsidized by government) through implementing TGLP and overseeing the fencing of communal grazing areas. Additionally, the MoA assesses and monitors range conditions (including fire and drought); monitors crop, forestry and animal health programmes; and evaluates Ministry projects. The DFID-funded GIS project spanned three departments – Range Ecology (RE), Remote Sensing and Cartography, and Monitoring and Evaluation (M&E) – with day-to-day management exercised by the head of RE, supported by an expatriate counterpart. In effect, the principle source of oversight and direction came from annual[6] project reviews.

Though the project was organized into teams to facilitate work, there were limited opportunities for interaction or mutual learning except at special workshops or annual reviews. On a day-to-day basis, project management acted as a gatekeeper by taking decisions without consultation, and by managing the flow of information between teams, between the project and the Ministry and potential users of project data. Heavy staff workloads, manpower shortages, and the split provision of technical assistance between two UK institutions[7] also constrained project work.

A slow project start-up and lack of leadership by the Project Manager, who distanced himself from the project, resulted in a series of problems including the exclusion of the head of the Monitoring and Evaluation Unit from project decisions. The expatriate Technical Cooperation Officer (TCO, a natural scientist) and the Project Manager narrowed the scope of the project by shifting the focus towards 'capturing' technical data (i.e. on vegetation change – vegetation status, soil erosion, land use, geology, etc. – meteorology, topography, wildlife, and remotely sensed data). Such actions shifted the use of the GIS from research to providing technical reports for the Range Ecology Department (i.e. on drought, desertification and fire). The net effect was to prioritize the collection of technical data and to confine the role of the GIS to producing maps (e.g. of fire scar, vegetation change, etc.). In effect, research on socioeconomic processes and changes in land use was sidelined.

Contending discourses on environmental change

Several possibilities existed for interdisciplinary collaboration, including an examination of the tenets of the 'new' range ecology which argues for a need to 'track' changes in livestock forage and fluctuations in the number of livestock herded on the rangelands (Behnke *et al.* 1993). Such research could have assessed the evidence for environmental variability and the need for new policies to support the livelihood strategies of livestock owners. A second possibility would have been to conduct research into the knowledge of rural peoples about their environment and how they manage local resources. This topic was proposed at the beginning of the project but was dropped in the first year due partly to problems with UK sociological support and to the Ministry's opposition to action that might bestow legitimacy or importance to the indigenous San/Basarwa hunter-gatherers.[8]

The above research programmes were not in conflict, and both could usefully have examined biophysical data with a view to complementing and exploring local environmental knowledge and rural household decision making (e.g. on stocking levels or sustainable resource use). However, neither possibility was pursued. Instead, project management privileged certain 'scientific' over other forms of knowledge (including social science, and local and indigenous knowledge). The manner in which this occurred can be illustrated with respect to decisions that defined the function of sociological research, and in relation to efforts by management to eliminate sociological research from the second phase of the project.

When the role of external support for sociological research was altered (approximately twenty months into the project cycle), the 'sociological team' was required to provide evidence to the Annual Review of its ability to undertake research and to demonstrate what it could contribute to the project. To this end, results of two exploratory village studies utilizing Rapid Rural Appraisal (RRA) were presented, together with basic data about indigenous knowledge of rangeland vegetation that included information regarding changes in the distribution of rangeland plant species.

Sociological research was required to provide data that complemented the biophysical data collected by the other teams. Against the wishes of project management, it was agreed that sociological research would focus on: (1) how different social strata make use of range resources (an analysis of rural livelihoods); and (2) the perception of environmental change at village level (which included collecting samples of rangeland plants). As the project proceeded, research on rural livelihoods was stymied by management's refusal to disseminate research findings (within and outside the Ministry) and by its attempt to undermine research findings. Village RRA research offered range ecologists the opportunity to verify satellite data and to collect data on local ecology. However, because sociological data were discounted there was no mutual learning between teams. Any notion that RRA data might suggest new lines of inquiry or a need to evaluate existing quantified datasets was rejected.

Work for the final project review provides another illustration of how management blocked interdisciplinary research. In a preliminary meeting, the entire project agreed that the final team demonstrations/reports should meet four criteria, namely that: (1) adequate data should already be on the GIS; (2) the demonstration should exhibit as many linkages as possible to other teams; (3) the work was feasible in terms of staff time and workloads; and (4) the demonstration should relate to Ministry policy. Three topics were agreed, namely:

1   Analysis and reporting of veld fires (by the Seasonal Monitoring Team).
2   Analysis and reporting on drought (by the Long-term Vegetation Monitoring Team).
3   Examination of the socioeconomic impact of fencing (by the Sociology/Range-user Team).

Each team defined its own proposal and identified the inputs it needed from the other teams. However, several months later management added a fourth topic, land degradation, about which there had been no discussion and for which no previous work had been conducted. The information required for topics 1, 2 and 4 called for significant sociological inputs. In particular, topic 4 on environmental degradation asked for data that would shed light on the possible socioeconomic causes and consequences of observable trends in land degradation. However, rather than use existing data, new sociological data was required. In effect, project management sought to use the sociology team to advance its interest in land degradation. Indeed, the sociologists were increasingly used to verify satellite imagery on veld fire and to assess the impact of drought despite the fact that RRA methods were not designed for such problems (local staff also lacked the training to adapt the methods).

It is useful to summarize the sociologists' report on the impact of fencing to illustrate the teams' much wider focus and to indicate why this line of inquiry was marginalized. The presentation was based on data from two villages and sought to demonstrate the variable impact that fencing would have on two different social strata: (1) female headed households (recognized as among the poorest); and (2) wealthy cattle-owning households (BRIMP 1998a, 1998b). The villages were of a similar population size and social composition, but one was located on the hardveld and the other on the sandveld. Data from the use of RRA demonstrated the following:

1   The importance of locally available range resources to each social stratum (i.e. female-headed households were heavily dependent on access to 'free' range resources).
2   The extent to which each stratum had access to non-range-based resources/opportunities (i.e. outside the district; thus cattle-owners moved their herds to better pasture and educated children left to earn money that was sent back, etc.).

3   The immediate impact which fencing would have in denying female-headed households' access to vital resources.
4   Because the majority of households depended upon the range, research concluded that the long-term impact of fencing would be to impoverish households and make them dependent on the state for assistance.

Furthermore, because the sandveld was a drier and less productive environment with few alternatives to earn a living or supplement a livelihood, and because such a large amount of land was already fenced and inaccessible (i.e. from leasehold ranches, game parks, etc.), fencing constituted an immediate threat to local livelihoods. The sandveld village was characterized by low levels of cattle ownership, limited access to wage work, and high numbers of female-headed households, even though it was relatively well served by basic services. The reasons for high levels of poverty in this village related to the allocation, between 1973 and 1980, of substantial areas to establish private, fenced ranches. An additional consequence of fencing had been the loss of access to veld products for home consumption and to earn cash. Continued population growth in an enclosed sandveld environment had also resulted in people converting marginal land to arable production at the expense of pasture, trees, etc., which, together with high livestock densities, degraded local pasture.

Project management opposed the fencing report on the grounds that it questioned Ministry policy. However, at the insistence of the head of the M&E unit, the report was presented to the Review. However, senior Ministry officials failed to attend and the Review failed to address central problems regarding the absence of agreement about the research agenda and the absence of an interdisciplinary methodology (Campbell 1999).

At the final Project Review, the three teams located in RE had not completed their presentations nor had project management drafted a proposal for a second phase. The Review attempted to resolve the first problem by rolling unspent budgets forward to allow time to complete work. However, despite external assistance, project management was unable to draft a viable funding proposal due partly to its desire to drop sociological research.[9] One conclusion I drew from the final Review, which failed to address the tensions and problems in the project, was that the need to institutionalize the project (and the investment made in the Ministry) took precedence over the project's failure to achieve its aims.

Rural livelihoods and sustainable natural resources

One reason for the project's failure to foster interdisciplinary research stems from DFID's assumption that more 'knowledge' would result in improved policy analysis and the formulation of sustainable policies. As already discussed, this did not occur because the GIS was not used to facilitate research. In effect, bureaucratic and policy interests used the GIS to pool technical data. In addition, the project did not critically evaluate the data placed on the GIS (work by the GIS team was limited to collecting data and confirming its 'integrity'). Basic concerns about data quality and validity were not addressed. This failure to agree criteria about the value of specific datasets resulted in an attempt to 'capture' every possible dataset that might provide 'national' coverage. For example, while the shortcomings of large government/social surveys are well known, no attempt was made to assess the quality of such information. Sources such as the agricultural census and data from Department of Wildlife aerial wildlife surveys were used regardless of their reliability, their value to social or ecological research, or the cost of converting such data into a useable form. Furthermore, no effort was made to train staff or policy analysts in how to interpret the data/maps provided by the GIS. Questions about the confidence limits of the datasets were not raised, nor were the limitations of spatially organized data (e.g. the problems of spatial coincidence, proximity and dependence; Goodchild 1996) or problems of generalizing from spatial data. In effect, quantitative data collection was the priority, and the GIS was used primarily to map remotely sensed data so that range ecology could report on fire and drought.

Such an environment seriously constrains research, which needs to be open-ended and able to pursue all lines of enquiry. A focus on rural livelihoods and/or IK would have had to be interdisciplinary in order to obtain and interpret many different kinds of knowledge. Such an approach would have offered the possibility of overcoming many biases – towards planners/government rather than people, scientists rather than social scientists, quantitative rather than qualitative, scientific rather than indigenous knowledge, etc. – that stem from a Western Cartesian visual bias that privileges cognitive understanding (Rundstrom 1995; IDS 1997; Davies and Hossain 1997; Clammer, chapter 3).

Returning to the problem of 'mapping' African land use, the shifting sets of entitlements to use land (and the resources located on it) require an analysis of how social relationships and socioeconomic and political processes intersect with a number of context-specific factors. Short of an in-depth study of land use, the possibility exists of combining qualitative social science (i.e. Participatory Rural Appraisal, interviews, group discussions, key informants, etc.) with 'scientific' methods (e.g. soil/ecological surveys, remotely sensed data, etc.) to analyse patterns of natural resource use. While there are only a few examples available to guide research, the prospects and problems are relatively clear and relate to the need: (1) to agree a common methodology; (2) to agree and develop joint research techniques; and (3) to agree about how to resolve 'incommensurable' findings (e.g. issues of spatial scale and the integrity of the sociocultural data). Finally, there is a need to respect and appreciate local knowledge as something that is qualitatively different from Western cognitive knowledge, and which has an important role to play in natural resource policy and research (Agrawal 1995; Sillitoe 1998).[10]

Payton *et al.* (n.d.) attempt to reconcile local and scientific forms of knowledge about land and water resources in East Africa and Bangladesh by combining qualitative research with chemical and physical analysis of soils in a GIS-managed analysis of spatially referenced data. Their findings indicate that the integration of methods to investigate different forms of knowledge demonstrate the strengths and limitations of scientific and indigenous knowledge. However, despite attempts to provide a tool to translate/'model' local terms into a classificatory system similar to that produced by soil scientists, the endeavour resulted in a loss of detail and context. Their findings appear to reflect generic problems involved in research that seeks to combine methods from different 'paradigms', namely:

- problems with the sequencing and degree of iteration between methods and the lack of fit between qualitative and quantitative data (i.e. the need to design research methodology carefully);
- problems of 'translation' (between local people and researchers and between social science and science); and
- problems with 'spatial cognition' in which local/cultural perception does not fit with the binary thinking (and data referencing) of GIS or of science.

The issue of spatial cognition is central to research on IK. Payton *et al.* (n.d.) argue that while local knowledge 'can be quantified and systematically organized by means of a GIS', nevertheless there is a clear lack of fit (and resultant distortion) when IK is placed on a GIS. They argue that 'the geometry of soils and environmental knowledge does not accord to a Euclidean metric' (*ibid.*: 13–14). It is worth reiterating Rundstrom's (1995) point that the geographic knowledge of indigenous peoples is cultural. As such, the dependence of the GIS on binary thinking and the idea that ambiguity is a liability, together with the failure to appreciate that IK is a distinct epistemological form of knowledge, results in the distortion and misrepresentation of IK. Indeed, Rundstrom argues that efforts to 'capture' and inscribe such knowledge transform it and result in fundamental misunderstandings. Thus, knowledge which is primarily transmitted through cultural idioms and social processes, as occurs in ritual, are subject to a

> high degree of probability that misunderstanding will occur and be 'represented' in the outside world, i.e. inscribed in textual, graphic or binary digital code. At the least, this again diminishes the power of knowledge and causes disharmony [for indigenous peoples] and at worst can be (mis)used against the people in a very destructive manner.
>
> (Rundstrom 1995: 53)

The problem with interdisciplinary endeavours is defining a methodology that can address the very different perspectives involved in understanding the 'natural' world (via quantitative methods and data), the 'social' world (via qualitative methods) and diverse 'local' worlds (which are experiential and are not systematized). Left to their own devices, the group that adheres to each form of knowledge is primarily aware of the strengths and limitations of its own methods and 'data'. To paraphrase Purcell, in such a situation each group regards its own knowledge as 'the truth' (1998: 267). A considerable body of scientific research into IK displays an implicit cognitive and cultural bias that devalues this form of knowledge, its explanations and the categories it employs. Instead of embracing difference with the aim of understanding it, Western knowledge commits conceptual 'violence' against such knowledge by denying its validity, reformulating its arguments and stripping ('technical' and environmental) knowledge from the social context in which it has meaning.

Concluding remarks

While the location of the GIS in the Botswana Ministry of Agriculture and the nature of the project management contributed to the failure to develop a methodology capable of analysing RNR and poverty, it is necessary to step back and examine the thinking that guided the project. Project work mirrored the bureaucratic mindset of Ministry politics that attempted to control rather than understand environmental change. This can be seen in the way that project management defined which kinds of knowledge were valid and worth studying, and the roles and work of the teams. Project management sought to keep to itself (and the Ministry) the power to define the research agenda, the policy issues to be investigated and the right to advance or block the flow of project-generated information (Hobart 1993).

This course of action prevented the use of the GIS to undertake research on the rangelands (reporting on veld fire or drought does not qualify as research). What is important is to understand the medium- and long-term processes responsible for ecological change, a task that requires carefully thought out research into the physical and social processes responsible for land use and environmental change. Such a task can best be accomplished by designing interdisciplinary research that draws upon the best traditions and methods of natural and social science.

What occurred in the Botswana GIS project was the prioritization of 'scientific' knowledge – defined in terms of its familiarity to range ecologists – over other forms of knowledge, and in particular over the knowledge of local people. Furthermore, information that addressed the costs of policy (e.g. fencing) was discounted and marginalized. The contribution of local people was limited to confirming satellite imagery (and the deductions based upon such images), and their knowledge was seen to be of little value in assessing the wider picture as defined by officials or outsiders. The value attached to sight, seeing and images are fundamental to GIS, range ecology and 'science', in the sense of verifying/'ground-truthing' satellite images or providing the information required by officials. This cognitive bias reveals the foundation on which 'scientific' discourse is founded, namely the cult of the expert/civil servant. The fact that project management chartered a plane to verify satellite images but was unable and unwilling to learn from villagers about environmental change underlines the inability of bureaucrats to progress beyond a grossly simplified, scientistic and manageable account of the world.[11]

A focus on GIS, a technology that ostensibly facilitates knowledge acquisition and learning, possibly accentuates the role of bureaucratic/government development narratives in resource management. Did the project contribute to a more sustainable use of rangeland resources? The unequivocal answer is no. The responsibility for this failure lies with DFID, various consultants (especially those who designed the project), project management and the Botswana Ministry of Agriculture. After all, a technology is only going to be as good as those who manage it. The central lesson is that placed in the hands of a line ministry, a GIS becomes a resource at the disposal of bureaucrats who, by training and orientation, function to serve existing policy ends. Bureaucrats are unable and unwilling to question conventional thinking, to investigate complex issues, or to critically examine official policy. In this context, a GIS is an inappropriate technology. Nevertheless, and regardless of the limited use to which it was put, the GIS in Botswana has strengthened the authority of administrators and has supported destructive forms of development pursued by government in the Kalahari.

Notes

1   I am indebted to Martin Byram and Paul Sillitoe for their comments.
2   The USAID-funded Range and Livestock Management Projects initiated in Botswana in the early 1970s failed precisely because 'of the lack of attention to traditional claims to grazing areas' and the absence of local consultation (Hitchcock 1985: 117).
3   The former name of DFID.
4   The Tswana royal clan.
5   The Kalahari, which stretches across Botswana, is divided into the eastern hardveld and the western sandveld. This east–west distinction is based on major differences in soil type, vegetation cover, rainfall distribution (e.g. availability of ground water) and seasonal temperature. The distinction is important in socioeconomic terms since the hardveld has better soils, vegetation and water, and historically was the home of the cattle-owning Tswana. The resource-poor sandveld, with its limited vegetation, sandy soils and lack of surface water was/is the home of hunter-gatherers. The advent of borehole technology in the 1940s allowed cattle owners to expand into the sandveld and resulted in its *de facto* privatization for cattle keeping (White 1992).
6   I was a member of the team that conducted the first annual Project Review and I attended subsequent reviews as a member of the project.
7   Because the UK support institution initially contracted to provide sociological assistance lost its contract, the University of Wales, Swansea and a local consultancy firm took over support arrangements twenty months into the project.

8 The Ministry barred investigation into the significance of ethnicity for local-level resource use. Constraints of time and resources also meant that the team was unable to go to the western sandveld to investigate Basarwa knowledge. This attitude is reflected in the government's refusal to recognize that the San/Basarwa have any claims (as its first occupants) in the Kalahari (see Good 1999).

9 Project management failed to consult with its teams, including the head of M&E; it prioritized work on drought and fire; and it sought to exclude sociology/anthropology (Project Memorandum, Botswana Rangeland Inventory and Monitoring Project, Phase 2. Draft. MoA. 1998). In a workshop held to agree a proposal for the second phase, the outside facilitator noted a 'lack of congruence about organizational objectives' between the project manager and M&E concerning the intention of the project management to drop fencing from the project (K. Higgins. 1998. Facilitation Workshop to agree Phase II inputs. June).

10 Not the least of which is that a failure to understand local knowledge, and to consult and plan with local people is achieved at the risk of compounding problems of poverty and resource degradation.

11 The need to simplify is linked to acceptable (i.e. manageable) 'scientific' views of range degradation based on (contested) estimates of livestock-carrying capacity as compared to more complex accounts that attempt to track ecosystem dynamics (Abel 1993; Behnke 1992; Dougill 1997; Thomas and Sporton 1997).

Bibliography

Abel, N. 1993. Reducing cattle numbers on Southern African communal range: Is it worth it? In R. Behnke and I. Scoones (eds) *Range Ecology at Disequilibrium*. London: ODI/IIED.

Abel, N. and P. Blaikie. 1990. Land degradation, stocking rates and conservation policies in the communal rangelands of Botswana and Zimbabwe. *ODI Pastoral Development Network* no. 29a. London: ODI.

Adams, M. 1996. When is ecosystem change land degradation? *ODI Pastoral Development Network* no. 39e. London: ODI.

Agrawal, A. 1995. Dismantling the divide between indigenous and scientific knowledge. *Development and Change* 26: 413–439.

Aldenderfer, M. 1996. Introduction. In M. Aldenderfer and H. Maschner (eds) *Anthropology, Space, and Geographic Information Systems* (pp. 3–18). Oxford: Oxford University Press.

Behnke, R. 1992. New directions in African range management policy. *ODI Pastoral Development Network* no. 32c. London: ODI.

Behnke, R., I. Scoones and C. Kerven. (eds) 1993. *Range Ecology at Disequilibrium: New Models of Natural Variability and Pastoral Adaptation in African Savannas*. London: ODI.

Booth, D., J. Holland, J. Hentschel, P. Lanjouw and A. Herbert. 1998. Participation and combined methods in African poverty Assessment: Reviewing the agenda. Social Development Division Africa Division, DFID. London. February.

Botswana Institute of Development Policy Analysis (BIDPA). 1997. *Study of Poverty and Poverty Alleviation in Botswana*. Vols 1 and 2. Gaborone: Ministry of Finance and Development Planning.

Botswana Range Inventory & Monitoring Project (BRIMP). 1998a. Gathwane. *RRA Field Report* no. 5. Gaborone: BRIMP & MoA. February.

——. 1998b. Sekoma. *RRA Field Report* no. 6. Gaborone: BRIMP & MoA. February.

Bryman, A. 1988. *Quantity and Quality in Social Research*. London: Unwin Hyman.

Campbell, J. 1999. The development and use of Rapid Rural Appraisal Research: Key findings. Ministry of Agriculture, Botswana & Botswana Range Inventory and Monitoring Project. *Range Users Team Report* Phase I. Gaborone. June.

Daplyn, P., J. Cropley, S. Treagust and A. Gordon. 1991. The use of Geographical Information Systems in Socio-economic Analysis. Natural Resources Institute, *NRI Socio-Economic Series* no. 4. London: Overseas Development Administration.

Davies, S. and N. Hossain. 1997. Livelihood adaptation, public action and civil society: A review of the literature. *IDS Working Paper* no. 57. Sussex: Institute of Development Studies.

DFID. 1994. *Project Memorandum: Range Inventory and Monitoring Project.* Gaborone: DFID.

Dougill, A. 1997. Ecological change on Kalahari rangelands: Permanent or reversible? Implications for sustainable agricultural use. Paper given to ESRC Workshop *Sustainable Livelihoods in Marginal African Environments.* University of Sheffield. April.

Downs, R. and S. Reyna (eds). 1988. *Land and Society in Contemporary Africa.* London: University Press of New England.

Dunn, E., P. Atkins and J. Townsend. 1997. GIS for development: A contradiction in terms? *AREA* 29(2): 151–159.

Freudenberger, K. 1998. The use of RRA to inform policy: Tenure issues in Madagascar and Guinea. In J. Holland (ed.) *Whose Voice? Participatory Research and Policy Change* (pp. 67–79). London: Intermediate Technology.

Good, K. 1999. The state and extreme poverty in Botswana: The San and destitutes. *The Journal of Modern African Studies* 37(2): 185–205.

Goodchild, M. 1996. Geographic Information Systems and spatial analysis in the social sciences. In M. Aldenderfer and H. Maschner (eds) *Anthropology, Space, and Geographic Information Systems* (pp. 241–250). Oxford: Oxford University Press.

Government of Botswana. 1998. *Strategic/Organisational Plan.* Division of Agricultural Planning and Statistics. Gaborone: Ministry of Agriculture.

Hay, R. 1988. Famine incomes and employment: Has Botswana anything to teach Africa? *World Development* 16(9): 1113–1125.

Hitchcock, R. 1985. Water, land and livestock: The evolution of tenure and administration patterns in the grazing areas of Botswana. In L. Picard (ed.) *The Evolution of Modern Botswana.* University of Nebraska.

——. 1995. Indigenous Peoples, resource management, and traditional tenure systems in African dryland environments. In D. Stiles (ed.) *Social Aspects of Sustainable Dryland Management* (chap. 9). Chichester: J. Wiley and Sons.

Hobart, M. 1993. Introduction: The growth of ignorance? In M. Hobart (ed.) *An Anthropological Critique of Development* (pp. 1–30). London: Routledge.

IDS. 1997. Community-based sustainable development: Consensus or conflict? *IDS Bulletin* 28(4) (October).

Jick, T. 1979. Mixing qualitative and quantitative methods: Triangulation in action. *Administrative Science Quarterly* 24: 602–611.

Loker, W. 1996. Land degradation in the Peruvian Amazon: Applying GIS in human ecology research. In M. Aldenderfer and H. Maschner (eds) *Anthropology, Space, and Geographic Information Systems* (pp. 19–43). Oxford: Oxford University Press.

Moran, E. 1992. Anthropology and remote sensing. *Culture & Agriculture* 43: 16–17.

Payton, R., J. Barr, A. Martin, P. Sillitoe, J. Deckers, J. Gowing, N. Hatibu, S. Naseem, M. Tenyewa and M. Zuberi. n.d. Methodological lessons from contrasting approaches to integrating indigenous knowledge and scientific soil and land resources survey. Unpublished ms.

Peters, P. 1994. *Dividing the Commons: Politics, Policy and Culture in Botswana*. London: University Press of Virginia.

Purcell, T. 1998. Indigenous Knowledge and applied anthropology: Questions of definition and direction. *Human Organization* 57(3): 258–272.

Ringrose, S., C. Vanderpost and W. Matheson. 1996. The use of integrated remotely sensed and GIS data to determine the causes of vegetation cover change in southern Botswana. *Applied Geography* 16(3): 225–242.

Rundstrom, R. 1995. GIS, indigenous peoples, and epistemological diversity. *Cartography and Geographic Information Systems* 22(1): 45–57.

Sechrist, L. and S. Sidani. 1995. Quantitative and qualitative methods: Is there an alternative? *Evaluation and Program Planning* 18(1): 77–87.

Shipton, P. and M. Goheen. 1992. Introduction. Understanding African land-holding: Power, wealth, and meaning. *Africa* 62(3): 307–326.

Sillitoe, P. 1998. The development of indigenous knowledge. *Current Anthropology* 39(2): 223–252.

Stonich, S. 1996. Integrating socio-economic and GIS: A methodology for rural development and agricultural policy design. In M. Aldenderfer and H. Maschner (eds) *Anthropology, Space, and Geographic Information Systems* (pp. 778–790). Oxford: Oxford University Press.

Thomas, D. and D. Sporton. 1997. Understanding the dynamics of social and environmental variability: The impacts of structural land use change on the environment and peoples of the Kalahari, Botswana. *Applied Geography* 17(1): 11–27.

Tsimako, B. 1991. The Tribal Grazing Land Policy (TGLP) ranches: Performance to date. Gaborone: Monitoring and Evaluation Unit, MoA.

Valentine, T. 1993. Drought, transfer entitlements, and income distribution: The Botswana experience. *World Development* 21(1): 109–126.

Weiner, D., T. Warner, T. Harris and R. Levin. 1995. Apartheid representations in a digital landscape: GIS, remote sensing and local knowledge in Kiepersol, South Africa. *Cartography & Geographic Information Systems* 22(1): 30–44.

White, R. 1992. *Livestock Development and Pastoral Production on Communal Rangeland in Botswana*. London: Food Production and Rural Development Division, Commonwealth Secretariat.

Chapter 10

Indigenous and scientific knowledge of plant breeding

Similarities, differences and implications for collaboration

David A. Cleveland and Daniela Soleri[1]

Indigenous or local knowledge and modern, scientific knowledge have become increasingly separated in the process of modernization, and have often been assumed to be fundamentally different. In a world with unprecedented human impact on the environment, characterized by biophysical and sociocultural globalization, both the necessity of this separation and the assumption of fundamental differences need to be problematized. The question of how similar or different scientific knowledge and indigenous knowledge are, and how they might work together to help solve the problems of 'development', has immense practical and ethical implications. It also has immense theoretical importance – for better understanding the relationship between knowledge, action and environment (the world of things and actions outside of the mind) has the potential for improving the efficiency of consciously directed (teleological) human adaptation, for example for 'sustainable' interventions. It can help us to discriminate the general from the particular, an essential prerequisite for policy at all levels. At the same time, an important test of theory is its practical efficacy – the results of its application to understanding and solving human–environmental problems.

We illustrate the potential of theory-based investigation of indigenous and scientific knowledge by comparing the knowledge and practice of small-scale maize farmers in Oaxaca, Mexico, with that of scientific maize breeders, using a holistic theory of knowledge and basic plant breeding theory. We focus on knowledge of heritability of maize traits as determined by interaction of genotype and environment, a fundamental concept in biology (often discussed in anthropology as 'nature versus nurture'), and the relationship between this knowledge and the practice of plant breeding. We ask two main questions. First, to what extent are farmers' and plant breeders' knowledges and practices similar or different regarding maize *genotypes* (varieties, populations and plants) and *growing environments* (fields, selection and test plots)? Second, how can answers to the first question contribute to the process of collaboration between farmers and plant breeders, with the goal of developing varieties that better fulfil farmers needs?

The problem: scientific maize breeding and local farmers

Many people continue to go hungry in the world even though enough food is produced to prevent hunger if it is adequately distributed. The huge increases in yields and production necessary to have kept up with a rapidly expanding population are commonly attributed to modern, scientific agriculture and plant breeding that has taken place largely in optimal growing environments. In many areas where there are food shortages, food is produced by small-scale farmers who continue to practise traditionally based agriculture. Given the eventual limits to food production in optimal environments, the negative environmental effects of industrial agriculture, the political and economic costs of food distribution, and the desire of many local communities to maintain their farming identity and independence, it is likely that much of the increase in food production needed adequately to feed people in marginal areas must come from those areas (Heisey and Edmeades 1999). There is increasing concern to improve the yields of these farmers by making plant breeding more appropriate to their needs (Evans 1998; Mann 1999).

Indigenous and scientific plant breeding

Plant breeding includes both (1) the development of new varieties through artificial selection of plants by farmers and breeders within segregating plant populations, which changes the genetic make-up of the population, and (2) the choice of germ plasm that determines the genetic diversity available within a crop as the basis for selection, and the choice (by plant breeders) of which varieties to release and (by farmers) of which varieties to plant (Cleveland *et al.* 2000). Since the first domestication of wild plants about 12,000 years ago, farmer plant breeders have been responsible for the development of thousands of crop varieties in hundreds of species (Harlan 1992). Plant breeding as a specialized activity began about 200 years ago in industrial countries, and modern scientific plant breeding developed in the early part of the twentieth century, based on Darwin's theory of evolution through selection, and on the genetic mechanisms of evolution elucidated by Mendel and others (Allard 1999; Simmonds 1979).

For the last 200 years scientific plant breeding has become increasingly separated from plant breeding by farmers (Simmonds 1979). The emphasis of modern, scientific plant breeders (hereafter simply *plant breeders*), has typically been on developing *modern varieties* (MVs) adapted to *optimal* (relatively uniform, low stress), geographically widespread growing environments, and giving high yields in these environments (Evans 1993; Fischer 1996). While they have also given attention to breeding for stress tolerance, this attention has focused on stresses in relatively large-scale, optimal environments, and on commercial farmers who can afford to purchase seed, not on the farmers who are the topic of this chapter (Bänziger *et al.* 1999; Ceccarelli *et al.* 1994; Heisey and Edmeades 1999). This contrasts with plant breeding by farmers, especially small-scale farmers in *marginal* (relatively variable, high-stress) growing environments with limited access to external inputs (hereafter simply *farmers*). These farmers often grow *farmers' local varieties* (FVs), which are usually assumed to have more narrow geographical adaptation to specific marginal growing environments, giving moderate yields in those environments (Harlan 1992; Zeven 1998).

Maize

As with other major grain crops, high-yielding maize MVs have been bred for relatively optimal environments across wide geographic areas, and are relatively lacking in genetic diversity – only limited work has been done on breeding for the marginal environments of many small-scale farmers where yields are relatively low (Smith and Paliwal 1997).

Mexico is the centre of maize domestication and diversity, and is also the home of the Green Revolution approach to plant breeding in wheat and maize, developed at the International Maize and Wheat Improvement Centre (CIMMYT). This approach is characterized by the transfer of industrial agriculture to the Third World based on MVs (Simmonds 1990). Although in Mexico 222 maize MVs have been released by the public sector during 1966–97, and 155 private-sector MVs were available in 1997, 77 per cent of maize area is planted to FVs, with relatively low yield (2.3 Mg/h) (Morris and López Pereira 1999). In the southern Mexican state of Oaxaca, 93 per cent of maize area harvested in 1990 was under FVs (Aragón Cuevas 1995). Grain yield in Oaxaca during this period averaged 0.8 Mg/ha (INEGI 1996: 32), 40 per cent of the average yield for Mexico as a whole, and 21 per cent of the world average (Figure 10.1).

The reasons for the low adoption rate of maize MVs given by researchers, and their implications for farmer and scientist knowledge, differ greatly. They tend to emphasize the farmers, the economic system, the environment and plant breeders: (1) a lack of farmer knowledge, for example that farmers are 'only dimly aware of the potential benefits of improved germ plasm and crop management practices', and lacking the education and skills needed to manage MVs 'properly' (Aquino 1998: 249); (2) a lack of appropriate economic profit incentive for farmers due to exogenous 'technical, economic, institutional, and political factors' (Morris and López Pereira 1999); (3) the marginal growing environments (drought stress, low soil fertility, low level of inputs such as irrigation and fertilizers) of small-scale farmers in Mexico (de Janvry *et al.* 1997; García Barrios and García Barrios 1994), who cultivate most of the land planted to this crop; and (4) lack of appropriate plant breeding, that is MVs have generally not been targeted on these farmers (and

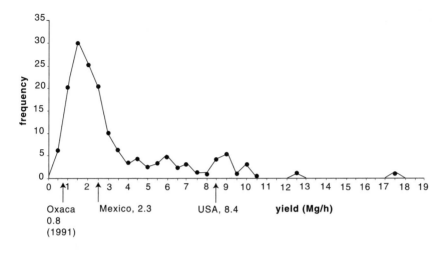

Figure 10.1   World maize yields by country, 1999

Graph based on data from FAO 2000

Note: n = 158

may, therefore, produce lower yields than FVs) (Aquino 1998; Heisey *et al.* 1998; Heisey and Edmeades 1999).

Comparing local and scientific knowledges as the basis for collaboration

The recent development of modern, scientific plant breeding, and its separation from farmers has resulted in a great divide between the maize breeding and production of small-scale farmers growing FVs in marginal environments (which is largely unknown to most plant breeders), and maize breeding programmes which are directed towards production by larger-scale farmers growing MVs in relatively optimal environments (largely unknown to small-scale farmers in marginal environments).

The first step in a comparison of indigenous and scientific knowledge is necessarily a definition of 'knowledge'. We define 'knowledge' as the non-genetic information possessed by an individual, as distinct from action or practice, though it can only be observed as expressed in behaviours or practice (including speech and writing) (Cleveland 2001). We define 'epistemology' as the process by which stimuli from the external physical world (e.g. from stars, wheat plants, yield trial data, journal articles, a colleague's or neighbour's verbal comments) are first received and then processed into physical patterns within a person's brain, which may subsequently be perceived subjectively as knowledge, or may remain as unconscious knowledge. This process is influenced by the biological structure and function of the brain, the technologies and practices used, and by pre-existing knowledge, as well as by the particular portion of external reality the individual experiences. Knowledge is shared to a greater or lesser degree within groups of different sizes to which individuals belong. Defined in this way, knowledge is similar to common concepts of culture in anthropology, which exists at the individual level and is shared to varying degrees with others (see, for example, Brumann 1999 and accompanying comments).

Indigenous knowledge as locally constructed skill versus scientific knowledge as generally verified theory

Many anthropologists and other social scientists often contrast scientific and indigenous knowledge in ways that seem to essentialize them, seeing the former as rationalistic, reductionist, theoretical, generalizable, objectively verifiable, abstract and imperialistic, in sharp contrast to the latter, which is seen to be organic, holistic, intuitive, local, socially constructed, practical and egalitarian (Escobar 1999; Scott 1998: 340). Ingold, for example, argues that indigenous knowledge is acquired through the process of 'enskillment', rather than through conscious conceptualization (Ingold 1996a, 1996b). Scott sees the 'basic procedure' of scientific plant breeding as 'exactly the reverse' of that of indigenous farmers, who are seen to have a much more complete and sophisticated understanding of objective reality in the development of their crop varieties, whose plant breeding knowledge he characterizes as 'craft', practice or 'mētis' (Scott 1998: 302, 340). Sillitoe sees indigenous knowledge as 'conditioned by sociocultural tradition, being culturally relative understanding inculcated into individuals from birth, structuring how they interface with their environments' (Sillitoe 1998b: 204), and as being more a 'skill' than conceptual, and as 'contingent and often local, not systematised and universal' as is scientific knowledge (Sillitoe 1998a: 229).

A closer reading of the literature suggests we need to reconsider these common anthropological ideas on empirical grounds and because they may impede theoretical understanding of knowledge, and potential collaboration between indigenous people and scientists (Agrawal 1995). It seems prudent to make as few a priori assumptions as possible, and formulate hypotheses about scientific knowledge and indigenous knowledge that can be empirically tested.

The universal as opposed to local nature of indigenous knowledge has been argued both from an evolutionary biological viewpoint, for example in terms of adapted epistemologies (Cosmides and Tooby 1996), and from an empirical viewpoint, as in the many studies comparing indigenous and scientific taxonomies of plants and animals (Berlin 1992). While many farmers' complicated practices observed by outsiders may appear to be untheorized responses to changing and unpredictable circumstances, concluding that indigenous knowledge is 'practice', this begs the question of the mental basis of behaviour, and equates farmers' inability to verbalize this basis to naive outsiders with the absence of theoretical understanding. As with scientific knowledge, theory and intuition are not mutually exclusive.

Indigenous and scientific knowledge also appear to be similar in being composed of different types of knowledge (substantive or empirical, formal or normative, theoretical or deductive, and intuitive or unconscious). Ellen reviews the results of research on subsistence of rainforest peoples, including his own with the Nuaulu of Seram, eastern Indonesia, in terms of their knowledge of nature. He concludes that observations of 'particular instances' (substantive knowledge of many individual species) leads inductively to 'knowledge of general principles', and in knowledge transmission these 'overarching deductive models of how the natural world works are privileged over accumulated inductive knowledge' (Ellen 1999: 106). These models (or theories) function at a macro-scale as a 'folk synecology', for example in connecting observations at the species level with forest structure and dynamics (Ellen 1999: 107).

We define theories as generalizable (not necessarily universal) concepts about the way things in the world relate to each other, including causal relationships, on which predictions and action can be based (c.f. Hull 1988: 485; Medin and Atran 1999: 9). According to some philosophers of science, 'Theory-free observation languages and classifications are impossible' (Hull 1988: 485). There is no such thing as a purely observational term, since our descriptions of our observations are necessarily affected by theory, and apparently non-theoretical terms such as 'animal' and 'dorsal' are theory-laden (Hull 1988: 8).

Limited theoretical understanding due to epistemological limitations (e.g. lack of microscopes) does not mean that conceptual indigenous knowledge cannot be the basis for effective practice. For example, Trutmann et al. (1996: 68) show that while farmers have 'no concept of the biological causes of individual diseases', their 'functional explanations for putrefaction' developed from 'thinking through their observations in their own cultural idioms' and result in management practices that are effective in reducing loss of yield from disease (Trutmann et al. 1996). However, this does not mean that these farmers' knowledge may not be theoretical, because all theory, including Western scientific theory, is always partial, and because operationalizing theoretical concepts always leave things out; they could not function unless they did (Hull 1988: 485).

On the other hand, scientific knowledge, like indigenous knowledge, can also be culturally relative, 'local' knowledge. Agrawal points out that criticisms of the failure of science-based approaches to Third World development on the grounds that they 'ignored the social, political and cultural contexts in which they were implemented' suggest that 'it is likely that the so-called technical solutions are just as firmly anchored in a specific milieu as any other system of knowledge' (Agrawal 1995: 425). Dove suggests that indigenous knowledge and scientific knowledge may also be alike in their limited ability to comprehend complex natural phenomena (Dove 1996). Work by social scientists, historians and philosophers on the nature of scientific knowledge since the 1920s has explicitly explored the role of personal psychology, historical contingencies and social context in its production (Giere 1999).

Perhaps one reason for the continued resistance by many social scientists to attempts to explore possible similarities between indigenous knowledge and scientific knowledge is that, if they are found, it will inevitably lead to the privileging of scientific knowledge (Sillitoe, this volume). The dominance of scientific knowledge in development projects based on assumed similarities between them (e.g. Sherwood 1997) continues the tradition of privileging scientific knowledge based on modernist ideas of differences between indigenous knowledge and scientific knowledge. It may be that many proponents of indigenous knowledge as different (and 'better') than scientific knowledge are using an essentialist definition of science similar to that of some advocates of positivist science. This definition ignores current research in social studies of science and the writings of scientists themselves, resulting in a situation similar to that in anthropology, where erroneous assumptions about the role of positivism in science cause some anthropologists to reject the notion of a 'science' of anthropology (Roscoe 1995).

Beyond participation: possibilities for collaboration

The deepening global human–environmental crisis has led to a sense of urgency in understanding the possible contribution of both indigenous knowledge and scientific knowledge to solutions. Nader, for example, writes that 'globalisation renders the search for a more balanced, indeed more scientific, treatment of disparate knowledge systems inevitable' (Nader 1996: 6–7). Sillitoe also sees indigenous knowledge as being able to challenge and thus advance scientific understanding of natural processes (Sillitoe 1998a: 227), and suggests the 'need to develop a coherent indigenous knowledge intellectual framework to interface effectively with Western science' (Sillitoe 1998b: 215, n.4). Yet, contrasting views of indigenous knowledge and scientific knowledge in an essentialized way make it difficult to conceive of the possibility of collaboration between indigenous peoples and scientists in the sense of mutual sharing of ideas. Scott, for example, sees farmers as capable of incorporating the results of scientists' 'epistemic work', but sees science incapable of acknowledging or including farmers' practice (Scott 1998: 304), and Sillitoe sees as problematic the possibility that 'local people can frame their problems in a manner intelligible to scientists', and that 'Science determines its own research agenda' based on 'models it used to understand the world' (Sillitoe 1998a: 230, 232).

Collaborative plant breeding (often referred to by its acronym, CPB, and also known as participatory plant breeding, PPB) has emerged in the last decade as a popular focus of development, with major initiatives, for example by the Consultative Group on International Agricultural Research (CGIAR) and several of its Centres (CGIAR 1997) and by the Community Biodiversity Development and Conservation programme (CLADES *et al.* 1994). Collaborative plant breeding is based on the critical assumption, often unexamined, that plant breeders' and farmers' knowledge is compatible.

However, most of the research on plant breeding has been done either (1) by social scientists focusing on the social aspects, who have not used biological theory or an empirical understanding of biophysical reality, or (2) by plant breeders and biologists focusing on the biological aspects, who have not used social theory or an empirical understanding of social reality and knowledge. The result is that little is known of plant breeding indigenous knowledge in relation to scientific knowledge. A review of key articles suggests that the data needed to address questions about farmer plant breeding (knowledge, practice, results) in terms of biological theory are often scant or non-existent, and that the answers to these questions that do exist in the literature are often very different, even contradictory, and may be based on unexamined and unrecognized assumptions (Cleveland *et al.* 2000). As a consequence, many collaborative plant breeding efforts appear to emphasize either the biological aspects of plant breeding, for example the transfer of technology, or the social aspects, for example empowering farmers (McGuire *et al.* 1999), with little integration of biological and social issues, theoretically or empirically.

For example, a four-level taxonomy of participation (contractual, consultative, collaborative and collegial) developed by Biggs (1989) is commonly used as a measure of participation, and reflects what many see as its goals. Participation is defined quantitatively, primarily by physical effort on the part of farmers; that is, the greater farmers' efforts the more they are participatory, and therefore the greater the impact in terms of social goals such as equity and empowerment. However, social goals may in fact be relatively independent of biological goals. For example, the introgression of alleles conferring disease tolerance into a local variety may produce biological and social benefits with no farmer participation, and farmer participation in improving mass selection may increase the self-esteem of local farmers, but have no biological benefits. An alternative is to consider 'participation' qualitatively, as a relationship between farmers and plant breeders characterized by ongoing interaction including discussion of the conceptual basis of plant breeding practice, mutual respect and the common goal of meeting local needs. This relationship could be present regardless of the specific plant breeding strategy or level of physical involvement of either farmers or breeders. Such a relationship may well require deeper understanding of similarities and differences between farmers' indigenous knowledge and plant breeders' scientific knowledge.

Methods

In exploring the nature of indigenous knowledge and scientific knowledge of plant breeding, we have used a naturalistic and holistic model of knowledge combined with a basic biological model of plant breeding (discussed below) to analyse farmers' knowledge of their maize varieties in Oaxaca, compared with maize breeders' knowledge.

A holistic, naturalistic approach to scientific knowledge and indigenous knowledge in plant breeding

The goal of our research is to find a way to compare conceptual (theoretical) scientific knowledge with indigenous knowledge by literally integrating social and biological theory. It requires collaboration between natural and social scientific disciplines that has been seen as necessary by others to further indigenous knowledge research (Sillitoe 1998b: 216). We start with the biological model that informs plant breeding theory and practice because it is accessible to us, a part of our culture, and because it appears to have a high level of objective accuracy and intersubjective validity, i.e. it appears to refer to an empirical reality that both farmers and scientists experience. In addition, at the level of classification of biological organisms, there appears to be a fairly high level of correlation between local and scientific systems, implying a common conceptual basis (Berlin 1992; Boster 1996). However, we assume that there is also indigenous knowledge of plants and growing environments that may be quite different from that of scientists, and may not be amenable to explanation in parallel scientific terms.

We use both a holistic theory of knowledge and plant breeders' biological theory as our theoretical base for achieving increased understanding of farmer and plant breeder knowledge of the relationship between crop plants and their growing environments. This is a simple model of the relationships between objective biophysical and social reality, epistemology, knowledge, practice (behaviour) and the effects of practice on biophysical reality, using terms and concepts found in the current literature (Figure 10.2).

We take a *holistic* approach, a middle ground between the objectivist (positivist, utilitarian, internalist) and constructivist (relativist, intellectualist, externalist) perspectives (Cleveland 2001). While the ideal of a 'holistic' approach has a long history in anthropology (and other disciplines), the current debate over indigenous and scientific knowledge seems to us to have strayed far from this ideal. The 'science wars' and the debate in the social studies of science about the superiority of internalist versus externalist approaches is also testimony to lack of a holistic approach.

As a result, a holistic approach is being advocated to counter the polarized divide in theoretical approaches to knowledge and practice in social studies of science (Bourdieu 2000; Harding 1998; Hull 1988), anthropology (Ellen 1996;

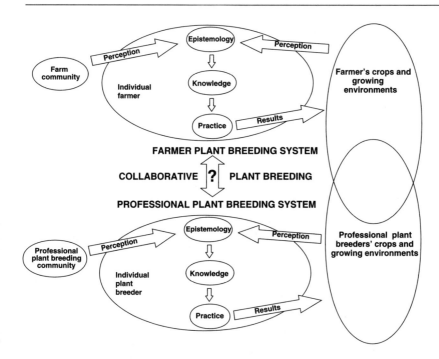

Figure 10.2   A holistic model of plant breeding knowledge

Schweizer 1998; Sillitoe, this volume), ethnobiology (Medin and Atran 1999) and natural sciences (Gould 2000). It sees scientific knowledge *and* indigenous knowledge as both constructed by epistemological processes influenced by social and historical factors which affect, for example, values and technologies. On the other hand, it also sees scientific knowledge *and* indigenous knowledge as a reflection of both the general patterns, and the local and individual variations of biophysical reality and of human cognition (Boster 1996). The result is a complex 'knowledge' which requires empirical investigation to understand its origins, nature and relationship to practice in any particular case.

Epistemology is defined in our model as the process by which stimuli from the external physical world (e.g. from maize plants, a journal article, a planting song, a colleague's or neighbour's verbal comments) are first received and then neurologically processed into physical patterns within a person's brain that are subsequently perceived subjectively as knowledge. This process is influenced by the biological characteristics of the individual, by the technologies and actions employed by the individual, and by pre-existing knowledge.

Plant breeders' biological model

As a framework for comparing farmer and plant breeder knowledge and practice we use the basic biological theory of evolution and development (e.g.

Falconer 1989), which is the explicit basis of modern scientific plant breeding (Allard 1999; Simmonds 1979), and underlies plant breeders' understanding of even the most complex phenomena they encounter (Cooper and Hammer 1996; DeLacy *et al.* 1996).

The core of biological theory and practice in plant breeding is the relative contribution to individual phenotypes (phenotypic variation, V_P) of the genotype (genetic variation, V_G), the environment (non-genetic or environmental variation, V_E), and genotype-by-environment (G×E) interaction. Thus, we have the equation $(V_P=V_G+V_E+V_{G×E})$. $V_{G×E}$ represents the degree to which genotypes behave consistently across a number of spatial or temporal environments. Quantitative G×E is characterized by marked changes in performance with changes in environmental factors. Qualitative G×E between two or more varieties is often referred to as a 'crossover' because in the commonly used regression analyses, the regression lines for yield (or other traits) cross over at some point (see Figure 10.7, below). Heritability (H, described here in the broad sense) is the proportion of V_P due to V_G, (V_G/V_P). Traits with high average H vary less with variation in the environment than traits with low average H. Heritability is a major determinant of the response to selection (R), which, for a specific trait, is the difference between the mean of the whole population from which the parents were selected and the mean of the next generation that is produced by planting those selected seeds under the same conditions. R is the product of two different factors, H and S (R = HS), where S is the selection differential, the difference between the mean of the whole population from which the parents were selected, and the mean of the group selected from that population to form the seeds for the next generation (Falconer 1989).

Using the biological model we seek to understand farmers' perceptions in breeders' terms and concepts in order to facilitate collaboration, including increasing farmers' status in plant breeders' eyes, and increasing farmers' ability to use their own knowledge of their FVs and growing conditions. Conceivably our research could also enable farmers to compare plant breeders' theories with their own. We are aware of the 'intimate links between knowledge and power' that have been ignored by many indigenous knowledge advocates who, perhaps unconsciously, privilege scientific knowledge while singing the praises of indigenous knowledge (Agrawal 1995: 430). We do not assume that when there are differences between farmers and breeders that the farmer is always 'wrong', nor, on the other hand, do we assume that outsiders have been negligent in understanding farmer knowledge and practice in their own terms (see Scoones and Thompson 1993; Uphoff 1992). We acknowledge that successful plant breeding, by either farmers or formal breeders, does not depend on a complete empirical or theoretical understanding of the biological mechanisms involved (Duvick 1996; Simmonds 1979). We also use the model in our research to understand plant breeders, and *differences among* plant breeders.

Case studies of maize breeding

We undertook the research with farmers as part of a larger study of farmer selection and the genetic structure of their maize populations, working with thirteen farming households in two communities in the Central Valleys of Oaxaca, Mexico for a period of sixteen months (June 1996–October 1998) (for details see Soleri and Smith 2002; Soleri, Smith et al. 2000b; Soleri and Cleveland 2001). We collected data in Spanish through participant observation, informal discussions, formal interviews, farmer selection exercises (in which they identified the best ears for planting from a sample of ears from plots in their fields) and on-farm experimental plot research. We used standard statistical tests for significance (P ≤ 0.05) wherever appropriate. We worked with eight farm families in Santa Maria (pseudonyms are used for communities throughout), a community in the Zimitlan Valley, and with five families in San Antonio, a community in the Mitla Valley. This is a marginal environment for maize production, with 88 per cent of summer production grown under rainfed conditions, and with most households experiencing harvest 'failure' about one out of every four years (Dilley 1993).

We carried out research on scientific plant breeding through informal interviews with an opportunistic sample of plant breeders (n ≈ 20), and through an analysis of the plant breeding literature. Our research with both farmers and plant breeders is ongoing, and is being extended to other families in the two communities, and to other locations and crops.

Farmers

Trait heritability and intrapopulation selection

The formal interviews presented farmers with hypothetical scenarios constructed with elements, some of which were familiar and some novel to them. The scenarios made use of traits with high average H (tassel colour) and medium-to-low average H (ear length) that were familiar and of interest to farmers. We asked about expression of these traits in both a variable, high-stress (*marginal*) field typical of the region and a hypothetical, uniform, low-stress (*optimal*) field, one that in no way limits plants' growth potential, an environment that farmers had not experienced. Our purpose was to present hypothetical situations that would facilitate discussion of the abstract concept of heritability, i.e. to improve our understanding of how farmers perceive the influence of V_G and V_E on maize phenotypes. The potential role of V_G was represented by the relationship between phenotypes of parental and progeny generations, and the potential role of V_E by the contrasting growing environments.

Tassel colour (including yellow, red and purple) is a highly heritable trait that farmers in both communities pointed out to us. In San Antonio a household sought out a yellow maize population with purple tassels because of the pleasure of looking across a field of green plants with purple tassels. In Santa

Maria a household had developed and grew a white maize population with purple tassels, cobs and husks. They did so because when making tamales (steamed maize flour dough) with these purple husks, the purple colour is transferred to the food – a desirable effect. The null hypothesis was that farmers see a relatively small contribution by V_G to total V_P, attributing V_P predominantly to V_E – that seeds from plants with a given tassel colour produce plants with a diversity of tassel colours when planted in a marginal environment, and mostly tassels of the given colour when planted in an optimal environment. The alternative hypothesis was that farmers see tassel colour primarily determined by V_G, that the tassel colour of the progeny plant would be the same as that of the parent regardless of the environment.

Using photographs to represent a local population of maize that included plants with both purple and yellow tassels, we asked farmers what tassel colour would result if seed were only taken from plants with purple tassels and those seed were planted in (1) a marginal field, and (2) an optimal field (Figure 10.3). The majority of responses to these scenarios stated that tassel colour would be purple in either field, that is, it would not be affected by the growing environment. The remainder stated that there would be a mixture of colours, and that after five years of isolation from cross-pollination with other populations and continued selection for that colour, the population would have all purple tassels.

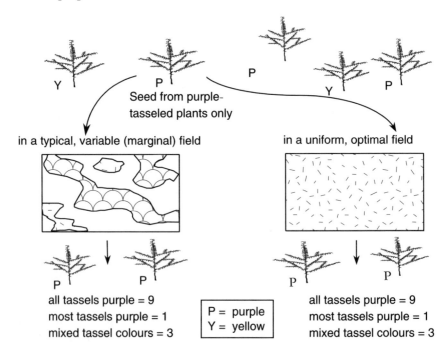

Figure 10.3   Genetic perceptions: responses to tassel colour scenario

Some farmers went further in their explanations. For example, two of the households pointed out that even after five cycles of isolation and selection for tassel colour, occasional non-selected phenotypes would still occur – a few yellow tassels among the population selected for purple tassels – a result that plant breeders would attribute to crossing and continuing segregation in a heterogeneous population.

Ear length is one of farmers' central selection criteria in both communities (Soleri, Smith *et al* 2000). The null hypothesis was that farmers see a relatively small contribution by V_G to total V_p, that seeds from long ear cobs produce plants with a diversity of ear lengths when planted in a marginal environment, and mostly long ears when planted in an optimal environment. The alternative hypothesis was that farmers see ear length primarily determined by V_G, with progeny phenotype for the most part the same as that of the parent, regardless of the environment. As with tassel colour, our hypotheses did not include the effects of the pollen parent or of segregation in progeny phenotypes, although these were noted by some farmers.

Using a variable sample of maize ears from a local field to 'demonstrate' the scenarios, we asked farmers what would be the length of the ears produced in a marginal environment as compared to those produced in a uniform environment, if they planted only seed from the long ears from a typical harvest of variable sized ears (Figure 10.4). The farmers stated that the marginal environment would produce a harvest of variable ear lengths while the harvest from the uniform environment would consist of uniformly long ears. One farmer noted that there would always be some variation present in any environment.

Responses to the scenarios (Table 10.1) showed general agreement among farmers regarding high and low heritability traits. Genetic variation and the capacity to select from it were clearly recognized for the high heritability trait, tassel colour. Here, farmers see phenotypic variation consistently expressed despite contrasting environments, and they attribute this variation to a non-environmental source. In contrast, for the low heritability trait (ear length), farmers see no V_G, attributing progeny phenotypes to their growing environment, not to their parental phenotype.

Table 10.1   Summary of farmer perceptions of heritability for two traits and effect on progeny performance for one trait in maize

Phenotypic trait selected for in parents	Heritability: Farmers' expectations for progeny phenotypic variation in an environment that is					
	Marginal			Optimal		
	none	some	much	none	some	much
Tassel colour	9	1	3	9	1	3
Ear length	0	0	13	12	1	0

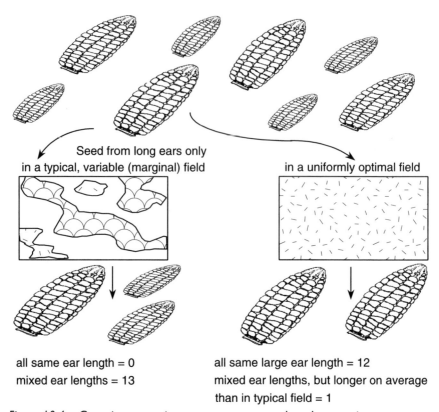

Seed from long ears only

in a typical, variable (marginal) field   in a uniformly optimal field

all same ear length = 0   all same large ear length = 12
mixed ear lengths = 13   mixed ear lengths, but longer on average
                                 than in typical field = 1

Figure 10.4   Genetic perceptions: responses to ear length scenarios

V_G, V_E and interpopulation descriptors

Differences between the perceptions of other aspects of their maize populations among farmers in the two communities expand our understanding of
farmer knowledge. Although Santa Maria and San Antonio are only approximately 65 km apart and both communities have good access to major
markets, there is a distinct difference in farmers' naming practices regarding
their white maize varieties in the two communities (Table 10.2). In both locations *blanco criollo* (local white) maize is the primary class of maize cultivated.

In Santa Maria varieties of *blanco* are categorized solely on features
observed in the ear after harvest – particularly kernel/ear type (*cuadrado* versus
bolita), as well as pigmentation of the cob, and tassel. No distinct local *blanco*
varieties were identified by farmers as maintained for cultivation in particular
environments (locations, years or management practices). In contrast, San
Antonio farmers categorize varieties of *blanco* on the basis of their cycle
length (*tardón*, long cycle, versus *violento*, short cycle), as measured by days to

Table 10.2   Summary of objectives, methods and findings* used in the investigation of farmers' perceptions and interpopulation variation of local *blanco* maize varieties

Question	Method	Findings	
		Santa Maria	*San Antonio*
What are farmers' declared varieties of local *blanco* maize?	Formal interviews	Two varieties based on ear and kernel morphology: *cuadrado* and *bolita*	Two varieties based on cycle length: *violento* and *tardón*
What are farmers' estimations of cycle length of their local *blanco* maize varieties?	Formal interviews	Cycle length estimates for *cuadrado* and *bolita* are not significantly different	Cycle length estimates for *violento* and *tardón* are significantly different
Is there a significant difference in reproductive phenology between farmer-declared long- and short-cycle *blanco* varieties in San Antonio?	Comparison with orthogonal contrast[1] of days to anthesis of varieties based on field trials	N.A.	The *violento* populations (n = 2) had significantly shorter days to anthesis than did the *tardón* populations (n = 2).

Notes:
* Significance set at P ≤ 0.05
[1] A method for analysing planned multiple comparisons, based on *t*-tests

anthesis and harvest, and say that they maintain these varieties because of their different performances in response to V_E, specifically year-to-year variation in amount and timing of precipitation. Based on farmer estimates, the differences in cycle lengths for *tardón* and *violento* in San Antonio are significant, whereas there are no significant differences in farmer estimates of cycle lengths for the main types of white maize in Santa Maria (Soleri and Cleveland 2001).

These findings suggest that intra field V_E appears greater to farmers in Santa Maria than V_E between fields/years and, therefore, that maintaining separate varieties (distinct 'sets' of V_G) for different fields/years is not worth their effort. This is not so in the eyes of San Antonio farmers. Rather, the findings suggest the hypothesis that one of the factors contributing to farmers' maintenance of distinct varieties of a class of maize (*blanco* in this case) is their assessment of the magnitude of V_E among their growing environments and the costs and benefits to them of maintaining each variety.

Attention to cycle length in San Antonio may be one reason why, despite gene flow through seed exchange and subsequent pollen movement, we found in field trials a significant difference in days to anthesis between white maize varieties from these two communities (Soleri and Smith 2002).

Conclusions about farmers' knowledge and practice

These findings suggest that farmers' theories must be understood in context. As with formally trained researchers, it appears that most farmers base their understanding of V_G and H on their own experiences. That they recognize V_G is evidenced by responses to scenarios regarding a trait with high average H (tassel colour). That they recognize V_E is evidenced by the farmers in San Antonio maintaining varieties with different cycle lengths. As such, farmers' responses may not so much deny the presence of V_G in their maize populations for traits of low average H, but reflect their unfamiliarity with optimal growing environments and indicate the overwhelming influence of V_E in local fields, obscuring V_G in low heritability traits (Figure 10.5). This may be a major reason why farmers do not express an interest in changing their existing maize varieties, only in maintaining them, or adopting new varieties if they want to improve production (Soleri, Smith *et al* 2000), a finding similar to that of research with farmers in Jalisco, Mexico (Louette and Smale 1998).

These findings are important for collaborative plant breeding because they suggest that the assumptions of plant breeders (and those of other outsiders

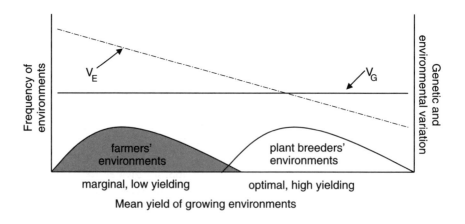

Figure 10.5   Graphic representation of the hypothesis of experience limiting perceptions and theory: V_E obscuring V_G in farmers' experience of V_P

based on plant breeding theory and practice) may underestimate and/or misunderstand farmers' plant breeding knowledge, including their interest in and expectations of plant breeding. Understanding farmers' plant breeding in terms of plant breeders' biological model is not straightforward, because the genotypes, environments and epistemologies of farmers and plant breeders are different in some ways, and similar in others. This means that if collaborative plant breeding projects based on invalid assumptions about farmers' plant breeding fail, outsiders may conclude that 'collaboration' does not work because farmers cannot understand the basic ideas of scientific plant breeding, or that scientific plant breeding is inappropriate for farmers' situations. Such conclusions are not justified without first understanding farmers' plant breeding knowledge, and to do this a methodology such as the one used here may be useful.

Plant breeders

There is a great deal of controversy among plant breeders' (including maize breeders) about the extent to which selection in optimal environments results in widely adapted MVs, that is varieties that also have superior yield in marginal environments, a phenomenon termed *yield spillover* (MV D, compared with FV B, Figure 10.6). When there is no spillover, there may instead be qualitative G×E, known as a *crossover*. A crossover is a change in rank of varieties across the range of environments in which they are grown, which in regression analysis means that their slopes cross over. For example MV C outyields FV B in the more optimal environments, but B outyields C in the more marginal environments (Figure 10.6).

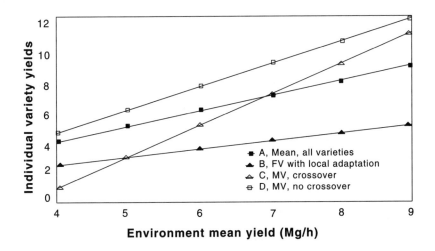

Figure 10.6   Spillovers and crossovers

Emphasizing selection in optimal environments

The more conventional approach is one that emphasizes selection and testing of new varieties in optimal environments, with the assumption that such varieties will also be higher yielding in farmers' marginal environments (Romagosa and Fox 1993). This approach is justified theoretically (in terms of genetic response, R) because it is more efficient (more rapid increase in R) to carry out selection in optimal environments where heritabilities are higher due to lower V_E, and empirically by the widespread adoption of MVs in the Third World (e.g. in the Green Revolution) (Byerlee 1996), including, for example, high adoption rates for maize hybrid MVs among limited resource farmers in more marginal environments in Zimbabwe (Heisey *et al.* 1998).

A review of on-farm trials in five Third World countries, comparing maize varieties containing improved CIMMYT germ plasm adapted to farmers' environments with FVs, found evidence of crossovers in a minority of cases, and concluded that MVs generally outyield FVs even in the 'worst environments studied' (Pham *et al.* 1989: 205). In another report of CIMMYT maize breeding research the authors concluded

> These observations suggest that CIMMYT's strategy [selection in relatively optimal environments] for population improvement and cultivar development has been successful for developing superior maize cultivars for the resource-poor farmers of the developing world, where most of the low-yielding environments occur.
>
> (Pandey *et al.* 1991: 289)

Three recent articles by plant breeders describing evaluation of maize genotypes across a range of environments (two reporting CIMMYT research) conclude that selection in optimal environments produces genotypes with higher yields than locally adapted genotypes in marginal target environments (Ceballos *et al.* 1998; Duvick 1992; Pandey *et al.* 1991). When the data reported in these studies are compared with those of the three articles described in the following section, the former appear to reflect a narrower range of environments, especially in the higher yielding environments (Figure 10.7).

Emphasizing selection in marginal environments

The major alternative to the yield spillover viewpoint asserts that yield in different environments can be negatively correlated and, therefore, that MVs selected in optimal environments may show qualitative G×E for yield when evaluated along with varieties adapted to low-yielding environments, resulting in crossovers between MVs and FVs. In fact, crossovers in performance between varieties are 'common' (Evans 1993: 165ff.). It has been suggested that one reason for crossovers is that plant breeders have targeted relatively

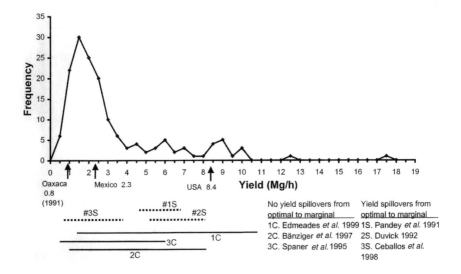

Figure 10.7   Yield spillovers in maize germplasm trials from optimal to marginal environments (compared with world maize yields by country, 1999, see Figure 10.1)

optimal environments (with high-input farmers), with the result that 'selection has inevitably, but unconsciously', been for high-yielding, high-response varieties that may often have low yields in marginal environments. For high performance in marginal target environments, selection must take place in these environments (Simmonds 1991). In contrast, crossovers are attributed by advocates of the spillover approach to a lack of conventional breeding effort in optimal environments, not to the failure of this approach (Pingali and Rajaram 1999).

Three recent articles by plant breeders describing evaluation of maize genotypes across a range of environments (two reporting CIMMYT research) conclude that selection should take place in marginal environments that have similar stresses to the target environments (Bänziger *et al.* 1997; Edmeades *et al.* 1999; Spaner *et al.* 1995). When the range of environments reported in these articles are compared with those of the three articles described in the previous section, they appear to be dealing with a wider range of environments, especially at the low yield end of the distribution (Figure 10.7).

Conclusions about plant breeders' knowledge and practice

The reasons why plant breeders disagree about the possibility of yield spillovers in maize breeding from selection in optimal environments may be partially dependent on their different experiences, namely: (1) the environmental stresses and corresponding genotypic adaptations they study (e.g. drought, acid soil, or low nitrogen levels); (2) the range of genetic diversity present among the varieties being compared; and (3) the degree of difference in the range and type of V_E, especially in stress levels, between the environments in which selection and testing occur (test environments) and those in which cultivation by farmers occurs (target environments) (Cleveland 2001).

The examples we present, based on preliminary analyses, provide some support for the third explanation (Figure 10.6), which has also been suggested for other crops (Ceccarelli 1996). If this explanation is valid, then plant breeders with little or no experience with farmers' marginal environments will be unlikely to anticipate the crossovers between MVs and FVs that can occur there (Figure 10.8). This has also been our experience in our informal interviews with plant breeders. Compare this with a parallel hypothesis based on farmers' knowledge illustrated in Figure 10.5.

In addition, there is some evidence to support the hypothesis that choice of selection environments is influenced by values, as reflected in statements plant breeders make about the goals of maize breeding (Cleveland 2001). On the one hand, those favouring selection in optimal environments tend to emphasize the need for farmers to modernize in order to make their farming systems appropriate for cultivation of the MVs that plant breeders produce. For example, 'Since improved varieties are usually better able to take advantage of this extra investment, they can thus be regarded as an incentive for farmers to raise their level of inputs and to improve their management of

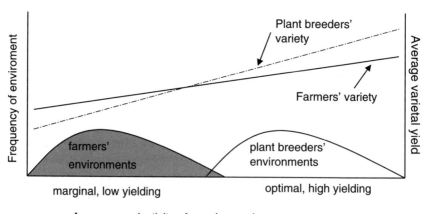

Figure 10.8   Graphic representation of hypothesis of experience limiting perceptions and theory: range of V_E limiting plant breeders' observations of G×E
Partially based on Ceccarelli 1989 and Ceccarelli *et al.* 1994.

maize' (Pham *et al.* 1989: 205). In terms of farmers' reasons for not adopting MVs, this emphasizes lack of economic incentives rather than economic, institutional or physical barriers. There may also be the assumption that there are cultural barriers, i.e. ignorance of small-scale farmers (Aquino 1998).

On the other hand, those favouring selection in marginal environments tend to emphasize the need for plant breeders to adapt their breeding goals to meet the needs of farmers' situations and environments, and emphasize the difficulty of reducing poverty via technical change (Heisey and Edmeades 1999). For example:

> Maize yields in farmers' fields in many tropical countries... [are] in stark contrast to yields ... reported on breeding stations in those same countries ... Farmers' fields are rarely characterised by only one abiotic stress ... Resource constrained farmers in many parts of the tropics may apply no fertiliser at all.
>
> (Bänziger *et al.* 1999: 1035)

The scientific knowledge of plant breeders that exists on an unconscious or intuitive level may also affect their practice, though this possibility has received much attention from researchers. Simmonds suggests that selection by conventional breeders has 'unconsciously' been for varieties with high response in optimal environments, and high-yielding, high-response varieties that have low yields in marginal environments (Simmonds 1991), or what some plant breeders have referred to as 'cryptic breeding' (Smith and Zobel 1991: 57). One prominent plant breeder has stated that:

> Modern methods of statistical design and analysis add precision to all of these decisions and quantitative genetic theory adds rationality to breeding plans, but art and experience − not precision genetics − are the key to successful use of these useful tools.
>
> (Duvick 1996: 543)

Conclusions

At the beginning of this chapter we asked two general questions. The preliminary answers from our research are summarized below.

First, to what extent are farmers' and plant breeders' knowledges and practices similar or different regarding maize genotypes (varieties, populations and plants) and growing environments?

1   There are *similarities* between farmers and plant breeders in their knowledge of the determinants of plant phenotypes, in that both recognize the joint contribution of genotype and environment. The knowledge of both

is theoretical because it includes causal relationships that are the basis of predictions and plans.

2   There are *differences* between farmers and plant breeders because of the differences in the specific kinds of genotypes and environments they work with, and differences in epistemological tools: for example, farmers' more holistic knowledge of genotypes and environments versus the plant breeders' more specialized knowledge of genetics, statistics, and their technological ability and resources to control environmental and genotypic variables.

3   These differences *between* farmers and plant breeders are paralleled by *similar* differences *among* both farmers and plant breeders that appear to be in part the result of working with different environments. For example, plant breeders differ from farmers in regard to their observations and theory regarding the possibility of yield spillovers from selection in optimal to marginal environments, while Oaxacan farmers differ from plant breeders in terms of theory for discriminating between genotypes in terms of growing cycle length.

Second, how can answers to the first question contribute to the process of collaboration between farmers and plant breeders, with the goal of developing improved varieties for farmers?

4   It is important to question the extent to which plant breeding 'theory' applied to collaborative plant breeding is in fact an elaboration of fundamental biological theory based on narrow interpretations and untested assumptions. Understanding the basis for disagreements among plant breeders about plant breeding theory and practice can help.

5   Plant breeders' assumptions may need testing by formulating hypotheses applied to (a) farmers' biophysical and sociocultural environments; (b) farmers' theoretical as well as empirical knowledge; and (c) disagreements about theory among plant breeders in terms of differences in assumptions and values (e.g. about the possibility and desirability of farmers adopting MVs), and in the genotypes and environments they work with.

6   Problematizing the relationship between farmer and plant breeder knowledge based on a holistic theory of knowledge can contribute to the formulation and testing of specific hypotheses within the context of collaborative plant breeding projects.

7   Both farmers' indigenous knowledge and plant breeders' scientific knowledge are important for collaborative plant breeding. Plant breeders who emphasize their technical epistemology often focus on genetic response to selection (R), and are puzzled when farmers reject their advice, just as farmers are puzzled that plant breeders do not understand that any improvement in yield, for example, has to be weighed against the costs of the extra time and resources required.

8   The search for generalizations about farmer and plant breeder knowledge and practice, and for policy based on them to guide collaborative plant breeding, is valid, but we need to be careful of superficiality.
9   If collaborative plant breeding projects fail, it may be because they are based on invalid assumptions regarding the interpretation of plant breeding theory. Therefore, it is not valid to conclude from such failures that farmers cannot understand the basic ideas of scientific plant breeding, or that scientific plant breeding is inappropriate to farmers' situations.

While farmers' knowledge is local, it can also be based on the same generalizable theories about crops and environments as plant breeders'. The contingencies of plant breeders' experiences with unique genotypes, environments and social contexts renders their knowledge local also. Understanding that farmer and scientist knowledges are both local and both generalizable may open up new possibilities for communication between farmers and scientists, and for understanding how these knowledges can complement each other to the benefit of both groups.

While plant breeders may all believe that the fundamental biological model is universally valid, they increasingly disagree on its interpretation as the number of variables and their relationships increase. We have suggested that claims for generalizability, especially by breeders unfamiliar with the situations of farmers, may be invalid, in the same way that claims of farmers based on locality may be invalid because they do no have wider experience of genotypes and environments. The minority of plant breeders with wider experience, and the minority of farmers with wider experience, may have conceptions of genotypes and environments different to the majority. This can form the basis for furthering theoretical understanding that can be communicated to a larger number of farmers and plant breeders.

Our holistic theoretical approach to understanding knowledge is meant to problematize assumptions about fundamental or inherent differences between indigenous knowledge and scientific knowledge, and facilitate investigation of possible similarities as well as differences. We have assumed that greater understanding can provide farmers and local scientists with conceptual tools they can use to adapt or develop their own innovations to best meet their needs. This is also an assumption that needs to be carefully tested, however. Though we are well aware that our application of holistic knowledge theory has so far been biased towards the scientific model, a holistic approach helps us to be cognizant of the limits of that model, and is leading us in the direction of more detailed investigation of the sociocultural and epistemological basis of farmer and plant breeder knowledge, including work with farmers and plant breeders in different areas of the world, working with different crops (Soleri, Cleveland et al. 2000).

Note

1   We thank the collaborating farm households in Oaxaca who taught us much and brought great patience and good humour to our work together; the municipal authorities of the study communities for permission to conduct this work; M. Smale and M. E. Smith for discussion and advice; and S. E. Smith for stimulating discussion and assistance in many forms. Our research has been supported in part by grants to Daniela Soleri from the American Association for University Women, Association for Women in Science; Research Training Grant for the Study of Biological Diversity (University of Arizona), Sigma Xi, the US–Mexico Fulbright Commission, and the USAID–CGIAR Linkage Program; grants to David A. Cleveland from the Committee on Research, Faculty Senate, UC Santa Barbara, the Institute for Social, Behavioural and Economic Research, UC Santa Barbara, and the National Science Foundation (SES-9977996); and the financial and logistic support of the Economics Program of CIMMYT through M. Smale, and of the Maize Program of CIMMYT through S. Taba.

Bibliography

Agrawal, A. 1995. Dismantling the divide between indigenous and scientific knowledge. *Development and Change* 26: 413–439.

Allard, R. W. 1999. *Principles of Plant Breeding* (2nd edition). New York: John Wiley and Sons.

Aquino, P. 1998. Mexico. In M. L. Morris (eds) *Maize Seed Industries in Developing Countries* (pp. 231–250). Boulder, CO; Mexico, DF: Lynne Rienner; CIMMYT.

Aragón Cuevas, F. 1995. La producción de maíz en Oaxaca, situación actual y perspectivas futuras (Report for Instituto Nacional de Investigaciones Forestales y Agropecuarias (INIFAP)), Centro de Investigacion Regional del Pacifico Sur, February.

Bänziger, M., F. J. Betrán and H. R. Lafitte. 1997. Efficiency of high-nitrogen selection environments for improving maize for low-nitrogen target environments. *Crop Science* 37: 1103–1109.

Bänziger, M., G. O. Edmeades and H. R. Lafitte. 1999. Selection for drought tolerance increases maize yields across a range of nitrogen levels. *Crop Science* 39: 1035–1040.

Berlin, B. 1992. *Ethnobiological Classification: Principles of Categorization of Plants and Animals in Traditional Societies*. Princeton, NJ: Princeton University Press.

Biggs, S. D. 1989. *Resource-poor Farmer Participation in Research: A Synthesis of Experiences from Nine National Agricultural Research Systems*. OFCOR Comparative Study Paper no. 3. The Hague: International Service for National Agricultural Research (ISNAR).

Boster, J. 1996. Human cognition as a product and agent of evolution. In R. Ellen and K. Fukui (eds) *Redefining Nature: Ecology, Culture and Domestication* (pp. 269–289). Oxford: Berg.

Bourdieu, P. 2000. *Pascalian Meditations*. Cambridge: Polity Press. First published as *Méditations pascaliennes*, Éditions de Seuil, 1997.

Brumann, C. 1999. Writing for culture: Why a successful concept should not be discarded. *Current Anthropology* 40 (suppl.): S1–S27.

Byerlee, D. 1996. Modern varieties, productivity and sustainability: Recent experience and emerging challenges. *World Development* 24: 697–718.

Ceballos, H., S. Pandey, L. Narro and J. C. Perez-Velásquez. 1998. Additive, dominant, and epistatic effects for maize grain yield in acid and non-acid soils. *Theoretical and Applied Genetics* 96: 662–668.

Ceccarelli, S. 1989. Wide adaptation: How wide? *Euphytica* 40: 197–205.

——. 1996. Adaptation to low/high input cultivation. *Euphytica* 92: 203–214.

Ceccarelli, S., W. Erskine, J. Hamblin and S. Grando. 1994. Genotype by environment interaction and international breeding programmes. *Experimental Agriculture* 30: 177–187.

CGIAR. 1997. CGIAR Systemwide Project on Participatory Research and Gender Analysis for technology development and Institutional Innovation 1997. *New Frontiers in Participatory Research and Gender Analysis: Proceedings of the International Seminar on Participatory Research and Gender Analysis for Technology Development.* Cali, Columbia: CGIAR SWP.

CLADES, COMMUTECH, CPRO-DLO, GRAIN, NORAGRIC, PGRC/E, RAFI, and SEARICE. 1994. *Community Biodiversity Development and Conservation Programme.* Wageningen, The Netherlands; Santiago, Chile: Centre for Genetic Resources, and Centro de Education y Tecnologia (Proposal to DGIS, IDRC and SIDA for Implementation Phase I – 1994–1997).

Cleveland, D. A. 2001. Is plant breeding science objective truth or social construction? The case of yield stability. *Agriculture and Human Values* 18(3): 251–270.

Cleveland, D. A., D. Soleri and S. E. Smith. 2000. A biological framework for understanding farmers' plant breeding. *Economic Botany* 54: 377–394.

Cooper, M. and G. L. Hammer. 1996. Synthesis of strategies for crop improvement. In M. Cooper and G. L. Hammer (eds) *Plant Adaptation and Crop Improvement* (pp. 591–623). Wallingford: CAB International in association with IRRI and ICRISAT.

Cosmides, L. and J. Tooby. 1996. Are humans good intuitive statiticians after all? Rethinking some conclusions from the literature on judgement under uncertainty. *Cognition* 58: 1–73.

de Janvry, A., G. Gordillo and E. Sadoulet. 1997. *Mexico's Second Agrarian Reform: Household and Community Responses.* San Diego: Ejido Reform Research Project, Center for US–Mexican Studies, University of California, San Diego.

DeLacy, I. H., K. E. Basford, M. Cooper, J. K. Bull and C. G. McLaren. 1996. Analysis of multi-environment trials – an historical perspective. In M. Cooper and G. L. Hammer (eds) *Plant Adaptation and Crop Improvement* (pp. 39–124). Wallingford: CAB International in association with IRRI and ICRISAT.

Dilley, F. B. 1993. *Climate Change and Agricultural Transformation in the Oaxaca Valley, Mexico.* Ph.D. dissertation. The Pennsylvania State University .

Dove, M. R. 1996 Process versus product in Bornean augury: A traditional knowledge system's solution to the problem of knowing. In R. Ellen and K. Fukui (eds) *Redefining Nature: Ecology, Culture and Domestication* (pp. 557–596). Oxford: Berg.

Duvick, D. N. 1992. Genetic contributions to advances in yield of US maize. *Maydica* 37: 69–79.

——. 1996. Plant breeding: An evolutionary concept. *Crop Science* 36: 539–548.

Edmeades, G. O., J. Bolaños, S. C. Chapman, H. R. Lafitte and M. Bänziger. 1999. Selection improves drought tolerance in tropical maize populations: I. Gains in biomass, grain yield, and harvest index. *Crop Science* 39: 1306–1315.

Ellen, R. 1996. The cognitive geometry of nature: A contextual approach. In P. Descola and G. Palsson (eds) *Nature and Society: Anthropological Perspectives* (pp. 103–124). New York: Routledge.

———. 1999. Models of subsistence and ethnobiological knowledge: Between extraction and cultivation in Southeast Asia. In D. L. Medin and S. Atran (eds) *Folkbiology* (pp. 91–117). Cambridge, MA: MIT Press.

Escobar, A. 1999. After nature: Steps to an antiessentialist political ecology. *Current Anthropology* 40: 1–30.

Evans, L. T. 1993. *Crop Evolution, Adaptation and Yield*. Cambridge: Cambridge University Press.

———. 1998. *Feeding the Ten Billion: Plants and Population Growth*. Cambridge: Cambridge University Press.

Falconer, D. S. 1989. *Introduction to Quantitative Genetics* (3rd edition). Harlow: Longman Scientific and Technical.

FAO (UN Food and Agriculture Organization). 2000. Database available at http://apps.fao.org/.

Fischer, K. S. 1996. Research approaches for variable rainfed systems – thinking globally, acting locally. In M. Cooper and G. L. Hammer (eds) *Plant Adaptation and Crop Improvement* (pp. 25–35). Wallingford: CAB International in association with IRRI and ICRISAT.

García Barrios, R. and L. García Barrios. 1994. The remnants of community: Migration, corn supply and social transformation in the Mixteca Alta of Oaxaca. In C. Hewitt de Alcántra (ed.) *Economic Restructuring and Rural Subsistence in Mexico: Corn and the Crisis of the 1980s* (pp. 99–118). Transformation of Rural Mexico no. 2. San Diego, CA and Geneva: Ejido Reform Research Project, Center for US–Mexican Studies, University of California, San Diego, and United Nations Research Institute for Social Development (UNRISD).

Giere, R. N. 1999. *Science Without Laws*. Chicago: University of Chicago Press.

Gould, S. J. 2000. Deconstructing the 'science wars' by reconstructing an old mold. *Science* 287: 253–261.

Harding, S. 1998. *Is Science Multicultural? Postcolonialisms, Feminisms, and Epistemologies*. Bloomington, IN: Indiana University Press.

Harlan, J. R. 1992. *Crops and Man* (2nd edition). Madison, WI: American Society of Agronomy, Inc. and Crop Science Society of America, Inc.

Heisey, P. W. and G. O. Edmeades. 1999. Part 1. Maize production in drought-stressed environments: Technical options and research resource allocation. In CIMMYT (eds) *World Maize Facts and Trends 1997/98* (pp. 1–36). Mexico, DF: CIMMYT.

Heisey, P. W., M. L. Morris, D. Byerlee and M. A. López-Pereira. 1998. Economics of hybrid maize adoption. In M. L. Morris (eds) *Maize Seed Industries in Developing Countries* (pp. 143–158). Boulder, CO; Mexico, DF: Lynne Rienner; CIMMYT.

Hull, D. L. 1988. *Science as a Process: An Evolutionary Account of the Social and Conceptual Development of Science*. Chicago: The University of Chicago Press.

INEGI, 1996. *La agicultura en Oaxaca*. Aguascalientes, Aguascalientes, Mexico: INEGI.

Ingold, T. 1996a. Hunting and gathering as ways of perceiving the environment. In R. Ellen and K. Fukui (eds) *Redefining Nature: Ecology, Culture and Domestication* (pp. 117–156). Oxford: Berg.

———. 1996b. The optimal forager and economic man. In P. Descola and G. Palsson (eds) *Nature and Society: Anthropological Perspectives* (pp. 25–44). New York: Routledge.

Louette, D. and M. Smale. 1998. *Farmers' Seed Selection Practices and Maize Variety Characteristics in a Traditional Mexican Community.* Economics Working Paper no. 98–04. Mexico, DF: CIMMYT.

Mann, C. 1999. Crop scientists seek a new revolution. *Science* 283: 310–314.

McGuire, S., G. Manicad and L. Sperling. 1999. *Technical and Institutional Issues in Participatory Plant Breeding – Done from the Perspective of Farmer Plant Breeding: A Global Analysis of Issues and of Current Experience.* Cali, Columbia: CGIAR Systemwide Program on Participatory Research and Gender Analysis for Technology Development and Institutional Innovation. Working Document no. 2, March.

Medin, D. L. and S. Atran. 1999. Introduction. In D. L. Medin and S. Atran (eds) *Folkbiology* (pp. 1–15). Cambridge, MA: MIT Press.

Morris, M. L. and M. A. López Pereira. 1999. *Impacts of Maize Breeding Research in Latin America.* Mexico, DF: CIMMYT.

Nader, L. 1996. Anthropological inquiry into boundaries, power, and knowledge. In L. Nader (ed.) *Naked Science: Anthropological Inquiry into Boundaries, Power and Knowledge* (pp. 1–25). New York: Routledge.

Pandey, S., S. K. Vasal and J. A. Deutsch. 1991. Performance of open-pollinated maize cultivars selected from 10 tropical maize populations. *Crop Science* 31: 285–290.

Pham, H. N., S. R. Waddington and J. Crossa. 1989. Yield stability of CIMMYT maize germplasm in international and on-farm trials. In J. R. Anderson and P. B. R. Hazell *Variability in Grain Yields: Implications for Agricultural Research and Policy in Developing Countries* (pp. 185–205). Baltimore, MD: The Johns Hopkins University Press.

Pingali, P. and S. Rajaram. 1999. Global wheat research in a changing world: Options for sustaining growth in wheat productivity. In P. L. Pingali (ed.) *Global Wheat Research in a Changing World: Challenges and Achievements* (pp. 1–18). CIMMYT 1998–99 World Wheat Facts and Trends. 1998/99. Mexico, DF: CIMMYT.

Romagosa, I. and P. N. Fox. 1993. Genotype x environment interaction and adaptation. In M. D. Hayward, N.O. Bosemark and I. Romagosa (eds) *Plant Breeding: Principles and Prospects* (pp. 373–390). Plant Breeding series. London: Chapman and Hall.

Roscoe, P. B. 1995. The perils of 'positivism' in cultural anthropology. *American Anthropologist* 97: 492–504.

Schweizer, T. 1998. Epistemology: The nature and validation of anthropological knowledge. In H. R. Bernard (eds) *Handbook of Methods in Cultural Anthropology* (pp. 39–87). Walnut Creek: Altamira Press.

Scoones, I. and J. Thompson. 1993. *Challenging the Populist Perspective: Rural People's Knowledge, Agricultural Research and Extension Practice.* Discussion Paper no. 332. Brighton: Institute of Development Studies, University of Sussex.

Scott, J. C. 1998. *Seeing Like a State: How Certain Schemes to Improve the Human Condition have Failed.* New Haven, CT: Yale University Press.

Sherwood, S. G. 1997. Little things mean a lot: Working with Central American farmers to address the mystery of plant disease. *Agriculture and Human Values* 14: 181–189.

Sillitoe, P. 1998a. The development of indigenous knowledge: A new applied anthropology. *Current Anthropology* 39: 223–252.

——. 1998b. What know natives? Local knowledge in development. *Social Anthropology* 6: 203–220.

Simmonds, N. W. 1979. *Principles of Crop Improvement.* London: Longman Group Ltd.

——. 1990. The social context of plant breeding. *Plant Breeding Abstracts* 60: 337–341.

——. 1991. Selection for local adaptation in a plant breeding programme. *Theoretical and Applied Genetics* 82: 363–367.

Smith, M. E. and R. L. Paliwal. 1997. Contributions of genetic resources and biotechnology to sustainable productivity increases in maize. In K. Watanabe and E. Pehu (eds) *Plant Biotechnology and Plant Genetic Resources for Sustainability and Productivity.* Austin, TX: R. G. Landes Company.

Smith, M. E. and R. W. Zobel. 1991. Plant genetic interactions in alternative cropping systems: Considerations for breeding methods. In D. A. Sleper, T. C. Barker and P. J. Bramel-Cox (eds) *Plant Breeding and Sustainable Agriculture: Considerations for Objectives and Methods* (pp. 57–81). CSSA Special Publication no. 18. Madison, WI: Crop Science Society of America and American Society of Agronomy.

Soleri, D. and, D. A. Cleveland. 2001. Farmers' genetic perceptions regarding their crop populations: An example with maize in the Central Valleys of Oaxaca, Mexico. *Economic Botany* 55: 106–128.

Soleri, D. and S. E. Smith. 2002. Rapid estimation of broad-sense heritability of farmer-managed maize populations in the Central Valleys of Oaxaca, Mexico and implications for improvement. *Euphytica*, in press.

Soleri, D., S. E. Smith and D. A. Cleveland. 2000. Evaluating the potential for farmer and plant breeder collaboration: A case study of farmer maize selection in Oaxaca, Mexico. *Euphytica* 116: 41–57.

Soleri, D., D. A. Cleveland, S. Ceccarelli and S. Grando. 2000. Farmers' knowledge as a conceptual component of collaborative plant breeding: Barley farmers of northern Syria. Presented at the International Symposium, *Scientific Basis for Participatory Improvement and Conservation of Crop Genetic Resources,* Oaxtepec, Morelos, Mexico.

Spaner, D., R. Brathwaite and D. Mather. 1995. Comparison of open-pollinated stress-tolerant and landrace maize for production under stress conditions in Trinidad. *Maydica* 40: 331–337.

Trutmann, P., J. Voss and J. Fairhead. 1996. Local knowledge and farmer perceptions of bean diseases in the central African highlands. *Agriculture and Human Values* 13: 64–70.

Uphoff, N. 1992. *Learning from Gal Oya: Possibilities for Participatory Development and Post-Newtonian Social Science.* Ithaca, NY: Cornell University Press.

Zeven, A. C. 1998. Landraces: A review of definitions and classifications. *Euphytica* 104: 127–139.

Chapter 11

'Déjà vu, all over again', again

Reinvention and progress in applying local knowledge to development

Roy Ellen

> Raymond Firth ... commented that he had a sense of *déjà vu*, *déjà connu* and *déjà conçu*.
>
> (Grillo 1985: 3)

The diversity and scope of the issues discussed at the millennial ASA conference – including those collected in this volume – defy a comprehensive treatment in a mere 'afterword'. Certainly, no useful purpose is served by reiterating and annotating the contents in the way in which Paul Sillitoe has already done most excellently in chapter 1. I shall, therefore, confine myself to four themes. The first concerns how we understand and reconstitute the boundaries between different kinds of knowledge; it is preceded by a historical preamble and concludes with a reflection on the relationship between science and indigenous knowledge. The second theme explores the advantages and disadvantages of contextualization; the third participation and power; and the fourth, the relationship between academic anthropologists and development work. These are, to some extent, selected idiosyncratically, mainly because they continue to pose puzzles for me personally, but also because they do seem, serendipitously maybe, conveniently to represent penetrating threads connecting some otherwise very different concerns amongst contributors. Even though the conference was large by comparison with most of its predecessors, there remained noticeable gaps in its coverage of relevant issues. Compared with their prominence in recent literature, there were, for example, no feminist issues or perspectives as such, there was surprisingly little about indigenous knowledge in green arguments, on intellectual property issues, on the transportability of knowledge, or on participatory mapping. If there is a substantive bias in my treatment, it is in the direction of natural resource management and local environmental knowledge, which seems to me to have forced the pace of recent developments.

Taken as a whole, the papers presented at the conference (some published here, others appearing in the companion volumes)[1] leave two indelible impressions. The first is the degree to which such a substantively heterodox collection can be unified by repeated reference to the terms 'indigenous knowledge', 'participation' and 'development'. The second, and this is what proved to be rather remarkable about the conference in particular, was the stark and challenging juxtaposition of so much that was undeniably new with so much that was palpably well trodden. What was new was: the mixture of contributions from academic anthropologists and professional practitioners, from natural scientists as well as social scientists; a critical engagement with the shibboleths of 'participatory development'; an acceptance that both participation and reliance on indigenous knowledge involve subtle and not so subtle power relationships; a recognition that in their engagement with 'indigenous knowledge' anthropologists have something which development practitioners really seem to want and about which anthropologists think they have sufficient expertise to offer; and the view that whatever indigenous knowledge might be, it cannot be crudely opposed to scientific inputs, which can, given appropriate opportunities, be productively integrated. What was not so new was: the resurrection of unresolved debates about applied anthropology; the continuing ambiguity in the relationship between anthropology and development practices; a diversionary excursus into the relationship between knowledge and culture; and the revisiting of some familiar intellectual territory linked to the rationality controversy of the 1970s. One measure of just how much things have changed is that in Grillo and Rew's (1985) *Social Anthropology and Development Policy*, itself the outcome of an earlier ASA Decennial Meeting (and one specifically organized to reposition anthropology away from the Ivory Tower), one finds none of the terms that are central in the present volume, and 'participatory approaches' in the contemporary sense barely hinted at. One way of examining why these issues arose in the way they did, and of establishing the extent to which the preceding papers might represent a new orthodoxy, is to look at the history of indigenous knowledge studies.

The history of indigenous knowledge

There has been much discussion elsewhere of what the most appropriate term might be to label that knowledge upon which this volume focuses: ethnoscience, folk science, citizen science, traditional knowledge, local knowledge, indigenous knowledge (IK), traditional environmental knowledge (TEK), indigenous environmental knowledge (IEK), traditional knowledge systems (TKS) or even 'cunning intelligence'. Although at one point during the conference a samizdat thesaurus was circulating which helpfully defined and elaborated some of these terms, and many others, it is a terminological debate which is ultimately irresolvable and therefore arguably futile. Each term has been generated in a particular discourse and nexus of social and professional interactions, none are homogeneous, and all have their uses, come with slightly different connotations (although many with a surprising degree of semantic overlap), and carry particular ideological and moral loads. All have their advantages and disadvantages. What term we use is in part a question of whether that term has become part of a particular local, sectoral, professional or national policy context, and in which specific debates it appears. Mindful of the intellectual ordure which is likely to be heaped upon me, I shall for convenience refer to indigenous knowledge (and sometimes in the interests of brevity, to IK), in a postmodern sort of way though bereft of ironic quotation marks.

It is now accepted that whatever indigenous knowledge may be, as a generic category it was invented in the second half of the twentieth century for a variety of ideological and practical reasons (Ellen and Harris 1997, 2000). During the seventeenth and eighteenth centuries European naturalists and medical practitioners would think nothing of assimilating knowledge from newly colonized or contacted people, in a way which today we would describe as biopiracy. It is only really with the rise of development in the twentieth century that such knowledge has been, by turns, muted, actively rejected and subsequently rediscovered and celebrated. Within anthropology, its tentative rise to academic respectability is largely linked to ethnoscience, the 'new ethnography' of the 1960s. In this context we see an indigenous knowledge innocent of its possible entanglement with intellectual property rights and practical applications; an indigenous knowledge without development. Anthropologists were engaged in research on subjects we would now define rather differently, without fully appreciating the potential significance of what they were doing. Much of the writing was scholarly, esoteric and fundamental, though in the work – for example – of Harold Conklin (1957) sponsored by the FAO, the fundamental and the practical found a critical cross-fertilization. One of the seminal articles from this period is Metzger and Williams's (1966) analysis of Tzeltal firewood categories, famous mainly for the ridicule poured on it by Marvin Harris (1969: 591), for whom it epitomized 'the science of trivia'. Almost forty years later, we find it surprising that people should think it an irrelevance to seek to understand how poor farmers facing upland resource depletion make decisions about the selection of fuel.

By the 1980s this innocence had been shattered by the twin impacts of the Western counter-culture and the failure of conventional top-down development, a response (as Croal and Darou, chapter 5, remind us) to the sheer ineffectiveness (and especially the cost-ineffectiveness) of projects involving large numbers of expensive expatriate 'experts', qualified by degrees of ignorance of their target populations (Hobart 1993; Richards 1985). Though it might not have seemed like it at the time, we can now agree that the revitalized interest in indigenous knowledge emerged out of a 'postmodern' discourse on development, one looking for ways which allowed other voices to speak for themselves, and was critical of established institutional, scientific and economistic models. Thus arrived what we might describe as the first *formative* phase of IK-inspired research and application, associated with the seminal work of pioneers such as Johannes (1989) and Chambers (1983), neither of whom were (embarrassingly for the profession) anthropologists. Of this generation, among the anthropologists, Warren and Brokensha (Brokensha *et al.* 1980) were most obviously standard-bearers for an anthropological contribution. The second phase, associated with the last decade of the twentieth century, has seen the *routinization* of indigenous knowledge in the world of development practitioners, and the (relatively late) arrival of anthropologists *en masse* (indicated by a plethora of edited collections, the teaching of the subject in university departments and contracted research of an applied character), and its final integration into academic and development orthodoxy. At the same time we have increasing reflexivity within the Academy, and with it critiques of earlier phases, the acknowledgement of the problems of participatory approaches, and a deconstruction of the category of indigenous knowledge itself. Thus, 'indigenous knowledge' acquires its ironic punctuation marks, no longer a methodology or a subject, but a 'discourse' riddled with contradictions (Hobart 1993). The 1996 European Science Foundation seminar on 'Indigenous Environmental Knowledge and its Transformations' held in Canterbury conveniently marks this turning point (Ellen *et al.* 2000), taking stock of developments, and, from a suitably critical distance, observing just how a reified 'indigenous knowledge' was itself influencing events. The meeting challenged the more ideologically driven and unsubstantiated claims for indigenous knowledge, while accepting the central role for local knowledge in development, together with the reflexive twist that 'The cross cultural study of their knowledge may advance our scientific understanding of natural processes by challenging our concepts and models' (Sillitoe 1998: 227).

Proliferating kinds of knowledge

Although participants at the conference thankfully largely avoided the more nomenclatural and scholastic subtleties of the indigenous knowledge debate, it was not entirely surprising that claims for the existence of indigenous knowledge as a meaningful and relevant category should be challenged, and prompt discussion of core anthropological issues as to what *knowledge* is anyway, and what its relation might be to *culture*. In order to avoid floundering in the mire, it is evident that we must draw some kind of distinction between the two. The confusion which permits the conflation of knowledge and culture arises largely because so much discussion of culture revolves around its mentalist conceptions, in which it is generally understood as a web of symbols or meanings; a characterization, of course, which equally applies to knowledge. But culture is always more than this, including as it does all those practices (active and latent) and their material outcomes which arise through, and are located in, non-genetic (both linguistic and non-linguistic) instantiations, and which are transmitted between individuals non-biologically. Knowledge, therefore, must always be an aspect of culture, and though perhaps contributing to its organization, it is also more than mere *information*. Knowledge is generated at the interface of cultural memory and individual intelligence, and in addition, therefore, always carries a moral and social load. John Clammer's (chapter 3) suggestion that the word 'ontology' might be preferable does not, I fear, solve the problems of conceptualizing different kinds of knowledge or of comparing them cross-culturally.

If we accept knowledge as a legitimate category and analytic device, then the problem of *kinds of knowledge*, or *ways of knowing* (to use a phrase which some have recently preferred for its processual bias), is easier to handle. I am not concerned in this section, however, so much with bodies of empirically constituted knowledge (knowledge *of* something defined in terms of a conventional etic grid, be it soil, disease or minaret-building). Rather, I shall discuss general qualitative distinctions based on the social or cognitive standing of such knowledge or knowledge-generating processes, and especially distinctions which have themselves been challenged and which, therefore, represent lines of analytic, methodological or ideological tension.

The first two lines of tension which have a bearing on matters discussed in this volume are between cognitive and non-cognitive, and linguistic (lexical) and non-linguistic notions of knowledge. These distinctions, though overlapping, are not necessarily the same. As a consequence of recent developments in anthropology and cognitive science, the default understanding of knowledge, at least in anthropology, is usually conscious, cognized or reflective knowledge: something we are aware of acquiring and using, and often do so purposely in order to solve various technical and social problems. However, people also acquire knowledge tacitly, unobtrusively and unreflectively as part of the process of socialization and growing up. Many would regard this as being no less knowledge than that which we consciously articulate or recognize. One example of this is *bodily knowledge*: knowledge acquired and coded as part of doing and recognizing in particular practical contexts, say learning how to harvest rice with a Javanese finger knife – which requires sensory and motor skills that are readily transmitted trans-generationally, but which are not explicitly formulated into a set of rules. Such techniques are acquired through mimicry, experience and informal apprenticeship. One difficulty here is that this subcategory cuts across another common distinction, that between knowledge and *skills*, which hinges on the idea that turning one into the other requires learning *to do things*, some kind of practice of an abstract preconception (Sigaut 1994: 436–439). Much knowledge of the first kind (*cognitive knowledge*) is encoded in language, is therefore *lexical* (such as we find in plant and animal nomenclatures), and where this yields regularities in how people conceive relationships between different living kinds, it becomes classificatory knowledge. However, much knowledge, particularly of natural processes is only partially lexically expressed. Where knowledge is manifestly evident, though not necessarily systematically expressed in language, we might rather speak of *substantive* knowledge (Ellen 1999). Skills are generally thought of in this way, and often difficult to clearly represent, abstractly and linguistically.

A third line of tension is evident in attempts to identify or deny the distinction between what has been described as *technical* (mundane) and *symbolic* knowledge (knowledge versus know-how, savoir versus savoir-faire, ontological knowledge versus practical knowledge), a distinction which goes back beyond Durkheim and Mauss to earlier philosophical dualisms, particularly mind/body theories. Attempts to make such distinctions are not completely separate from attempts to distinguish knowledge from skills, and the difficulty with virtually all such qualitative contrasts is that they are never hard and fast. Those anthropologists who have accepted the legitimacy of distinguishing the technical from the symbolic have, on the whole, been those who have undertaken specialized studies of kinds of 'indigenous knowledge', the ethnosciences in the sense used above. By contrast, those anthropologists who have avoided analysing technical knowledge, or who reject the distinction between technical and symbolic in the first place, have been more interested in symbolic and social knowledge *per se*. For a long time, technical knowledge was an unfashionable thing for social anthropologists, at least to study, and was thought not to pose the same rigorous intellectual challenges as symbolic knowledge. Fortunately, such a narrow view no longer exists, partly because – it must be said – the technical has become symbolic. The long-standing disinterest in technical knowledge amongst anthropologists must surely be one reason why studies of indigenous technical knowledge have seemed to be more important to non-anthropologists than to anthropologists. Among non-anthropologists, such as development consultants and natural scientists, the tendency until quite recently has been to deny that others have any technical knowledge worth knowing, and that if there is, then this is hopelessly compromised by contamination with symbolic knowledge. A few, however, have been amongst those most enthusiastically endorsing the relevance of indigenous knowledge.

Part of the problem is that many pragmatists are wary of endorsing the utility of indigenous knowledge because this may question their own credentials as scientists and professionals. To put it differently, several generations of Western scientists have failed to learn any lessons from the folk because of what John Bousfield once described as 'epistemological chauvinism'. A dramatic example of this is Paul Richards' (1985) investigation of variegated grasshopper infestation of manioc in West Africa. Laboratory scientists made a significant research investment to discover what local farmers already knew, but which nobody had thought to ask them, perceiving farmer failure to solve the problem of infestation as ignorance. In fact, the situation was precisely the opposite: farmers well understood the ecology of the pest and had taken action to eradicate it, although without success. Their helplessness stemmed not from lack of understanding, or emphatically not *mis*-understanding, but rather from the magnitude of the problem they knew they faced, and the absence of resources to cope with it. A similar story could be told for many agro-ecological problems encountered by farmers.

Of course, the symbolic and metaphysical merges with the mundane, and both may be truly *local* knowledge, to be understood processually and recursively; but this is no reason to ignore the other, deconstruct it out of existence, nor is it a justification for not tackling real practical issues. Local people themselves simultaneously embed their practical knowledge in the symbolic, and their symbolic knowledge in the practical, but are nevertheless often quite able to separate the two when it matters (see, for example, Worsley 1997: 3, 74–75, 120–121). There is a tension between this view, which stresses the pragmatic ability of people to separate the mundane and the symbolic, and what others are telling us about the way empirical knowledge is really structured around 'cosmovisions'. By emphasizing the merging of local symbolic knowledge (e.g. worldviews) and technical knowledge, those who criticize the use of anything less than fully symbolically contextualized knowledge sometimes seem to be avoiding the problem of practicalities altogether and denying the possibility of there being solutions.

A fourth line of tension in anthropological studies of indigenous knowledge in development is evident in the assumption of common human responses to problem solving, versus an emphasis on cultural diversity. We can detect the beginnings of the new emphasis on heterogeneity in 1980s development policy (Long 1996: 39), with its shift away from standard solutions in favour of flexible and local strategies, just as in the wider economy 'Fordist' dogma was giving way to decentralized and loosely structured modes of economic organization. Just how entrenched this emphasis has now become more generally in business is evident from a recent UK Audit Commission advertisement seeking a 'Head of Diversity'. It is interesting that this celebration of cultural diversity should be linked to a parallel growth in the sacralization of biological diversity (Maffi 2001). As Alexiades (in press: 5) puts it: 'In this new context, local and traditional knowledge, and more generally cultural diversity, acquire new and powerful meanings', at the very moment when they are being absorbed into an ever-expanding capitalism reinvigorated by a shift towards an information based economy. This latter has profoundly altered the meaning of information (which must in part have undermined older assumptions as to what constitutes knowledge). Many have now internalized an infocentric perspective on the world, through a process of commodification of bits of nature (reflected in gene patents) and the commodification and revitalization of traditional knowledge. Both are linked to the hegemonic decline in the ideology of modernization (Alexiades in press: 7).

Against this trajectory we must balance a growing acceptance of what used to be called 'the psychological unity of mankind', but which is now expressed either through anecdotal platitudes of the kind 'all farmers are hard-headed pragmatists', or through the subtle and not-so-subtle mantras of cognitive science and evolutionary psychology. We see it in the assertion that some classificatory knowledge – what Brent Berlin called *general purpose* knowledge – reflects universal cognitive regularities (which for some are even 'hard-wired'), in contrast to other more functionally adapted and local *special purpose* knowledge. In a paradoxical way, the celebration of the localness, specialization and diversity of environmental knowledge as 'science' gives credence to assertions of commonality of response, especially when researchers demonstrate effectively how farmers facing similar problems in widely separated parts of the world have developed basically the same dynamic understandings of the relationship between elements in an agro-ecological system (Sinclair *et al.* in press), a position echoed in Cleveland and Soleri's contribution to this volume (chapter 10).

The old universalist/relativist debate takes on methodological and ethical dimensions when considered in terms of the tension between the need for uniformity in order to translate unambiguously, and the dangers of mistranslation where there is diversity and a polyphony of indigenous voices. Anthropologists in general, and students of ethnobiological knowledge in particular, have long recognized the dangers of assuming that local knowledge – that stock held by a single population – is static and uniformly distributed socially. While there is 'common knowledge' shared by the majority, much is shared only by sections of a population, according to gender, age, occupational specialization and experience. This variation does not always appear evident at the level of popular rhetoric, nor in the hands of those well-meaning publicists and practitioners of indigenous knowledge who have relatively little experience of social realities in actual communities. The failure of indigenous knowledge in development is often linked to assumptions about the communal character of that knowledge, assumptions which are groundless. In his contribution, Clammer (chapter 3) rightly observes that indigenous knowledge is subject to precisely the same stratification as other forms of knowledge, and when 'obtained by conventional methods is almost certainly ideological (class-, gender- and position-specific) rather than shared, and [that] much of what is shared is actually imposed by patterns of authority'. Clammer here reminds us of the omniscient speaker–hearer fallacy, of the interlinkages between symbolic and technical aspects of knowledge, and of how social position influences what we accept as knowledge and how we use it. But, however well-intentioned his cautionary remarks might be, it is clear that he is addressing knowledge of social rather than of technical practices. Thus, what is *quantitatively* demonstrable for technical knowledge in most small-scale peasant societies, exemplified say by the reading of vegetative indicators of seasonality or how to sow seeds, is the greater extent to which it *is* shared (and in a different way, and more openly) than more esoteric social or symbolic knowledge, which is also necessarily more ideological, rule-bound and proprietorial.

Finally, we might identify a fifth tension between the view of indigenous knowledge as bounded, tied to particular spaces, intrinsic and changeless (so powerfully evoked when we use the near-synonym 'traditional knowledge'), and the growing recognition of its dynamic character, its ability to utilize new ideas, respond to evidence, change and move around. As both Clammer (chapter 3) and Sillitoe (chapter 6) emphasize, it is not hermetically sealed from other kinds of knowledge, and local populations constantly absorb new knowledge (including scientific knowledge), sometimes transforming it in remarkable ways. Such a process is sometimes described as *hybridization, syncretization, blending, incorporation* or *integration*, though defining what this might mean in formal and cognitive terms has proved elusive, partly because we cannot clearly specify the 'units' or 'processes' which are hybridizing, and because recombination and reinterpretation are intrinsic to all knowledge systems. Certain understandings of hybridization are easier to grapple with than others, say the superficial sense in which we speak of the combination of particular *bits* of know-how from different traditions. This understanding is particularly apparent when we think of innovation in physical equipment, as when sago processors in Pasar Usang in West Sumatra replace rattan and bamboo with fine wire mesh sieves to press and filter starch (Ellen 2001). Indeed, the idiom of technical hybridization may be the way most of us model hybridization of more abstract knowledge. Similarly, in what must count as one of the most extraordinary studies of local farmer knowledge yet undertaken, as well as a remarkable example of how local people can successfully restore agro-ecologies which science-driven farming has rejected, Phillips-Howard (1993) describes how Delimi on the Jos Plateau created a viable agricultural medium out of an old tin-working area, partly through the use and evaluation of twenty-four kinds of manure and artificial fertilizer (Figure 11.1).[2] But understanding hybridization in the sense of how different ways of knowing are integrated is much more difficult to specify. And of course, at every turn, how hybridization works or is defined depends on how different bodies of knowledge are identified, labelled and valued. Thus, hybridization is not simply operating at the cognitive level, it is often material, and almost always a social process in which moral evaluations are brought to bear. Hybridization can appear to take place simply by moving the boundaries between representations of different kinds of knowledge. It also raises problems of equity, where particular kinds of knowledge are preferred over others and convey more status (for example, Western biomedicine over Ayurveda, or Ayurveda over shamanism). The same problem occurs through commoditization, whether preferences are exercised through the market, legal processes, or both. To assert intellectual property rights over knowledge is to assume that it comes in chunks, and to speak of hybridization (meaning the recombination of complexes and 'bits') is, therefore, in one sense, to challenge its intrinsic fluidity. Moreover, what is hybrid knowledge for one generation is indigenous in the next.

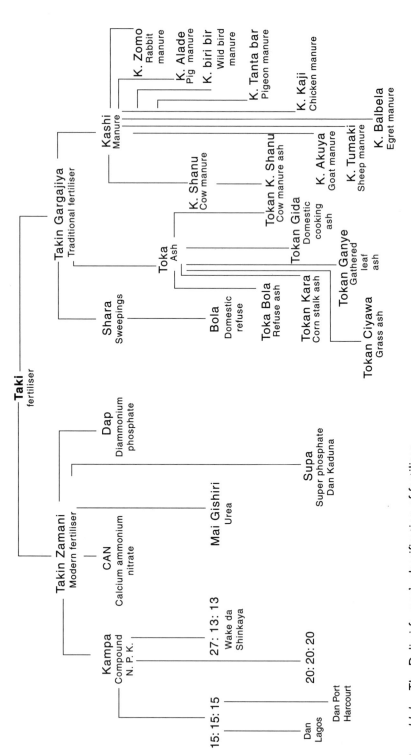

Figure 11.1 The Delimi farmer's classification of fertiliser

Source: From Phillips-Howard (1993)

There are, then, many different ways in which we might cut up the knowledge cake, none of which are mutually exclusive of others, and all of which reveal latent and manifest lines of tension. All of us manage, quite competently and often unconsciously, to operate multiple knowledge systems in parallel, and we readily move and convert between one and the other, and recombine their various elements. We are all specialists in several different knowledge systems, some formally (through paper qualifications) in the sense that Sillitoe is both an anthropologist and a soil scientist, Posey was both an anthropologist and entomologist, and Bicker is both an anthropologist and farmer. It is only when we start being reflexive or seek conversions between specialized knowledges embedded in particular divisions of labour, or between linguistically, culturally or ecologically remote contexts, that the distinctions between the multiple knowledges we carry around with us become self-evident and important. It is, however, true that some practical knowledge (e.g. minaret-building) is difficult to translate into systems of abstract knowledge; and we cannot transparently convert all substantive knowledge into formal (lexical) knowledge. That Penan hunters in Brunei have fewer words for plants than neighbouring Dusun agriculturalists is not because they *know* less, but probably because they have less need of words (Ellen 1999). By contrast, *feng shui* well exemplifies a kind of magisterial practical mastery and 'folk' tradition, and yet is clearly also part of a well-articulated literary and pre-eminently lexical corpus of spiritual knowledge.

The concept of hybridization is of special interest when we come to examine the strained relationship between indigenous knowledge and science.

Science and indigenous knowledge

One specialized form of knowledge with a specific cultural embodiment, but which has achieved a well-earned reputation for reliable evidence-based technology is science. While this book is not explicitly about the anthropology of science, by focusing on how anthropologists and natural scientists interact, and particularly on the failures of allegedly 'science-driven' development, it inevitably draws attention to the opposition between the two, which most chapters in this volume actively seek to overcome. As one speaker at the conference put it: 'Science is powerful cognitive stuff'. But science is powerful not just because of the calories it can release through engineering, but through its intellectual (and legal) hegemony. It is not powerful because it is particularly 'rational, objective and produced according to the canons of scientific method, and … consequently universal' (Turnbull 2000: 6), and certainly not because it is 'inherent and autonomous', though these representations in turn have served to promote and sustain its authority. On the contrary, it is polythetic, 'messy, contingent, unplanned and arational' (Turnbull 2000: 3), a conditional 'assemblage' of local knowledges, for ever 'trying to get the world to fit a particular kind of solution' (*ibid.*: 6, 14). On the face of it, this is a bizarre form of reverse engineering, for it is not the solution which is ordinarily considered the best starting point, but the objective: locate the destination and then explore all means of getting there, regardless of the route. GIS, in John Campbell's terms(chapter 9), is an example of such a solution in search of a problem, or a method in search of an application. This is one of the major problems in applying science to development, and in explaining the differences between science and indigenous knowledges. And yet despite all the difficulties, science has given us a remarkably reliable model of the world. This is partly because it ideally attempts to explain parts of the world transparently, through experimentation, collecting and measuring systematic data, and by seeking to verify testable, theory-generated hypotheses, but also because its predictions are *sufficiently* accurate to innovate narrowly specified kinds of technology.

Without rehearsing all the arguments in the 'Science war' controversies, the subject matter of this volume has necessitated the careful rethinking of what – in a participatory development context – science might contribute. There has always been, for example, a concealed tension in the easy elision between science, a supposedly 'universal' body of objective knowledge, and *Western* science, a body of knowledge having specific and unique origins in 'the scientific revolution' of seventeenth century Europe, which in turn grew out of European folk knowledge systematized through the scholarly disciplines of theology and classical philosophy – botany from horticulture, chemistry from alchemy, physics from practical mechanics, and so on – reinforced through later incorporation of other foreign knowledge facilitated through European geopolitical expansion. The eighteenth-century British agricultural revolution, for example, was not based on science, but on local technological and economic innovations which achieved new economies of scale; and as Cleveland and Soleri (chapter 10) point out, scientific plant breeding in turn grew out of farmer knowledge combined with Darwinian and Mendelian theories of inheritance. Only in the early twentieth century was the umbilical cord between science and folk tradition effectively cut. So, given that 'science, in the general sense of systematic knowledge, was never uniquely Western' (Turnbull 2000: 3–4), and given what we now know about the cross-fertilization of different knowledge traditions, it might better be described as 'transmodern' (*ibid.*: 227–228), or 'global' knowledge. It is, I suggest, increasingly absurd to speak of 'Western' science in a postmodern world, and evokes postcolonial arrogance in an epoch of the 'Indian bomb' and numerous Asian Nobel laureates. We would not dream of talking of Western football, even though historically it was first formalized and institutionalized as a game in Europe. To continually speak of 'Western science' and, even worse, of 'Science as a kind of Western indigenous knowledge' is untenable and dangerous.

Because 'indigenous knowledge' is so protean and extensive (everything, it would seem, that is left when we remove systematic science and scholarship), to claim that it is comparable or not comparable to science is misleading, a diversion from the real issue. It is not, in my view, particularly helpful to define indigenous knowledge as everything science is not, or in terms of tables of discrete opposing characteristics. So, for Cleveland and Soleri (chapter 10), following Escobar and Scott, and many others, it may be useful as a beginning to characterize indigenous knowledge as local, performative, organic, holistic, intuitive, socially constrained, practical, incremental and egalitarian; in contrast to science which is rationalistic, reductionist, theoretical, generalizable, objectively verifiable, abstract, non-contextual, universal, based on cause and effect, and imperialistic. However, given the diversity of indigenous knowledge, these sets of opposites do not take us very far, and exceptions and additions can always be found. Indigenous knowledge can include propositional statements, experimental evidence, mathematical thinking and literacy. Kasepuhan farmers in the Mount Halimun region of West Java keep a written record of the traditional landraces they plant, precisely to compare how they respond to different annual growing conditions (Soemorwoto, pers. comm.). In Bali, long before scientific attempts to understand the dynamics of irrigation systems, traditional institutions (in this case temples) served as foci for the systematization and aggregation of local ecological knowledge (Lansing 1991). Although science may challenge the credibility of 'indigenous knowledge' as science, the diversity of all that purports to be, or is by default treated as, indigenous knowledge makes any kind of generalization hazardous. Professional scientists and others have coped with this diversity and fluidity (as we have seen) by essentializing it, freezing it (Semali and Kincheloe 1999: 21), breaking it down into conveniently absorbable, observable and representational modules. But what we have to deal with as a result of such transformations and manipulations, even in some of the anthropological descriptions of indigenous knowledge, is something different, almost chimerical.

It is true that science is often presented in ways which make it difficult to connect with more informal knowledges. There was some discussion at the conference of the way in which different kinds of scientific knowledge obfuscate messages, interfere with the flow, set up social and cognitive barriers, and sometimes prevent altogether an engagement with critically important local knowledges. Medical knowledge becomes, for example, a matter of charts, tests and analyses, but no *stories*. Campbell (chapter 9) provides, in his treatment of GIS, an excellent example of how the *a priori* structuring of scientific representations prevents absorption of data on informal, flexible and serial land tenure arrangements of Namibian agropastoralists. Scientists themselves are often ambiguous in the degree to which they permit non-scientific considerations explicitly to influence their work. Some are intrinsically ethical creatures. Others, it seems, always like to keep their distance and claim that science is neutral, not always for reasons which make scientific sense, and leaving it to technologists and engineers to make the real ethical decisions. There is no reason why, as the Navajo biologist quoted by Croal and Darou (chapter 5) suggests, science should not incorporate ethics. Whether a scientist is acting ethically or non-ethically makes no difference to the quality of the science. However, to suspend belief in the interest of good analysis is a different matter. Darrell Posey took exception to my use of the word 'dispassionate' in this context at the 1996 Canterbury meeting. Sadly, he cannot have the last word on the matter, but I am convinced that to retain credibility with scientists, decision makers, the sentient subjects of our research and the indigenous peoples we advise, we just cannot allow our findings to be compromised by political correctness. This does not mean that we should not engage in the real world and be passionate, committed and partisan. We can, I think, put forward an excellent case for the use of science in development, but it is not always necessary, is frequently neutral in its consequences, often counterproductive, sometimes manifestly immoral, and never sufficient.

Given the complexity of knowledge, I am suspicious of flow-charts and three-dimensional diagrams to model the relationships between science and other kinds of knowledge. It is helpful to imagine 'a spectrum' between the indigenous knowledge of poor farmers and the knowledge of scientists, and it is undeniable that we need to recognize and reinforce the two-way flow of information. However, despite Paul Sillitoe's (chapter 6) brave attempt to show the epistemological and practical interconnections between science and indigenous knowledge in his mandala model, it is perhaps too formal and complicated. Given all that has been said of the polythetic character of science, the fuzziness of its boundaries and the complexity of its historic interconnections with other knowledge systems, the knowledge spectrum might better be modelled as a Molybius strip than through spheres with intersecting meridians; or – to employ contrasting artistic metaphors – with reference to one of those surreal Escher prints in which a bird imperceptibly metamorphoses into a fish, rather than with reference to a neat seventeenth-century Dutch landscape which describes everything with the precision of the cartographer and architect. But just because representing the totality of relations between kinds of knowledge is so formidable that it cannot be reduced to a simple geometric model, this does not mean that it is impossible to describe or compare the cognitive, representational and social contours of different knowledge systems. That there is variation must be a matter of conviction based on experience for any anthropologist, and textually organized knowledge is always going to be very different from knowledge which is orally transmitted. But we are in danger of disappearing into our own navels if we believe it is necessary to classify and compare all kinds of knowledge in order to justify, demystify or utilize them. For every metaphor is accompanied by its own special obfuscation, and in the end we might find that every meta-model we invent to accommodate all possible types and connections will, like Hercules and the Lernaean hydra, maniacally create yet more kinds of knowledge as fast as we can deconstruct them.

Although some of us may protest that we are thoroughly postmodern (and therefore less interested in explanation than interpretation), or may be portrayed as such by our critics, we all conspire to varying degrees in the possibility of science and to attesting its truth value, otherwise there is little point to anthropology. We accept there is a discourse and set of concepts which are sufficiently shared to enable the common pursuit of understanding and the forming of judgements whose standing can be measured against data. Most of us also accept science-driven development for ourselves, so when it comes to ascertaining the correct balance of science and indigenous knowledge in projects in less developed countries, we have to be careful that we do not deny to others what we would accept for ourselves. If we do not believe science − social or natural − has something to offer, then we must ask why we are assisting with development in the first place. In advocating a role for indigenous knowledge, we should not appear to tell indigenous people that what they already know is sufficient, nor imply that science is appropriate for us, but that others can manage well enough on indigenous knowledge. Such views and assumptions merely serve to perpetuate an invidious and pernicious social and pseudo-cognitive divide, echoing anthropologically discarded notions of 'the primitive'.

Context, context, context ...

It has become commonplace to demonstrate, and even more commonplace to assert, that what indigenous people know cannot be disembedded from its context, that their thoughts are not free-floating, that we must examine the circumstances of their social production and recognize their relational, contextual and perspectival character. And, equally, it is anthropologists who are widely regarded as the experts in the provision of context, as much of it as clients require (and often much more). This obsession with context is in part a response to enthusiastic early ethnographers who tended, like the Anglo-Saxon historian Nennius in his *Historia Brittonum*, to tip everything they knew into 'a big heap', without differentiating degrees of significance or subject from context. Context, where the relationship to critical variables is not explored, is not context in any helpful sense at all. In the framework of development consultancy, applied anthropologists have long recognized the dangers of stripped-down social profiles and rapid evaluations, under pressure for ill-advised, quick-fix solutions. Similarly, checklist Rapid Rural Appraisal has been adopted by some as a convenient means of describing knowledge, scientizing it and transferring it to other places where it might be useful. The continuation of this process is commoditization, which occurs when markets and lawyers get involved. What we have learned about indigenous knowledge is that you cannot just plug it in to a development project. It is not simply that the relevant context is removed through selection, simplification and modularization; it is generally agreed that many kinds of indigenous knowledge, as Purcell and Onjoro (chapter 8) stress, are just not amenable to specification and formalization in the way scientific knowledge or other particular kinds of folk knowledge are. The elastic soil categories used by Wola sweet potato cultivators in the Papua New Guinea Highlands cannot be readily translated into the US Department of Agriculture hierarchical pedological classification (Sillitoe 1996), and as Campbell (chapter 9) demonstrates in this volume, the variety and fluidity of cultural conceptions and social arrangements in Africa (particularly fuzzy, nested, rights to land) are incapable of being captured by GIS models, which can only handle clearly bounded groups. While it is frequently impossible to systematize and formulate indigenous knowledge in ways which written, GIS or other database approaches require, it is not always necessary either. There are times when the pressure to use state-of-the-art techniques and justify large budgets needlessly results in the application of inappropriate technologies.

However, having stressed the dangers of decontextualization, it is important to recognize that, in practice, there is really no end to the amount of context which might be provided and the difficulties faced in describing context in ways which are consistent and intelligible. The position is somewhat reminiscent of the way in which, in real world systems (social or ecological), causation always seems to regress infinitely away from the variable the condition of which has measurably changed. In this view, complaints about the insufficiency of context, just like the regression of causation, become so many lame excuses for an inability to draw any conclusions about what knowledge *can* be adequately described or explained. Although it is clear that modularization can so transform knowledge that it is rendered meaningless and ineffective, there can be little doubt that much knowledge *is* successfully modularized, decontextualized and transferred, for example to the labs of pharmaceutical companies as well as via local diffusion between 'indigenous' populations. The biopirating of traditional knowledge is a problem precisely because it is sufficiently successful for biopirates to make a good living from it. Biopiracy – the acquisition of particular bits of knowledge and their unacknowledged repackaging in a different knowledge system – is the measure of just how successful the transference and repackaging of bits of knowledge can be.

Participation and power

The problem with power in anthropological studies is that it comes and goes depending on the subject under investigation, the level and unit of analysis selected, and the methodology employed. Nowadays, anthropologists increasingly inhabit an analytic space with political scientists, political economists and sociologists, from where they capably analyse power abstracted to the level of nation state and global relations. However, other anthropologists continue, quite legitimately when addressing many issues, to aggregate and compare local instances and populations independent of their relationship to encompassing states, regions and the globe. When such anthropologists seeks to be comparative, generalizing and nomothetic, local power relations get ignored; when they are idiographic, ethnographic and societal, ethnography can provide masterful descriptions of power in all its disguises and in nuanced detail. In studies of indigenous knowledge it is, in principle, no different. When generalizing there is an understandable emphasis on what is shared, either within populations or between them: the process of analysis can itself eliminate the power element which is embedded in network relations of people as both individuals and groups. When there is an emphasis on the specific and the relational, power as a dimension and explanatory factor reappears.

Pioneer efforts to record indigenous knowledge and integrate it into development projects gave scant attention to power issues, as Purcell and Onjoro (chapter 8) and others remind us. At the most fundamental level, an inability to register the unequal social distribution of knowledge, as exemplified in the discussion above of the omniscient speaker–hearer fallacy, has often led to a failure to recognize relations of power in society which influence the distribution of that knowledge, or which define, say, what is 'knowledge' and what is not. In this respect it is, I think, no coincidence, that in her work among the Krisa of northwest Papua New Guinea, Stefanie Klappa can report (Ellen 2000: 194) that local people say sacred clan histories and land rights constitute 'knowledge', in its Tok Pisin gloss ('save'), in a way which widely shared know-how about the right soil requirements for growing yams palpably does not. Similarly, care of the forest, in Tok Pisin ('lukautim bus'), is always interpreted in terms of boundary issues rather than in terms of environmental issues as such. Knowledge, then, can be emically latent and neutrally valued, or it can – when reified – be negatively or positively valorized. Positive valorizations encourage sacralization, its transformation into property, and ultimately commoditization.

Like power, participation has moved from being hidden or assumed (as in 'classic' participant observation) to being up front (in the *Writing Culture* sense), and universally accepted as the ethically preferable way to formulate and conduct all research involving human subjects. Everything, it seems, can nowadays be redescribed as being in some sense 'participatory', and, paradoxically, participatory approaches have proved to be quite compatible with top-down projects masquerading as bottom-up ones. Clammer (chapter 3) even suggests that participatory development produces a new kind of knowledge, managed and directed from above. In the contemporary research environment, informants have become our co-researchers, folk healers front-line experts, and the medical ethnographer is apprenticed to the shaman. One can well understand the political and moral point which is being made here, but the problem with this kind of *Through the Looking Glass* redesignation, and of typologies of the kind borrowed from Biggs (1989) by Cleveland and

Soleri (chapter 10) – 'contractual, consultative, collaborative and collegial' – is that they are innocent of any real power relations which might exist between individuals. Who, we begin to ask, is participating with whom?

The power relations in indigenous knowledge discourse reveal themselves in several ways. First of all, local knowledge was innocently appropriated in the development of European scientific traditions, in ways which were made easy by the unequal power relationship between Europeans and (generally colonized) subjects. With the reification of the modernist project of science-driven progress during the middle part of the twentieth century, the traditional became widely accepted as irrelevant, and indigenous knowledge was used much more selectively. In pharmacology, as folk knowledge of herbal remedies, it was virtually abandoned for several decades, though ethnobotanical screening has since the 1980s become more important, if controversial. Under 'high modernism', science becomes the superior *a priori* standard by which all truths, including those derived from traditional teachings are measured, validated and valued (Pfaffenberger 1992; Turnbull 2000). This point is developed in this book by Purcell and Onjoro (chapter 8). The same is even true of postmodern IT approaches, which tend to reinforce narrow disciplinary approaches at the expense of developing and testing more appropriate interdisciplinary methodologies to better understand the impact of environmental change on rural poverty. As Campbell (chapter 9) suggests, in the context of a participatory ethos, GIS is a palpably *inappropriate* technology, functioning in the case he analyses only to serve existing political ends.

But even when the important role that indigenous knowledge can play is acknowledged, and procedures are put in place to ensure its appropriate protection, it is often plugged into a model of understanding and a set of norms dictated from outside. What is acceptable 'indigenous knowledge' is defined in official terms, which may radically differ from those understood and preferred by local people. But even official definitions of indigenous knowledge must be differentiated, as between those enshrined in law, those which are accepted in state or administrative discourse, and those 'official' versions defended by, say, indigenous political leaders or specialists *against* the shared knowledge of most ordinary people. We can observe the articulation of these distinctions in the current dispute between Brent Berlin's National Institute of Health-funded bioactivity screening project and the organized Tzeltal folk healers of Chiapas who are supported by local and international political groups (Zarembo 2000). Similarly, participatory approaches can be a source of other kinds of local political dispute, as when participatory mapping leads to new 'official' versions of boundaries for land disputed by other people not consulted as part of the exercise. It is easy enough to accept that locals must control their own knowledge, but the problem here is that those individuals who serve as channels with outsiders and servants of the state are often cultural brokers who may already be persuaded of official interpretations of indigenous knowledge, or may be crudely self-seeking. There are, always, power differences within the community. The local knowledge that is heard is sometimes only that of the wily players; or, alternatively, it is the wily players who manage to protect their knowledge, and the guileless ones who get exploited. People should, of course, speak for themselves, and indeed multiple voices must be encouraged, but which ones to listen to can become a methodological and ethical dilemma, and a potential source of conflict. Moreover, even if a researcher is confident of having selected or sampled the appropriate voices, people will – in the end – provide the knowledge which they are prepared to share. There are communities, it is said, so experienced in handling requests for and in marketing 'indigenous knowledge', that it can be suitably packaged into, say, MA or Ph.D. versions, depending on the sophistication and depth required, and the payment on offer. And all of this may soon be available, if it is not already, on the Web.

Where government departments or their agencies are involved in projects involving indigenous knowledge, the imbalance is self-evident. The position with NGOs is more varied ideologically, politically and economically, and it is difficult to generalize about their role. Kassam (chapter 4) notes that both northern and southern NGOs are interested in involving indigenous knowledge, but southern NGOs are much more into identity politics and are culturally embedded: for them, indigenous knowledge is often an expression of patrimony and of resources to be protected rather than a pragmatic strategy or conviction ideology to achieve development. The power exercised by NGOs and aid-giving bodies can, however, be more subtle. I have already argued that by the 1990s indigenous knowledge was consolidating itself in development work. This had involved a great deal of romanticizing and mythologizing, in which indigenous knowledge became something akin to an anthropological arts and crafts movement, which saw virtue in indigenous knowledge because of its aesthetic qualities, and because it is both morally uplifting for local people and for the anthropologist to promote. Such toe-curling and patronizing effusions of the 'indigenous' provided a convenient target for later deprecating deconstructions of indigenous knowledge, attempting to portray it as the latest bid to maintain neo-colonial hegemony. But such critiques themselves often end up essentializing indigenous knowledge, and often come from those who have least experience of development issues at the grassroots.

As the use of indigenous knowledge has expanded, so the tables have turned, and local knowledge itself becomes a source of legitimation, a form of resistance, identity and power, sometimes in quite crude ways, as where financial compensation is received for its transfer. Anthropologists, lawyers, development practitioners, environmental NGOs and political activists, having created indigenous knowledge in a particular form, now find that the indigenous are wreaking their righteous revenge, not only by claiming it back, but by deploying the concept in ways often not anticipated by the non-indigenous. Although many (perhaps most) poor rural peoples of the developing world have themselves internalized the view that they are the passive recipients of 'development', and many have a negative or entirely neutral evaluation of their own technical knowledge, others have learned to use the language of the sacred, science and the law to advance, protect and generally make the most of their knowledge. If local peoples have, in the past, been disinterested in their own knowledge, then this has often been magnified in the research communities of their own countries. Sinclair and his colleagues (in press) show how extension workers in Nepal were not aware of the sophisticated knowledge of ecological processes that was general amongst farmers. Fortunately, things are changing and many research centres, (and as we have seen) NGOs and governments in the South have now adopted the indigenous knowledge mantle, spawning regional indigenous knowledge networks, bureacratizing knowledge and seeking a legal apparatus to protect it on behalf of the state, and sometimes on behalf of local people themselves. It has developed into a rhetorical mode which itself actually challenges the authority of professional scientific and disciplinary thinking in fundamental ways, and therefore contests its value and status. No wonder that science has begun a rearguard action to challenge indigenous knowledge as useful knowledge, and as scientific in particular.

Anthropology's unresolved relationship with development

Anthropologists have proved that they are good at identifying problems, saying why projects have failed and why things cannot be done, and that they are even better at providing infinite context for whatever it is that is being proposed. Unfortunately, many are still not so good at committing themselves to particular solutions, or at communicating what they know and directing it along appropriate channels. To me, it is surprising that professional social scientists should continue to be surprised that organizations are complex and comprise wilful political networks, and are not just benign instruments for the implementation of planned social change. Perhaps we should hope that when we next hear colleagues berating the leaden weight and political manoeuvring of bureaucracies, it is merely posturing, or a deliberate attempt to wake up decision makers or a public audience, and not naiveté. And in speaking of such issues, anthropologists still talk a different language: often obscure, elusive, allusive, and sometimes downright unhelpful. I have often heard more that is positive from non-anthropologists on the subject of indigenous knowledge in development than I have from anthropologists, and this I put down to misplaced disciplinary loyalty to some spurious notion of professional intellectual purity among the latter (combined with the infinite relativist regress of postmodernism) less than some attempt to defend the moral high ground. Development, planned and unplanned social change, will continue regardless of what happened at the ASA 2000 conference, despite the sceptics who were present, and the cynics who were not. It must also be conceded that planned change can be executed well enough, badly, or very badly, and that the advice decision makers accept can make a difference. Our attitudes towards and use of indigenous knowledge may be crucial. It is true that plugging indigenous knowledge into projects is often an avoidance of the real problem, an opting out of difficult decisions, but we must believe that by using the jargon of participation, community-based management and indigenous knowledge we are doing more than simply repeating meaningless mantras, that this is more than the triumph of hope over experience.

In order to move forward I believe we need to recognize a number of inevitabilities, especially if we are to guard against indigenous knowledge becoming either everything or nothing, a Panglossian panacea or a Pandora's box.

First, the indigenous knowledge option in development projects is about finding practical, simple and local solutions: reducing the incidence of malaria, or increasing productivity – very material things. This requires serious engagement with peoples' knowledge systems, understanding the interconnectedness of the technical and the symbolic, and the provision of sufficient social and cultural context. Though none of this need be intrinsically complex, we face social obstacles at every stage. In working on appropriate ways to integrate natural science and indigenous knowledge, we must continually resist the tendencies of organizations and many scientific disciplines to apply generic solutions without first exploring the local. As Turnbull (2000: 14) nicely puts it: 'Malaria is irredeemably messy and local, yet we continue to try for mono-cultural, global solutions at the expense of local knowledge and local people.'

Second, we must combine a sophisticated analysis of organizations (funding bodies, project sponsors and project teams) with an ability to identify appropriate bodies of indigenous knowledge. By now, anthropologists and others have learned enough about how local knowledge works in general terms, on the basis of a hundred years of ethnography and fifty years of specialist technical reports, to accept that it should not always be necessary to recommend that what is required is yet *more* research. In many cases it might be better and more effective to deploy, paradoxically, that generic experience of localness and the accompanying critical approach, than screening general development policy guidelines. It depresses me when I see manuals for social forestry reinventing techniques which anthropologists have known about and used for decades. This is why anthropologists must learn to work as part of interdisciplinary teams, perhaps even serving as the organizational 'glue', developing an appropriate language as they go, not being high-handed or sulking when things go wrong, or adopting an 'I told you so' approach. They need to use multiple methods to triangulate and verify findings and viewpoints. Although more diplomacy and hearts-and-minds work is clearly still necessary at the indigenous knowledge–science interface, and there is no stable language of knowledge integration, applied indigenous knowledge need not be controversial.

Finally, we need to instil a mindset that *there is no alternative*, that there can be no retreat from indigenous knowledge. It must always be the point of departure and the final destination. This is partly a moral and political point: people must control their own knowledge (whatever social problems this may give rise to) – it is the indigenous who must decide what indigenous knowledge is and how that knowledge is used; and what material and cultural objectives local people wish to pursue is entirely for them to decide. But there is also no alternative for another reason. Though many are rightly concerned at the disappearance of much local wisdom for its own sake, and with it a reduction in the diversity of cultural responses, indigenous knowledge of a very important kind is ever present and constantly being reinvented to cope with new circumstances. I have developed elsewhere the idea of 'indigenous knowledge' as a *buffer* (Ellen and Harris 2000), though we might equally well use the metaphor of a software conversion program or of lubricating oil, because in so many instances the role of this kind of intuitive, informal, knowledge is to make technologies based on more formal abstract knowledge work. It is this kind of knowledge which allows us to use new technologies in a pragmatic way: the know-how of Icelandic fishermen facilitating use of the latest sonar equipment, any one of us trying to make a data-projector work, the indigenous knowledge of the oil industry, or British farmers coping with the barrage of conflicting official (scientific and political) advice from government and veterinary professionals about foot-and-mouth disease.

In this concluding chapter I have emphasized the diversity of indigenous knowledge, not just in the sense of the diversity *between* cultures, but also in the sense of diversity of meanings which we attach to the category, in terms of cognitive organization, substantive components, material embodiments, and so on. I take the view that the category arises by default, as a counterpoint to what we call science, and is constructed largely on the basis of the kind of knowledge it is not. So, paradoxically, while as flexible intuitive understanding it is bound to endure and inhere at every technical and social interface, as a profession anthropologists can render a service by arguing for fairer terms of engagement with development, which include ensuring that the conditions for the preservation of its more endangered varieties persist. While only time will tell whether ASA 2000 will prove to have been a benchmark in the integration of indigenous knowledge and participatory development, on the evidence of the papers collected here there is some hope that anthropologists might now become constructively critical without being deconstructively oppositional.

Notes

1   *Development and Local Knowledge*, edited by Alan Bicker, Paul Sillitoe and Johan Pottier; and *Negotiating Local Knowledge*, edited by Johan Pottier, Paul Sillitoe and Alan Bicker.

2   Kevin Phillips-Howard died in 1995. I met Mike Warren at a meeting in Venice in 1997 at which he informed me that he thought this paper remained unpublished, but he promised to check. Unfortunately, Mike Warren himself was dead within the week, and despite further enquiries I cannot confirm that the paper has not been published, though see Phillips-Howard 1999. The figure which appears here is that presented to a conference in Leiden in 1993.

Bibliography

Alexiades, M. N. in press. Ethnobotany and globalization: Science and ethics at the turn of the century. In L. Maffi, T. Carlson and E. Lopez-Zent (eds) *Biocultural Aspects of Ethnobotany and Conservation*. Advances in Economic Botany. Bronx, New York: The New York Botanic Gardens.

Biggs, S. D. 1989. *Resource-poor Farmer Participation in Research: A Synthesis of Experiences from Nine National Agricultural Research Systems*. OFCOR Comparative Study Paper no. 3. The Hague: International Service for National Agricultural Research (ISNAR).

Brokensha, D., D. M. Warren and O. Werner (eds). 1980. *Indigenous Knowledge Systems and Development*. Lanham, MD: University Press of America.

Chambers, R. 1983. *Rural Development: Putting the Last First*. London: Longman.

Conklin, H. C. 1957. *Hanunóo Agriculture: A Report on an Integral System of Shifting Cultivation in the Philippines*. Rome: FAO.

Ellen, R. F. 1999. Modes of subsistence and ethnobiological knowledge: Between extraction and cultivation in Southeast Asia. In D. L. Medin and S. Atran (eds) *Folkbiology* (pp. 91–117). Cambridge, MA: MIT Press.

——. 2000. Local environmental knowledge. In S. Bahuchet (ed.) *Les Peuples des Forêts Tropicales Aujourd'hui. Volume II. Une Approche Thématique* (pp. 187–200). Bruxelles: Programme Avenir de Peuples de Forêts Tropicales.

——. 2001. The distribution of *Metroxylon sagu* and the historical diffusion of a complex traditional technology: Towards the resolution of some unanswered questions. Paper presented at the 2001 EUROSEAS conference held at the School of Oriental and African Studies, London. Unpublished.

Ellen, R. and H. Harris 1997. *Concepts of indigenous knowledge in scientific and development studies literature: A critical assessment*. APFT Working Papers no. 2, 15pp.

——. 2000. Introduction. In R. F. Ellen, P. Parkes and A. Bicker (eds) *Indigenous Environmental Knowledge and its Transformations: Critical Anthropological Perspectives* (pp. 1–33). Amsterdam: Harwood.

Ellen, R. F., P. Parkes and A. Bicker (eds). 2000. *Indigenous Environmental Knowledge and its Transformations: Critical Anthropological Perspectives*. Amsterdam: Harwood.

Grillo, R. 1985. Applied anthropology in the 1980s: Retrospect and prospect. In R. Grillo and A. Rew (eds) *Social Anthropology and Development Policy* (pp. 1–36). ASA monographs no. 23. London: Tavistock.

Grillo, R. and A. Rew (eds). 1985. *Social Anthropology and Development Policy*. ASA monographs no. 23. London: Tavistock.

Harris, M. 1969. *The Rise of Anthropological Theory: A History of Theories of Culture*. London: Routledge and Kegan Paul.

Hobart, M. 1993. Introduction: The growth of ignorance? In M. Hobart (ed.) *An Anthropological Critique of Development* (pp. 1–30). London: Routledge.

Johannes, R. E. (ed.). 1989. *Traditional Ecological Knowledge. A Collection of Essays*. Gland, Switzerland, Cambridge: IUCN.

Lansing, J. S. 1991. *Priests and Programmers: Technologies of Power in the Engineered Landscape of Bali*. Oxford: Princeton University Press.

Long, N. 1996. Globalization and localization: New challenges to rural research. In H. Moore (ed.) *The Future of Anthropological Knowledge* (pp. 37–59). London and New York: Routledge.

Maffi, L. (ed.). 2001. *On Biocultural Diversity: Linking Language, Knowledge and the Environment*. Washington, DC and London: Smithsonian Institution Press.

Metzger, D. and G. E. Williams. 1966. Some procedures and results in the study of native categories: Tzeltal firewood. *American Anthropologist* 68: 389–407.

Phillips-Howard, K. D. 1993. Management of soil fertility among small-scale farmers on the Jos plateau, Nigeria. Paper presented at the Pithecanthropus Centennial 1893–1993, *Human Evolution and its Ecological Context* Leiden, The Netherlands, 26 June–1 July.

——. 1999. The indigenization of exotic inputs by small-scale farmers on the Jos Plateau, Nigeria. In G. Prain, S. Fujisaka and M. D. Warren (eds) *Biological and Cultural Diversity: The Role of Indigenous Agricultural Experimentation in Development* (pp. 80–91). London: IT Publications.

Pfaffenberger, B. 1992. Social anthropology of technology. *Annual Review of Anthropology* 21: 491–516.

Richards, P. 1985. *Indigenous Agricultural Revolution: Ecology and Food-crop Farming in West Africa*. London: Hutchinson.

Semali, L. and J. L. Kincheloe. 1999. What is indigenous knowledge and why should we study it? In L. Semali and J. L. Kincheloe (eds) *What is Indigenous Knowledge? Voices from the Academy* (pp. 3–57). New York and London: Falmer Press.

Sigaut, F. 1994. Technology. In T. Ingold (ed.) *Companion Encyclopaedia of Anthropology: Humanity, Culture and Social Life* (pp. 420–459). London: Routledge.

Sillitoe, P. 1996. *A Place Against Time: Land and Environment in the Papua New Guinea Highlands*. Amsterdam: Harwood.

——. 1998. The development of indigenous knowledge: A new applied anthropology. *Current Anthropology* 39(2): 223–252.

Sinclair, F. L., D. H. Walker, B. Thapa, L. Joshi, P. Preechapanya and A. J. Southern. In press. General patterns in indigenous ecological knowledge. In A. Bicker, P. Sillitoe and J. Pottier (eds) *Development and Local Knowledge*. London: Routledge.

Turnbull, D. 2000. *Masons, Tricksters and Cartographers: Comparative Studies in the Sociology of Scientific and Indigenous Knowledge*. Amsterdam: Harwood Academic.

Worsley, P. 1997. *Knowledges: Culture, Counterculture, Subculture*. New York: The New Press.

Zarembo, A. 2000. Magnet for globophobes: Chiapas is happy to attract protest, not profit. *World Affairs*, Atlantic Edition (9 April): 29.

Index